For David

With very best wishes

Judith N Browning

November 1998

New York City, circa 1796. Lower Manhattan, from Trinity Church at far left, to the houses on State Street at the Battery. At left: A French man-of-war. Line engraving by Archibald and Alexander Robertson, circa 1796. (Courtesy of the Eno Collection, The New York Public Library, New York City)*

New York City
Yesterday & Today

30 Timeless Walking Adventures

Judith H. Browning

Corsair Publications, Inc.

First published November 1990 by Corsair Publications, Inc.,
Connecticut.

Designed by CHEUNG/CROWELL Design, Connecticut.
Printed in the United States of America by Eastern Press, Inc.

10 9 8 7 6 5 4 3 2 1

Library of Congress Catalog Card Number 90-081118

Publisher's Cataloging-in-Publication Data
(Prepared by Quality Books Inc.)
Browning, Judith H.
   New York City, Yesterday & Today : 30 Timeless Walking
Adventures / Judith H. Browning.—
   p. cm.
   Includes bibliographical references and index.
   1. New York (N.Y.)—Description—Guide-books. 2. New
York (N.Y.)—History. 3. Restaurants, lunchrooms, etc.—
New York (N.Y.) I. Title. II. Title: New York City, Yesterday
and Today.
F128.18   974.7'1   ISBN 0-9626067-0-7

Manhattan circa 1854. Lithograph by J. Bornet. (Courtesy of The New-York Historical Society, New York City)

C O N T E N T S

Introduction

S ometimes as I hurry along the crowded sidewalks of New York City, I imagine a startlingly different time and place. The traffic-choked streets and towering skyscrapers vanish, and they are replaced by narrow, crooked dirt paths lined with crude thatched-roof timber cottages. A colorful patchwork of orchards and gardens, a sprinkling of windmills, and a delightful canal give the rolling landscape a distinctly Dutch look. On the East River the masts of seagoing sailing ships bristle, and nearby the business of trade is carried on at the bustling, noisy waterfront called the Strand.

This is Dutch New Amsterdam, founded at the southernmost tip of Manhattan in 1625. The tiny, boisterous outpost will one day become the international metropolis, New York City.

In this book of walking adventures, I invite you to come along with me to visit New York City today — teeming with millions of people, a carnival of color and noise, and electric with excitement. Then we will return to the 17th century and those that followed to visit Manhattan when it was another place — as rich in adventure and promise, and just as colorful and fascinating — the New York City of yesterday.

t' Fort nieuw Amsterdam op de Manhatans

The earliest known view of New Amsterdam as it

appeared between 1626 and 1628, during the early

years of the Dutch settlement on Manhattan Island.

Fort Amsterdam, as depicted here, existed only in

the artist's imagination. In reality the fort was just

a simple earthen-walled square, around which the

first settlers' tiny wooden shelters were clustered.

(Courtesy of Museum of the City of New York).

Sailing Aboard *Petrel*

The Statue of Liberty by sailboat

Above: Bartholdi, standing at bottom center, oversees construction of the full-scale plaster model of Liberty's arm holding the tablet. This photograph clearly shows the intricate wooden framework. (Courtesy of The New York Public Library, New York City)✦

Left: The symbol of freedom and hope, *Liberty Enlightening the World.* Although this is her formal name, the world chose another one — The Statue of Liberty. (Photograph © Jeffrey Jay Foxx, 1990)

What better way to begin a book about New York City than at Manhattan's southern tip, the Battery, where the city began. And what better way than to see the Statue of Liberty in the harbor, the symbol of hope and new beginnings for millions of immigrants.

And the adventure? A sail into the harbor aboard Petrel, *the sleek two-masted racing yawl that President Kennedy sailed.*

The Statue of Liberty: the History

The French sculptor Frédéric-Auguste Bartholdi (1834-1904) was just 22 years old when he first saw Egypt's Sphinx and the pyramids, an experience that contributed to the young artist's admiration for ancient, colossal monuments. After he returned to Paris, Bartholdi began to use these and other ancient works of art for inspiration, completing a number of larger-than-life statues during the next 10 years.

Historians often attribute the design for *Liberty Enlightening the World* — the name chosen by Bartholdi — to the sculptor's unrealized design for a Suez Canal lighthouse in the form of a female colossus. However, Bartholdi always insisted that the idea was kindled in 1865 during a dinner party in Versailles, France. The host, Edouard de Laboulaye,

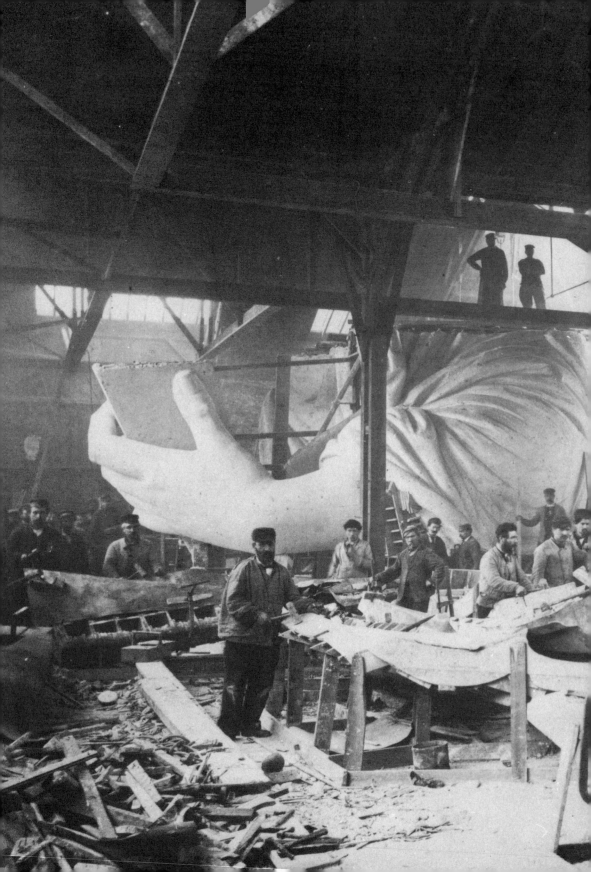

was a highly respected law professor and historian, who in 1875 would play a key role in formulating a democratic constitution for France. Laboulaye, an ardent admirer of America, told his guests he believed that France had made a crucial contribution to American liberty by providing ships and soldiers during the Revolution. The professor felt that a lasting friendship had been forged between the two nations because of that contribution, and if a monument were ever built to commemorate America's 1776 Declaration of Independence, the project should be a joint effort as well. That conversation, Bartholdi would later write, fired his imagination and remained fixed in his memory.

Bartholdi began to design a colossal figure, and by 1870 he had prepared initial drawings and models for the statue, which he hoped to complete in time for the 1876 centennial celebration of American independence. Then, encouraged by Laboulaye, the sculptor sailed to America in May of 1871 to share his vision of *Liberty Enlightening the World*.

As the ship sailed into New York Harbor, Bartholdi noticed Bledloe's Island, an islet still covered with the remains of star-shaped Fort Wood, which had been completed in 1811 and abandoned by 1877. Bartholdi later decided that *Liberty Enlightening the World* must stand on that site, holding aloft her great torch of freedom and hope.

The 37-year-old sculptor met with many influential Americans, among them the poet Henry Wadsworth Longfellow, President Ulysses S. Grant, and the editor of the *New York Tribune*, Horace Greeley, all of whom listened politely as Bartholdi described the great statue dedicated to American independence and explained that the project would be a joint effort: France would donate the statue, and America would build the pedestal on

which the towering figure would stand.

After this first visit to America, Bartholdi returned to his Paris studio to continue refining his vision of Liberty, and by 1875 he had completed his design. The great figure would be draped in robes of antiquity. Broken shackles and chains of tyranny would lie at her feet. She would hold the torch of freedom in her upraised right hand, while she would cradle in her left arm a tablet inscribed July 4, 1776, the date of America's Declaration of Independence. Liberty, whose classically handsome face was modeled on that of Bartholdi's mother, would wear a crown with seven rays, symbols of the seven continents and seven seas of the world, over which her torch of freedom would cast its light.

And Liberty's size? The statue would rise 151 feet from the pedestal. Her waist would be 35 feet thick and her nose more than four feet long. Each index finger would extend eight feet, and each eye would measure two-and-a-half feet wide in her 10-foot-wide face.

With the 1876 centennial deadline fast approaching, Bartholdi was faced with the realization that *Liberty Enlightening the World* would never be completed in time for the American celebration. The sculptor did, however, manage to complete a portion of the figure, the forearm and hand holding the torch, in time to display it at the Philadelphia Centennial Exhibition beginning in August of 1876, and afterward, in New York City's Madison Square Park on Fifth Avenue and 23rd Street. In both cities the 30-foot-high forearm and hand drew enthusiastic visitors, who patiently stood in long lines for a chance to climb the interior ladder for a view from a balcony surrounding the torch. Liberty's forearm remained in Madison Square Park for seven years, after which it was shipped back to Paris in 1884 and ultimately incorporated into the statue.

Bartholdi attended the 1876 centennial celebration during his second visit to America, staying nine months to tour cities and make speeches. Afterward, encouraged and excited by the American response, he returned to a large Paris workshed he had acquired for construction of the statue and began work on Liberty's head. (The copper head was displayed at the Paris Exposition Universelle on the Champ de Mars in 1878 to the delight of fairgoers, who climbed an interior stairway to look out through windows of Liberty's crown.)

As construction continued, Bartholdi addressed important structural concerns. How would the gigantic metal figure withstand the winds that buffeted New York Harbor? In 1880 the sculptor turned to the eminent engineer and bridge builder Alexandre Gustave Eiffel for answers.

Eiffel, who would later complete the Eiffel Tower for the 1889 World Exhibition, used his bridge-building experience to advise Bartholdi to construct a freestanding, reinforced, wrought-iron pylon as the central support for the figure. To this 96-foot-high pylon would be attached a secondary iron framework, which would surround the pylon. Hundreds of flat iron bars with springlike flexibility would be bolted to the secondary framework and would project upward and outward, attaching to the backs of copper plates forming Liberty's skin.

Liberty's iron skeleton, designed by Alexandre Gustave Eiffel. (Drawing by Mark Cheung, 1990)

Previous pages: Artisans at work hammering the copper plates of Liberty's skin into shape inside the Paris workshed in 1882. (Courtesy of The New York Public Library, New York City)✦

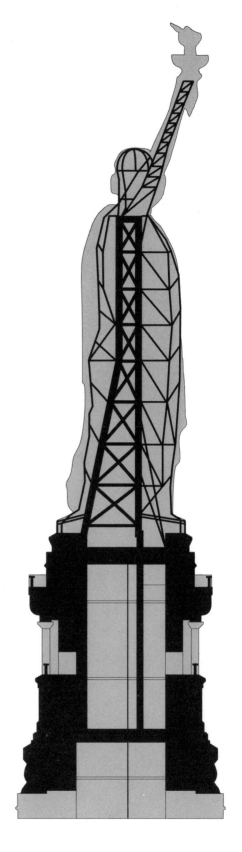

The 200,000-pound skin would be a marvel of engineering — a gigantic jigsaw puzzle composed of 300 large, very thin copper plates (approximately the thickness of a silver dollar). The curvature of the plates would be meticulously formed by gently hammering the pieces against precisely curved wooden forms.

In order to provide a way for bolting the copper plates to the iron skeleton, an armature (a mesh of vertical and horizontal iron bands) would be attached to the back of each copper plate. This armature would be bolted to one or more of the projecting flat iron bars, which in turn would be bolted to the secondary framework of Liberty's iron skeleton.

However, another difficult problem remained to be solved. The copper plates could not be attached directly to their iron armatures, because the rates of contraction and expansion caused by temperature changes are different for iron and copper. The copper skin had to be flexible enough to adjust to those changes and also flexible enough to withstand the fierce harbor winds.

Eiffel's answer was a design utilizing copper "saddles," which were attached to the back of each copper plate, allowing the iron bands of the armature to slip back and forth through the saddles when ad-

justments were needed.

This problem solved, construction of the skeleton proceeded outside in the Paris workyard, while inside the cavernous shed, work on the copper figure went forward in a piecemeal fashion rather than from head to foot. (Visitors were often astonished to see the workroom strewn with various parts of Liberty's huge body — the toes, a finger, the head, or a piece of the arm.)

By July 1882 the statue had been completed to her waist in the workyard. Growing crowds of curious onlookers watched as Liberty began to rise slowly above the rooftops of Paris, surrounded by

her wooden scaffolding. In August 1883 the great head was lifted into position. During the winter the upraised arm was hoisted into place over a separate girder, which was attached to the central pylon. Finally the scaffolding was dismantled.

In February 1884 Bartholdi reported that the figure was finished at last. France formally presented *Liberty Enlightening the World* to the people of the United States on July 4, 1884 — but she still stood on French soil.

In January 1885 dismantling began. Scaffolding was reconstructed around the 450,000-pound copper and iron figure, and Liberty was carefully taken apart, numbered, and packed into 214 giant crates, some of which weighed as much as 6,000 pounds. The French three-masted warship *Isére* was selected to carry the precious cargo to New York.

There were many problems yet to be solved. Although the French donation had materialized, Americans lagged woefully behind in collecting funds for the pedestal. To make matters worse, Americans were surprisingly uninterested in the project, and there were many who looked on the whole affair with distrust and cynicism, wondering just why France would give such a gift.

In 1885 newspaper publisher Joseph Pulitzer intervened, using his newspaper the *World* to build reader enthusiasm for the project, to shame the wealthy into donating funds, and last — but certainly not least — to increase newspaper circulation. Pulitzer succeeded on all counts. He raised $100,000 from rich and poor alike and made the *World* the most widely

Liberty Enlightening the World, surrounded by scaffolding, rises slowly above the rooftops of Paris, 1882-1883. (Courtesy of The New York Public Library, New York City)✦

circulated newspaper in the Western Hemisphere.

On June 17, 1885, *Isére* sailed into New York Harbor. Although the pedestal was still being constructed (completed in April 1886), the painstaking work of uncrating, checking, and assembling the statue began at once. Work was completed on October 25, 1886, when the last sheet of copper — the bottom of Liberty's right sandal — was riveted into place. *Liberty Enlightening the World* stood at last on the 89-foot-high pedestal and 65-foot foundation, rising from star-shaped Fort Wood.

Bartholdi attended the October 28, 1886, unveiling ceremony, at which President Grover Cleveland presided. Although the day was rainy and gray, more than a million people watched the festive parade of 20,000 marchers stream down Fifth Avenue while a naval procession of approximately 300 vessels sailed down the Hudson and into the harbor.

Within a few years, Lady Liberty would be known around the world as a beacon of hope. Millions of immigrants would see the monumental figure holding the upraised torch of freedom as their ships sailed through the Narrows and into New York Harbor.

★

In 1903 a plaque inscribed with a poem would be attached to an interior wall of the Statue of Liberty's pedestal. That poem, "The New Colossus," by New York City poet Emma Lazarus, would proclaim to the world:

Not like the brazen giant of Greek fame,
With conquering limbs astride from land
    to land;
Here at our sea-washed, sunset gates
    shall stand
A mighty woman with a torch, whose
    flame
Is the imprisoned lightning, and her name
Mother of Exiles. From her beacon-hand
Glows world-wide welcome; her mild
    eyes command
The air-bridged harbor that twin cities
    frame.
"Keep, ancient lands, your storied
    pomp!" cries she
With silent lips. "Give me your tired,
    your poor,
Your huddled masses yearning to
    breathe free,
The wretched refuse of your teeming
    shore.
Send these, the homeless, tempest-tost
    to me.
I lift my lamp beside the golden door!"

Liberty's head on display at the Paris International Exposition in 1878. (Courtesy of The New York Public Library, New York City)✦

The Statue of Liberty by Sailboat

The sailboat's mainsail ballooned gently in the late summer breeze, and the teak decks gleamed under the setting sun. We were sailing aboard *Petrel*, graceful and swift as the powerful seabird for which she was named.

President John F. Kennedy had once sat exactly where we were sitting and had raised *Petrel's* sails. He loved this sailboat, and as often as his tight schedule allowed, he sailed her out of the United States Coast Guard Academy in New London, Connecticut. If tragic events hadn't intervened, *Petrel* would have become the President's official yacht.

Today *Petrel* brings pleasure to New York's visitors who happen to discover her, and to New Yorkers, who often feel that they are sailing on a private yacht. Sometimes there are as few as 10 or 12 passengers aboard *Petrel*, although she can carry up to 35.

We sailed *Petrel* on a balmy August afternoon. It was one of those perfect days for sailing, with warm and soothing breezes. There were 10 passengers ambling around the deck, watching the parade of colorful boats and the historic landmarks documenting America's past.

The breezes picked up, and *Petrel* swiftly glided far out into the harbor. We were offered an incomparable view of Manhattan's skyscrapers silhouetted against a dazzling blue sky.

A replica of a 19th-century sloop sailed by, American flag riding high, sails

Petrel, the 1938 racing yawl once sailed by John F. Kennedy. (Courtesy of Bring Sailing Back)

flared in the afternoon breeze.

She was headed back toward Battery Park, on which we could see the brownstone walls of Castle Clinton, completed in 1811 as the "West Battery" to defend New York against the British, although it was never used for defense. Once located 300 feet from shore, landfill gradually surrounded the fort, attaching it firmly to Manhattan.

Looking east, we could see the shores of Brooklyn; and straight ahead, Staten Island. (Arching between those two New York City boroughs is the steel span of the Verrazano-Narrows Bridge, the longest suspension bridge in North America.)

"Isn't that Ellis Island?" somebody asked, pointing to the west.

It was indeed, and on that island we could see the immigration station through which an estimated 12 million immigrants passed between 1892 and 1924.

By this time we had struck up a conversation with two lively and interesting New Yorkers, and before long we were talking about the passing scene, the history of New York, and the city today. We all agreed that sailing on *Petrel* made us realize how many little-known adventures are hidden in the city. They often turn out to be the most fascinating of all.

We wondered about *Petrel*. What kind of sailboat is she? Who built her, and when?

I sauntered over to a crewman and began to quiz him. As he hoisted a sail, he cheerfully explained that *Petrel* is a yawl, a two-masted sailing vessel with a mainmast and a smaller mizzenmast aft (to the rear) of the helm. He added that *Petrel* is 70 feet long, weighs 32 tons, has a mainmast 90 feet high, and can carry up to 3,000 square feet of sail.

I learned that *Petrel* was designed by Sparkman and Stephens and was built in

Making friends aboard *Petrel*. A New
Yorker tells the author a favorite story
about an immigrant relative's first view
of Liberty as he stood on the ship's
deck at dawn. (Photograph by David
Browning, 1989)

Brooklyn, New York, in 1938 for a
Canadian, who raced her for nearly eight
years. After the Canadian sold *Petrel*, she
changed hands several times until she was
finally donated to the United States Coast
Guard Academy, where she was a training
vessel and also competed in and won
many ocean races.

It was during this time that John F.
Kennedy was often aboard, sailing the
sleek racing yawl out of New London,
Connecticut — and *Petrel* captured his
imagination. He decided to have her as
his own, to requisition her as his presidential yacht. It was not to be. Not long
afterward he was assassinated.

I thanked the crew member for the
information, then turned to watch a 19th-
century sailing vessel gliding through the

rippling harbor waters. She was the
1885 schooner *Pioneer*, with her passengers from the South Street Seaport
crowding the deck.

Following in her wake was an old
wood-paneled Staten Island ferry noisily
churning the water. In the distance I
could see a giant oceanliner silhouetted
against the sky, dwarfing a Circle Line
sightseeing boat as it stoically chugged
around Manhattan.

All of this motion and sound and
color seemed a fanfare for the minutes
that followed. *Petrel* sailed near the
Statue of Liberty. Nearer — nearer still.
Suddenly the Lady was looming high
above us, beribboned by pink and orange
striations of sunset. She was a soul-
stirring figure, a regal colossus, framed
by *Petrel's* billowing sails.

As *Petrel* turned, then sailed toward
shore, the passengers talked together
quietly. The air was cooler now, the
harbor tranquil. Battery Park was shadowed in twilight as we shook hands with
the crew, said good-bye to the other
passengers, and headed back home.

History of the Battery

The tiny Dutch trading post of New Amsterdam was founded by the Dutch West India Company as a commercial venture in 1625 and stood here, at the toe of Manhattan Island. The settlement's first 30 families were actually employees of the company, and their primary responsibility was to build a lucrative fur trade with the Indians, as beaver, otter, and mink pelts commanded extremely high prices in Europe.

The outpost's largest structure was the earthen-walled Fort Amsterdam, around which the settlers' crude timber and mud-walled huts were clustered. Gradually other rudimentary structures were built along the dirt paths, including a thatch-roofed counting house with a second-floor religious hall and a horse-mill for grinding tree bark used in tanning hides. As the colony was expected to become self-sustaining, *bouweries* or company farms were tilled to provide food for the settlers and a few animals.

It was from these simple beginnings that the City of New York began to grow.

Additional Historical Sights at Battery Park

Bowling Green, the grassy plot visitors see today at the foot of Broadway, was originally an open area used by the early Dutch settlers as a marketplace, parade ground, and children's play area. Legend has it that in September of 1626 New Netherland's Director-General Peter Minuit stood on this spot and, after handing the Indians 60 guilders' worth of beads and trinkets (about $24), purchased the island of Manhattan.

Bowling Green became the city's first park in 1733, used for lawn bowling. On July 9, 1776, the green was the scene of political unrest when the statue of King George III, erected in 1770, was knocked down by disenchanted patriots and melted to make bullets. The fence surrounding the green today dates from 1771 and was built to protect the statue.

Across from Bowling Green on the site of the first Dutch fort stands the *Custom House*, completed in 1907, a Beaux-Arts masterwork designed by Cass Gilbert, architect of the Woolworth Building and the United States Court House. Apart from the building's beauty, it had an important governmental function as well. At the turn of the 20th century, the United States Customs Service levied millions of dollars in taxes and was the greatest source of revenue for the United States government.

The Custom House, unused for many years, has recently been chosen to house an exhibition space for the National Museum of the American Indian.

Battery Park, the great wedge of greenery at Manhattan's southern tip, was named for the 17th-century battery of cannon that once defended the harbor. The southern tip of Manhattan ended approximately at present-day State Street until it was gradually extended with landfill through the centuries. After the American Revolution, when distintegrating Fort George (originally Fort Amsterdam) was demolished, the rubble from the fort was used as landfill, and the island was pushed outward again. In the late 18th and early 19th centuries, the Battery was a fashionable area, offering a delightful promenade from which strollers enjoyed splendid views of the harbor.

Castle Clinton, built in 1811 to defend the harbor, has served New York City in various ways through the years. The structure was transformed into a concert hall in 1824 and renamed Castle Garden.

From 1855 to 1890 it was used as an immigration depot, processing nearly eight million immigrants. From 1896 to 1941 the building functioned as the New York Aquarium. It is now used primarily as a ticket booth for trips to the Statue of Liberty.

The wide avenue of Broadway, the first major road built by the Dutch, begins at the Battery. At *1 Broadway* Kennedy House stood from 1771 to 1882, used by General Washington as headquarters at the beginning of the Revolutionary War and later occupied by British Generals Howe and Clinton.

A short distance away is *39 Broadway*, the site of the second mansion occupied by President Washington from February to August 1790, when his home at 3 Cherry Street proved to be too small for his large staff.

Finally, I hope you will take time to visit the *New York City Vietnam War Memorial*, a long overdue tribute to Americans who fought and died in Viet Nam. The memorial is located at the Vietnam Veterans Plaza near Water Street at Coenties Slip.

View of Bowling Green, looking south. This 1898 photograph shows the Battery in the distance between Steamboat Row on the left, which housed shipping offices in former townhouses, and the very beginning of Broadway. The grand Custom House, completed in 1907, replaced Steamboat Row. The tent in the foreground was used for recruiting during the Spanish-American War, which had just begun. (Courtesy of The New-York Historical Society, New York City)

Note: A sail aboard *Petrel* does not include a tour of the Statue of Liberty. For tours of Liberty Island, see information at the end of this section.

To sail aboard *Petrel*, call or write:
Bring Sailing Back
c/o *Petrel*
Battery Park
New York, NY 10004
212-825-1976

Petrel sails from mid-April to mid-October (depending on the weather) from the far west side of Battery Park shore. Important: *Petrel* sails promptly. Be sure to allow at least an extra 30 minutes for travel delays and the walk across Battery Park.

Sailing Times:
Monday-Friday
   Departures from noon until 7:30 p.m.
Saturday & Sunday
   Departures from noon until 8:00 p.m.

Tickets:
Prices vary from $8.00 per person for a 45-minute lunchtime sail to $20.00 per person for a two-hour Saturday evening sail. Other sailing adventures are offered, including special moonlight sails for two and private parties. Tickets are sometimes available for spur-of-the-moment sailing — often the nicest adventure of all! You are invited to take picnic meals aboard, although all beverages must be provided by *Petrel*.

   If writing for tickets, allow time for your check to reach the company and to receive your tickets by return mail — at least 10 days.
   No refunds or date transfers.

(Want to learn more about sailing? Ask about the courses available through the Petrel *Sailing School.)*

Additional Harbor Tours

Staten Island Ferry
(Does not go to Liberty Island)
State & Whitehall Streets
(next to Battery Park)
718-390-5253

One of the best bargains around at 50¢ for a round-trip. The ferry, which has been running for 175 years, leaves New York City from the foot of State Street every 30 minutes on the hour and half-hour for a scenic 25-minute trip past the Statue of Liberty to Staten Island.

Circle Line
(Does not include a tour of the Statue of Liberty)
Pier 83 (west end of 42nd Street at 12th Avenue)
212-563-3200

Although it does not depart from the southern tip of Manhattan, this three-hour boat tour offers wonderful views of Ellis Island and the Statue of Liberty as it circles Manhattan. $15.00 per adult; $7.50 for children under 12.

Statue of Liberty Ferry to the Statue of Liberty National Monument
Battery Park
212-269-5755

Boats leave Manhattan hourly on the hour from 9:00 a.m.-4:00 p.m. with extended hours in summer for the 20-minute trip to the Statue of Liberty and Ellis Island, which opened to the public in September 1990. Ferries return to Manhattan hourly on the half-hour. $4.00 (adults) and $2.00 (ages 3 to 11). Price includes statue and island admissions.

A view from *Petrel* looking north at the Battery and the splendid Manhattan skyline. (Photograph by David Browning, 1989)

R E S T A U R A N T S

There are many small cafes along Broadway, quick and inexpensive.

D I R E C T I O N S

Subway:
- IRT Lexington Avenue #4 & 5 to Bowling Green
- #1, 9 to South Ferry
- BMT N, R to Whitehall Street

Bus:
- M1 (Fifth / Madison Avenues) to South Ferry (5:00 a.m. to 4:30 p.m.)
- M6 (Seventh Avenue / Broadway between 59th Street & South Ferry)
- M15 (First / Second Avenues) to South Ferry

Car:
- FDR Drive & West Side Highway, Battery Park / South Ferry exit

The Day George Washington Became President

Following the inaugural parade route, April 30, 1789

The place: *The southern tip of Manhattan island, the oldest part of New York City, first settled by the Dutch in 1625.*
The time: *One historic day in American history — April 30, 1789 — the day George Washington was inaugurated as the first President of the United States.*

ow step back more than 200 years. Join me for an imaginary 18th-century stroll along the narrow streets of old New York. We will follow the stately inaugural parade, visiting three historic landmarks along the way — Fraunces Tavern, Federal Hall National Memorial, and St. Paul's Chapel.

The grand procession began in front of President-elect Washington's home at 3 Cherry Street, demolished long ago. The land on which that house once stood lies beneath the approach to the Brooklyn Bridge near South Street Seaport.

The parade continued down Pearl Street, passing Fraunces Tavern, which must have been brimming with cheering celebrants on that last day of April 1789, as the popular tavern stood directly on the parade route at Pearl and Broad Streets and afforded its patrons a fine view of the white inaugural coach, drawn by six matched horses. We will join the parade

Above: Federal Hall National Memorial today. (Photograph © Phil Cantor, 1990)

Right: The Sub-Treasury Building rising where Federal Hall once stood on Wall Street. This photograph shows the bronze figure of George Washington looking down on Wall Street at the turn of the 20th century. (Courtesy of The New-York Historical Society, New York City)

Fraunces Tavern as it looked in 1777.
From Hollyer's *Views of Old New York*.
(Courtesy of The New-York Historical
Society, New York City)

at the historic tavern, the scene of General
George Washington's farewell to his
officers in 1783 at the end of the Revolutionary War. The setting for that famous
gathering, the Long Room, has been re-
created as part of an interesting museum.
We will browse through the second-and
third-floor galleries, perhaps stopping for
a meal in one of the handsome dining
rooms downstairs, as Fraunces Tavern is
also a very popular restaurant today.

The tavern, a red brick Georgian
building with mustard-yellow trim, is a
restoration and reconstruction, built by
the Sons of the Revolution in 1904.
The original structure had been severely
damaged by five major fires during the
18th and 19th centuries and, conse-
quently, had also been restored and

altered many times through the years.

From Fraunces Tavern the parade
route continued northward on Broad
Street. The original Federal Hall, the
nation's first capitol, stood on Wall Street
and faced south, looking down Broad
Street. It was in that building on the
second-floor balcony overlooking Broad
Street that George Washington took the
oath of office, becoming the first President
of the United States on April 30, 1789.

Today Federal Hall National
Memorial stands at the corner of Wall and
Nassau Streets — slightly to the east of
the site of the original Federal Hall. This
building houses a museum that celebrates
the birth of the new nation and the
Constitution. The museum, which opened
its doors during a gala bicentennial
celebration on April 30, 1989, will be the
second stop on the parade route.

The inaugural parade continued along
Wall Street. The new President walked
with the members of both houses of
Congress, and we will follow his foot-

steps, turning north on Broadway to pass in front of historic Trinity Church and its surrounding churchyard, crowded with blackened tombstones. (A separate chapter is devoted to Trinity Church.)

We will follow the parade route a few blocks up Broadway, stopping to visit beautiful St. Paul's Chapel, the only surviving Colonial church in Manhattan. It was in this small church that the new President stopped to say prayers, and it was here that the inaugural procession ended so long ago.

Fraunces Tavern: the History

The original house on the Pearl and Broad Street site was built in 1719 by a prosperous New Yorker, Stephen Delancey, on land extended into the harbor by fill. Even then, the crowded city was looking for new ways provide land for an ever-growing population.

As the story goes, a Delancey descendant lost the family fortune, and with it, the Pearl Street house. The structure was used for various purposes by successive owners until 1762 when Samuel Fraunces, an immigrant from the West Indies, bought the house and turned it into Queen's Head Tavern in honor of Queen Charlotte of England. With the defeat of the British, the reference to the monarchy was removed, and the establishment became simply Fraunces Tavern.

Taverns such as the Queen's Head played an important part in the lives of 18th-century Americans, particularly in small, isolated villages in which taverns functioned as the only social centers. In these tiny communities a tavern became a place in which people starved for social contact could meet and hear the news, which was often weeks or months old. In

a warm, convivial tavern a patron could raise a glass of ale, eat a hot meal, smoke one of the long white clay pipes rented from the tavernkeeper, and pick up his mail from a tavern table, as the tavern also functioned as a post office. (Although it was considered poor manners, some tavern customers passed the hours reading letters addressed to their neighbors!)

Serious matters were decided in taverns as well. Many a defendant's future was decided in a crowded, smoke-filled tavern by a judge and jury. Even the course of American history was determined several times within dimly lit tavern walls. The Boston Tea Party was secretly planned in Boston's Green Dragon Tavern, and at the Queen's Head in New York, George Washington and his officers planned battle strategy in July of 1776. (Admiral Lord Howe's fleet had just arrived and had landed British troops on Staten Island, adding to the thousands already assembled there.)

Business was transacted as well: The New York Chamber of Commerce was founded at the Queen's Head in 1768.

General Washington could have chosen another tavern, of course, since in 1776 New York City was bustling with approximately 22,000 citizens and hundreds of taverns. Fraunces Tavern was chosen because it was one of the city's finest taverns, known for the excellent meals prepared by the tavernkeeper, Samuel Fraunces.

However, according to a number of historical accounts, General Washington was nearly murdered at the tavern in 1776. The general was attending a court martial at Fraunces Tavern when several guards tried to season his favorite pea soup with poison. Congress concluded that Fraunces was "instrumental in discovering and defeating" the sinister Tory plot, later dubbed the Hickey Conspiracy,

taking its name from Sergeant Thomas Hickey, one of the guards. Following a court martial ordered by Washington, Hickey was hanged in June.

Fraunces further aided the patriot cause during the war when he was forced into service as cook for British General Robertson. Apparently, Fraunces kept one ear to the door as he stirred his cake batter and basted his roasts, because he was given a reward after the war for his efforts, possibly for funneling British battle strategy to General Washington.

An intriguing man was Fraunces, although most of his life remains a mystery to this day. Records do show, however, that Fraunces had a rare talent for tavernkeeping, although he viewed it as a "base profession," quite beneath his station as a gentleman.

General Washington's farewell to his officers on December 4, 1783 at Fraunces Tavern. (Courtesy of The New-York Historical Society, New York City. Copy of a lithograph from a painting by Harry A. Ogden)

Unfortunately, by 1775 the tavern owner's social ambitions began to exceed his bank account. Although he was having financial problems, Fraunces decided that he needed an impressive New Jersey country estate. That need was his undoing. Bankruptcy ended his social climb, and Fraunces was finally forced to sell his prized tavern.

Fraunces joined the President's staff as chief steward in 1789, supervising 14 servants and overseeing numerous official functions. He later wrote that the dinners he prepared at the presidential mansion were "bountiful and elegant," offering an array of courses that began with soup, followed by fish, fowl, meats, and vegetables. Desserts were served in courses as well: a selection of pastries, for which Fraunces was renowned, often followed by "iced" creams, fruits, and nuts.

Fraunces served the President for five years, moving with Washington to the nation's second capital, Philadelphia, in 1790. Fraunces later opened a tavern in Philadelphia and lived quietly in that city until his death at the age of 72.

★

As you browse through Fraunces Tavern Museum, I hope you will imagine that you are actually living in the 18th century. Perhaps then you will be able to see the firelight dancing on the paneled walls of the Long Room, hear the slap of cards hitting the tavern table, and smell the aroma of Virginia tobacco smoke.

The porcelain bowl on the side table would be filled with punch, the staple drink of taverns, a warm mixture of rum, sugar, spices, and lime or lemon juice. A servant would be standing behind the rough wooden bar dispensing a variety of drinks popular during that time: hard cider, beer, brandy, or the more expensive drink, wine, which was imported from Spain and Germany.

The men sitting in this room, leaning over the table playing cards, would be attired in the English fashion, although their waistcoats, knee breeches, and stockings would be simpler in cut and fabric, having been made in America. Hair would be drawn back and bound into a queue with a black ribbon called a solitaire.

It was in the Long Room that General George Washington said farewell to his officers on December 4, 1783, shortly after the evacuation of the British. It was later recorded that there were tears in all eyes, even in those of the general, as he raised his glass and said, "With a heart full of love and gratitude, I now take leave of you. I most devoutly wish that your latter days may be as prosperous and happy as your former ones have been glorious and honorable."

The Clinton Room, across the hall from the Long Room, features rare hand-blocked wallpaper depicting scenes of Colonial New York. There are many amusing inaccuracies in this paper, which was designed by a Frenchman who had never been to America.

You will see General Washington's triumphant return to New York City after the war, which shows him on horseback in front of the Boston State House! Another scene depicts British General Cornwallis surrendering to General Washington on October 18, 1781, in the Hudson River Valley instead of York-town, Virginia.

The wallpaper is dated about 1838 and is not original to the Clinton Room. (The private dining room in the White House is decorated with the same pano-ramic paper.)

The Clinton Room was the setting for another historic event, for it was here that New York Governor Clinton held a gala dinner for General Washington on November 25, 1783, the day the British finally sailed out of New York Harbor after the Treaty of Paris was signed in September of that year.

★

Now let us return to the imaginary 18th-century New Yorkers seated in the Long Room. They are probably looking forward to a memorable dinner prepared by Fraunces and his staff. Perhaps the aroma of the first course drifts into the room — a fish and corn chowder, spicy and delicious. In the kitchen below Fraunces prepares the other dishes: fried and pickled oysters, a Queen's Head specialty; a brace of roasted pheasants basted to a golden turn in butter and wine; and a juicy leg of mutton surrounded with turnips. Finally, Fraunces' famed des-serts: cinnamon-apple tarts, syllabub (beaten cream, sugar, and liquor), a pear "iced" cream, and a rare treat — fresh pineapple, just off the boat from the West Indies. Two bottles of expensive Madeira wine wait on the sideboard, glowing ruby red in the firelight.

★

And now we will leave these 18th-century gentlemen as they proceed to dinner. Follow me upstairs to browse through the galleries investigating life in Colonial New York through engravings, original letters, and other historical documents. Then it is just a short stroll up 18th-century Broad Street to Federal Hall and the inauguration of George Washington.

Federal Hall:
the Inauguration

Federal Hall and Wall Street, circa 1789, showing the second Trinity Church at the head of Wall Street. (Courtesy of The New-York Historical Society, New York City. Drawing by Archibald Robertson)

Federal Hall, April 30, 1789 — splendidly restored and festooned with colorful swags of red, white, and blue. A blustery afternoon, this last day of April, wrapped in a bright blue sky. A chorus of joyous cheers rises from the multitude. General Washington has arrived at last.

The President-elect's dignified form is seen briefly by the celebrants as he emerges from the inaugural coach, proceeding slowly between two columns of soldiers before he enters Federal Hall.

All eyes are fixed on the second-floor portico now. Another great explosion of cheers as the great general suddenly appears above the crowd. His tall, distinguished figure is enhanced by a well-tailored brown suit made from homespun cloth woven in Connecticut, chosen to encourage the purchase of goods manufactured in America. The suit is decorated with silver buttons emblazoned with spread-winged eagles and 13-starred cuff buttons, symbols of the 13 Colonies. The general wears a ceremonial sword sheathed in a steel scabbard.

Among the dignitaries surrounding the President-elect are Robert R. Livingston, Chancellor of New York State, who will administer the oath; Samuel Otis,

Secretary of the Senate, who holds the Bible on a red velvet cushion; Vice President John Adams; New York Governor George Clinton; and Secretary of War Henry Knox.

Washington turns his head, listening to Robert Livingston, and for the first time today Americans see the famous patrician profile. Then he steps forward, leaning his hand for a moment on the lacy wrought-iron railing. Some of those looking up intently from the packed street below, from every window, and from the surrounding rooftops sense that the great man is tired. But then that is to be expected after eight long years of war.

For a moment General Washington scans the crowd, perhaps looking for familiar faces of his soldiers. Undoubtedly there are many standing there, and others lie buried just a short distance away in the churchyards of Trinity Church and St. Paul's Chapel.

A cool breeze ruffles bright banners and flags held by the cheering masses below and sweeps into the open portico, chilling the President-elect. George Washington is not in good health this inauguration day. War has taken its toll here, too.

George Washington has reluctantly accepted the office of President. Even today his thoughts are of Mount Vernon, his beloved home in Virginia. He fought eight long years, waiting for the day when he could at last go home — to walk through his fields, to tend his grapevines, to sleep in his own bed. And he *did* go home; he *did* enjoy life at Mount Vernon again — for a short time.

But the years Washington sacrificed to win the war were not enough for the new nation's leaders and the people. They insisted that George Washington must lead the new nation. They begged him to accept his destiny and become

Inauguration of George Washington as the first President of the United States of America at Federal Hall on April 30, 1789. (Courtesy of The New-York Historical Society, New York City. Photo-lithograph by Joseph Laing)

34

the father of the republic. Finally, "...with a mind oppressed with more anxious and painful sensations than I have words to express,"* General Washington left his Virginia plantation once again.

The time has come. With his hand on the Bible, George Washington takes the oath of office to become the first President of the republic. Livingston announces, "It is done," and turns to the great assemblage to shout, "Long live George Washington, President of the United States!"

A 13-gun salute is followed by the roar of cannon booms and tumultuous cheers from the jubilant throng. President

* These words were recorded in Washington's diary. Unfortunately another journal, in which he wrote his thoughts during his journey by coach from Mount Vernon to the inauguration, has been lost or destroyed.

General George Washington returns
to New York City after the British
evacuation on November 25, 1783.
Behind him is Federal Hall, at which
he will be inaugurated in 1789.
(Courtesy of The New-York Historical
Society, New York City)

Washington bows several times, then
surrounded by dignitaries, walks slowly
into Federal Hall. In the Senate Chamber
he delivers his inaugural address to both
houses of Congress.

Afterward members of Congress
surround the new President as he joins the
procession once more. The soldiers are
resplendent in uniforms of red, navy,
and white, some playing fifes and drums,
while others hold long-barreled muskets
with bayonets spiking upward toward the
bright sky.

Blasts of fireworks fill the air even
now, anticipating the greatest display ever
seen in America. Every church bell in
the city tolls joyously.

The splendid inaugural coach remains
empty, because the President decides to
walk the short distance to St. Paul's
Chapel. Celebrants make way on narrow
Wall Street as the procession moves
slowly by, allowing the people to catch a
glimpse of their new President. The
parade turns north on Broadway, passing
the second Trinity Church, nearly completed now, rising from the foundation of
the first church, burned during the Great
Fire of 1776.

In the distance to the north President
Washington catches a glimpse of Corporation Yard.* It was on this green that the

* The present-day City Hall Park in front of City Hall.

36

general and his soldiers listened to the Declaration of Independence being read on July 9, 1776. Later the British built the infamous Brideswell Prison there, imprisoning many of Washington's soldiers. Nathan Hale was one of those men, spending his last days behind the forbidding walls until he was executed.

At last the inaugural parade stops at St. Paul's Chapel on Broadway. Fortunately, this little parish church escaped the 1776 fire. President Washington worships here often, and it is here that he will attend a service of thanksgiving for the new federal government.

The President climbs the steps of St. Paul's, listening to the nearly deafening cheers that fill the April air. Once inside the chapel he enters his pew and kneels beneath the sparkling crystal chandeliers. Sunlight pours through the clear panes of the long windows and dances along the turquoise and pink walls.

President Washington bows his head and says a prayer for the future of his country.

Here we leave George Washington, head bowed in a small parish church. We know, as he cannot know, the difficult years that lie ahead. He will serve his country as President for another eight long, trouble-filled years. When he finally returns to Mount Vernon in 1797, he will do so as a tired old man who has been dangerously ill twice during his years as President, once from a tumor lying deep in his thigh and then from a near-fatal bout with pneumonia.

After leaving office, the President will have only two years left to ride horseback over his beautiful land, to walk through his ripening fields, to sit before a peaceful fire in his drawing room. But this time he will remain at Mount Vernon. When he dies in 1799, his body will be laid to rest in the garden crypt.

Federal Hall National Memorial: the Tour

One of the most exciting views in New York City is here, in front of Federal Hall National Memorial. Flags are fluttering high on buildings all along Wall Street, their colors brightening historic Trinity Church's timeworn façade at the end of the busy street.

Across narrow Wall Street stand the 1903 New York Stock Exchange Building, which resembles a Roman temple with its frieze of fallen warriors, and the vaultlike walls of Morgan Guaranty Trust Company (1913), originally J.P. Morgan & Co.

High up on a pedestal in front of Federal Hall National Memorial, the monumental figure of George Washington towers above the crowded sidewalk, his right hand reaching forward, his great bronze cape flowing behind. More than 12 feet high and weighing six tons, this figure, created by John Quincy Adams Ward and dedicated in 1883, is considered the finest sculptural representation of George Washington ever made.

This is Federal Hall National Memorial in the 1990s. Now, step back to 18th-century Wall Street.

★

The building that stood on this site in 1703 was simple, unadorned City Hall, which housed the legislative body, courts, jail, and fire department.

In 1765 delegates from nine Colonies met at City Hall in protest of the Stamp Act imposed by Britain, requiring Colonists to buy stamps and attach them to a wide variety of articles. Dubbed the "Stamp Act Congress," the meeting was the first formal political protest leading to the American Revolution.

With the American victory came the decision to make New York City the nation's capital. Suddenly there was a need for a capitol building, and the leaders of the fledgling republic elected to renovate City Hall for that purpose, deciding to enlarge and transform the unassuming structure into something grand, a building worthy of the new nation.

Pierre Charles L'Enfant, who later designed the city plan for Washington, D.C., was commissioned in 1788 to remodel and enlarge City Hall, transforming it into a more majestic Federal Hall. The result was a classical building influenced by Roman architectural models, having Doric columns, a second-floor balcony, and a pediment emblazoned with an eagle and 13 stars, representing the 13 Colonies. The renovated structure was considered worthy of the new government and admirably suited for General Washington's inauguration.

Federal Hall served as the first capitol from March 4, 1789, when the republic first began to function under the Constitution, until the nation's capital was moved to Philadelphia, Pennsylvania, in August 1790. It was at Federal Hall that Congress enacted laws creating the federal judicial system, the Departments of State, War, and Treasury, and the first Cabinet. It was there that 12 constitutional amendments were approved by Congress, 10 of which were later ratified by the states, becoming the Bill of Rights.

After 1790 Federal Hall resumed its former role as City Hall until a new City Hall was completed in 1811 a few blocks north at the present City Hall Park. The original City Hall/Federal Hall, which was in a poor condition, was demolished.

In 1842 a granite and marble United States Customs House was completed on the site of the former Federal Hall. The

Wall Street during the festive celebration of the 147th anniversary of the inauguration of George Washington, April 30, 1936. (Courtesy of The New York Public Library, New York City. Photograph by the Associated Press)✦

Greek Revival building with its fluted
Doric columns was designed to resemble
the Parthenon. The interior's dramatic
marble rotunda, whose balcony was
supported by Corinithian columns, was
modeled after the Pantheon in Rome.

This grand neoclassical building,
which houses the Federal Hall National
Memorial Museum today, functioned as
the Customs House until 1862, and
afterward as the most important unit of
the United States Sub-Treasury system,
serving as the repository for 70 percent of
the government's revenues. Thick-walled
vaults filled the building, even penetrating
the walls of the rotunda. So immense
was the amount of money handled during
the 1870s that the basement floor had to

be reinforced to withstand the crushing weight of as much as $200 million worth of coins. Protecting such vast sums posed a problem as well. During the 1873 Panic, for example, the building was guarded by gun turrets.

The Sub-Treasury Building took on a new role as Federal Hall National Memorial in 1955, a role that has continued to this day, with one important change: A museum celebrating the birth of the United States and its Constitution opened on April 30, 1989, exactly 200 years after George Washington took the oath of office at Federal Hall.

Models of the first City Hall/Federal Hall may be seen in the museum, as well as the suit George Washington wore the day of his inauguration and the Bible on which he took the oath of office. Recorded lectures, accompanied by the sounds of cheering and cannon booms, detail the history of the inauguration, drawing visitors into events of that momentous day, April 30, 1789.

St. Paul's Chapel: the tour

After leaving Federal Hall National Memorial, walk west on Wall Street toward Trinity Church, then turn north on Broadway. As you walk toward St. Paul's Chapel a few blocks up Broadway, just imagine how New York City looked during George Washington's inauguration.

Approximately one quarter of the area you have just seen, from the Battery to Trinity Church, had burned in the Great Fire of 1776, erasing much of early Dutch New Amsterdam from the Manhattan landscape. Seven years of British occupation, which ended in 1783, had also taken its toll.

However, the city was well on the way to recovery. Although some of the narrow, crooked streets still showed the effects of war and fire, attractive new neighborhoods with substantial brick houses had sprung up — and these were decidedly English in design. Businesses were also beginning to prosper, and the city was developing into an international trade center. The 29,000 inhabitants living in New York City in 1789 would see their number double within 11 years.

Yet you can gauge just how small the city of New York still was in the late 18th century when you realize that St. Paul's Chapel was located near the northern edge of the city in 1789 and had actually been built outside the city limits in 1766 on rolling farmland owned by Trinity Parish. The chapel was built to meet the needs of a growing Trinity Parish congregation, which included residents of a little village north of the city limits in the Manhattan countryside — the same Greenwich Village we know today.

St. Paul's Chapel appears almost exactly as it looked on April 30, 1789, when President Washington climbed the steps.[*] Nearly everything is original, down to the iron hinges on the doors and the leaded-glass windows, thanks to a sensitive restoration completed in 1926 — but not without an intensive treasure hunt!

---

[*] Only the spire and clock tower were erected later. The addition, designed by James Crommelin Lawrence, completed the exterior in 1794, 32 years after the chapel was completed.

St. Paul's Chapel and churchyard, view from the southwest. (Courtesy of The New-York Historical Society, New York City. Photograph by Irving Underhill, 1899)

The 14 cut-crystal Waterford chandeliers that originally hung in the nave and galleries of the chapel had been given to the parish churches and other organizations in the late 19th century. All but one were discovered, and they were brought back to St. Paul's Chapel.

The windows had suffered as well. For example, heavy Victorian stained glass darkened the window behind the high altar. Luckily, the original glass had been spared, packed away for more than 40 years. By 1926, sunshine filtered through the original window once again.

Dark brown paint was removed from the walls, and it was discovered that the original colors had probably been lively shades of pink and turquoise. The walls were repainted, and once more St. Paul's Chapel glowed with the vivid colors of Colonial days.

Today, as in 1766, the elegant, light-filled interior is punctuated by soaring handcarved columns with Corinthian capitals that support the graceful galleries. The handcarved, gilded pulpit with a winding stair is original. It is still crowned with the symbol of nobility, the British coronet with six feathers, a reminder of pre-Revolutionary days.

The altar was designed by Pierre L'Enfant, who designed Federal Hall. He also designed the decoration above the altar that depicts Mount Sinai surrounded by sheets of lightning and thunderclouds, and the Tablets of Law with the Ten Commandments.

A reproduction of Washington's pew is located in the north aisle. The Great Seal of the United States hanging above the pew is original and is the first representation of the Great Seal ever made. But you will have to imagine the elegant canopy that once decorated the pew and the upholstered chairs on which the President and his family once sat.

New York State's first govenor, George Clinton, sat in the stately pew in the south aisle. This pew is also an exact reproduction.

Hanging at the rear of the nave is George Washington's regimental flag a design of white stars on a navy field. This design was incorporated into the first flag of the United States and has remained a part of American heritage to this day.

And just to prove that research still goes on and new information is still being discovered about this venerable church, it was always believed that Scottish architect Thomas McBean designed St. Paul's Chapel, modeling it after a Georgian-Classical Revival masterwork by English architect James Gibb — the Church of St. Martin's-in-the-Field in London. Recent information unearthed in Trinity Parish archives indicates that perhaps Thomas McBean did not design the chapel — and, surprisingly, that a man named Thomas McBean may never have existed at all! Then who *was* the architect of St. Paul's Chapel? Only time and further delving into the 18th century will tell.

★

And so ends a journey into the past and a single day in America's history — George Washington's inauguration. Fraunces Tavern, Federal Hall National Memorial, and St. Paul's Chapel all pay homage to that momentous day, celebrating the nation's first President, the nation's first capital, and the new nation itself.

The World Trade Center buildings tower above St. Paul's Chapel today. (Photograph by David Browning, 1990)

Fraunces Tavern Museum
54 Pearl Street at corner of Pearl &
Broad Streets
New York, NY 10004
212-425-1778

Hours:
Monday-Friday 10:00 a.m.- 4:00 p.m.

Admission: (Suggested donation)
• Adults $2.50
• Children & seniors $1.00

Group Tours:
Call for information

Federal Hall National Memorial
26 Wall Street at Nassau Street
New York, NY 10005
212-264-8711

Hours:
Monday-Friday 9:00 a.m.-5:00 p.m.

Admission: Free

Group Tours:
Call for information

St. Paul's Chapel
Broadway & Fulton Streets
New York, NY 10007
212-602-0874

Hours:
Monday-Saturday 8:00 a.m.- 4:00 p.m.
Sundays 7:00 a.m.-3:00 p.m.

Admission: Free

Tours:
Free daily with verger — just ask
when you visit

Additional Tours and Sights in Lower Manhattan

See following chapters: Trinity Church,
Federal Reserve Bank, City Hall, the Statue of
Liberty by sail boat, Sitting in on a Trial (Civic
Center), Brooklyn Bridge, and South Street
Seaport.

New York Stock Exchange
20 Broad Street
New York, NY 10005
212-656-5168

Hours:
Weekdays 9:00 a.m.- 4:00 p.m.
Last tour starts at 3:00 p.m.

Admission: Free

Tours:
Call for information

Woolworth Building
233 Broadway
New York, NY 10279
212-553-2000

Built in 1913 as headquarters for the five-and-
dime-store chain, the Woolworth Building is
still owned by the company. From 1913 to
1930, the building was the world's highest.

The Woolworth Building was designed by
Cass Gilbert, who skillfully combined modern
skyscraper design with Gothic design elements
to create a structure of beauty and grace. Take
a look at the three-story vaulted marble lobby
with the intricate glass mosaic ceiling.

Cass Gilbert also designed the Custom
House at Bowling Green and the U.S. Courthouse at Foley Square.

R E S T A U R A N T S

Fraunces Tavern Restaurant
54 Pearl Street at corner of Pearl &
Broad Streets
212-269-0144

Breakfast:
　Monday-Friday 7:30-10:30 a.m.
Lunch:
　Monday-Friday 11:30 a.m.-4:00 p.m.
Dinner:
　Monday-Friday 5:00-9:30 p.m.

* All major credit cards
* Reservations suggested

Fraunces Tavern Restaurant always seems to be busy. People love the atmosphere, because it gives a real 18th-century flavor to dining.

The restaurant has several large dining rooms, each with its own character. On our last visit, we sat in the inviting Lafayette Room, lined with humorous Hogarth prints.

The menu is extensive. We like the grilled offerings, which include veal chops, lamb chops, and hamburgers. A nice alternative is the fixed-price breakfast for $12.95 — a more modest price and you can still soak up the charming atmosphere. Or stop at the Trophy Room for a light lunch or dinner (sandwiches, soups, etc.) at about $10.00-$15.00 per person.

Lunch & dinner:
　Appetizers $5.00-$8.00
　Entrees $14.00-$25.00

Fraunces Tavern today. (Photograph ©
Phil Cantor, 1990)

D I R E C T I O N S

Subways:
* IRT #1 to South Ferry
* IRT 4, 5 to Bowling Green
* N, R (weekdays only) to Whitehall Street

Bus:
To South Ferry
* M1 (Fifth / Madison Avenues)
* M6 (Seventh Avenue / Broadway / Avenue of the Americas)
* M15 (First / Second Avenues)

To reach Fraunces Tavern, take a bus or train to Battery Park — designated by Whitehall, South Ferry, and Bowling Green above. Fraunces Tavern is a short walk up Pearl Street.

Car:
* FDR Drive & Henry Hudson Parkway, Battery Park / South Ferry exit

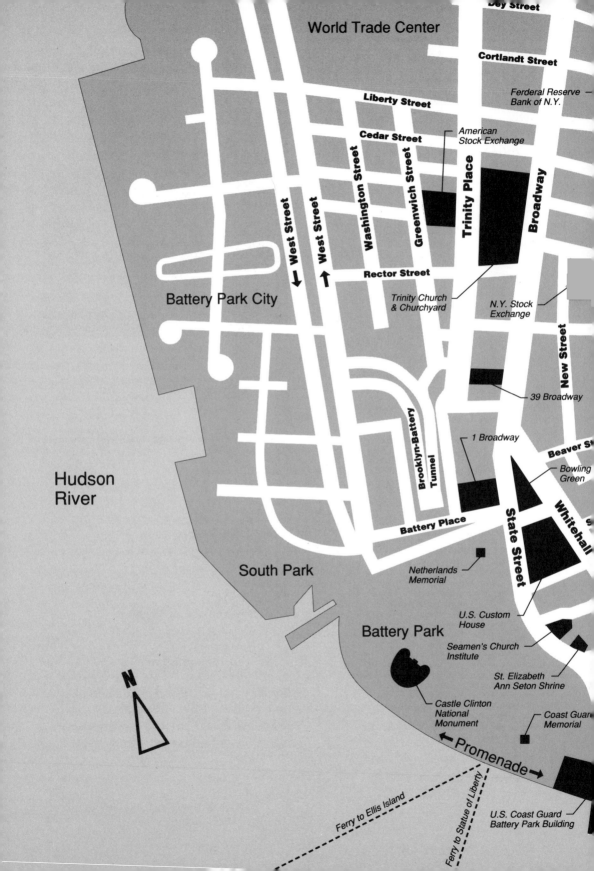

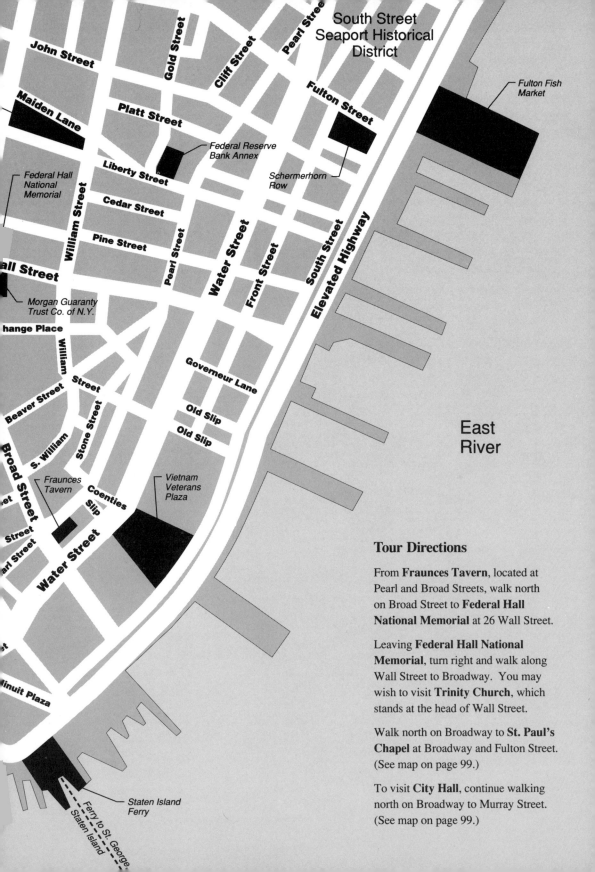

John Street

Gold Street

Cliff Street

Pearl Street

South Street
Seaport Historical
District

Fulton Fish
Market

Maiden Lane

Platt Street

Fulton Street

Federal Reserve
Bank Annex

Liberty Street

Schermerhorn
Row

Federal Hall
National
Memorial

William Street

Cedar Street

Pine Street

Pearl Street

Water Street

Front Street

South Street

Elevated Highway

all Street

Morgan Guaranty
Trust Co. of N.Y.

hange Place

William

Street

Governeur Lane

Beaver Street

Stone Street

Old Slip

Old Slip

East
River

S. William

Broad Street

Fraunces
Tavern

Coenties

Slip

Vietnam
Veterans
Plaza

et Street

rl Street

Water Street

inuit Plaza

Ferry to St. George,
Staten Island

Staten Island
Ferry

Tour Directions

From **Fraunces Tavern**, located at
Pearl and Broad Streets, walk north
on Broad Street to **Federal Hall
National Memorial** at 26 Wall Street.

Leaving **Federal Hall National
Memorial**, turn right and walk along
Wall Street to Broadway. You may
wish to visit **Trinity Church**, which
stands at the head of Wall Street.

Walk north on Broadway to **St. Paul's
Chapel** at Broadway and Fulton Street.
(See map on page 99.)

To visit **City Hall**, continue walking
north on Broadway to Murray Street.
(See map on page 99.)

Historic Trinity Church

The stories her tombstones tell

Above: Trinity Church sat at the head of a far different Wall Street in this circa 1890 photograph. At right are the steps of the Sub-Treasury building, site of the former Federal Hall. (Courtesy of The New-York Historical Society, New York City)

Left: Trinity Church today. (Courtesy of the Parish of Trinity Church)

The History

rinity Church, surrounded by a peaceful green churchyard and enclosed within the marching spears of a black wrought-iron fence, presides serenely over Wall Street's clutter, confusion, and noise. Her slender spire is framed in front by the Wall Street corridor. Behind her the mammoth World Trade Center soars. Yet for most of New York City's life, nearly 200 years, Trinity Church's spire was the tallest structure on the island and was used as a beacon by ships until 1890.

The story of Trinity Parish spans nearly 300 years. Come with me as I peel back those layers of time — until it is 1697 once more — the year in which the first Trinity Church was completed.

★

You are now standing on a narrow dirt road looking at a little rectangular church with a mansard roof and a simple entrance. There are tombstones in the small, shaded churchyard that predate this structure, evidence that this site was a burial ground even before there was a church.

Looking northward at the 17th-century landscape, you will see hilly, lightly wooded countryside, uninhabited save for a sprinkling of windmills and a few houses. Just to the south of the

church you will find the remnants of a combination stockade/earthworks/wooden plank wall that ran straight across the island — built by the Dutch as the northern defense against the British and the Indians. However, it has already outlived its purpose, since the British successfully invaded in 1664 and the last Indian rampage against Dutch settlers occurred in 1655. This disintegrating *waal* will be completely dismantled in a few years, leaving Trinity Church at the head of a street appropriately called Wall Street.

The small seaport village of New York lies just behind the dilapidated wall, spreading southward to the tip of the island. Come take a leisurely stroll along these 17th-century streets.

Even though New York is British now, it still resembles a quaint Dutch village in 1697. Neat little houses, backed by garden patches, fruit trees, and bright flower beds, line both sides of narrow, winding, mostly dirt roads. The earliest houses are small, one-room structures. These once had thatched roofs, but they were prohibited in 1657 — too much of a fire hazard.

Tidy Dutch brick houses are the rule, with attractive steep roofs made of black or red tiles. Gables are cut in a stair-step pattern and face the street. The Dutch home is tightly constructed and cozy inside, kept even warmer by a large tile-decorated fireplace used for cooking. Numerous small-paned windows let in sunlight, and there is often a front "Dutch" door, whose top half opens to let in breezes and sunshine in good weather.

View of Trinity Church and Wall Street from South Street, circa 1890. (Courtesy of Museum of the City of New York)

As you walk along, followed perhaps by a roaming goat or pig, you will notice that London-style row houses are beginning to jostle for position along the crooked, often muddy roads. British influence is increasing daily, beginning to replace that of the Dutch.

This small seaport village, which boasts a few thousand citizens and more than a thousand slaves, carries on a brisk, lucrative fur trade with the Indians, shipping valuable pelts and other natural resources to England and returning with necessities and luxuries unobtainable here.

A walk southward along Gentlemen's Way, also known as Public Wagon Road or Broad Way, will lead you straight through the village to a fort that hugs the tip of the island. Built by the Dutch, who called it Fort Amsterdam, it is a simple, earthen-walled compound containing a prison, church, governor's house, and barracks. The fort is in a state of disrepair and will slowly deteriorate until it is finally torn down around 1789.

Until 1676 there was a delightful Dutch canal flanked by roads at the tip of the island. It has been filled in now, creating another pleasantly wide road called Broad Street. Broad Way and Broad Street, as well as many other streets built by the Dutch and English, will one day be an integral part of 20th-century New York City.

Turn back now and walk north along Broad Way, returning to the first Trinity Church of 1697. There we will watch the unfolding of nearly 300 years of Trinity Church history on that same plot of land at the head of Wall Street.

Small and unadorned, this 17th-century church was important because it was the first Anglican Church, the Church of England, built in Manhattan, the result of a charter granted by the Crown in 1697. Along with that charter, the new parish received a large tract of land in the uninhabited northern part of Manhattan.

Another gift followed, this one granted by Queen Anne, who in 1705 gave to the parish a tract of Manhattan land called the Queen's Church Farm. It just so happened that this farm's acreage covered much of the west side of Lower Manhattan, from latter-day Fulton Street to Christopher Street and from Broadway to the Hudson River. Trinity Parish eventually became quite prosperous and, as the congregation grew, subsidiary churches called chapels were built in outlying areas of the island. One of these was St. Paul's Chapel, constructed in 1766 on a plot of Trinity farmland a short distance up Broadway but still outside the city limits.

From the first, Trinity Church attracted influential parishioners, and at least one who was infamous — an interesting story. It seems that the Scottish privateer Captain William Kidd (who lived on in folklore) had settled into New York society, marrying Sarah Oort, a wealthy, prominent widow. It was during these pleasant days that Captain Kidd provided the tackle to raise the steeple of Trinity Church.

Unfortunately, the captain did not live long enough to enjoy worshipping in his private pew. As the story goes, although Kidd was hired by the British

The first Trinity Church as enlarged in 1737. (Courtesy of Museum of the City of New York)

The second Trinity Church, built after the 1776 fire destroyed the first church. (Courtesy of Museum of the City of New York. Lithograph for *D.T. Valentine's Manual for 1859* from a drawing)

The present Trinity Church, consecrated in 1846. (Courtesy of Museum of the City of New York. Lithograph for *D.T. Valentine's Manual for 1859* from a drawing by George Hayward)

Crown to seize the cargo and crew of any enemy ship he encountered on the high seas, those very acts were used by the Crown as proof of piracy. In 1701 Captain Kidd was arrested, taken to England, and hanged, his body left in chains as a warning to other wrongdoers.

As New York began to grow into a city during the early 18th century, Trinity Parish developed a number of outreach programs, among them numerous religious programs and a school for slaves and Indians, the first in New York. Through the years, Trinity Parish aided churches and institutions worldwide, finally totaling more than 1,500.

In 1709 Trinity founded a charity school for poor children, which eventually became the prestigious private Trinity School (now located on West 96th Street). Trinity provided land for King's College in 1754, dedicated to "Belles Lettres, Breeding, and Some Knowledge of Men and Things." This first college was built on five acres near the church but later moved to upper Manhattan, where the fine new campus was given a new name — Columbia University.

In September 1776, just after the outbreak of the American Revolution, a great fire of unknown origin raced through the city. The conflagration engulfed nearly a quarter of the city, including Trinity Church. Only the churchyard with its charred tombstones bore witness that a church had stood on the spot. Since St. Paul's Chapel had been spared, it was used by Trinity Church members, among them President George Washington, first Chief Justice of the Supreme Court John Jay, and first Secretary of the Treasury Alexander Hamilton.

After the Revolution a new church was built on the foundation of the first, completed in 1790. Trinity was no longer an Anglican church, of course, as ties with England had been severed. The new Trinity was an Episcopal church, which served a growing congregation until 1839, when heavy snows revealed serious structural defects, and the church was torn down.

The third Trinity Church built at the head of Wall Street on Broadway was to be the last, a jewel of Gothic Revival architecture, designed by the talented, self-taught English architect Richard Upjohn. Upjohn was determined to create a church that would reach to the heavens. All elements, from the pointed arches and pinnacles to the great spire, would draw the spirit upward.

Upjohn had his critics, who complained that his design was simply too splendid and too *English*. Why not have good, honest clear glass instead of those flamboyant stained-glass windows? Vaulted ceilings belong in a cathedral, not in a simple church! Why is there to be a cross atop the spire instead of the traditional weather vane?

Upjohn's response to the critics? He installed stained-glass windows, a soaring vaulted ceiling, and a golden cross at the spire's pinnacle. Then he quickly dismantled the spire's scaffolding, ensuring that the cross would not be taken down.

It was fortunate indeed that Richard Upjohn had the courage to ignore those 19th-century critics. When Trinity Church was consecrated in 1846, it was immediately acclaimed one of the most beautiful buildings in 19th-century New York. And it is still considered one of the most beautiful buildings in 20th-century New York City.

Trinity Church interior, circa 1897. (Courtesy of Museum of the City of New York)

Tour of Trinity Church

Bronze doors flank the main entrance, as well as the north and south entrances. The doors were designed by Richard Morris Hunt, a noted architect of the day, and were erected in 1896. All were donated in memory of John Jacob Astor II, grandson of John Jacob Astor (1763-1848), who founded the Astor dynasty by building an immense fortune in real estate and the fur trade.

The bronze doors at the front and north entrances depict Biblical scenes. The south doors depict historical scenes of New York and Trinity Parish. One scene represents Trinity Parish's ministry to the Indians, while another relief is of President Washington at St. Paul's Chapel after the April 30, 1789, inauguration.

The baptistry near the north door (to the right) features a reredos (altar screen) inset with a rare early 15th-century Italian altarpiece.

Walk to the center aisle.

Take a moment to look at the majestic sweep of the nave, both upward — 80 feet to the vaulted ceiling — and forward — a length of 202 feet to the chancel, with its intricately carved altar, reredos, and the arched chancel window. The floor and the pews in the nave are original. The carved oak organ case and loft are examples of flamboyant Gothic decoration (having a flamelike design).

The vaulted stone ceiling is actually made of plaster, carefully painted to give the illusion of stone and suspended below the real ceiling with a gap in between. The expense of an authentic vaulted ceiling was prohibitive, but architect Richard Upjohn did not let that keep him from creating a Gothic Revival interior.

Walk down the aisle to the chancel.

To the left is the canopied oak pulpit, richly carved, lacy, and intricate. To the right is the lectern, where lessons are read. Rising behind a marble altar, inset with glass mosaics and precious stones, is a remarkable Normandy limestone and white marble reredos, which resembles the façade of a Gothic cathedral. The altar and reredos were given by the Astor family in 1877 in memory of William B. Astor, son of John Jacob Astor.

The reredos is highlighted by a carving of the *Crucifixion of Christ*. To the left and above is *Christ's Resurrection at Easter*. To the right is *Christ's Ascension to Heaven*. At the pinnacle of the reredos is *Christ in the Kingdom of Heaven*. On either side of the Crucifixion scene are figures of the Twelve Disciples. Below are scenes from *The Passion of Christ*, including *The Last Supper* after Leonardo de Vinci's masterpiece.

The great chancel window, worked in stained glass of brilliant hues, rises from the reredos and arches beneath the vaulted ceiling. This window is original, as are the other stained-glass windows in the church — a rarity, since Victorian tastes demanded more ornate designs and early windows were often replaced in New York churches. (The stained glass in the church windows was made in a small shed erected in the north churchyard.) The central figure of Christ is flanked by:

- St. Peter with the keys to the Kingdom of Heaven
- St. Matthew with a youth at his side
- St. Mark with a lion
- St. Luke with an ox
- St. John with an eagle
- St. Paul with a sword

If you look closely, you will detect a variance in the stained glass used in St. Matthew's face. During the Civil War, when Union troops were garrisoned at Castle Clinton at the Battery, a few soldiers decided to use the windows for target practice. Fortunately, only one was a marksman!

Walk to the right of the chancel and enter the Chapel of All Saints.

This small chapel was dedicated to Reverend Dr. Morgan Dix, Rector of Trinity Church from 1862-1908, who was the guiding force behind many outreach programs for the poor, including a great number of immigrants.

The Chapel of All Saints is an inner sanctum of quiet beauty. Delicate stained-glass windows in soft colors offer muted light. There is a fine rood screen surmounted by a crucifix, which separates the nave from the chancel. The carved bishop's chair at the right was made in the 1920s for a visit by the Archbishop of Canterbury. The tomb of Dr. Dix rests beneath the altar. As you leave the chapel, notice the sensitive carving of the Madonna and Christ surmounting the door.

Walk to the museum on the opposite side of the church.

Exhibitions change regularly and may include such treasures as the charred Bible that was saved from the flames when the first Trinity Church burned to the ground in 1776, a set of 17th-century communion silver given by the British monarchs William and Mary when the Anglicans worshipped in the chapel of Fort Amsterdam before Trinity Church was built, and the original grant in which Queen Anne granted land to Trinity Parish in 1705.

The Chapel of All Saints in Trinity Church. View of Cenotaph of Dr. Morgan Dix, ninth Rector of Trinity Parish, dedicated in 1913. (Courtesy of Museum of the City of New York)

Tour of Trinity Churchyard

Trinity churchyard, with its blackened, age-old tombstones, is a tranquil relief from the clamor of swirling traffic beyond its enclosing wrought-iron fence. Whether you walk here in summer, when snowball bushes are in bloom and the plane and silk trees cast cool shadows over the graves, or in winter, when the darkened tablets rise from a bed of snow, the experience is restful, peaceful.

Begin your walk in the north churchyard.

1 *Francis Lewis (1713-1803)*
Lewis is the only signer of the Declaration of Independence buried in New York City. His unmarked grave is in this area of the north churchyard and is indicated by a small marker located opposite the church's north door.

2 *William Bradford (1660-1752)*
Bradford was Colonial America's father of the printed word. The tall, narrow tombstone (a replica; the original is at The New-York Historical Society) catalogs Bradford's 70 years of "firsts" in America. After arriving from England at the age of 22, Bradford started the first paper mill, was the first printer south of Boston, brought the first printing press to New York City in 1693, printed the first paper money in the Colonies, and founded the first newspaper, the *New York Gazette*. After a busy and productive 92 years, Bradford's tombstone testifies that ... *being quite worn out with Old age and labor he left this mortal State in the lively Hopes of a blessed Immortality.*

3 *Richard Churcher (Died 1681)*
This is the oldest identified grave in the churchyard, that of a five-year-old boy.

4 *Charlotte Temple (1756-?)*
According to legend, the young woman who lies here died during childbirth while in her early twenties. A naval officer promised to marry her, but at the same time he was secretly courting a young woman with money and position. The story ended at Charlotte's graveside, when the officer unsuccessfully begged the girl's father to kill him.

The tale, said to be based on truth, became a best-selling 19th-century American novel, *Charlotte: A Tale of Truth*. (The truth is that no one will ever know if the young woman who lies here is indeed *that* Charlotte.)

5 *Mary Dalzell (Died 1764, age 28)*
An epitaph that underlines the fragility of life in Colonial America:

Adieu my dearest Babes and tender
  Husband dear
The time of my departure is now
  drawing near.
And when I'm laid low in the silent
  grave ...

6 *Sidney Breese (Died 1767)*
To prove there is humor even in a graveyard, one Sidney Breese obviously carved this epitaph for himself:

Made by himself
Ha Ha Sidney Sidney
Layest though [sic] here
Till time is flown

7 *Firemen's Monument (1865)*
Honors six volunteer firefighters who died while serving in the Union army during the Civil War.

8 *Soldiers' Monument*
The monument resembles a Gothic church steeple surmounted by a gilded eagle.

North Churchyard

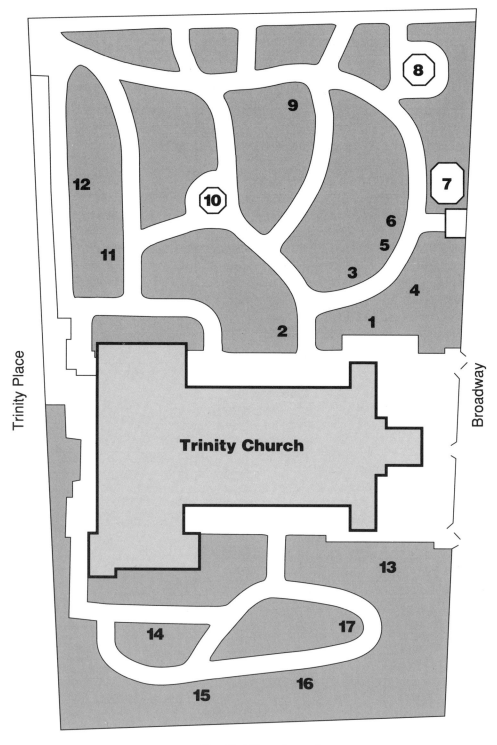

Trinity Place

Trinity Church

Broadway

South Churchyard

Commissioned in 1852 to honor the soldiers and sailors buried here, many of them in unmarked graves.

9 *Adam Allyn*
His honest epitaph was carved by fellow actors. They avowed that the comedian *... possessed many good qualitys [sic]. But as he was a man he had the frailities [sic] common to man's nature.*

10 *Caroline Webster Astor (1830-1908)*
This 39-foot-tall monument, richly carved with Biblical figures, commemorates the life of a woman who understood exactly how to harness wealth and use it to create ultimate social power. She was the same Mrs. Astor who not only ruled New York society's glittering "Four Hundred," but actually created the list with the help of Ward McAllister — whom she later dropped from the list as unworthy. Caroline Astor is not buried here. She lies in the Astor family vault at Trinity Cemetery uptown.

11 *Albert Gallatin (1761-1859)*
This impressive brownstone memorial marks the life of an illustrious American who held governmental positions under Presidents Washington, Adams, Jefferson, Madison, Monroe, and John Quincy Adams. He served as a diplomat, Congressman, Secretary of the Treasury, and Minister to France and Great Britain. Gallatin also founded New York University. He is buried with his wife, Hannah Nicolson (1766-1849), in her family vault.

★

Trinity Churchyard today. (Photograph by David Browning, 1990)

60

As you walk along the path bordering the church's north façade, you will see blackened, half-buried tombstones rising from a bed of groundcover. These tombstones illustrate an interesting fact: Some tombstones were charred and were even exploded by the 1776 fire, but many are black because during an attempt at preservation they were coated with paraffin, which attracted soot and dirt. Until recently Trinity Church was covered with grime because it was also "preserved." However, the original pink sandstone façade is now slowly being revealed, thanks to a $6.8 million restoration project.

Several tombstones are replicas. Vandalism, pollution, and weathering threatened to destroy the originals, which have been safeguarded.

12 *Robert Fulton (1765-1815)*
Fulton was one of America's great innovative minds. As a young man, Fulton was an accomplished artist who studied with Benjamin West. Fulton abruptly changed careers, first designing canals, then, in a leap into the future, designing a submarine named *Nautilus*, which he unsuccessfully offered first to Napoleon about 1801, then to the British in 1804.

Fulton is best remembered for his invention of the steamboat. In later years, Fulton promoted this last invention and founded steamboat lines. He also spent a great amount of time trying to protect his patents in court.

Fulton died at 49 and is buried in his wife's (Harriet Livingston) family vault in this part of the churchyard. A memorial to Fulton is located in the south churchyard. Harriet Livingston's grave is in upstate New York.

★

Before you walk to the south churchyard, take a moment to look through the wrought-iron fence to the city street below, a reminder that Manhattan was once a much hillier island than it is today. The stones forming the retaining wall are said to be the remains of the second demolished church.

By the way, there are many unmarked graves in Trinity churchyard. During frequent yellow fever and smallpox epidemics, swift burial was a necessity, and mass graves were hastily dug. These mass burials may have caused a rather macabre problem — possibly unrealized at the time. An underground pool used for drinking water lay beneath the graveyard, drawing its water from rain that filtered through the graves. Whether officials began to fear contamination or simply decided that the existing graveyard was too crowded, burials were prohibited south of Canal Street after 1830.

Trinity Parish opened another cemetery in 1876 (155th Street between Broadway and Riverside Drive), using land that had once been a farm owned by J.J. Audubon, the artist-naturalist. Audubon lies beneath the hilly land overlooking the Hudson River — one among thousands.

13 *Captain James Lawrence, USN (1781-1813) and Augustus C. Ludlow (1792-1813)*
Captain Lawrence, Commander of the frigate *Chesapeake* during the War of 1812, has lived on in American history for his famous dying words, "Don't give up the ship!" Augustus C. Ludlow, who served as second-in-command, died at the age of 21 during the same sea battle. The impressive monument is guarded by eight cannons linked by chain, said to have been taken from a captured British ship.

14 *Commodore Silas Talbot (1751-1813)*
First Commander of the *USS Constitution,*
the frigate that became famous during the
War of 1812 as "Old Ironsides."

15 *Robert Fulton Monument*

16 *Alexander Hamilton (1755-1804)*
A pyramid surmounts the striking memorial to the most illustrious person buried
at Trinity churchyard.

Hamilton was one of two illegitimate
sons born in the British West Indies to
beautiful Rachel Fawcett Lavien, who
while married to a planter, John Lavien,
began to live with James Hamilton.
Abandoned by their irresponsible father,
James Hamilton, Alexander and his
brother James soon lost their mother, who
died when Alexander was just 13.

The two young boys began working,
Alexander as a clerk and James as a
carpenter. The ambitious Alexander
impressed the local minister, who sent the
boy to the United States to study, after
which Alexander entered King's College
(Columbia University).

At the outbreak of the Revolutionary
War, Alexander enlisted, soon rising to
the rank of lieutenant colonel and aide-de-
camp to General George Washington. A
brilliant soldier, Hamilton led a successful
charge at Yorktown in 1781, crowning his
military career, during which a lasting
relationship developed with Washington.

Building one political power base
upon another, Hamilton married Betsy
Schuyler, daughter of General Philip
Schuyler — an enduring marriage, which
produced eight children.

In the years following the war,
Hamilton's star rose steadily — first in
law, then in government. Hamilton was a
proponent of a strong federal government
and was influential in laying the foundation for the new government. He was an
author of *The Federalist Papers*, became
Secretary of the Treasury under Washington, and was responsible for establishing
a national banking system.

Hamilton also had many enemies,
among them Aaron Burr. Hamilton
worked actively to ensure that Burr lost
the presidency to Thomas Jefferson as
well as the governorship of New York.
Enmity intensified until at last Burr
challenged Hamilton to a duel on July 11,
1804. Hamilton was mortally wounded
and died the following afternoon. Ironi-
cally, Hamilton's son Philip had been
killed in a duel two years before, in the
same location and holding the same gun.

17 *John Watts (1749-1836)*
In his judicial robes and wig, a bronze
John Watts stands guard over his own
grave. Watts was a Congressman, first
judge of Westchester County, Speaker
of the New York Assembly, and the last
Royal Recorder of New York City.

Parish of Trinity Church
Broadway at Wall Street
New York, NY 10006
212-602-0700

- The Reverend Daniel Paul Matthews, D.D., Rector
- The Reverend Canon Lloyd S. Casson, Vicar
- Phyllis Barr, Parish Archivist & Museum Curator

Mass:
Monday-Friday 8:00 a.m. & noon

Services:
Sunday 9:00 a.m. and 11:15 a.m.

Tours:
Daily 2:00 p.m. by a verger

★

Recommended Reading:
For an interesting guide to all of New York City's cemeteries, pick up *Permanent New Yorkers* by Judi Culbertson and Tom Randall.

RESTAURANTS

For nearby restaurants, see listings in Lower Manhattan.

DIRECTIONS

Subway:
- IRT #2, 3, 4, 5 to Wall Street
- BMT RR to Rector Street
- BMT J, M to Broad Street

Bus:
- M1 (Fifth / Madison Avenues) to Broadway & Fulton Street
- M6 (Seventh Avenue / Broadway / Avenue of the Americas) to Broadway & Fulton Street

Car:
- FDR Drive, Pearl Street exit
- West Street, turn at Rector Street

The blackened tombstones in Trinity churchyard. (Photograph by David Browning, 1990)

Stately 19th-Century City Hall

Where the mayor holds court with reporters and city business gets done!

ity Hall, completed during the early years of the American republic, is the historic centerpiece of New York City's Civic Center. Perhaps the building looks a little out of place in the gritty, noisy city — an aristocratic blend of French Renaissance and Federal architecture on her pedestal of steps. Yet her dignified 19th-century presence is somehow reassuring.

The building's refined lines are enhanced by an impressive cupola. *Justice,* holding the symbolic scales in one hand and a sword in the other, stands at the apex. However, the figure is different in one respect — *Justice* is not wearing a blindfold.

When City Hall was completed in 1811, just one mile north of Manhattan's southernmost tip, it was considered the very last northern boundary of New York City. The city fathers were so certain of it, in fact, that they ordered the back of City Hall sheathed in cheaper brownstone rather than the expensive marble used for the rest of the exterior. After all, they reasoned, who would ever see City Hall from the back? As it turned out, even the choice of soft Massachusetts marble was

Above: City Hall today. (Photograph © Jeffrey Jay Foxx, 1990)

Right: City Hall in gala dress for an unrecorded 1895 celebration. (Courtesy of The New York Public Library, New York City)✦

a poor one. By the turn of the 20th century it had almost completely eroded and was finally stripped off and replaced with the limestone you see today.

★

The work of city government goes on within the walls of 19th-century City Hall. If you go through one of the four pairs of doors, you may catch a glimpse of the lively proceedings.

Just inside is a beautiful rotunda with a double swirl of marble stairs winding up to a fine columned gallery. Perhaps you will even find the mayor in the rotunda, carrying on with reporters; or then again, he could be down the hall in the Blue Room in which he signs legislation, holds press conferences, and conducts various meetings.

This first floor isn't used solely by the executive branch of city government. City Councilmen's offices are down the hall, while in the press room, Room 9, you will hear typewriters clattering, the buzz of voices, and the jangling of telephones as reporters go about the business of getting and giving the news.

Now climb one of the stairways to the second floor. On the left is the original City Council Chamber, in which the legislative branch of city government still meets about twice a month. This is where the City Council president and 35 Council members enact city laws, hold public hearings on legislation, and approve the city budget, among other legislative responsibilities.

The City Council Chamber is grand indeed, with a ceiling bordered by heavily carved and gilded moldings, centered with a painting set like a jewel in a gilt frame high overhead. An ornate railing encircles the gallery from which visitors are welcome to listen to the proceedings

View of Broadway and palatial City Hall as they appeared in 1819. View looking north from Ann Street. From an original watercolor by Swedish Baron Axel Leonhard Klinckowstrom, who visited New York in 1818-1819. He wrote that Broadway was the most frequented promenade in the city "where all new fashions can be admired." A column of St. Paul's Chapel can be seen in the left foreground. The second building on the left belonged to John Jacob Astor. And those dogs roaming the cobblestone street? Some of them are pigs! (Courtesy of The New-York Historical Society, New York City)

when City Council is in session — often very lively entertainment!

On the opposite side of the second floor is the airy and elegant Board of Estimate Chamber. Through the years this 19th-century room has been the unlikely setting for the hurly-burly of city business carried on by the Board of Estimate, a body composed of the mayor, city comptroller, president of the City Council, and the five borough presidents. Within this chamber city deals and contracts have been hashed out and public hearings held about city financial matters.

All of that changed when the Board of Estimate was abolished in 1990. The City Council took over responsibilities concerning land use and the budget, while the executive branch was given the power

to award various contracts. And how will the beautiful Board of Estimate Chamber be used? Only time will tell.

Between these two chambers is the Governor's Room, designed as the New York City office of the New York governor after the state capital was moved from New York City to Albany. The Governor's Room and two flanking chambers are used today as a museum of New York City history as well as a reception room.

As soon as you enter the Governor's Room, you will see the desk used by President George Washington at Federal Hall when New York City was the nation's capital. Washington's 1789 silk inaugural flag is displayed nearby. Standing guard by the desk is an American flag

City Hall draped in mourning in preparation for Abraham Lincoln's funeral procession in New York City on April 25, 1865. President Lincoln lay in state for 24 hours in City Hall. Lincoln's body was transported by train from Washington, D.C., to Springfield, Illinois, for burial. (Courtesy of The New-York Historical Society, New York City)

from Marquis de Lafayette's grave in Paris, a reminder that the brilliant French statesman and soldier served in America's Continental Army and was a friend of Washington.

The remaining furnishings in all three rooms were originally made for the Governor's Room or for the City Council Chamber.

Now take a look at the large portraits lining the walls of all three rooms. This outstanding collection was begun in 1792 by the Common Council, which predated the City Council. If you have ever wondered how the first American leaders really looked, how they dressed, and how their faces revealed their characters — now is your chance to find out. The paintings really do portray the personalities of these early leaders.

There is George Washington, of course, "distinguished" and "noble" and "regal," as he was described repeatedly by writers of the day. Even the new Senate suggested that the President's title should be "His Highness, the President of the United States of America, and Protector of their Liberties"!

The portrait of Washington by the renowned American artist (and Revolutionary War soldier) John Trumbull was commissioned by the Common Council in 1792, along with the portrait of George Clinton, first governor of New York, which also hangs in the Governor's Room. General Washington is depicted splendidly dressed in his uniform and standing beside his battle horse.

Another John Trumbull portrait depicts handsome Alexander Hamilton, a major-general during the Revolutionary War and afterward first Secretary of the Treasury. Hamilton was plagued by whisperings of his illegitimate birth and disliked by some of the nation's leaders who thought him imperious, overbearing, and cold; but even his detractors often admired his brilliance. It is interesting to speculate how high his star would have risen had he not been killed in the duel with Aaron Burr.

Aristocratic Thomas Jefferson gazes from his frame with an intelligent, worldly expression. Author of the Declaration of Independence, first Secretary of State, and third President of the United States (1801-1809), Jefferson was

also another man — architect, inventor, botanist, and Virginia landholder.

Jefferson, an important figure in the new government, was soon pitted against Hamilton in a bitter power struggle over national policy. Jefferson said he did not like controversy, but as you can tell from his eyes, he was an able, clever, and determined adversary. There were even some — Aaron Burr, for instance — who said he was ruthless.

I think you will find the other portraits just as interesting, from bossy, iron-willed Peter Stuyvesant, who arrived from Holland in 1647 to lead the new Dutch colony of New Netherland (New York State) and its village port, New Amsterdam, to gaunt, tough Andrew Jackson, who as major-general decisively defeated the British at the Battle of New Orleans in January 1815 and served as President of the United States from 1829 to 1837.

Throughout the history of City Hall, many of these men and the leaders who followed in their footsteps have walked through the wide double doors of the Governor's Room to attend official receptions. And there were others who lay in state at City Hall, among them Ulysses S. Grant and Abraham Lincoln.

★

As you leave City Hall, take a few minutes to read the historical plaque at City Hall Park across the street. This green plot of land exemplifies the many ways in which New York City land has been used through the centuries.

Under 17th-century Dutch rule, the area was windmill-sprinkled farmland. During the 18th century alms houses for the poor stood on this ground, and public executions were held in an exotic red pagoda structure.

The British built Brideswell Prison

here in 1775, which stood until 1838, and in 1842 a fountain 100 feet in diameter dominated the park. This was demolished to make way for a huge post office, which stood from 1875 until 1938.

    Numerous political demonstrations also took place here, including a protest led by Alexander Hamilton on July 6, 1774, as well as the reading of the Declaration of Independence to Washington and his troops July 9, 1776.

Above: An interesting view of City Hall during construction of the subway. This photograph was taken on April 19, 1901. Beneath City Hall Park today is a relic of the past — a grand subway stop, cut off and silent. The IRT southbound local offers a nostalgic view of this early 20th-century station. Just stay on the train at the end of the line at Brooklyn Bridge. The train will loop around, passing the former station as it begins the trip uptown. (Courtesy of The New York Public Library, New York City, the William B. Parsons Collection)✦

Right: A post office was built in 1875 at the south end of City Hall Park, blocking the view of City Hall behind it. In 1938-1939 the building was demolished. This photograph was taken at the intersection of Vesey Street, Broadway, and Park Row, circa 1890. The roof of St. Paul's Chapel is seen in the left foreground. (Courtesy of The New-York Historical Society, New York City)

City Hall

City Hall Park
Near Broadway & Murray Street
New York, NY 10007
212-566-2326

Hours:
Monday-Friday 10:00 a.m.-4:00 p.m.

Admission: Free

Tour City Hall on your own or join a weekly tour.

Call to confirm that the Governor's Room is open: 212-566-8681.

To find out when the City Council is in session, call 212-566-8681 or 212-566-2354.

Want to watch one of the mayor's public functions at City Hall? Call the Mayor's Press Office, 212-566-5090.

DIRECTIONS

Subway:
- #2, 3 to Park Place
- #4, 5, 6 to Brooklyn Bridge
- A, C to Chambers Street
- N to City Hall

Bus:
- M1 (Fifth / Madison Avenues)
- M6 (Seventh Avenue / Broadway / Avenue of the Americas)
- M101, M102 (Third / Lexington Avenues)

Car:
- FDR Drive, Civic Center exit
- West Street, turn at Chambers Street

Gold! Gold! Gold!

A visit to the gold vault of the New York Fed

Above: This fascinating circa 1921 photograph shows the New York Fed site after demolition of numerous small buildings. The entire block was excavated to bedrock, in some areas as far as 117 feet below street level. (Courtesy of The New York Public Library, New York City)✢

Left: A Wells Fargo armored truck waits at the New York Fed. (Photograph © Phil Cantor, 1990)

he immense Federal Reserve Bank of New York has been compared to a moat-ringed fortress hiding a vast subterranean cache of gold. An apt comparison. The treasure of gold bricks is certainly there. And the block-square building does resemble a fortress, the narrow streets that encircle it suggesting a moat.

The New York Fed might resemble a centuries-old fortress, but a 20th-century world of finance goes on behind the thick stone walls. Go through the Liberty Street doorway now and take a look at the Federal Reserve System, past and present.

★

A new American government was just barely in place in 1791 when angry voices filled President George Washington's office in New York City's capitol building, Federal Hall. Alexander Hamilton, the young and brash Secretary of the Treasury, and Thomas Jefferson, the 48-year-old Secretary of State, shouted across the desk of the startled President.

The quarrel was about money — the new government's money and the money of the new nation. How was it to be managed? Hamilton insisted that there must be a central bank, empowered by Congress to manage the government's money and regulate the nation's credit. Jefferson loudly disagreed, uncharacteristic behavior for the dignified Virginian. Jefferson steadfastly asserted that the

Constitution did not give Congress the power to create such a bank.

Hamilton won the first bout. The first Bank of the United States was created in 1791, chartered for 20 years. However, a sharply divided Congress failed to re-charter the bank in 1811, foretelling an up-and-down struggle for a flexible and safe monetary system that was to last 100 years.

Although a series of financial panics rocked the United States during the 19th century, a severe panic in 1907 finally jolted Americans into the realization that banking reform was essential. Woodrow Wilson, sworn in as President in 1913, was instrumental in bringing about that reform.

Surrounded by well-chosen advisers who expounded diverse views, Wilson proved himself a wise and skillful leader and negotiator, using every trick in his presidential arsenal to encourage compromise on a number of issues. After a long and difficult fight, the Federal Reserve Act was passed on December 23, 1913, providing the guidelines for the Federal Reserve System.

How is the Federal Reserve System Organized and What does it do?

The Federal Reserve System is the nation's central bank, whose operating arms are its 12 regional Federal Reserve Banks and their 25 branches. Each of the Federal Reserve Banks has a nine-member board of directors, which over-

The mammoth New York Fed. Date unknown. (Courtesy of The New York Federal Reserve Bank, New York City)

sees operations under the supervision of the seven-member Board of Governors who meet in Washington, D.C.

The goal of the Federal Reserve System is to maintain a safe and flexible banking system in the United States. To do so, the Federal Reserve System has many responsibilities, one of which is the formulation and administration of mone-tary policy designed to keep the economy healthy and growing by balancing money and credit with the demand for goods and services.

The Federal Reserve is the govern-ment's banker as well. The Treasury and other government agencies keep their mammoth checking accounts in Federal Reserve Banks, and each year billions of dollars are deposited and withdrawn from these accounts. For example, federal unemployment taxes and corpo-rate income taxes flow into Federal Reserve Banks.

The Federal Reserve System is also the central bank used by other commercial banks and thrift institutions, offering similar banking services to those deposi-tory institutions that they in turn offer to individuals and businesses. Federal Reserve Banks make loans, hold cash reserves, move currency and coins to and from banks, and process billions of checks for these banks and thrifts.

Federal Reserve Banks generate billions of dollars in income for the federal government each year, primarily from interest earned on government securities and services offered to banks and thrifts.

The Federal Reserve System func-tions in numerous other ways. For example, it administers federal consumer credit protection laws.

The Fed is also responsible for maintaining adequate amounts of paper money and coins to meet fluctuating banking needs and seasonal public demand. This responsibility includes sorting, examining, counting, and discarding worn currency and ordering replacements from the U.S. Bureau of Engraving and Printing.

The Federal Reserve System functions as a central check-clearing system, processing about 40 percent of all checks cashed in the United States. The Fed handles nearly 17.6 billion checks (1988) every year.

The Federal Reserve makes investments, receives deposits, and holds gold for foreign governments, central banks, and international monetary institutions. It is this gold, of course — the stacks and stacks of gleaming bars — that draws thousands of visitors to the New York Federal Reserve Bank each year, making its tour one of New York City's most popular attractions.

Two powerful bodies of the Federal Reserve System formulate key monetary policies. They are the Federal Open Market Committee (FOMC) and the Board of Governors.

Under law state-chartered and national depository institutions are subject to reserve requirements of the Federal Reserve System, obliging them to hold in reserve a percentage of their customers' deposits. These reserves are then deposited in a Federal Reserve Bank or can be held as vault cash. The Board of Governors can increase that percentage, thus restricting the banks' lending, decreasing business activity. On the other hand, that percentage can be decreased, giving banks more money to lend, thus increasing business activity. (Because the effect of changing reserve requirements is so far-reaching, it is seldom used. The percentages were last changed in 1980.)

The Board of Governors and the Federal Reserve Banks have a combined role in determining a second powerful method for restricting or expanding credit and the money supply. It is the discount rate. Banks and thrift institutions borrow from Federal Reserve Banks just as individuals borrow from banks. They are charged an interest rate, called a discount rate, which is determined by the board of directors in each Federal Reserve Bank, subject to approval by the Board of Governors.

When the discount rate is increased, credit is restricted, as it is more expensive for banks to borrow, and in turn, it is expensive for individuals or businesses to borrow from banks — thereby slowing the economy. On the other hand, when the rate is lowered, it is less expensive for banks to borrow, and they can charge a lower rate to their customers, encouraging borrowing and more money in circulation.

The Federal Reserve System's most powerful policy-making body is the Federal Open Market Committee. The FOMC is composed of the seven members of the Board of Governors and five of the 12 Federal Reserve Bank presidents, who serve on a rotating basis for one-year terms (except the president of the New York Fed, who is a permanent member).

Meeting approximately every two months in Washington, D.C., the FOMC determines the most important monetary policy — the purchase and sale of U.S. Government and Federal Agency securities, called Open Market Operations.

Millions — or billions — of dollars flow when securities are bought or sold, directly affecting depository institutions'

A closeup view of the Fed's massive building stones. (Photograph © Phil Cantor, 1990)

reserves, and in turn affecting the availability and cost of credit and money in the marketplace.

The Federal Reserve is indeed a powerful mechanism, which plays an important role in safeguarding the American economy through its policies that control credit and the money supply. But there are other forces at work as well. Among them are the spending and saving habits of consumers, taxing and spending by federal and local governments, wage and price policies of business and labor, economic policies of foreign governments, even the emotional outlook of the American public — all important factors in the final economic equation.

The Tour

Most people come to the Federal Reserve Bank of New York for one reason — to see gold. However, the entire tour is fascinating, and it is worth the trip just to see the building. Fourteen stories high and covering an entire block, the Fed is monumental in size, even down to the building stones, which resemble great rounded sarcophagus lids.

There is an interesting story attached to the construction of the New York Fed. In 1918 a site three blocks north of Wall Street was chosen. The only problem was that the block was already crowded with a jumble of small 19th-century buildings. Gradually the building owners agreed to sell — that is, except one, who owned the Montauk Building fronting William Street. When that owner was offered $400,000, he refused, choosing instead to

The gold vault. (Courtesy of The New York Federal Reserve Bank, New York City)

sell to a speculator for $425,000.

The speculator immediately demanded $1.25 million for the property. The government, biding its time, completed the Fed around the Montauk Building in 1924. Then in 1933 during the Depression the speculator was more than glad to sell the building for $326,250. The building was razed, and the Fed at last occupied the entire block in 1935 — a patiently awaited 17 years later!

The Federal Reserve Bank of New York is a powerful presence in the financial district. It actually gives the impression of a gigantic impregnable fortress isolated on an island bounded by Nassau, Liberty, and William Streets and by Maiden Lane. The architectural firm York & Sawyer designed the building to impart the feeling of security and power, reaching for inspiration into 15th-century Florence and the fortified *palazzos* of the wealthy banking and merchant families.

Excavation was begun in 1921, a herculean task in itself, since the entire block had to be excavated down to bedrock as far as 117 feet below street level and 60 feet below water level. The reason? Only solid bedrock could support the incredible weight of the gold that would ultimately be stored in the depths of the building. It was also a dangerous business, as there was a risk that the surrounding buildings might teeter forward and collapse into the gaping pit because the streets were so narrow.

In 1924 the Federal Reserve Bank was complete, a kind of New York Renaissance palace, down to the massive chiseled blocks of limestone and sandstone, the 30-foot-high vaulted ceilings, the great arches, and over 200 tons of ornate wrought-iron grillwork and decoration, including huge hand-wrought iron lanterns flanking the Liberty Street en-

trance — exact copies of lanterns at the Strozzi *palazzo* in Florence.

★

The monumental scale of the Federal Reserve is probably the first thing visitors notice as they wait just inside the 33 Liberty Street entrance for the tour to begin. The lobby is imposing, with shiny travertine floors and a soaring vaulted ceiling, and with great filigreed handwrought iron gates, which give access to the upper floors.

After an introductory lecture about the New York Fed, its powers and responsibilities, the tour group is ushered to the third floor, passing through a barred jail-like entry to the currency verification department. There, behind a large window is a room filled with paper money. This is where the New York Fed processes more than 2.6 billion bills (notes) deposited each year by banks and thrift institutions — excess currency held by the Fed until it is needed by the depositors.

Using high-speed automatic sorters, bills are fed at a rate of 60,000 an hour through optical scanning devices, which can detect denomination, condition, and whether a bill is counterfeit by reading different densities of ink on each bill. Bills totaling about $160 million a day pass through these sorters.

Bills that are in good condition are fed into slots and tied into 100-note stacks. Counterfeit bills — about 100 a day — are separated automatically and sent to the U.S. Secret Service. Worn or otherwise unfit bills are fed into automatic shredders. (Each visitor is given a little package of shredded money to take home as a souvenir.) The shredded currency will be replaced by paper money — officially known as Federal Reserve notes printed by the U.S. Bureau of Engraving and Printing. The new bills arrive at the Fed in 4,000-note stacks which are called "bricks."

There is a display area in the currency verification department in which various notes are exhibited, ranging from a Colonial bill emblazoned with the warning *To Counterfeit is Death* to a case full of counterfeit money.

There is also an interesting display of coins. For example, there is a Spanish *dolare*, originally accepted as currency in the American Colonies, which led Congress to choose the word "dollar" to designate the nation's basic monetary unit. Also displayed are an 1850s Liberty Head gold dollar and an early one-cent copper coin, the first coin authorized by the United States Congress.

Visitors do not see the processing of coins, which is yet another service performed by the New York Fed for depository institutions. Around 4.5 million coins are sent by banks and thrifts (and the Metropolitan Transit Authority) each day, separated by denomination, and put into large bags. Arriving by armored truck, the coins are processed by weighing the bags, since counting millions and millions of coins each day would be an overwhelming task. The Philadelphia Mint provides the New York Fed with replacement coins. Also unseen by tour groups are the New York Fed's paying and receiving tellers, who provide another important service, handling about $146 million in deposits each day and approximately $167 million in withdrawals.

Next on the tour — and without a doubt the highlight — is an excursion 80 feet below the crowded sidewalks of Manhattan to the silent and heavily guarded gold vault, stretching half the length of a football field.

One-seventh of all the known monetary gold reserves in the world rests here on solid bedrock — 830,000 bars weighing between 27 and 28 pounds each, or 10,500 tons. There is more gold resting in this gold vault than in any other single place in the world — at least any known repository!

And the value of all of this gold? The market price fluctuates according to supply and demand, of course. In mid-1990 it was valued at $136 billion in the world market. Most of the gold stored in this vault is foreign gold, sent to the United States for safekeeping prior to World War II.

There is very little United States gold stored here. Instead, U.S. bullion is stored at Fort Knox, Kentucky, and at West Point, New York, as well as at the Denver and Philadelphia mints and the San Francisco Assay Office.

The gold stored here by 80 foreign countries and some international organizations is kept in one or more of 122 separate triple-locked compartments within the vault, where it is neatly stacked in an overlapping pattern for stability — rather like building a brick wall.

Visitors get a chance to peer into Compartment 86, which contains 5,160 bars. Each bar is worth about $160,000 (mid-1990), with a total value of approximately $825 million. Compartment 86 is one of the very smallest. In contrast there is a compartment (the owner is kept secret, of course!) that holds $16 billion in gold, forming a block 18 feet wide, 10 feet high, and 18 feet deep!

Transactions between nations storing gold at the Fed may be carried out right here in the gold vault. (However, there are very few transactions of this type, as nations generally do not pay their debts in gold anymore.) The gold bars would be physically moved from one country's compartment to another, a far less dangerous and less expensive method for trans-

acting business, costing just $1.75 for each bar moved.

However, moving gold is hard work for the gold stackers. Hydraulic lifts help, of course, but stacking thousands of heavy bars is backbreaking work. Even the workers' feet must be protected with strong magnesium safety shoe covers worn over steel-tipped work shoes. A dropped 27-pound brick is painful, even if the brick is made of gold.

And what about security? The vault has 12-foot-thick walls, and the floor rests on solid bedrock. Above the gold vault are two more floors of impregnable concrete and steel-walled vaults. In addition, there is just one entry to the gold vault, and it is a marvel of engineering, a design for ultimate security.

To understand the entry mechanism, imagine a tin can that has been cut in half vertically and the halves spread slightly to create a narrow rectangular opening. The can, which is designed to rotate, is set into a frame. When the can rotates 90 degrees, the open section is moved from the center of the frame and turned sideways to face the frame itself. A solid curved side of the can now faces front, sealing the frame shut.

Now just imagine that the tin can is a 9-foot-tall, 90-ton steel cylinder, rotating in a 140-ton steel frame. The giant cylinder is rotated by a large hand-turned wheel. A second hand-turned wheel lowers the 90-ton cylinder three-eighths of an inch into the floor, creating a water-

The impressive three-story-high Liberty Street entrance, opened for the day. (Photograph © Phil Cantor, 1990)

tight, airtight seal, similar to pushing a cork into a bottle. Finally, a series of time locks and multiple combinations control access to the entrance of the vault.

Then, of course, there is literally an army of guards protecting the Fed. The protection staff is comparable to the police force of many medium-sized American cities. A majority of these guards are ranked as experts in marksmanship, the highest rating given.

Added to these measures are several procedures that seal the entire building from top to bottom — stairs, elevators, doors — within seconds after an alarm has been activated. These and many other safeguards have made the Fed and the vault impregnable. No one has even attempted to break into the New York Fed or any other Federal Reserve Bank.

Visitors leave the vault filled with facts and stories about gold. Here are just a few of them:

The United States is the only country that casts rectangular bricks, which are always 7 inches long, 3-5/8 inches wide and 1-5/8 to 1-3/4 inches thick. The bars cast in other countries are trapezoidal, and some U.S. firms are also changing to the trapezoidal shape.

A seal is stamped on each and every bar, which tells where and when that bar was cast. Another number tells its purity, which must be at least 99.5 percent pure gold to be considered "good delivery" for monetary gold.

All gold bars must weigh between 350 and 430 troy ounces — except under one condition. If there is not enough gold to make a complete bar at the end of a casting process, a slimmer bar is cast. What is it called? A Hershey bar!

And finally, about 90,000 tons of gold have been mined throughout history. If all of that gold were cast, it would form a cube 54 feet on each side.

The Federal Reserve Bank of New York
33 Liberty Street
New York, NY 10045
212-720-6130

Important:
Try to reserve as far in advance as possible
(two to three months), as the tour is extremely
popular. Book group tours four to six months
in advance.

Admission: Free

Tours:
Weekdays at 10:00 a.m., 11:00 a.m., 1:00 p.m.,
and 2:00 p.m. School groups must be 16 years
of age or juniors in high school.

R E S T A U R A N T S

La Tour D'Or
14 Wall Street, 31st Floor
212-233-2780

Lunch:
   Monday-Friday noon-3:00 p.m.
Dinner:
   Monday-Friday 4:00-8:00 p.m.

• All major credit cards
• Reservations suggested

You couldn't find a more appropriate place to
have lunch after the tour of the gold vault than
La Tour D'Or. The delightful French restaurant is located just a stone's throw from the
New York Stock Exchange and Trinity Church
in a building once owned by J.P. Morgan.
Morgan controlled such a vast financial empire
during the late 19th and early 20th centuries he
more than once bailed out the impoverished
U.S. government. What is more, this restaurant is located in a penthouse-apartment
hideaway once maintained by Morgan. What
secrets these walls could tell!

And speaking of walls, they are a soft
delicate pink now, enhancing the turn-of-the-
century remnants of Morgan's apartment —
carved walnut doorways, ornate moldings, and
a fireplace with a carved walnut mantel. A
nice touch added by the owner is a tile wall
painted with a 19th-century scene of the Paris
stock exchange.

There is also a delightful vintage bar, and
there are small private dining rooms, which
are eagles' nests in the sky.

The prix-fixe lunch is a winner. We started
with a creamy and bright carrot soup and a
flavorful watercress soup. Another good
choice was a delicately seasoned salad, crisp
and colorful.

Main courses were traditional Continental
offerings, well-prepared and presented. There
was a thick veal chop, crispy on the outside
and pink and juicy inside, bathed in a red wine
sauce and garnished with shredded carrots
with ginger and spicy apple slices. Beef
Wellington was a welcome change from the
usual sodden disaster often served in restaurants. The crust was flaky and crisp, the beef
tender. A filet of sole almondine was perfectly
prepared.

Desserts included a chocolate mousse, a
Grand Marnier mousse, and raspberry, peach
and strawberry tarts — satisfying endings to a
more than satisfying lunch.

Service was friendly and efficient. The
waitresses added to the mood of 19th-century
New York in their long black skirts, high-
necked blouses, and long aprons.

Prix-fixe lunch $28.95
Prix-fixe dinner $38.95

D I R E C T I O N S

The Gold Vault. (Courtesy of The New York Federal Reserve Bank, New York City)

Subway:
- J, M, Z to Fulton Street Station
- #2, 3, 4, 5 to Fulton Street Station or Wall Street Station
- A, C to Broadway-Nassau Station

Bus:
- M1 (Fifth / Madison Avenues)
- M6 (Seventh Avenue / Broadway / Avenue of the Americas)
- M15 (First / Second Avenues)

Car:
- FDR Drive, Civic Center / Pearl Street exit

Parking:
- Extremely limited

A Courtroom Adventure

Sitting in on a trial

Surprisingly, this tour, which might seem most stringently regulated, turns out to be one of the most spontaneous, exciting, and — yes — fun! We will explore the Civic Center of Manhattan, choose a courthouse or two, walk right in, ask questions, and see several trials. It is advisable to start the day early, as there is so much to see.

The Tour

Lower Manhattan is a mixed bag of federal, state, and city government buildings, apartment buildings, and warehouses — some distinguished, some nondescript. They crowd an area vaguely bounded by Broadway to the west, White Street to the north and Fulton Street to the south.

There is certainly no shortage of courthouses — two imposing, classical ones on Foley Square (the New York Supreme Court and the United States Courthouse), the Civil Court Building, the Criminal Courts Building (housing the Men's House of Detention, The Tombs) and Surrogate's Court. Also within the Civic Center complex are the mammoth Police Headquarters, the Old New York County Courthouse (the infamous Tweed Courthouse), the handsome Municipal Building, and historic City Hall.

Where to begin? Since the object of this day is spontaneous adventure (not all court dockets are made public in

Above: The Tombs, circa 1880. This Egyptian-style building, thought to resemble a pharaoh's tomb, was located across Centre Street from the present Criminal Courts Building and Men's House of Detention (The Tombs). This was the main city jail from 1838-1892. Demolished. (Courtesy of Museum of the City of New York)

Right: Today's Criminal Courts Building also houses The Tombs, named for the demolished 19th-century jail. (Photograph © Phil Cantor, 1990)

advance), we decide to enter the first courthouse we pass, which happens to be the Civil Court Building, a plain-looking 1960s structure. Once inside, we head for the information desk and ask to sit in on a criminal trial. (Some felony cases are heard here.) We are directed to the clerk's office, Room 911.

As we walk along the ninth-floor corridor, we are prepared for brusque, negative answers to our questions. Instead, the clerk whips out a blank sheet of paper and writes down the courtroom number for each of the morning's trials he thinks will interest us. What is more, he gives us a rundown of each one.

"Oh, here's a good one!" he exclaims as he ticks off a trial in Part (Courtroom) 1212. "The attorneys are summing up today. A drug trial. Colorful defense attorney on that case!"

The clerk leans on the counter. "I used to sit in on trials on my day off when I worked nearby. I enjoyed them so much that I finally decided to work here ... . The funny stories I could tell you!"

Without pausing for breath, he launches into this story: The judge in a recent trial was asking the jurors if there was anything unclear to them about the evidence presented so far.

"No, Your Honor," replied a frowning Juror #2, "but I've got to tell you something. I've been looking at Juror #9, and now I know why he looks familiar. He mugged me last year, and as soon as this trial is over, I'm pressing charges!"

And she did.

The clerk hands us the sheet of promising trials and gives us a few tips:

In each courthouse, specify whether you want to see a criminal or civil trial when you ask for information. You will be directed to the correct clerk's office.

There are often long delays in court proceedings. Get a list of two or three trials from the clerk's office so that you won't waste your day waiting.

After you enter a courtroom, a court officer will probably ask you if you are involved in the proceedings of the trial. Don't be concerned. That procedure is just part of his job, as witnesses and jurors aren't allowed to sit in the courtroom as spectators. Simply answer, "I'm just observing."

Don't be afraid to ask questions. There is always someone willing to help you learn about courtroom procedure.

"Oh, listen. I meant to tell you," the clerk adds as we are walking away, "when you go across the street to the Criminal Courts Building, be sure to sit in on arraignments! Very interesting!"

We find Part 1212 without any trouble and quietly open the door. The jurors look up as we tiptoe in and sit down. Sure enough, the court officer asks us if we have a part in the proceedings.

The defense attorney is strutting back and forth, starched and pressed and in fine form, stabbing the air with his index finger to punctuate his message to the jury that his client is poor and honest — an innocent who has never sold drugs. The jurors are not so convinced. Their eyes seem steely as they glance at the defendant, a disreputable-looking individual who slumps in his chair, keeping watch over his shoes.

We listen to the prosecutor next, a tiny young woman with fragile hands and a rich voice. Finally, after some minutes, she turns to the jurors and reaches

---

United States Courthouse, Foley Square. Cass Gilbert's temple-skyscraper, completed in 1936. To the left is the Supreme Court of the State of New York. (Courtesy of Museum of the City of New York)

forward, palms up, making two fans with her spread fingers. "Ladies and gentlemen, take a good look at this man. Do you actually believe his story? Or do you believe the accounts of our four witnesses, one of whom, you will recall, is [pause] a minister's wife."

At this, we get up quietly and leave the courtroom. We can guess the outcome of this trial!

We watch one more trial in this courthouse, then cross the street to the Criminal Courts Building at 100 Centre Street. The huge granite and limestone building resembles a prison for a good reason: Part of the mammoth stern-faced structure is The Tombs, the Men's House of Detention, so-called because its demolished predecessor across the street resembled an ancient Egyptian tomb. That name still fits this building.

We pass through the three-story entrance into a wide lobby crowded with the gamut of humankind. We must walk through a metal detector here, and our bags are searched. We watch in amazement as an officer takes an ice pick away from a cringing young man.

"Does this happen often?" we ask in disbelief.

The officer shrugs his shoulders. "Oh, we get a little of everything in here. You should have been here 10 minutes ago. Some guy actually thought he could get through with 41 vials of crack! Can you beat that? Anyway, he's on his way to the pokey now!"

A guard directs us to the clerk's office on the 10th floor, which is far larger and busier than the previous office. We stand around a few minutes until we finally catch the eye of a man who scurries back and forth behind the grill-fronted counter.

"Sure," he answers amiably when we tell him we'd like to sit in on a trial. "Hey, Lennie! Call up and see if the trial

in Part 1115 is still in session." He turns back to us. "Now, that's a good one," he confides. "Good judge."

Lennie yells that we're in luck. The trial is still going on. We ask for a backup trial and are on our way.

The courtroom is quiet, but we immediately feel the tension. The judge, a blond, svelte woman, slides a quick glance at us, then turns to nail the defense attorney with a cold stare. Obviously she does not like something he has just said.

The prosecutor doesn't like it either. She leaps to her feet. "Objection again, Your Honor!" she cries in an exasperated voice, leaning forward on the table with outstretched arms.

The judge coolly summons the defense attorney to the bench, where she speaks inches from his nose. We can't hear the quiet words, but a court reporter, who has hurriedly gathered up her recorder and scurried to the bench, is trying valiantly to capture every word on her machine. Finally the defense attorney shuffles back to his table. Will he try once more? He does. The judge leans forward. She speaks evenly, her eyes narrowed. "No *more* of this, Counselor — and you know I *mean* it."

At this, the defense attorney drops resignedly into his chair, sticks his legs out in front of him, and crosses them neatly at the ankles, darting a quick glance at the jury. Two of the jurors shake their heads gently. One is examining his fingernails, while three others relax against their seat backs. One yawns.

Meanwhile, the defendant, a lean, fox-faced individual, calmly stares at the ceiling, arms folded.

We watch the trial for half an hour, then, following the first clerk's advice, we head down to watch arraignments in Arraignment Part 129. We hear a muffled commotion behind the heavy double doors, and once inside, we see why.

What a noisy melee! Arraignment Part 129 is packed with observers, attorneys, and officers. Prisoners, some handcuffed, are constantly being brought from cells just beyond the rear door. Once inside the courtroom, they fill the empty spaces on a long, narrow bench that runs along one side — resembling nervous birds on a wire. Again and again, the rear door swings open, revealing holding cells crowded with prisoners awaiting their turns on the bench.

We sit down on one of the hard, stiff-backed benches and look around. The courtroom is harsh and dismal under the fluorescent lights. The judge looks tired.

I decide to find out more about arraignment procedure. I get up and walk back to ask a guard, who is leaning against the wall, arms folded. He explains that the man seated behind the thick stack of papers on the battered table is an assistant district attorney. From the top page he is reading the charges being brought against the prisoner now standing before the judge. An attorney, either court-appointed or private, stands beside the accused man, giving any evidence he has to support the prisoner's innocence. The judge will at that time decide whether there is enough evidence to charge the prisoner with a crime and whether bail is warranted.

As I turn to walk back to my seat, I nearly collide with a wiry, menacing individual — dirty jeans, dingy sweatshirt emblazoned with palm trees, and heavy black boots. I scurry to my seat as he saunters up the aisle, straight for the judge's bench. He leans forward, speaking rapidly to the judge. Then he turns, and that is when we see the badge swinging heavily from a brass chain around his neck. He is an undercover cop.

Next a swaggering sliver of a man takes his turn before the judge. The assistant district attorney begins to read a long list of charges: possession of drugs, robbery, assault with a deadly weapon, and threatening the undercover arresting officer. In short order the prisoner is charged, a hefty bail is set, and he is taken out, his sandals slapping furiously on the scuffed floor.

We watch this peculiar circus until lunchtime, then stroll a short distance to Chinatown, window shopping along Mott Street with its bright jumble of signs and lively mix of people, stopping for a fortifying lunch along the way.

Afterward we walk toward Foley Square, and seeing the United States Courthouse, we decide we should end the day by watching a federal trial. We stand back a minute and look up at the Grecian temple, which supports a skyscraper tower, capped in turn by a gilded pyramid. This is another Cass Gilbert building, but unlike his graceful, rather fanciful Woolworth Building, the U.S. Courthouse is soberly clad in heavy granite — a no-nonsense structure, grand and imposing. There will be no lighthearted talk with guards here, we suspect.

We make the trek up the steps and pass between the portico's huge Corinthian columns. Once inside the marble lobby we encounter four guards, somber both in dress and expression. Wordless, we pass through inspection. Once on the other side, I timidly ask, "Is it possible to sit in on a federal trial today?"

As if jolted by an electric current, the eyes of all four guards light up at once. "Lovey, are you in luck today! Come along with me," chortles one guard, sprinting ahead of us. "You'll have to check your camera and tape recorder in the security office, and then I'm going to show you to the courtroom."

We lope along behind the gesturing

guard, straining to hear his words, which float behind — "bribery ... loan sharking ... organized crime ... " We park our camera and tape recorder and follow the guard, who strides ahead again. Then with a parting "Enjoy yourselves!" he disappears down the deep corridor. We go in.

What a courtroom this is — spacious, dignified, somewhat overwhelming. The walls are veneered in black marble and walnut paneling. The ceiling is at least three stories above us. Fifteen-foot-high arched windows line two walls of the chamber.

We sit down, but not before the defense attorney, apparently in the middle of cross-examination, wheels around 180 degrees and stares at us. Then, without pausing in motion or in the flow of his speech, he pivots another half-circle, facing the judge once again. Peculiarly, each time the courtroom door opens, he pivots gracefully, studying each person who enters. This rather dainty maneuver is even more surprising because the defense attorney is a burly, squared-off man with a large square head anchored to a heavyset cube of a body. Shiny black eyes. Well-groomed silver hair worn long, almost to the collar of his expensive gray suit.

The judge, high up behind his massive walnut bench, looks small in contrast. Small face, small glasses, small hands. But looks can be deceiving.

The prosecution? His well-padded

The Municipal Building, completed in 1914, was designed by McKim, Mead & White. Photograph by George Hall & Son, 1914. City Hall is shown in the foreground. Just behind is Surrogate's Court. (Courtesy of Museum of the City of New York)

frame, encased snugly in a navy three-piece suit, exuberantly crisscrosses the floor, heels clicking. He has thoughtful, quizzical eyes above a glossy brown moustache that turns up in a smile.

The defendant? Quiet, unassuming, he could be anybody's grandfather.

A witness is called. He is long-limbed, sleek, with an easy, languid walk, wearing a very expensive suit. He takes the oath and sits down, smiling slightly.

The judge peers over neat gold spectacles. Suddenly we are startled to hear his loud, bass-drum voice reverberate around the courtroom. "You had my direct order to appear in this court yesterday. You are in contempt. I will deal with you later!" The witness sinks into the wooden chair, the last traces of a smile slipping off his face.

As interrogation begins, our attention is drawn to a scenario that is being played out three rows ahead of us. From our position we see only a man's silver head and his arm casually draped along the back of the bench. A heavy jeweled cufflink winks in a ribbon of sunlight.

From the bench behind him a younger man strains forward to receive a slip of paper as it drops gracefully from the manicured fingers resting on the back of the bench. The silver head swings into profile for a few seconds, and four or five words are soundlessly mouthed to the young lackey, who grabs his briefcase and hurriedly leaves the courtroom.

Meanwhile the finely honed performances continue before the judge and jury. The prosecutor explodes with indignant energy as he rapidly wheels across the floor, words and arms flying. Beneath the sober navy suit jacket, we catch a flash of red striped suspenders. Clearly, the jurors like him.

And the defense — a skater without skates, gliding, pivoting to the music

of his own words. Bright eyes are gliding too, measuring the reactions of the jury. He mesmerizes with his velvet voice.

The judge, with his Harry Truman face, peers over his spectacles, his expression changing rapidly from indulgence to irritation to forcefulness as he keeps this drama within the confines of law.

We spend the rest of this autumn afternoon in the courtroom, staying until the shadows lengthen and the sunlight moves out of the long windows. Then, with recorder and camera in tow once more, we head out toward the massive front doors.

"I hope you had a good time," smiles one of the guards, shaking hands cordially, a host seeing his guests to the door. Who would have guessed that a day at criminal trials would turn out to be one of the friendliest adventures of them all?

The Collect. A 1920 engraving of a 1798 drawing shows the spring-fed pond that was once located in the Civic Center area. The large pond, which provided water for Manhattan's first settlers, was finally filled in by 1817. Even today pumps work 24 hours a day beneath some of the Civic Center buildings to keep them dry! (Courtesy of Museum of the City of New York)

The Civic Center — Historical Information

An interesting 1878 photograph of the City Hall area looking north on Park Row when it was known as "Newspaper Row." (Courtesy of The New-York Historical Society, New York City)

When the Dutch settled Manhattan Island in 1625, they found a large spring-fed pond located in the hilly countryside north of the New Amsterdam settlement. This pond, which reached a depth of 60 feet in places, was known as the Collect and was a source of drinking water for the growing village. The Collect, which covered an area between present-day Centre and Worth Streets in the Civic Center area, gradually became polluted during the 18th century. The pond became so poisoned from tannery waste that it was filled in, using soil from the surrounding hills.

This section of New York City became the center of civic government in 1811 when the distinguished new City Hall was completed. Gradually, other government buildings joined City Hall, the first of which was the New York County Courthouse, familiarly known as the Tweed Courthouse, a symbol of 19th-century civic graft and corruption. Government buildings have sprung up alongside ever since, creating a motley mix of architectural forms, from Italianate to starkly modern.

Beginning in the 1840s newspaper publishing houses began to flourish in the Civic Center area, and slowly a chain of impressive newspaper buildings stretched along Park Row and dotted other streets near City Hall. By the 1890s there were 19 daily newspapers published for New York City alone. This era of newspaper publishing lasted into the early 20th century. Unfortunately almost all of the buildings were later demolished.

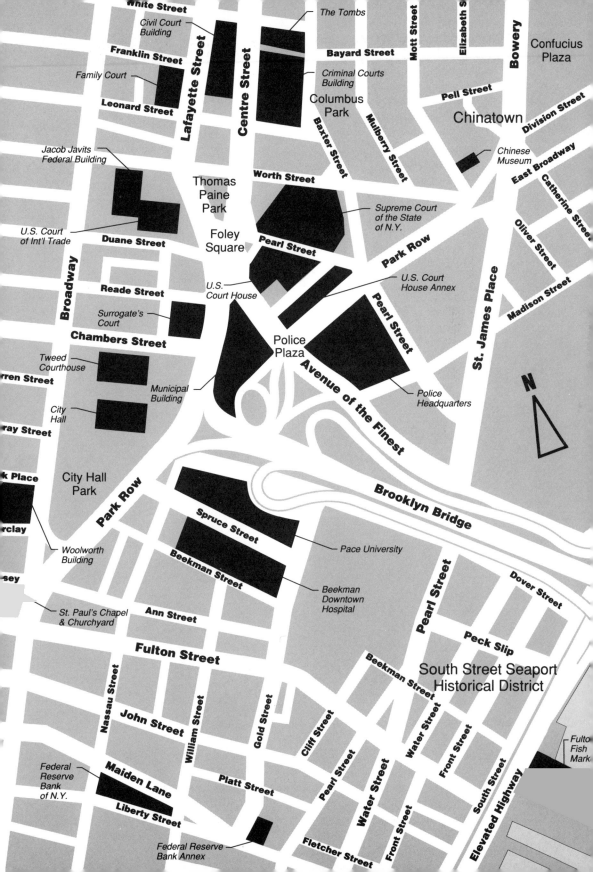

White Street

Civil Court Building

The Tombs

Franklin Street

Family Court

Leonard Street

Lafayette Street

Centre Street

Bayard Street

Mott Street

Elizabeth S

Bowery

Confucius Plaza

Criminal Courts Building

Columbus Park

Pell Street

Chinatown

Division Street

Jacob Javits Federal Building

Thomas Paine Park

Baxter Street

Mulberry Street

Worth Street

Chinese Museum

East Broadway

U.S. Court of Int'l Trade

Duane Street

Foley Square

Pearl Street

Supreme Court of the State of N.Y.

Park Row

Catherine Street

Oliver Street

Broadway

Reade Street

U.S. Court House

U.S. Court House Annex

Madison Street

Surrogate's Court

Chambers Street

Police Plaza

Pearl Street

St. James Place

Tweed Courthouse

Municipal Building

City Hall

Avenue of the Finest

Police Headquarters

N

rren Street

ray Street

k Place

City Hall Park

Park Row

Brooklyn Bridge

rclay

Spruce Street

Pace University

Dover Street

Pearl Street

sey

Woolworth Building

Beekman Street

Beekman Downtown Hospital

St. Paul's Chapel & Churchyard

Ann Street

Peck Slip

Beekman Street

South Street Seaport Historical District

Fulton Street

Nassau Street

William Street

Gold Street

Cliff Street

Water Street

Front Street

Fulto Fish Mark

John Street

Pearl Street

South Street

Elevated Highway

Federal Reserve Bank of N.Y.

Maiden Lane

Platt Street

Water Street

Front Street

Liberty Street

Federal Reserve Bank Annex

Fletcher Street

Trial-watching is a spontaneous adventure simply because trial calendars are not published in advance (except in the *New York Law Journal*, a newspaper available by subscription only: 212-741-8300), but there is absolutely no need to study a calendar in advance. Just walk into one of the courthouses listed below, visit the clerk's office, and ask for a list of the day's interesting trials.

To find out the trial's outcome, go back to that courthouse and requisition the file from the file room. The simple procedure will be explained to you when you arrive. The clerk's office might also have information about the outcome of the trial.

Courthouses

Criminal Courts Building
100 Centre Street
Between Worth & Leonard Streets

Completed in 1939. Overwhelming flat-faced behemoth with 1930s art deco design elements. The Tombs, the Men's House of Detention, is located in this building.

Criminal court cases (initial arraignment of almost all cases and disposition of misdemeanors and violations) and Supreme Court cases (felonies) are handled here. Criminal court arraignments are processed at Arraignment Part from 9:00 a.m.-5:00 p.m. and at night court after 5:00 p.m., running 24 hours a day and seven days a week.

★

Civil Court of the City of New York
111 Centre Street
Southwest corner of White Street

Civil court cases involving amounts not exceeding $25,000, landlord-tenant matters, small claims court, as well as some felony cases (New York Supreme Court cases) are handled in this courthouse.

★

United States Courthouse
40 Centre Street at Foley Square

Completed in 1936. Cass Gilbert's classical temple-skyscraper.

Inside this courthouse, which hears federal civil and criminal cases, is the U.S. District Court for the Southern District of New York and the U.S. Court of Appeals for the Second Circuit, with jurisdiction over New York State, Vermont, and Connecticut. The U.S. Bankruptcy Court for the Southern District is also housed in this building.

★

Supreme Court of the State of New York
60 Centre Street at Foley Square

Classical architecture, inspired by Rome's Pantheon and designed by Guy Lowell. Completed in 1927. The stately façade features 100-foot-wide steps, rising to a portico fronted by 10 granite columns. A 140-foot-long pediment, decorated with classical reliefs, is surmounted by three statues, *Law, Truth,* and *Equality*.

The interior is highlighted by a 75-foot-high rotunda decorated with a 1936 WPA mural, *Law Through the Ages*, in which 300 historical figures are depicted. There are additional murals on the third floor and in the fourth-floor jury assembly rooms.

The Supreme Court of New York hears civil cases for amounts exceeding $25,000.

★

Surrogate's Court
31 Chambers Street
Northwest corner of Centre Street

Considered a splendid example of Beaux-Arts architecture and completed in 1911, this building was originally the Hall of Records, and part of the building remains so today, housing public records that date back to the 17th century — wills, deeds, etc.

The figural groups at the entrance are *New York in its Infancy* and *New York in Revolutionary Times*. Numerous other large figures embellish the façade, all important leaders in the history of New York City. Of special interest is the lavish central hall, modeled on the foyer of the Paris Opera House. Open weekdays.

Surrogate's Court has jurisdiction over probate of wills, guardianships, and adoptions.

★

Appellate Division of the Supreme Court of the State of New York
First Judicial Department
25th Street & Madison Avenue

Although this court is not in the Civic Center area, it is well worth seeing. The classical building, the last important work of James Brown Lord, was completed in 1900.

Architectural elements include a fine portico with columns. On the Madison Square side, the two statues are *Confucius*, representing Chinese Law, and *Moses*, representing Hebraic Law. In the middle is *Peace*.

In the pediment on the 25th Street side is a figural group, *Triumph of Law*. On the pediment is *Justice*. Seated statues to the right and left of the 25th Street portico are *Power* and *Wisdom*. Numerous large figures embellish the roofline and represent Persian, Athenian, French, Indian, Anglo-Saxon, and Roman law.

Interior: In the foyer is a fine frieze, *Transmission of Law,* showing the development of law from ancient times to the 20th century. In the beautiful courtroom are three large panels, *Justice of Law*, *Power of Law*, and *Wisdom*. There is a splendid stained-glass dome in the courtroom as well as a number of beautiful stained-glass windows.

The Appellate Division of the Supreme Court is the intermediate court that hears trial appeals. (The highest court in New York State is the Court of Appeals in Albany.) The court located in this building is one of four courts comprising the intermediate appellate court of New York State. Of the four, this court is the busiest, as it has jurisdiction in New York and Bronx counties. For the most part, the court hears appeals from the Supreme Court, Surrogate's Court, and Family Court in New York and Bronx counties. The court's 13 justices hear over 3,000 appeals a year.

Arguments on appeals are heard on Tuesday, Wednesday, and Thursday afternoons beginning at 2:00 p.m. and on Friday mornings at 10:00 a.m. All sessions are open to the public.

★

Family Court Building
60 Lafayette Street

Matters involving children, including child protective proceedings, foster care proceedings, delinquencies, as well as family support proceedings, adoptions, paternity proceedings and family offense proceedings are heard in this courthouse. (Note: Of the courthouses listed, only this one generally does not allow casual visitors to watch court proceedings.)

Additional Sights in the Civic Center Area

City Hall, a New York Architectural Jewel
(See City Hall chapter.)

St. Paul's Chapel
The beautiful little church is the only Colonial church in Manhattan. (See George Washington chapter.)

Old New York County Courthouse (The Tweed Courthouse)
52 Chambers Street
Between Broadway & Centre Street

Sometimes described by architects as an English Renaissance country house in design, this building has made the full circle from shabby treatment through the years, barely escaping demolition, to a new status as one of the finest examples of Italianate architecture in the city.

The courthouse has long been considered a prime example of New York City civic corruption. Estimated to cost $150,000 when construction began in 1863, the work continued for nine long years, finally costing between $8 million-$12 million. At least 75 percent of that amount went into the pockets of notorious "Boss" William Marcy Tweed and his "ring" (who also had their hands in the Brooklyn Bridge construction till. See Brooklyn Bridge chapter). The building is now used as overflow for City Hall offices and houses the city archives.

Hours:
Monday-Friday 9:00 a.m.-4:30 p.m.

Admission: Free

Woolworth Building
233 Broadway

Built by Frank W. Woolworth as headquarters for his chain of "five and dime" stores. A work of Cass Elliot, completed in 1913.

Municipal Building
1 Centre Street at Chambers Street

Graceful in design in spite of its size, the 1914 Municipal Building rises high above City Hall, cradling the smaller structure and echoing the stately City Hall design. The building houses city government offices.

Police Headquarters
Between Park Row, Pearl, Henry & New Streets

This building, completed in 1973, seems appropriate as the headquarters for "New York's Finest," as it is strong and spartan, a great red brick cube. A three-acre Police Plaza connects the Municipal Building to Police Headquarters.

Chinatown
Chinatown, a tantalizing — and sometimes confusing — blend of colors, sights, and sounds, borders the Civic Center area. Save some time to stroll along the busy streets and sample some of Chinatown's delicious fare.

R E S T A U R A N T S

Say Eng Look
5 East Broadway
212-732-0796

Weekdays 11:00 a.m.-10:00 p.m.
Weekends 11:00 a.m.-11:00 p.m.

• All major credit cards

Say En Look is representative of the many Chinatown restaurants offering delectable dishes at inexpensive prices.

The menu is quite extensive and imaginative. Many dishes, such as the crispy whole fried fish, are prepared with seaweed. For the more adventurous, carp tail in casserole and fish maw with straw mushrooms.

We asked the chef for suggestions. He prepared a flavorful seafood soup brimming with delicate fish and shrimp. Next we sampled fried rolled puffs — well-seasoned and filled with tender white fish. A chicken dish in a dense orange sauce, delicately sweet, was also delicious.

The dining room, decorated in red and

black, was quite relaxing, quiet, and spacious — a real plus during a day of hectic touring in this area, which can be noisy and crowded. Service was cheerful.

Say Eng Look, which specializes in Shanghai cuisine, has been in business for 27 years and still has the same chef.

Main courses around $7.00

Other Suggested Restaurants in Chinatown

20 Mott Street
Between Mulberry Street & the Bowery
212-964-0380

• Excellent dim sum at moderate prices

★

Y.S. (Hop Woo)
17 Elizabeth Street
South of Canal Street
212-966-5838

• Inexpensive & good

★

Bo Ky
80 Bayard Street
Between Mott & Mulberry Streets
212-406-2992

• Well-prepared Vietnamese food at inexpensive prices

★

Tai Hong Lau
70 Mott Street
Between Canal & Bayard Streets
212-219-1431

• Good Cantonese food at a modest price

DIRECTIONS

Subway:
• #4, 5, 6 to City Hall
• J, M, Z to Chambers Street
• #1 to Chambers Street & West Broadway
• N, R to City Hall

Bus:
• M1 (Fifth / Madison Avenues)
• M6 (Seventh Avenue / Broadway / Avenue of the Americas)
• M101, M102 (Third / Lexington Avenues)

Car:
• FDR Drive, Manhattan Civic Center exit

Nighttime in Chinatown. (Photograph © Phil Cantor, 1990)

An Early Morning at Fulton Fish Market

In historic South Street Seaport

Above: The 1908 harbor lightship *Ambrose* was a stationary beacon for vessels sailing through Ambrose Channel into New York Harbor — one of many interesting museum sights offered to strolling visitors. (Photograph © Phil Cantor, 1990)

Left: South Street, 1887, showing Piers 9 and 10 on the East River. Although South Street Seaport still bristled with the masts of sailing vessels in the late 19th century, the seaport had declined in importance since the Civil War. (Courtesy of The New-York Historical Society, New York City)

The History

 ulton Fish Market, in continuous operation since 1831, is one of the last surviving links to South Street Seaport's maritime golden age. The era began at the end of the 18th century, reached its apex during the middle of the 19th century, and began a slow decline after the Civil War. By the turn of the 20th century the shops, offices, and restaurants that had once catered to the affluent had degenerated into a crime-infested area of dismal hotels, bars, and seedy boarding houses.

But during the glory days, when great sailing vessels crisscrossed the seas laden with rich cargoes, New York City was the center of American commerce, and it was along the East River that the great shipping lines docked, the influential merchants established their businesses, and the profitable trading deals were made.

That was South Street, the "Street of Ships," as it was known in the 19th century. However, not until the ambitious cultural/commercial project began in the

1970s would this area be called South Street Seaport.

Now step back nearly four centuries ... and enter the year 1625.

★

In 1625 the first Dutch settlers carried their belongings onto the Manhattan shore. They found a lush, hilly island with forests of hickory and oak, whose trunks stretched 70 feet into the sky and whose deep shade hid a plentiful supply of game, from turkey and elk to deer and black bear. Ponds dotted the verdant terrain, and streams coursed through it. Marshes teemed with birds and fish, and tidelands rimmed the island. Although those first Dutch settlers used the East River as a port, much of the land on which South Street would flourish some 200 years hence did not exist. It lay beneath the river as tidelands area.

Beginning in the late 17th century, colonists slowly pushed the original eastern shoreline outward from Pearl Street, creating land where there had been only water by dumping earth, rubble, trash, or any combination that could be gathered together for landfill. Gradually that shoreline was pushed outward, creating Water and Front Streets, and finally, by the beginning of the 19th century, it was South Street that fronted the river. By 1810 this outward thrust was completed, and the port, which had been rapidly developing since the end of the American Revolution, burst into the 19th century

Weighing and packing fish in the early morning at Fulton Fish Market. Photograph circa 1935. (Courtesy of The New York Public Library, New York City. Gift of Dr. Michael Wishengrad. Photograph © Ewing Galloway, Inc.)*

ripe for maritime prosperity.

There were many factors that led to 19th-century development of the seaport. One of these was the acquisition of land by one family, the Schermerhorns. For generations this family had purchased land along the East River, but it was an enterprising fifth-generation member, Peter Schermerhorn, a shipowner and merchant, who bought up all of his family's properties, including the lots that lay under the East River at high tide. He filled these in, and by 1812 he had built a string of brick buildings lining the entire block of Beekman Slip (renamed Fulton Street in 1816) between Front and South Streets and around both corners. (Restored by South Street Seaport Museum, these buildings now contain numerous shops and restaurants.)

Schermerhorn's timing was perfect. Having already made one fortune as a ship chandler (a merchant providing goods for the shipping industry), Schermerhorn increased his real estate holdings by building stores along South Street in 1818.

The Fulton Ferry Company had also approached Schermerhorn for permission to build a landing at the foot of his wharf. In 1814 the Manhattan terminal was completed, linking the prosperous city of Brooklyn to Manhattan and increasing business dramatically for Schermerhorn and for the seaport.

South Street's most influential change occurred in 1818 when the first regular trans-Atlantic shipping and passenger line began operations north of Schermerhorn Row, an example that was quickly followed by competing lines. Soon the port bristled with the masts of sailing vessels carrying freight and passengers.

It was not long before merchants recognized the need for a marketplace convenient to seaport traffic. In 1822 the first spacious Fulton Market opened across from Schermerhorn Row on Fulton Street, providing in one large structure a wholesale outlet for meats, produce, fish, and countless other goods and services, dispensed from 163 stands. This first market was replaced in 1883 by a rather grand Victorian building (see photograph), demolished in 1950, which the impressive 1983 Fulton Market was designed to resemble.

By the 1840s South Street was flourishing. Vessels great and small crowded the harbor, unloading such luxuries as bone china from England, tapestries from France, oranges from Spain, and chocolate from the West Indies. The China trade brought silks, tea, porcelains, and drugs. Of course, the ships rarely left the port with empty holds. They sailed out of the harbor laden with America's natural wealth, including cotton, corn, tobacco, wheat, and coal.

These were South Street's glory days. Each year more and more offices, shops, warehouses, and restaurants lined side streets. Swarms of people filled the port, clambering around or over stacked crates, bales, and boxes, which waited for harried clerks to drag them into the shops and warehouses.

Many sounds added to the unsettling din: shrieks and whistles, the clanging of bells and the bellowing of stevedores who loaded and unloaded the ships' holds, street vendors crying "Hot sausages! Ginger-beer!" and the constant clattering of horses' hooves and wheels over paving stones.

Servants from fashionable neighborhoods uptown scurried from shop to shop or from stand to stand in the Fulton Market, clutching their purchases of produce, pastries, or other goods. Merchants haggled over business in the Fulton Market's restaurants, their lively conver-

South Street, circa 1883. View of the second brick and terra-cotta Fulton Market, which opened April 2, 1883, an impressive Victorian-style building. Fulton Fish Market, located across the street (not shown) gradually took over this Fulton Market. The ornate building was finally torn down in 1950. The seaport's handsome new Fulton Market, completed in 1983, was modeled on the market pictured here. (Courtesy of Museum of the City of New York)

sations mixing with the other noises.

The fish dealers, who had been selling at the seaport since the 1820s, began to add color and confusion to Fulton Market in 1831. Unfortunately, they also added fishy smells and a pungent seepage, which drained into the butchers' stalls downstairs. The butchers complained bitterly until the fish dealers moved into their own market in 1834, a long wooden shed bordering the East River, with frontage on South Street. There the Fulton Fish Market stayed until the first dilapidated

building was replaced by a second wooden shed, the latter managing to stand through the Civil War. Finally, in 1869 the fish dealers moved into a graceful two-storied wooden building, capped with cupolas and a brass fish weather vane.

Throughout the 19th century the Fulton Fish Market carried on business from long tables that ran from front to back on the ground floor and from offices in the rear overlooking the East River. The market opened directly onto South Street, where horse-drawn delivery

wagons pulled up for loading by journey-men, whose handcarts were piled high with crates and boxes of fish.

The dealers sold incredible quantities of fresh fish during the 19th century. In the 1830s, for example, more than 200 million pounds of fish passed through the market each year. Tons of fish were sold each day. Deliveries were made directly to the market by fishing smacks and schooners, and the live fish were kept in holding "fish cars" in the East River until sold by the fishmongers, whose stalls opened onto the river.

The prosperous days of American merchant shipping in foreign trade began to wane after the Civil War and did not start to rebuild until World War I. Al-though New York City continued to enjoy brisk activity as a port used by foreign shippers, particularly those of Great Britain, South Street lost importance as foreign ships began to dock at other terminals, including south Brooklyn and Elizabeth, New Jersey. In addition, the countless small vessels that had once been used within the port for transporting goods were no longer needed. Slowly South Street began to decline.

Shops that had once catered to affluent customers turned into dingy saloons — and worse; buildings that had once contained the stores and warehouses of merchants became boarding houses — and worse. Crime began to fester in disreputable cafes and flophouses.

In spite of the seaport's decline, Fulton Fish Market tenaciously held on in the same location. In 1907 the dealers moved into a new Tin Building, which they use to this day, a rather ramshackle affair now but architecturally important as one of the four remaining tin buildings in New York City. In 1939 a new building, tagged the New Market, joined the old Tin Building, subsequently renamed the Old Market.

Even now the Fulton Fish Market operates in much the same way it has carried on business since the 1830s. Almost everything is done by hand, from the filleting of fish to weighing it on hanging scales. Even though the quantity of fish has steadily dwindled each year (88 million pounds of fish in 1988 com-pared with 384 million pounds processed in 1924), Fulton Fish Market is still the largest wholesale seafood market in the United States.

The 20th century has intruded in a few ways. Mechanized trucks have replaced the horse-drawn wagons, of course, and forklifts rumble through the market. In addition, by the 1920s East River pollution ended the practice of keeping live fish in fish cars.

But perhaps the market's most pro-found break with 19th-century tradition is that fishing boats no longer deliver their catch directly to Fulton Fish Market. Instead, all fish deliveries are made by truck from coastal fishing towns, or the fish are flown in from as far away as Africa, then trucked to the market from the airport. Although Fulton Fish Market vigorously lives on, its direct link to fishermen and their boats has vanished forever.

South Street, circa 1898. An interesting view of the bustling activity at Fulton Fish Market, the building with three cupolas, which was completed in 1869. The handsome cast-iron building in the foreground is the old Fulton Ferry terminal, built in 1863. You can see the masts of ships on the East River, and no doubt some of them are fishing smacks. Both buildings were demolished long ago. (Courtesy of The New-York Historical Society, New York City. Photo-engraving by George Schulz)

The Tour

5:45 a.m.
The dark streets are quiet. We see just a few people here and there, strolling un-hurriedly. Several coffee shops are open, sending aromatic tendrils of fresh coffee and hot rolls into the street.

Remnants of an old brick street run smack into the side of a 20th-century building, cut-off and silent. Where did it lead? Must have echoed to hoofbeats and carriage wheels once.

Moon is still up, a star or two. A workman at a construction site starts up a crane engine, which rumbles softly, just waking up.

5:55 a.m.
Catch the salty scent of the sea as we enter South Street Seaport. A real feeling of an 18th-century seaport this early. Very few people around in modern dress to break the spell.

6:00 a.m.
Arrive at the Children's Center and join 25 people waiting to take the tour.

M.J. Shaughnessy greets us. Bright yellow wooden fish earrings dangle rakishly from her ears. Sitting on little boxes, we listen to the fish market's history — interesting and to the point.

Next we get a picture of a night's work at Fulton Fish Market:

Beginning as early as 9:00 p.m., big refrigerated trucks loaded with fish start rolling in. By 1:00 a.m. unloading is in high gear. Wholesalers bawl out com-plaints if unloading isn't moving fast

Early morning at Fulton Fish Market. Readying a gaff hook to unload a swordfish from a hand truck.
(Photograph by David Browning, 1989)

113

enough. Friendly and not-so-friendly insults exchanged.

By 4:00 a.m. the market is in full swing, lit up like an amusement park. Fish are everywhere — in long stacked rows of boxes, cartons, and crates — spilling out into the middle of the street. Tables inside piled high with fish. Individual wholesalers set day's prices by walking around, checking with other dealers. Most orders called in a day or two ahead. Everything is done on credit — no money changes hands buying wholesale.

Most buyers come around 4:00 or 5:00 a.m. — from restaurants, hotels, etc., some arriving in tuxedos to paw through ice, seaweed, and fish. Market is at full tilt — crowded, noisy, colorful — unloaders, loaders, journeymen with hand trucks, salesmen, fillet men (who work all night cutting up fish), boxers, watchmen. It is hard, hard work, especially on those freezing winter mornings.

"Can we buy fish?" someone asks hopefully.

"Sure," says M.J. She shows us some large bags that say "dogfood" or "fertilizer." "Not to worry. They've never been used. They're seconds, imperfects. Just the right size for a big fish, tail hanging out of the top!"

6:30 a.m.
Time to see the market. A word of warning from M.J. "When you hear 'Watch your back!' find anywhere to stand, but give a clear path because what's coming through is a hand truck loaded with crates of fish, which are *extremely* heavy. The journeyman who's pushing it has been working many hours, and he wants to get that delivery to the truck. This is the end of his workday, and he wants to get out of here."

Dawn is pink above the East River as we follow M.J. outside. Air is soft and cool. We pass rows of buyers' small vans, each with a number on the back to ensure that the journeymen deliver fish to the correct vans.

We hit the Tin Building first — hurly-burly, exciting, intense, mass confusion. Yelling between stalls, some for business, some just passing the time.

"Watch your back! Coming through!" We make way in a hurry. The journeyman seems very small for such a load. Eyes exhausted, forehead smeared with grime and sweat. Even empty, the hand truck has to be heavy, but now it's loaded high with heavy crates. There is a wide, beaten-up leather belt wrapped around his narrow waist for support, a vicious-looking gaff hook slung over his shoulder — a steel claw on a wooden handle.

M.J.: "They fling those hooks into the fish to get them onto the scales and fling them into the crates to move them around, then they fling them over their shoulders. All the older men have callouses on their shoulders, but they don't even feel them any more. Stand back when they're using them!"

7:00 a.m.
So many species of seafood here. As many as 600 species go through in a year, 150 of them imported. Everywhere we look, we see a different variety, some we've never seen before.

Stacks and stacks of red net onion sacks bulge with clams. A table overflows with yellow-bellied Florida pompano and rows of great swordfish, their weights scrawled in white on gleaming gray sides — *120, 145, 129.* One is already cut into sections, resembling a huge tree, rings and all, two feet in diameter or more.

A loader ambles by, bantering with the group. Weighs 250 pounds at least,

and all muscle. He sports wide red suspenders, and a thick leather belt protects his middle. A much-used gaff hook with "Jake" on the handle is slung over his shoulder.

The dealers, also called fishmongers, visit with us when not busy hoisting fish onto large steel scales swinging on chains, or calling orders back to the office on primitive square call boxes strung up overhead, or making sales pitches.

"What's that?"

Proudly, "Tuna! I've got the best! Just look at that 150-pound tuna — over five feet long! And the one that looks like a silver torpedo is a mackerel — 130 pounds."

M.J. reaches into a box, drapes an African octopus over her hand. Tentacles curl down to her elbow. And in another box, hundreds of tiny squid. These are netted by the millions.

Work at Fulton Fish Market is still in full swing at 5:00 a.m. Here, cutting up a fish for a restaurant customer. (Photograph by David Browning, 1989)

7:15 a.m.
Stop to watch Japanese workers from Tsukiji Market in Tokyo, largest market in the world, selling 1,800 million pounds of fish a year! In spotless white coats they look like surgeons but are wielding razor-sharp long knives. Only yellowfin tuna sold here, much of it for sushi. Men so skilled they can cut up a huge yellowfin in five minutes.

7:30 a.m.
Above the din we suddenly hear a clear, rich voice singing an aria. Up there, standing on a table — a salesman, arms spread wide. Wonderful voice, but is he

kidding? Yes. He laughs, hops down.

7:45 a.m.
On to the 1939 building, more space,
wider aisles. We see a large shark,
disdainful even in death, with deadly saw
teeth and skin like an emery board.

Pass a table of striped bass — dapper
gray-and-silver striped bodies, red-
accented bellies. Great quantities of flat
flounders, a staple of the market. A
brawny salesman flings a heavy brown
grouper with pendulous pink mouth onto
the steel scale, its tail lopping over the
side. I pick up a fat little butterfish with
narrow yellow stripes and touch the rough
skin of a hammerhead shark. Nearby are
boxes of wiggling blue crabs, neatly
arranged in rows and covered with straw.

M.J. shows us some turquoise and
peach tropical parrot fish with beaklike
mouths for chomping away on coral reefs.
And another strange specimen: a red and
orange robin fish — batlike wings on the
head and spindly insect legs.

8:00 a.m.
Phew! Out of the noise and hustle-bustle
into morning sunshine. Still masses of
fish in boxes, crates lining the street.
Cleanup time. Washing down the street.

Sitting down to breakfast with M.J.
and others, we chat together like old
friends, enjoying little flaky rolls, steam-
ing bowls of savory Manhattan clam
chowder, cups and cups of fragrant
coffee. What fun!

Fulton Street today, looking east at
South Street Seaport. Schermerhorn
Row, completed in 1812, on right. On
left, shops and restaurants of the 1983
Fulton Market. (Photograph © Jeffrey
Jay Foxx, 1990)

Fulton Fish Market Tour

c/o South Street Seaport Museum
207 Front Street
New York, NY 10038
212-669-9400 or 212-669-9416

Tours are offered the first and third Thursdays from April through October and meet at 6:00 a.m. Cost is $10.00 a person ($8.00 for museum members). Reserve well in advance.

Although breakfast is not part of the tour, among the restaurants opening early is the Bridge Cafe (see review following). Or try Carmine's, at the corner of Front and Bleekman Streets, where the fishmongers hang out.

★

Also recommended are tours given by Richard Lord, who is in charge of an information service for Fulton Fish Market. These tours, designed for the professional, are offered to others by appointment. 212-962-1608.

South Street Seaport Museum

The museum, actually a combination of many historic buildings covering a seven-block area, offers many indoor and outdoor activities, tours, and films. 212-669-9400. Recorded information for tours and current exhibits: 212-669-9424

Hours:
Daily 10:00 a.m.-5:00 p.m.
(until 6:00 p.m. in summer)

Admission:
- Members free
- Nonmembers
    Adults $6.00
    Seniors $5.00
    Students with valid ID $4.00
    Children 4-12, $3.00

Tickets are available at the Visitors' Center at 12 Fulton Street and at the Pier 16 Ticketbooth in the seaport. Maps and tour information are given with the tickets. You may also book tours at the same time.

Following are tours that are free with the price of admission to the seaport museum:

Self-guided tour of Peking, *the second-largest sailing ship in existence.* The steel four-masted bark was built in 1911.

★

Tour of the 1885 Wavertree, *an iron-hulled, full-rigged, 293-foot sailing ship.* View its restoration in progress.

★

Tour of the back streets of the seaport — the interesting history and architecture.

★

Tour of working life in the old port, which investigates the seaport as it once was and examines the commerce it fostered.

★

There is an additional charge for the following tours:

Sails aboard the two-masted schooner Pioneer. Built in 1885, it was originally designed to carry cargo. Now it carries up to 40 passengers into New York Harbor, offering a grand view of the Statue of Liberty. Many sailing times. April-mid-September. $16.00 adults, $10.00 children.

A Christmas Walk with the Ghost of Herman Melville, 19th-century author of *Moby Dick*, among other works. Fascinating return to the nautical life of bygone days. Tour is led by Melville's "ghost" (Jack Putnam). Putnam also manages the Museum Book & Chart Store located on Water Street — very helpful in finding just the right book. Tours begin around the middle of December.

Ninety-minute cruises aboard the replica 19th-century paddlewheeler Andrew Fletcher *and steamboat* DeWitt Clinton. $12.00 adults, $6.00 children. All excursions leave from Pier 16.

R E S T A U R A N T S

Bridge Cafe

279 Water Street at Dover Street
Next to the Brooklyn Bridge
212-227-3344

Breakfast:
    Monday-Friday 7:00-11:45 a.m.
Brunch:
    Sunday 11:45 a.m.-3:30 p.m.
Lunch:
    Monday-Friday 11:45 a.m.-5:00 p.m.
Dinner:
    Tuesday-Saturday 5:00 p.m.-midnight
    Sunday & Monday 5:00-10:00 p.m.

• All major credit cards
• Reservations suggested

Built in 1801 as a residence, this historic building later became a bar called the Hole in the Wall, infamous for depravity and the number of murders committed. (It is said that the bar had 200-pound barmaids. One of these was notorious for her steel suspenders, billy club, and the pistol she kept under her skirt!)

The mirror-backed mahogany bar is still a centerpiece in the interesting old red wooden building — leaning a little askew now, understandably! The restaurant is popular with the Wall Street and City Hall crowds and

has been a favorite of former mayor Ed Koch.

Every dish we tried at the Bridge Cafe was remarkably good. For appetizers we ordered fragrant, colorful carrot ginger soup and piquant red pepper bisque. Salads were pretty and delicious. Rigatoni with sun-dried tomatoes and wild mushrooms was marvelous.

Now the entrees. My fried soft-shell crabs were the best I have ever had, decorated with a colorful array of bright, crisp vegetables. The seared yellowfin tuna was perfectly moist. Roast chicken with prosciutto, mozzarella, red wine, and cream was luscious. The angel-hair pasta with Manila clams and white wine sauce was robust and garlicky. There is also a nice selection of sandwiches at around $8.00.

The chocolate grand marnier cake and bourbon pecan pie were sinfully rich and delicious.

Breakfast under $10.00
Lunch:
    Appetizers $4.95-$7.95
    Entrees $12.95-$16.95
Dinner:
    Appetizers $4.95-$7.95
    Entrees $12.95-$18.50

D I R E C T I O N S

Subway:
• #2, 3, 4, 5, J, or M to Fulton Street Station
• A, C to Broadway-Nassau Station
• Walk east on Fulton Street into South Street Seaport

Bus:
• M15 (First / Second Avenues to Fulton Street)

Car:
• FDR Drive, South Street exit

A Walk Across the Brooklyn Bridge

A spectacular view and a spellbinding story

The Story of the Bridge

ince ancient times there has been a superstition among bridge builders that a bridge must take a life in sacrifice if it is to endure. Pagan? Barbaric? Of course. Yet early in construction the Brooklyn Bridge took its first life, that of its creator John A. Roebling. In 1869 the Brooklyn newspaper *Eagle* wrote " ... Henceforth we look on the great project of the Brooklyn Bridge as being baptized and hallowed by the life blood of its distinguished and lamented author."

And so began the story of the building of the Brooklyn Bridge.

John A. Roebling was at the top of his profession in 1867, when his proposal for a great bridge spanning the East River was adopted, and he was named chief engineer of the project. At the age of 61, Roebling was a successful architect and engineer, a millionaire with a lucrative wire manufacturing company in New Jersey, and an acknowledged master of suspension bridge design.

Above: Brooklyn Bridge today.
(Photograph © Jeffrey Jay Foxx, 1990)

Right: A marvelous photograph, circa 1890, of the Brooklyn Bridge promenade. (Courtesy of Museum of the City of New York)

German-born Roebling was proud, willful, and reserved, and many felt he was extremely arrogant. He was driven by work, always a perfectionist. Roebling was as stern with himself as he was with others, never giving in to illness or injury — a trait that would cause his death.

John A. Roebling's masterpiece was to be the East River Bridge, the name he used in his proposal. It would be the longest suspension bridge in the world, a shining arc beginning at City Hall Park at Chatham Street in Manhattan and terminating in Brooklyn at a block bounded by Fulton, Washington, Sands, and Prospect Streets.

There were other names given to the bridge at the time — the New York and Brooklyn Bridge, the Great Bridge, the Brooklyn Bridge, or simply the Roebling Bridge, but by any name it was to be a grand monument to the two cities, among the highest structures built in America up to that time, as well as the longest suspension bridge at 5,989 feet — a little longer than a mile, including the two approaches.

A system of specially constructed trains would cross the bridge, pulled by an endless cable. Traveling at speeds up to 40 miles an hour, these trains would connect with the elevated train systems of New York City and Brooklyn and would carry millions of passengers a year.

Other vehicles such as carriages and horse-drawn wagons would have their own lanes on either side of the railroad tracks. Roebling also provided pedestrians with an elevated promenade 18 feet above the traffic.

Planning for the future, Roebling designed the Brooklyn Bridge to be six times stronger than necessary — strong enough, as it turned out, to bear 20th-century cars and trucks that would someday stream by the millions across the bridge. In fact, the bridge would even

continue to carry Roebling's train system until 1944.

The Great Bridge would at last connect the first and third largest cities in America, allowing their people and their commerce to flow freely over the expanse of the East River.* The bridge would become a proud symbol shared by these two cities, a modern masterpiece. Indeed, for many years after its completion, the bridge would be called the Eighth Wonder of the World.

In 1869 newspapers all over America heralded the beginning of construction. Amazed readers learned that two gigantic wooden boxes called caissons, each measuring half the size of a city block, would be buried deep within the earth of the East River bed. These caisson foundations would be filled with cement.

Tremendous stone towers would rise from the mammoth caissons. They would be built of limestone below the high-water mark and of granite above. Soaring above the water, each tower (276-1/2 feet above the high-water mark at completion) would separate into a pair of 117-foot-high Gothic arches resembling windows in a colossal cathedral, through which twin roadways would thread. Finally, each great tower would be crowned with a cornice and three giant capstones.

As the towers were slowly rising from beneath the water, work would begin on two huge masonry structures called anchorages, one on the Manhattan shore and the other in Brooklyn. These block-square empty boxes, each more than 80 feet high and weighing 120 million pounds, would function as the name

* At that time Brooklyn had a population of more than one million and was the third largest city in the United States. In 1898 Brooklyn became a borough of New York City.

implied — that is, they would anchor the immense bridge cables. Roebling suggested that fireproof spaces in the tremendous hollow anchorages could also be used as treasury vaults, which could hold more than 75 percent of all securities and investments in America, an idea that was never realized.

When the anchorages were in place, four giant cables, each with a diameter of 15-3/4 inches, would be stretched across the tops of the two gigantic towers and secured to the anchorages. At completion each cable would be 3,578 feet long, with a load strength of nearly 25 million pounds, and composed of 5,434 pencil-thick wires, laid like stacked logs, then wrapped with a covering of more than 243 miles of fine wire. The total length of wire in each cable would ultimately be 3,515 miles. The cable wire would be made of steel instead of iron, a daring innovation, as steel had never before been used in an American building or bridge.

Next, heavy wire-rope suspenders would be strung vertically from the four horizontal cables and would connect to the suspended bridge roadway. Then inclined stays made of wire rope would be strung on the diagonal from the top of each tower down to the roadway in each direction, creating diamond patterns as they intersected with the suspenders. The inclined stays and the suspenders would be much smaller than the four great cables and would be woven just as a hemp rope is woven, with hundreds of fine, twisted wires.

Roebling called the bridge a perfect harmony of opposing forces — the powerful steel cables in tension, the awesome mass of granite towers in compression as the cables passed over, exerting an incredible downward force.

And so it was that John A. Roebling began in 1869 to build his masterpiece, which he said would be known as "... the greatest engineering work of the continent, and of the age." However, Roebling would never live to see the completion of the Brooklyn Bridge. He would die as the result of an accident during the summer of 1869 just as construction was beginning.

Roebling and his son Washington were in Brooklyn, making the final decision for the location of the Brooklyn tower. The elder Roebling, concentrating on his work, failed to get out of the way of a docking boat, and his toes were crushed between the boat and the piles. Although Roebling permitted amputation of the toes, the iron-willed engineer refused medication and a doctor's care. Too late it was discovered that he had a deadly tetanus infection — lockjaw. Rigidity and convulsions followed, and Roebling died in agony a month later.

As the two cities mourned, 32-year-old Washington Roebling quietly took his father's place. Although Washington had a much different personality — kind, relaxed, and friendly — he was a very intelligent and capable man. And he was absolutely the only person who knew from start to finish how to build the Brooklyn Bridge.

It is interesting to speculate whether Washington Roebling would have undertaken the monumental task of building the Brooklyn Bridge if he had known what misery lay ahead. The bridge would take three times longer than projected, finally opening May 24, 1883, and would cost $15 million — more than twice his father's estimate. The years in between dragged on, full of disappointments, bitter confrontations, wholesale corruption, and perhaps more than 20 deaths (although the number was never officially recorded).

Personal tragedy lay ahead for Washington Roebling as well. He would spend the rest of his life as a cripple and

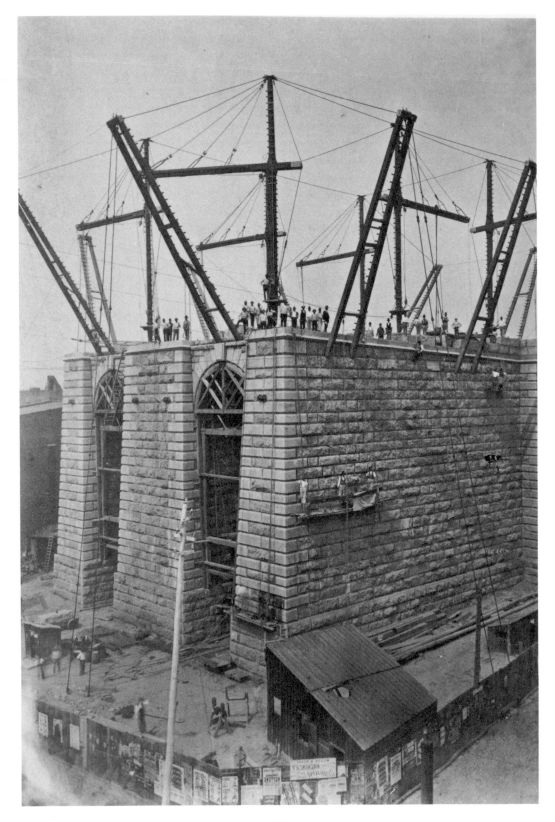

recluse as a result of a terrible accident in December 1870 during work on the Brooklyn caisson.

The gigantic six-million-pound timber box had been towed out to the construction site, and the mind-boggling task of submerging and burying the caisson had begun. In order to make the huge structure, which was open at the bottom, slowly sink to the river floor, courses (layers) of masonry were stacked on the five-foot-thick timber roof, one at a time. When at last the gigantic caisson rested on the river bottom, dredging began from inside the caisson, and slowly the massive box sank into the river bed and was covered, safe from water damage and destruction from water worms.

Compressed air filled the caisson to keep the walls from collapsing as it submerged and to keep water and mud from rushing in from beneath. Workmen entered from the roof, which was kept above the water line by the ongoing layering of masonry, and they went through a hatch down into an airlock. After compressed air was released into the airlock from the caisson to equalize air pressure, the men descended by ladder into the muddy caisson through an iron shaft. Excavated material was removed through ingenious water shafts.

However, little was known of the dangers of compressed air and the manner in which rapid decompression caused the mysterious malady called "the bends" by releasing nitrogen bubbles into the bloodstream. As the caisson sank deeper and deeper, atmospheric pressure in-

creased, and so did the terrible effects. The workmen suffered from splitting headaches, joint pains, convulsions, and paralysis. Some began to die.

The caisson was 43 feet down, with more than 56 million pounds of masonry resting on the timber roof, when another calamity struck — fire. The blaze, set unintentionally by a workman, began to burn unnoticed in a roof seam. Compressed air drove the flames deep into the roof timbers, hidden from sight and smell, and rapidly spreading for several hours.

Approximately 30 minutes after the fire was discovered, the news reached Roebling, who rushed to the scene. Acutely aware of the terrifying danger caused by the crushing weight of tons of material overhead, Washington Roebling nevertheless felt it was his duty to stay hour after hour in the heavily pressurized caisson. Finally, he collapsed in agony, temporarily paralyzed. Roebling had saved the caisson by completely flooding it, but he had lost his health forever.

Although Roebling was in constant pain, he was determined to continue as chief engineer. Under his direction the Brooklyn caisson reached its resting place and was filled with cement by 1871. The New York tower foundation was completed in July 1872.

The great towers grew slowly, layer by layer, as courses of masonry were added to the caissons. At last they rose high above the water, finally soaring above the rooftops on both shores.

Washington Roebling's health deteriorated steadily during construction of the towers. Severe pain, dizziness, and nausea increased until he was no longer able to go to the bridge site. A nervous condition developed as well, making it impossible for him to be around people.

And yet Roebling continued on as chief engineer, first from his home in

New York anchorage, July 31, 1876. On August 11, shortly after this picture was taken, the first steel-wire cable was stretched into place over the two towers. (Courtesy of Museum of the City of New York)

Trenton, New Jersey, and after 1877 from
a house at 110 Brooklyn Heights, which
had a spectacular view of the bridge.
There he sat, telescope in hand and often
bundled in blankets, watching the progress of his bridge. During the 14 years
of construction, he never went to the
bridge, and he rarely talked to the engineering staff. How then did he supervise
such an overwhelming project? Many
people wondered then, and many wonder
to this day.

Without a doubt Roebling was an
intelligent man, but beyond that, he had
a unique ability to transmit orders in the
most intricate detail by letter. These
letters were dictated to his wife Emily,
who in addition to writing them, made
certain they were understood by the
engineers, with whom she met on a
regular basis. The engineers dealt with
Emily directly on all matters. They told
reporters that she understood everything
about bridge building and could answer
any questions.

But because Washington Roebling
was seldom seen, stories began to circu-
late that he was hopelessly insane, ad-
dicted to drugs, or perhaps even dead, and
that his beautiful and accomplished wife
was actually the chief engineer. The few
who actually met with Roebling said
otherwise — that although he was terribly

The New York tower is completed,
1876. From the Beal Panorama of
1876. This photograph, taken from
the Brooklyn tower, shows the masted
ships that cluster at South Street. At
left: The mammoth domed building is
the New York City Post Office, just
completed in 1875 at the foot of City
Hall Park, dwarfing City Hall. The
spire of St. Paul's Chapel rises at the
far left. (Courtesy of Museum of the
City of New York)

ill, his mind was sound. Emily Roebling's real role in the construction of the bridge would never be known. She would never write about her contribution.

Meanwhile, construction continued on the two anchorages, which were completed in 1875 and 1876. The first wire for cable-making was stretched across the two towers in August of 1876, and cable-spinning was completed in October 1878. The long approaches leading to the anchorages were finally finished, sloping above the city streets of Brooklyn and New York. The bridge roadway was completed in 1881, 12 years after the start of construction, and the pine planks of the pedestrian promenade were laid in April 1883, just before the opening of the bridge in May.

At long last Washington Roebling's work was finished. The glorious undertaking had turned into bitter drudgery, not only because Roebling was ill, but because there had been ugly revelations of graft and corruption. Although Roebling had not been involved, many board members had been incriminated. Even the supremely corrupt William Marcy (Boss) Tweed and his cohorts had managed to line their pockets with bridge funds during the first years of construction — that is, until 1871, when Tweed was indicted on 120 counts by the Grand

Suspending the bridge floor beams, 1881. These beams will eventually bear the weight of four roadways, the two outer lanes for horses, wagons, and carriages, and the inside lanes for a cable-driven railroad system. There will also be an elevated walkway for pedestrians. Note the vertical suspenders. The two men are probably engineers, overseeing the work against the backdrop of Manhattan. (Courtesy of Museum of the City of New York)

Jury for various New York swindles.

The deepest humiliation of all came when the bridge was nearly finished. In 1882 some members of the bridge's board of directors tried to strip Roebling of honor by replacing him as chief engineer. They did not succeed. Roebling would be given the acclaim he deserved.

And so on a splendidly sunny day, May 24, 1883, the Brooklyn Bridge opened to unprecedented fanfare. Buildings were draped with red, white, and blue bunting; the river was a solid mass of gaily flagged vessels; and both cities swarmed with joyful celebrants. There was music everywhere, and cannon salutes, and ringing bells.

President Chester A. Arthur and New York Governor Grover Cleveland led a procession across the bridge to pay homage to Washington and Emily Roebling at their home in Brooklyn Heights. When night fell, a mile-long ribbon of lights sparkled across the expanse of the bridge while 14 tons of brilliant fireworks exploded in the black sky, culminating in a glorious display of 500 rockets that burst into showers of silver and gold. The spectacular display was accompanied by a jubilant chorus of bells, brass bands, thousands of people singing, and horns blasting from every ship and boat on the East River.

Shortly after the great celebration, 46-year-old Washington Roebling, a shadowy figure for so many years, resigned as chief engineer and slipped quietly away to New Jersey. There he built a grand mansion for Emily and resumed his life as a semirecluse.

As for Emily, she filled her life with adventure, receiving a law degree, writing a book, and traveling widely, even attending the coronation of Czar Nicholas and the Czarina Alexandra. Scintillating and spirited, Emily brought the world back to her cloistered husband until she was finally conquered by cancer in 1903.

Roebling lived for years in virtual seclusion until a crisis at the Roebling wire manufacturing plant made him suddenly decide to take control at the age of 84. To everyone's surprise, Roebling began putting in long, arduous days at the plant, a duty he continued until his death on July 21, 1926, at the age of 89. Amazingly, this man, who had suffered so long, had outlived almost everyone — his wife, most of his family, and almost all who had played major roles in the building of the Brooklyn Bridge.

The Tour

The short walk along the historic pedestrian promenade of the Brooklyn Bridge begins at the intersection of Centre and Chamber Streets near the beautiful 1914 Municipal Building.

Walk south a short distance. You will see a large sign "Brooklyn Bridge," indicating the bridge approach, which climbs gradually to the pedestrian walkway.

In short order, you will be strolling along the pleasant wooden walkway 18 feet above the stream of cars and trucks. The view is spectacular in every direction — a splendid panorama of New York City, Brooklyn, and New York Harbor, with a fine view of the Statue of Liberty.

The Brooklyn Bridge is quite overwhelming when seen close up — the huge granite blocks used in the mammoth towers, the monumental Gothic arches, the cables stretched into a gigantic steel macramé.

Within 25 minutes, you will see the immense Brooklyn anchorage and begin walking down the Brooklyn approach. If you plan to visit Brooklyn Heights, take

Grand bird's eye view of the Brooklyn Bridge published by Currier & Ives, 1885. (Courtesy of The New-York Historical Society, New York City)

the Cadman Plaza West exit. The pedestrian promenade will split into two walkways. Take the left, going down a stairway. Instructions in the following chapter will direct you to the first stop on the Brooklyn Heights tour.

A Few Tips:
Wear a hat on warm, sunny days and, of course, wear comfortable shoes, espe-

cially if you are taking the tour of Brooklyn Heights. Take along a jacket on cool days, as the promenade can be quite breezy.

Early Sunday morning is an ideal time to take this walk. There is less traffic on the bridge then, and your experience will be closer to the one enjoyed by 19th-century strollers.

Recommended Reading:
McCullough, David, *The Great Bridge,*
New York, Simon and Schuster, 1972. This
carefully researched, fascinating book about
the building of the Brooklyn Bridge is superb-
ly written and tells not only about the saga of
construction but also about the 19th-century
life in New York City and Brooklyn. Great
fun to read.

R E S T A U R A N T S

River Cafe
1 Water Street
718-522-5200

Brunch:
  Saturday noon-2:30 p.m.
  Sunday 11:30 a.m.-2:30 p.m.
Lunch:
  Monday-Friday noon-2:30 p.m.
Dinner:
  Monday-Saturday 6:00-11:00 p.m.
  Sunday 6:30-11:00 p.m.

• All major credit cards
• Reservations necessary
• A la carte menu at lunch; prix-fixe menu at
  dinner. If you prefer, you may come for a
  drink on the terrace after 5:30 p.m.

Our friends Judith and Steve joined us at
twilight, just as Manhattan was turning into a
sequined pattern of lights across the East
River. We all leaned forward to sniff the com-
pact ball of roses on the table as Gershwin
tunes were being played softly on a piano.
Subdued light pooled around lush flower
masses, the noise level was on a low simmer,
and the Manhattan nightscape lay beyond the
wall of windows — the soaring Brooklyn
Bridge and the East River, alive with boats.

But was the food worthy of all of this
glamour? Yes!

For appetizers we chose a pecan and shitake
consomme garnished with cinnamon-smoked
quail and apple ravioli, a spicy crab and black
olive gazpacho perfumed with a cumin
mousse, and a velvety sweet pea soup laced
with chanterelle mushrooms and lobster.

Main courses had the same flair, with unusual combinations of ingredients and flavors
that worked every time. Salmon seared with
ginger, burgundy butter, and leeks was
delicious, as were seared shrimp seasoned
with onion, tomato, and ginger in a rich and
spicy broth. Monkfish was roasted and garnished with poached oysters and bathed in a
lively horseradish and sorrel sauce, while a
tender squab cutlet was combined with
cracked mustard seed, arugula, and Chinese
cabbage flan.

And what desserts! Sublime stir-fried
fruits were crowned with ginger ice cream and
praline caramel. A sprightly glazed lemon
mousse was garnished with raspberries and
papaya purée, and the dense chocolate
whiskey cake nestled in a silky vanilla-bean
custard.

Lunch:
  Appetizers $8.00-$18.00
  Entrees $19.00-$30.00
Dinner:
  Prix fixe $55.00

If you are combining lunch with a walk
across the bridge and/or a Brooklyn Heights
tour, you should know that most people dress
up to come to the River Cafe. You might
carry a small tote bag with you — big enough
for a change of shoes and any other small
festive addition.

Harbor View

1 Old Fulton at corner of Water Street
(Columbia Heights leads straight to the
restaurant. From bridge exit, turn left,
walk toward river.)
718-237-2224

All-day dining:
    Sunday & Monday noon-10:00 p.m.
    Tuesday-Thursday noon-11:00 p.m.
    Friday & Saturday noon-11:30 p.m.

- All major credit cards
- Piano music every evening except Monday

This old-fashioned Italian restaurant, with its
whirling fans overhead, painted tin ceiling,
wood-paneled walls, and cheerful pink and
forest green linens, is a pleasant and casual
place to have a nice lunch or dinner and a nice
view of the New York City skyline. Located
near the historic Fulton Ferry landing, the cozy
little restaurant is in the shadow of the
Brooklyn Bridge, near the River Cafe.

From the large windows you will have an
interesting view of the comings and goings of
river traffic. At one point, we saw a huge
tanker, a 19th-century schooner, and a green-
and-white Circle Line boat outlined against the
fluttering flags and buildings of South Street
Seaport; just in front there was a parade of
fashion-conscious New Yorkers piling into
nearby River Cafe, followed by a nattily
attired duo who parked their bicycles and
strolled in.

Harbor View serves traditional fare such as
linguini with red or white clam sauce; red
snapper with capers, tomatoes, onions, and
peppers; veal with marsala wine sauce; and
pasta primavera in a rich and spicy tomato and
onion sauce. Salads are large and tasty.

Lunch:
    Appetizers $6.50-$8.50
    Entrees $7.95-$14.95
Dinner:
    Appetizers $9.50-$11.50
    Entrees $10.95-$17.95

D I R E C T I O N S

*Begin tour at intersection of Chambers and
Centre Streets near the Brooklyn Bridge
approach.*

Subway:
- IRT #4, 5, 6, N (The City Hall stop is
  quite close to the sloping approach to the
  Brooklyn Bridge promenade)
- J, M to Chambers Street

Bus:
- M15 (First / Second Avenues)
- M101, M102 (Third / Lexington Avenues)

Car:
- FDR Drive, Civic Center / Brooklyn
  Bridge exit

Correction page 123, paragraph 4: It was David
McCullough in *The Great Bridge* who described the
bridge as a harmony of opposing forces.

Strolling Through the 19th Century

In historic Brooklyn Heights

Above: View of #3 (corner) and 2 Pierrepont Place, located at the entrance to the Brooklyn Heights Esplanade. (Photograph © Jeffrey Jay Foxx, 1990)

Left: A circa 1922 view of the connecting Renaissance Revival mansions on Pierrepont Place, first owned by wealthy merchant traders. (Courtesy of The Brooklyn Historical Society)

arly Sunday morning in Brooklyn Heights. So quiet. Just a few people here and there ambling along the tree-shaded sidewalks. We have stepped into 19th-century New York, a neighborhood lined with rows of clapboard, brick, and brownstone houses. There are dignified stone mansions as well, and stately 19th-century churches.

We stop to admire a square 1876 carriage house set deep into 151 Willow Street. It is a sturdy red brick, fronted with elongated arched windows and double doors that once served as the carriage entrance. In a narrow side yard a worn brick walk meanders through dense ground cover to a little side door.

A sleepy-eyed man saunters up the street toward us. He is cradling a Sunday newspaper with one arm and clutches a bag of doughnuts in the other.

"Nice, isn't it?" he murmurs proudly, his head cocked to one side as he gazes at the restored carriage house. "And guess who lived at 155 Willow next door? The playwright and novelist Arthur Miller."

Shifting the bulky Sunday *New York Times* to his other arm, the stranger chats on happily. "A lot of famous people used

to live here. Truman Capote, for one.
Kinda odd, but real nice. He gave me a
copy of his book *Breakfast at Tiffany's*,
and he put a really nice inscription in it. I
think I still have it somewhere. Oh, yes
— and I know Norman Mailer — another
famous writer. He still lives in Brooklyn
Heights. Has a nice big house."

The man's eyes narrow thoughtfully.
"I've seen a lot of changes here since I
was born 55 years ago. Used to swim in
the East River when I was young, and my
brother even swam to the Statue of
Liberty and back one summer! Yeah, a lot
has changed, but it's still nice living here,
mostly because a few couples got together
in the late 1950s and started a conservation movement. They managed to preserve a bunch of 19th-century houses that
were about to be torn down. Thanks to
them, there are more than 600 original
19th-century houses in Brooklyn Heights
today. You know, you have to come here
to see how New York City actually
looked in the early 19th century, because
the wrecking ball got almost all of the
houses in Manhattan!"

The friendly stranger pauses, then
tugs at his shirt collar in sudden embarrassment. "My wife always says I talk too
much ... better be moving along! I hope
you enjoy your visit!" Then with a quick
smile he lopes off down the street and
disappears around the corner.

Old Fulton Street, showing the
Brooklyn Bridge and the old Fulton
Ferry terminal (demolished), from
which passengers were ferried to Fulton
Street at South Street Seaport. From
this site General George Washington
and his troops escaped across the East
River after their disastrous defeat in
August 1776 at the Battle of Long
Island. (Courtesy of Museum of the
City of New York)

Henry Ward Beecher, famous and influential pastor of Plymouth Church from 1847 to 1887. Reverend Beecher is shown in his prime here, about 45 years old, many years before the damaging Beecher-Tilton trial of 1875. Engraved from a photograph, circa 1858. (Courtesy of The Brooklyn Historical Society)

★

So this is Brooklyn Heights. We are standing on land that for centuries the Canarsee Indians called home. Their "long houses" were strung together into a necklace along the high bluffs of Long Island facing the East River — that is, until Dutch settlers arrived in the early 17th century, driving the Indians away from their ancestral home. Eventually the Dutch built a small village on the land, calling it "Breukelen" after a province in Holland.

The British followed. Four English ships anchored off the Manhattan shore in 1664, and the British demanded immediate surrender of New Amsterdam, the small trading village that clung to the tip of Manhattan Island. Peter Stuyvesant, the strong-willed and crusty Director General, was forced to surrender the poorly fortified town without a fight. "New Amsterdam" became "New York," while across the East River "Breukelen" was renamed "Brooklyn" by the British.

The British finally relinquished New York once and for all following the Revolutionary War when they sailed out of New York Harbor in 1783, but not before Brooklyn had once again played an important role in American history. It was during the Battle of Long Island, when General George Washington and his troops, many of whom were raw recruits, were resoundingly defeated by General Howe's well-trained British and Hessian soldiers. The Revolutionary War might have ended on August 27, 1776, but the British did not push the assault (a blunder for which General Howe would later be harshly criticized), allowing the American soldiers to escape from Brooklyn Heights to Manhattan under cover of a dense fog.

At the end of the Revolutionary War, the prime strip of Brooklyn fronting the East River across from Manhattan's financial district was still peaceful countryside, divided among a few large landholders. No doubt there were scores of Manhattanites who looked longingly across the river at the choice slice of Long Island, with its direct access to the East River and its phenomenal views of Manhattan; yet in 1807 there were just seven houses there. So near and yet so inaccessible.

In 1814 Robert Fulton's first steam ferry crossed the East River, soon joined by other ferry lines. At last there was a fast and reliable means of transportation to Brooklyn. Brooklyn landowners began dividing their land into 25-by-100-foot lots, which were quickly snapped up by prosperous residents of Manhattan and Brooklyn. Brooklyn Heights, the first Manhattan suburb, was born.

One after another, fine two-and three-storied houses rose from the grid of streets. Constructed of brick, stone, and wood, they stood in orderly rows behind wrought-iron fences bordered by tree-lined sidewalks. These well-appointed row houses and mansions were the homes of industrialists, bankers, shipping tycoons, and merchants who were wealthy enough to afford homes that were close to the fast-paced life of Manhattan but were far enough away to offer the advantages of a peaceful village.

★

There is still a feeling of 19th-century tranquility in Brooklyn Heights, which fortunately has been bypassed by the major thoroughfares. The bridges and tunnels leading to Long Island allow subways and cars to zoom over and under, leaving the Heights relatively undisturbed.

The Tour

As you will soon discover, Brooklyn Heights is just the right size for a stroll: about eight blocks wide and 14 blocks long. The houses, office buildings, apartments, churches, and shops are set into a neat webbing of streets, a design that is still almost exactly the same as it was when first laid out by landholders in the early 19th century.

A severe alteration occurred in 1951 when the Brooklyn-Queens Expressway sliced through the Heights, lopping off the northwest and southwest corners. A number of early houses were destroyed in the process, and Brooklyn Heights was cut off from direct access to the East River. As consolation for the expressway's mutilation, the residents were given an esplanade, which stretches along the East River above the traffic lanes, providing a marvelous promenade on which to stroll or sit and watch the passing East River traffic and take in the incomparable view of Lower Manhattan.

★

This walk through Brooklyn Heights highlights some of the popular architectural styles of the 19th century as they are exemplified by early houses, ending with a stroll along the delightful esplanade. Our tour begins at the corner of Orange and Hicks Streets.

Walk west on Orange Street. In the middle of the block is Plymouth Church of the Pilgrims (tour available; see information at the end of the chapter).

Behind this severe red brick façade, the sanctuary once rang with the fiery, impassioned sermons of Plymouth Church's first minister, Henry Ward Beecher. Beecher, with his flowing silver hair and resonant voice, was minister from 1847 to 1887 and was one of the most revered American public figures in the 19th century. In fact, Abraham Lincoln, who attended Beecher's sermons twice in 1860, once called the minister the greatest man in America. (Abraham Lincoln's pew, #89, left center aisle near the front, is marked with a plaque.)

Reverend Beecher was considered an oracle to the millions of Americans who avidly read his sermons in their local newspapers and to the lucky 2,000 followers who managed to get seats in the church sanctuary every Sunday morning.

They accepted Beecher's views on virtually every subject — from the way to build the Brooklyn Bridge to the way to achieve salvation. His influence was felt throughout the nation — that is, until his fall from grace.

An outraged husband (and church officer) accused Reverend Beecher of adultery, a devastating accusation during the strait-laced 19th century. At the subsequent sensational Beecher-Tilton trial in 1875, the jury finally returned a verdict of "no decision." Although the Plymouth Church congregation remained steadfastly behind Beecher, the minister's reputation was shadowed for the rest of his life. Was he guilty? We still don't know for certain!

Tour of the Church Sanctuary.

The interior is graceful and quite dignified in its simplicity. Slender, fluted Corinthian columns support the balcony that garlands the sanctuary. Above the simple raised platform is a richly carved Gothic Revival organ case.

The windows may remind you of 16th-century Dutch paintings — except that the radiant colors are created by stained glass and sunshine. The windows, which were made by Frederick S. Lamb Studios (circa 1907), depict Puritan history and American freedoms.

A fragment of Plymouth Rock and portraits of Abraham Lincoln, Harriet Beecher Stowe, and Reverend Beecher are displayed in the adjacent arcade.

Five large stained-glass windows by Tiffany Studios line the walls of Hillis Hall, located next to the sanctuary.

In an enclosed courtyard in front of the church is a large bronze sculpture of Henry Ward Beecher and a bronze frieze of Abraham Lincoln. The sculptor was Gutzon Borglum, better known for his monumental busts of Presidents Washington, Jefferson, Lincoln, and Theodore Roosevelt at Mount Rushmore.

★

As you stroll along, you will see a number of examples of Federal architecture, a style that became popular after the American Revolution and continued until about 1830, when revival styles, primarily Greek Revival, came into vogue in the United States. Federal architecture, named for the new American federation following the Revolution, was based on English Georgian architecture, which in turn drew inspiration from Italian and French Renaissance architecture.

Characteristics of American Federal design include a flat, smooth façade and a low-pitched roof. Architectural elements such as windows, doors, and moldings emphasize symmetry and harmony. Other characteristics include multipaned windows, as well as fanlights, colonnettes and sidelights surrounding doorways. Also louvered shutters, bowed bays, and simple rectangular lintels above windows.

The classical ornamentation can be quite splendid and formal, having such elements as great columns and porticos; or as found in Brooklyn Heights, simple and restrained — having narrow cornices, slender colonnettes, and uncomplicated moldings, for example. Whether simple or elaborate, the design is often well-proportioned and graceful, as exemplified by a house at 24 Middagh Street, described below.

Walk west on Orange Street and turn right to Hicks Street (named for John and Jacob Middagh Hicks, brothers who developed much of Brooklyn Heights). Walk two blocks north to Middagh Street and turn left.

#31-33. A charming clapboard dual residence, built about 1847 and painted a deep olive green with autumn-leaf red detailing. Originally merchants lived here above their shops: a paint store and a men's "hairdressing parlor," as listed in the 1847-1848 city directory. A simple, handpainted wooden sign hangs outside the door today, which advertises that an artist lives and works here — comforting proof that some traditions continue!

#24. Here it is, and what a beauty! Perhaps the best and oldest example of Federal architecture in Brooklyn Heights (circa 1824). A muted brown two-and-a-half-story clapboard on a Flemish-bond brick basement. (Flemish bond is a pattern created when the long side of the brick, the stretcher, alternates with the end, the header, making a "dot-dash" pattern, often in contrasting colors. Very popular in the 19th century.)

This house has been carefully restored and is virtually unaltered. The doorway, flanked by slender colonnettes and surrounded by leaded-glass sidelights and a transom window, is a trifle lopsided now, adding to its charm. Other characteristics of the Federal house found here: double-pitched roof with dormer windows, a house width that accommodates three bays, and basement kitchen shutters.

Turn left at the corner of Middagh and Willow Streets.

Take a peek at the peaceful garden behind #24. Feathery willow branches droop over the high wooden wall. A beautifully restored carriage house is just beyond the garden.

Continue walking along Willow Street past the carriage house (south).

#22. Home in which Henry Ward Beecher resided for several years. This house is a unit in a continuous façade of Greek Revival houses built from about 1830-1860, when Americans were enamored with everything from ancient Greece, from philosophy to architecture. Greek Revival buildings could be stately, having rows of great columns, grand pedimented entry porches, and friezes of fallen Greek heroes. Some were veritable Greek temples! On the other hand, the design could be quite pared down, with simplified classical detailing, exemplified by these row houses. Notice the flattened, wide moldings around doors and windows — more masculine than the Federal moldings. Flat projections called Greek ears decorate tops of recessed doorways.

Continue walking on Willow to the next corner. Turn right at Cranberry Street.

13, 15, 17 Cranberry, at corner. Circa 1830. More examples of the dignified and clean-lined Federal style of architecture. Lovely, simple ornamentation. Notice the graceful arched doorways with fanlights, as well as the smooth-faced brick façades, rectangular stone lintels, narrow moldings, and low-pitched roofs.

There are more than a dozen circa 1820-1840 houses on Cranberry Street. Very interesting to see, if you have a little extra time.

Return to Willow Street, continuing south to Clark Street.

At this corner is the former Towers Hotel, built in 1928, an imposing building set on a foundation of huge granite stones, which resembles a medieval castle with its arched windows and four octagonal towers. The building shows the influence of Romanesque Revival, which had a limited popularity during the last half of the 19th century, as it could be heavy and rather forbidding.

Brooklyn Heights on a quiet Sunday
morning. (Photograph by David
Browning, 1989)

Continue walking south on Willow.

101, 103 Willow. Greek Revival
houses. #101 (circa 1835) has a pleasing
wrought-iron railing, which terminates
in a vertical swirl design, a popular design
in Brooklyn Heights, and rarely seen
elsewhere — undoubtedly the work of
a Brooklyn foundry. Greek Revival
wrought-iron decoration was more elaborate than the Federal designs that
preceded it. Note the attractive wrought-
iron fence with stylized pineapple finials,
a symbol of hospitality. Again, the Greek
ears decoration on the doorway. #103

was built around 1848.

109-112 Willow. Whimsical houses
built in 1883, said to be the finest examples of Queen Anne architecture in
New York City. Although the style carries the name of the English queen who
reigned from 1702-1714, it was chiefly
the result of the fertile imagination of
Richard Norman Shaw, a late 19th-
century English architect. Queen Anne
style draws liberally from medieval and
Renaissance architecture. Surprisingly,
the result is quite pleasing. The style
became popular in America during the
last quarter of the 19th century and led to
a vogue for collecting early 18th-century
furniture and silver. Reproductions,
especially furniture with cabriole legs,
became popular.

151 Willow Street. The charming

1876 red brick carriage house discussed in the introduction.

155, 157, 159 Willow Street. Fine examples of Federal-style row houses, circa 1825. Eight-paneled doors flanked by Ionic colonnettes and leaded-glass transoms with side lights; elegantly simple stone lintels; Flemish-bond brick façades and arched dormer windows in a peaked roof. If you look at the pavement near the gate of #157, you will see a glass skylight, said to have shed a little sunshine into a tunnel that supposedly led to 151 Willow Street — some say to a vault!

Continue walking on Willow Street to Pierrepont Street, named for Hezekiah Beers Pierrepont, owner of a large estate in this area, who offered lots to the public in 1832. Turn left (east).

#27, corner of Willow and Pierrepont Street. One of the oldest Greek Revival houses in Brooklyn Heights, circa 1834. Façade altered extensively. The Flemish-bond brick and wrought-iron side fence with Greek-key design are noteworthy.

Continue walking east on Pierrepont Street.

36 Pierrepont Street. The George Hastings residence, named for its first owner, a merchant, and a prosperous one, no doubt. Circa 1845. A nice example of Gothic Revival architecture.

How to describe Gothic Revival? If you picture medieval cathedrals and castles with their pointed arches, buttresses, ornate stained-glass designs, intricate iron work, steeply pitched roofs, towers and battlements, you can imagine the inspiration for Gothic Revival architecture, which took America by storm around 1840.

The George Hastings House, a solid-looking square brick home, is embellished with such medieval detailing. Note the intricate tracery designs modeled on Gothic stained-glass windows, seen here in panels above the windows and in the wrought-iron fence. Lancet arches (spear-like arches) decorate the brownstone entrance, the balcony railing, and the fence. Note also the Gothic trefoil and quatrefoil designs, stylized three-leaf and four-leaf clovers.

82 Pierrepont Street at the corner of Henry Street. Here is an interesting example of Victorian Romanesque architecture, which, like Gothic Revival, took its inspiration from medieval architecture. This style was seen from about 1870-1890 but was never extremely popular, as it tended to be massive and overwhelming.

Characteristics include the use of numerous building materials in one structure, often alternating in wide bands that wrap around the building. Also, moldings in contrasting colors and decorated bricks, terra-cotta, and tiles. Sometimes the exterior takes on a colorful checkerboard appearance. Finally, there are arched openings, dormers, towers, columns — even gargoyles and other mythical creatures galore!

82 Pierrepont Street, known as the Herman Behr House after its first owner, was built in 1890. Here you see an entire façade banded in stone, brick, tile, and terra-cotta. Doors, windows, and a jigsaw of steep roofs are outlined by narrow bands in contrasting colors. The overall effect is somehow pleasing and fanciful in this day of spare, often undistinguished architecture.

Continue walking east on Pierrepont Street to Clinton Street.

The Brooklyn Historical Society, 128 Pierrepont Street, corner of Clinton Street, formerly called the Long Island Historical Society, has occupied this site since 1878. Designed by George B. Post, architect of the New York Stock Exchange Building, this venerable three-storied, arcaded brick building is lavishly decorated with red and yellow terra-cotta detailing, the first time the soft material was used extensively on a New York building.

Of interest are the numerous sculpted portrait heads decorating the exterior. Above the entrance are a Viking, representing the discovery of America, and an American Indian, representing the original inhabitants. On Pierrepont Street are heads of Christopher Columbus and Benjamin Franklin, while on the Clinton Street side are Shakespeare, Gutenberg, Beethoven, and Michelangelo, all representing exploration and unique achievement in various fields.

Be sure to see the beautiful second-floor library with its tiers of alcove bookcases, columns, and the high-ceilinged gallery with stained-glass windows.

The 4,000-square-foot Shellens Gallery of Brooklyn History recently opened on the first floor of the Historical Society. Once an auditorium in which such notables as Sir Arthur Conan Doyle, Henry Cabot Lodge, Woodrow Wilson, and Horace Greeley spoke to great crowds, this sun-filled, 22-foot-high space houses a museum devoted to Brooklyn history.

Turn right at corner of Pierrepont Street and Clinton Street, then turn right at the next corner to Montague Street.

Montague Street bustles with the activity of numerous small shops and restaurants. Stroll westward to the breezy esplanade bordering the East River.

Stop one block west of the esplanade at a short street with two names: called Pierrepont Place on the right side of

The Brooklyn Heights Esplanade today. (Photograph by David Browning, 1989)

144

intersecting Montague Street and called Montague Terrace on the left side.

This short street has two names because Montague Street once inclined sharply to an East River landing where the Wall Street Ferry docked. A small footbridge connected Pierrepont Place to Montague Terrace. (See opening photograph.)

Nos. 2 and 3 Pierrepont Place are examples of Renaissance Revival architecture, popular from approximately 1840-1890, inspired by English, Italian, and French architecture of the 15th to the 17th centuries. (Just imagine a great cube with symmetrical detailing. Strong, straight, regal lines — the great *palazzi* of Renaissance Italy, for example.) There was a third mansion, demolished in 1946.

The two surviving 1856 brownstone mansions, whose rear windows overlook the esplanade and the East River, have been attributed to Richard Upjohn, the distinguished architect of several New York churches, including Trinity Church. They are masculine and strong, with wide entrance steps flanked by impressive balustrades. Doorways are framed with ornamental Corinthian pilasters, and window moldings have a wide linen-fold design. Deep entablatures and corner quoins add additional strength and importance to the exteriors.

No. 2 Pierrepont Place belonged to a wealthy fur merchant, Alexander M. White. #3 was the residence of Abiel A. Low, whose great wealth came from the merchant trade in China and Japan. Low's son Seth was mayor of Brooklyn, president of Columbia University, and mayor of New York City.

Cross Montague Street to Montague Terrace.

Here is a beautifully preserved street of late 19th-century townhouses, connected in an English style of architecture called a terrace. These houses are in mint condition, a flowing, graceful unit. Thomas Wolfe wrote *Of Time and the River* in 1935 when he lived in #5.

Return to Montague Street and walk the short distance west to the esplanade.

Notice a stone tablet in a grassy plot marked by an American flag. On this site Four Chimneys stood, the house in which General George Washington was headquartered during the Battle of Long Island in August 1776, at the beginning of the American Revolution.

★

Here, at last, is the delightful esplanade, built in 1951 — a wide, straight ribbon, edged by the East River on one side and bordered by fenced gardens and historic tree-shaded houses on the other — a lovely contrast. I hope you will spend some time here, sitting on a bench in the sunshine or strolling beneath the tall honey-locust trees. You couldn't find a better place to watch the people and take in the colorful parade of boats, not to mention that fabulous view of Manhattan!

A relaxing walk along the Brooklyn Heights Esplanade and the striking view of Manhattan across the East River — a combination that is hard to beat! (Photograph by David Browning, 1990)

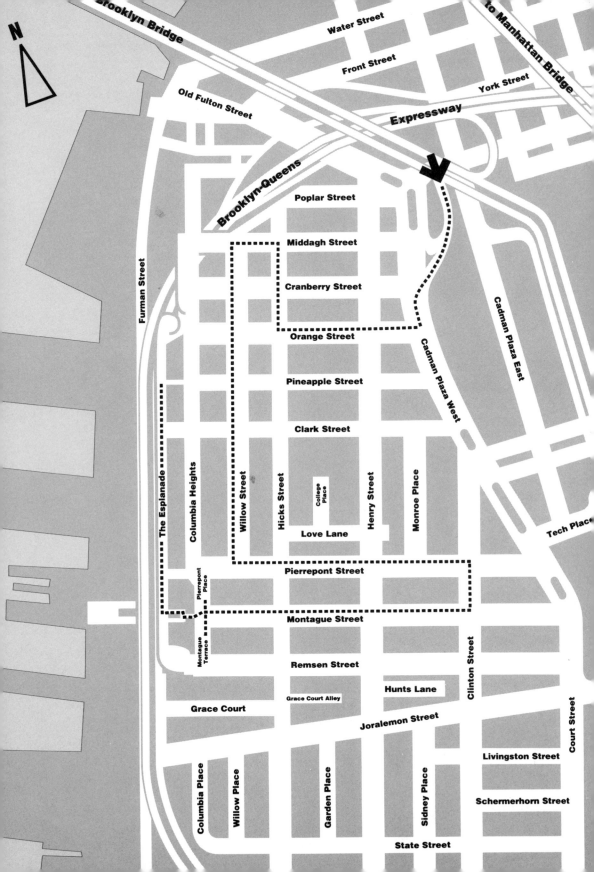

Plymouth Church of the Pilgrims
Orange & Hicks Streets
New York, NY 11201
718-624-4743

Sunday service 11:00 a.m. (This is a nice way to start the Brooklyn Heights walk.)

Tours:
Given by appointment

Brooklyn Historical Society
128 Pierrepont Street at Clinton Street
New York, NY 11201
718-624-0890

Hours:
Tuesday-Sunday noon-5:00 p.m.

Library Hours:
Tuesday-Saturday 10:00 a.m.-4:45 p.m.

Admission:
• Adults $2.50
• Children $1.00

★

Recommended Reading:
Two well-written books relate the history of Brooklyn Heights and offer extended tours: *Old Brooklyn Heights, New York's First Suburb,* by Clay Lancaster and *A Guide to the Metropolis, Walking Tours of Architecture and History,* by Gerard R. Wolfe.

RESTAURANTS

Slade's
107 Montague Street
718-858-1200

Brunch:
    Saturday & Sunday 11:00 a.m.-4:00 p.m.
Lunch:
    Daily 11:00 a.m.-4:00 p.m.
Dinner:
    Daily 6:00 p.m.

• All major credit cards

Slade's, a small, casual storefront cafe, is representative of many restaurants along Montague Street — good food at a modest price. Specials are written on a large blackboard.

Salads make a nice beginning, as do spicy gazpacho and old-fashioned chicken noodle soup.

Spinach fettuccine with shrimp and mussels in marinara sauce is nicely prepared, while chicken in a strawberry wine cream sauce is imaginative and tasty. Charbroiled burgers with a choice of such toppings as chili and onions, bacon, and cheese and mushrooms are satisfying and filling.

Try the strawberry tarts and cheesecake, both well-prepared.

Brunch $11.95 & $13.95
Lunch $6.00-$9.00
Dinner $8.00-$20.00

River Cafe and Harbor View Restaurants

For reviews, see the Brooklyn Bridge chapter. To reach these two restaurants from the esplanade, walk one block east to Columbia Heights. Turn left (north). Columbia Heights will lead you straight to the restaurants, which are located on the site of the old Fulton Ferry landing (see photograph in this chapter).

The restored 1876 carriage house at 151 Willow Street. (Photograph by Judith H. Browning, 1989)

D I R E C T I O N S

If beginning tour after Brooklyn Bridge walk (described in chapter 8):

As you walk down the bridge's sloping Brooklyn approach, you will see two walkways divided by a fence. Take left, down the stairs. You will see a small park on your right. Follow path that curves through park to the other side — you will be on Cadman Plaza West. Cross over. At Park Plaza Restaurant take a little tree-shaded path on the left to next street — Henry Street. Turn right one block. This is Orange Street and Henry Street, your starting point.

Subway:
- IRT Seventh Avenue Express #2, 3 to Clark Street Station at Henry Street. Walk north two blocks on Henry Street to Orange Street.
- IND Eighth Avenue, A or C to High and Cranberry Streets. Walk west one block on Cranberry Street to Henry Street. Turn left one block to Orange Street.

Car:
- Take Cadman West exit off Brooklyn Bridge. West on Middagh Street one block. Turn left to Henry Street. Park on one of the adjacent streets near starting point of tour.

The Brooklyn Museum and the Brooklyn Botanic Garden

Two adventures – back to back

First, The Brooklyn Museum and its History

 t was 1893. The eminent architectural firm of McKim, Mead & White had just completed Washington Arch in Washington Square Park. Plans for the entire Columbia University campus were on the drawing board. Now the firm had a challenging new commission: a splendid museum for Brooklyn. The monumental building would have a million-and-a-half square feet of floor space. Classical in style, it would be a colossal square, 550 feet on each side, and would dominate a 10-acre site.

The museum's crown would be a central dome. The inner space would be broken into four great quadrants, each one centered with a glass-enclosed courtyard 100-feet square. Three floors of galleries would surround the courtyards.

It was not to be. Construction continued until 1925. One-sixth of the building was completed — 250,000

Above: The Brooklyn Museum today. (Photograph © Jeffrey Jay Foxx, 1990)

Right: This May 30, 1896, photograph shows the first section of the museum, the northwest wing on Eastern Parkway, nearing completion. The building is decorated with flags for the Fourth of July celebration. (Courtesy of The Brooklyn Museum)

Above: A case of pottery objects and gold jewelry representing tribes of the northern Andes. At center: Two burial urns from the Magdalnea River Valley (1200-1500 A.D.). Among the gold objects: a gold flask, tweezers, and a pectoral disc (500-1000 A.D.). (Photograph by David Browning, 1990)

Below: In the sculpture garden — art saved from razed buildings. (Photograph by David Browning, 1990)

square feet. Then for many reasons, among them Brooklyn's earlier absorption into New York City as a borough and slowly dwindling funds, priorities changed. Fortunately, the museum had been designed as a complete and handsome structure at each stage of construction. And so it stands today — a distinguished fragment of Brooklyn's 19th-century dream.

The Tour

The Brooklyn Museum is spacious, uncrowded, and well-organized. The galleries have high ceilings, and many are carpeted, creating a tranquil, quiet atmosphere. Each work of art is given ample room in well-lighted display cases. The exhibits represent just a fraction of the museum's holdings, estimated at nearly two million objects.

First Floor

- Large-scale contemporary works
- African, Oceanic, & New World Art
- Special Exhibitions
- Exhibitions from the Permanent Collection
- Frieda Schiff Warburg Memorial Sculpture Garden
- Museum Shops & Museum Cafe

Begin in the African, Oceanic, and New World Art Gallery, in which you will find an outstanding and diverse collection of artifacts and works of art. The presentation is sleek and dramatic. Four large 28-foot freestanding cubes highlight remarkable pieces from the Americas, Africa, and the Pacific Basin.

Among the numerous displays representing North American art is an exhibit documenting the life of the Plains Indians. One series of cases overflows with buckskin dresses, shirts, and moccasins from the Blackfoot and Sioux tribes.

The Zuni Indians of New Mexico are represented by brightly painted and feathered Kachina dolls and masks. These early 20th-century pieces represent the gods who were thought to live and dance at the bottom of a sacred lake.

Artworks from Central and South America include gold jewelry from the northern Andes; an amazingly vibrant Peruvian hat, decorated with the feathers of birds now extinct; a 15th-century relief of the Aztec corn goddess Chicomecoatl, somberly clutching a serpent staff; and a rare, circa 1000 A.D. life-size limestone figure of Quetzalcoatl, the creator god, with an eery skeleton attached to his back, once worshipped by the Huasteca, a tribe descending from the Maya.

There is an embroidered wool mantle, woven in Peru between 100 B.C. and 100 A.D. Its intricate repeat pattern of stylized killer whales with human arms

The hornblower, a beautifully rendered bronze figure cast between 1500 and 1700 A.D., from the Benin Kingdom in Nigeria. (Photograph by David Browning, 1990)

153

was embroidered with more than a half-million stitches.

An expressive green stone mask stares with sightless eyes that once held gleaming inlays. Discovered in Teotihuacan, the ancient city near Mexico City, the circa 400 A.D. work of art represents the zenith of Teotihuacan power and influence.

From the gallery devoted to African art: a towering bead-embroidered crown (Nigeria, late 19th-early 20th century), encircled by three-dimensional figures and surmounted by Okin, the royal bird; intricate mortuary figures from Gabon; dance masks from the Ivory Coast and Guinea; a refined bronze hornblower (the attendant who announced the king's movement about the court), from the Benin Kingdom, Nigeria, cast between 1500 and 1700 A.D.; and a large, somber "power" figure (Zaire, 19th or 20th century), meant to protect the village from evil forces.

Two sculptures from New Guinea, a 1,300-mile-long island in the galaxy of islands forming Melanesia in the South Pacific: At left: A rattan mask. At right: A wooden canoe prow. Both 20th-century objects are from the Sepik River region on the northern coast. (Photograph by David Browning, 1990)

And from the Pacific Basin, a treasury of artifacts. Robust and lively are the carved masks, tools, weapons, carved ceremonial figures, and other objects representing such far-flung islands as New Caledonia, the Solomon Islands, New Ireland, New Guinea, New Zealand, and the Marquesas Islands of Polynesia.

Before heading upstairs, take just a few minutes to visit several galleries devoted to special exhibitions. There is also a sculpture garden, which contains a collection of architectural sculptures taken from demolished New York buildings.

Second Floor

- Art of Korea, Japan, Southeast Asia, Himalayas, India, China
- Islamic Art

The small but select collection of Islamic art spans 1,300 years, from the seventh century to the early 20th century. It includes fine 16th- and 17th-century Turkish and Iranian ceramics, which were acquired by the museum nearly 100 years ago. Many of these ceramic pieces filling the free-standing cases have lustrous designs in vivid turquoise, deep blue, and yellow. Hanging carpets in rich hues of red and blue accent the walls.

The Indian galleries hold numerous lively red sandstone figures, from 100 to 1100 A.D., as well as elaborately detailed bronzes and miniature paintings.

The art of Southeast Asia and the Himalayas is featured in an adjoining gallery. Among the pieces are a standing sandstone figure of Vishnu (9th century, Cambodia), an imposing 14th-century bronze seated Buddha from Thailand, and a voluptuous four-armed goddess of wealth (16th century, Nepal).

The adjacent Japanese galleries are small and intimate. From the museum's superlative collection of scrolls and screens, a recent exhibit included two six-fold screens entitled "Scenes of Kyoto," masterfully rendered scenes surrounded by swirling clouds of gold (Edo Period, circa 1645).

Other noteworthy pieces include rare 6th-century potteries; a sensitive 12th-century wooden carving of a Buddhist monk, his ascetic life revealed by the sharply defined rib cage and corded muscles; and a pair of carved wooden guardian lion-dogs, which once stood in an early 13th-century Shinto shrine.

The Chinese galleries house examples of Sung Dynasty celedon porcelains and an array of Tang Dynasty tomb figures (618-906 A.D.) splashed in green, brown, and gold glazes. A gallery was recently devoted to carved jade pieces and examples of the famous Ming Dynasty blue-and-white porcelains, while another special exhibition highlighted a collection of 18th-century cloisonné works of art.

Third Floor

- Ancient Middle Eastern Art
- Classical Art
- Egyptian Art

These lofty galleries are well-suited for the exhibition of monumental sculptures. The Egyptian collection, considered one of the finest in the world, spans more than 4,000 years, from the Predynastic period (4000-3000 B.C.) to the Moslem conquest in 700 A.D.

The museum's Egyptian wing owes its strength to a large annual income restricted to the purchase of Egyptian art: the Charles Edwin Wilbour Fund. Wilbour, an immensely wealthy 19th-century collector, dedicated his time and fortune to Egyptian art. Although Charles Wilbour willed his collection to The Metropolitan Museum of Art, the museum considered the antiquities of mediocre quality and turned down the bequest. The entire collection was accepted by The Brooklyn Museum, and a huge endowment from Wilbour's only son followed. That endowment built the museum's world-class collection.

The Ancient Middle Eastern Art gallery is devoted to artifacts dating from 5000 B.C. to 300 A.D. Of special importance are the 12 large alabaster reliefs from the palace in Nimrud, Iraq, of Assyrian King Ashur-nasir-pal II (883-859 B.C.)

The galleries displaying Greek and Roman antiquities offer the same peaceful, spacious setting for numerous works of art, including fine sculptures, beautifully preserved mosaics, gold jewelry, and the red-figured and black-glazed pottery of ancient Greece.

Fourth Floor
- Period Rooms
- Decorative Arts
- Costumes and Textiles

If you are interested in antiques, you could easily spend several hours on this floor, leisurely studying the period rooms, furniture, pottery, glass, pewter, porcelains, and silver.

You will actually walk through the history of the decorative arts when you visit the period rooms, which are presented in an informative, imaginative manner. Beginning with early 17th-century clapboard cottage settings with scrubbed pine floors and rough oak furniture, you will follow the progression of the decorative arts. The elegance of 18th-century design is exemplified by Southern and New England interiors. Then on to the early 19th century to see rooms designed in the refined Federal style, followed by the ornate clutter of late 19th-century Victorian settings. Finally, you will see the evolution of 20th-century modern design.

Of special interest is an entire reconstructed gray clapboard Dutch cottage, the Jan Martense Schenck house. Built in 1675 in Brooklyn, this charming two-room cottage is in mint condition, including the delicate blue-and-white tiles surrounding the Dutch open hearth. The "turkey-work" upholstered chairs and carpet-draped table, the burnished brass andirons, and the important carved wardrobe all date from the 17th century.

The 18th-century rooms are quite beautiful and rich in color, with handsomely paneled walls and distinguished furnishings. One noteworthy installation is a plantation house built in 1768 in North Carolina. The parlor sparkles with a deep robin's-egg blue paneling in charming contrast to the dazzling sunflower-yellow upholstered furniture and matching festoons (balloon shades), which crown the windows.

Representing early 19th-century design are rooms taken from a New Jersey house built in 1818. These settings reflect the fashionable colors popularized by the reign of Napoleon I of France and feature Empire furnishings, the ornate and gilded reflection of Napoleon's admiration for ancient Egypt, Greece, and Rome. Furniture by the eminent New York cabinetmaker Duncan Phyfe enriches the parlor, displayed against peach walls and forest-green draperies — fashionable colors of the day.

There are 28 period rooms. In addition, numerous galleries are devoted to antique porcelains, pottery, silver, pewter, glass, and textiles — the best examples from England, the United States, and Europe.

Fifth Floor

• American and European Paintings, Prints, Drawings, and Sculptures

Included in the impressive American collection are works of art by John Singleton Copley, Charles Willson Peale, Thomas Cole, Frederic Edwin Church, George Inness, Thomas Eakins, Winslow Homer, John Singer Sargent, Georgia O'Keeffe, and Larry Rivers.

European art holdings span a period from the Italian Renaissance to the Post-Impressionist period. The collection is excellent and diverse, including works by Albrecht Dürer, Rembrandt, Aelbert Cuyp, Vincent Van Gogh, Jean Honoré Fragonard, Paul Cézanne, Toulouse-Lautrec, Edgar Degas, Claude Monet, Paul Klee, and Pablo Picasso.

★

Parlor-bedroom from the Jan Martense Schenck House, a two-room Dutch cottage built in Brooklyn in 1675. The entire cottage may be seen in one of the museum's fourth-floor galleries of period rooms. (Photograph © Jeffrey Jay Foxx, 1990)

Before you leave the museum, take a few minutes to browse through the first-floor gift shop. Items from 65 countries crowd every shelf and case to overflowing and include reproductions of ancient jewelry, elaborately embroidered silk kimonos from Japan, Egyptian scarabs (for good luck), handmade pottery from Peru, and African carvings.

A smaller gift shop adjoining the main lobby offers unusual books, toys for children, and many handcrafted items.

The Brooklyn Botanic Garden

A three-minute stroll from the back entrance of The Brooklyn Museum will take you to the main entrance of the Brooklyn Botanic Garden. Ask for an information leaflet and a walking map as you enter.

To the right of the entrance is the herb garden, its feathery plants accented by bright flowers in jellybean colors. The centerpiece of this attractive garden is an Elizabethan knot garden designed with interlocking boxwood arcs and circles, the open areas filled with contrasting brown and white gravel.

Just ahead along the winding path is the Japanese garden, whose placid lake is edged with huge weeping cherry trees. A Torii, a sacred wooden gateway from a Shinto temple, stands in the center of the lake, its faded red-orange hue reflected in the quiet water, mingling with the flashes of orange carp swimming beneath.

The path winds to the Shakespeare Garden, whose plants are found in the plays and sonnets of William Shakespeare. Rest a minute on a seat beneath the white trellis archway, then follow the narrow brick walk through the garden. Yarrow, lavender, cuckoo, leak, violets, and fleur-de-lis irises are planted in little nosegays. A marker in front of each plant quotes the Shakespearean passage in which the plant is mentioned.

In the Fragrance Garden each plant is labeled in braille. Spicy peppermint geranium and lemon geranium vie with candytuft and golden wallflowers to fill the air with fragrance in the little jewel box of vibrant colors and heady scents.

A celebrity path begins opposite the Fragrance Garden. An inscription on

The exquisite Japanese Hill-and-Pond Garden, designed in 1914 by Takco Shioto. View of the Torii. (Photograph by David Browning, 1989)

the first stone in the walk says this is a
path that will never end because it is
composed of the names of those artists,
performers, and athletes who were born in
Brooklyn. Climb the gentle slope of the
shady hill, stepping from one flat stone to
another, and read the celebrated names:
Walt Whitman, Danny Kaye, Floyd
Patterson, Mickey Rooney, Woody Allen,
Mae West, Neil Simon, Mary Tyler
Moore, and Jackie Robinson — all sons
and daughters of Brooklyn.

Now the pathway circles past the
1913 administration building designed by
McKim, Mead & White — a soft green
antique that seems to rest comfortably in
its vast garden. Just behind — in space-
age contrast — three gigantic crystal
prisms are clustered, pavilions of the new
$25 million Steinhardt Conservatory.

Enter the conservatory terrace, then
walk through a long building housing an
incomparable collection of bonsai trees,
many of which are rare specimens hun-

dreds of years old. There is an aquatic greenhouse at one end of this long gallery, as well as the Trail of Evolution exhibit, which follows the evolution of plant life.

The three free-standing glass prisms are reached by way of a staircase leading downstairs, through a lobby, then into the three pavilions, each of which highlights a different climate. There are tropical, desert, and temperate pavilions. In addition, there is a dramatic palm conservatory, used for catered affairs.

After you leave the conservatory, a 50-acre landscape awaits you, scattered with hundreds of rare, old specimen trees and inlaid with a mosaic of seasonal gardens.

Springtime brings drifts of sunshine yellow on Daffodil Hill, and wisteria vines, with their drooping clusters of purple blossoms, line another path. Showers of sunny forsythia brighten the hillside. And everywhere — the pink-and-white clouds of blossoming dogwood.

In late spring the glossy green domes of rhododendron are blanketed in pink, white, or red flowers. There is also an iris garden, planted into a long, winding river of lavender, purple, and yellow.

Blossoming cherry trees are everywhere — dotting the meadows, climbing the hillsides, lining meandering pathways. There is an old orchard of stately cherry trees called the Cherry Esplanade, and in the Japanese garden huge weeping cherry trees abound, their lacy branches nearly drooping into the grass.

Summer brings the scent and silky blooms of peonies, big as tea cups. In the Cranford rose garden there is a tapestry of roses in every color and variety, the third largest public display of roses in the United States.

Swaths of bright summer flowers — many rare and unusual — define every area. When we toured the garden one hot July day, we saw hundreds of giant cleomes, their globes of purple, pink, and white bobbing on yard-long tubes of green.

Autumn brings the blaze of small, feathery spider maples and giant sugar maples, which rise hundreds of feet in a burst of crimson foliage.

In the fall the Brooklyn Botanic Garden is a riot of color, with bed after bed of orange, yellow, and bronze flowers. There is a rock garden too — mounds and cascades of green nestled among glacial boulders and spangled with gold, scarlet, and purple flowers.

There is a different kind of beauty in the winter landscape: the stands of shiny, prickly holly trees, waxy with red berries; towering pine trees, rising from a bed of snow; a somber *allée* of huge maples, planted on Armistice Day 1918 in memory of America's soldiers who fought and died in World War I — indeed resembling soldiers, standing tall and straight in their ranks, season after season, year after year.

Two glass pavilions of the new Steinhardt Conservatory. (Photograph by David Browning, 1989)

The Brooklyn Museum
200 Eastern Parkway
Brooklyn, NY 11238
718-638-5000

Hours:
Wednesday-Sunday 10:00 a.m.-5:00 p.m.
Except New Year's Day, Thanksgiving &
Christmas

Admission: (Suggested donation)
- Adults $4.00
- Seniors $1.50
- Students with a valid I.D. $2.00
- Children under 12 free

Tours:
Gallery tours given throughout the week.
Call for information.

Group Tours:
Call extension 221 for appointment

Note: The works of art and antiquities discussed in this chapter are representative of
objects on view in each gallery. Exhibits
change periodically.

Brooklyn Botanic Garden
1000 Washington Avenue
Brooklyn, NY 11225
718-622-4433

Hours:
April 1-September 30
  Tuesday-Friday 8:00 a.m.-6:00 p.m.
  Saturday, Sunday, & Holidays
  10:00 a.m.-6:00 p.m.
October 1-March 31
  Tuesday-Friday 8:00 a.m.-4:30 p.m.
  Saturday, Sunday, & Holidays
  10:00 a.m.-4:30 p.m.

Closed Monday except on a public holiday

Admission:
- Free to the garden
- $2.00 for Steinhardt Conservatory

Shop:
The gift shop offers the world of nature in
every form, from a nice selection of gardening
and nature books to jewelry, pottery, trays, gift
items — all with designs of flowers, birds, etc.

Open 10:00 a.m.-4:30 p.m.

Tours:
Free tour Saturdays at 10:30 a.m. and Sundays
at 1:30 p.m., given by a Botanic Garden guide.
Meet at the gift shop.

R E S T A U R A N T S

Brooklyn Museum Cafe
First floor

Open 10:00 a.m.-4:00 p.m.

Offers a selection of salads, sandwiches, and
other cafeteria-style dishes.

- Modern, airy setting

★

Botanic Garden Terrace Cafe
Simple dishes such as chicken and tuna salads,
soups, desserts, and coffee served outside on
the terrace.

Open April-October
10:00 a.m.-5:00 p.m., weather permitting

D I R E C T I O N S

Subway:
From Manhattan
- #2 or #3 IRT to Eastern Parkway Station in front of museum

Car:
From Connecticut and Westchester
- Cross Whitestone Bridge. Take Grand Central Expressway to Route 278 West (Brooklyn-Queens Expressway) to Exit 29 (Tillary Street). Follow Tillary to second light. Turn left onto Flatbush Avenue. At Prospect Park go 3/4 way around Grand Army Plaza circle and turn right onto Eastern Parkway. Pass in front of the museum and turn right at Washington Avenue to park.

From Manhattan
- Brooklyn Bridge, left to Tillary Street, right to Flatbush Avenue. Continue, using directions from Connecticut.

Manhattan Bridge to Flatbush Avenue
- Continue as above. (Getting to the bridge from the FDR Drive involves taking a maze of streets. Just follow the signs.)

From Long Island
- Long Island Expressway to Route 278. Exit Atlantic Avenue. Right onto Washington Avenue.

Parking:
- Ample parking between the museum and Botanic Garden behind the museum on Washington Avenue. $5.00 per day.

The elegant Elizabethan knot garden, the centerpiece of the herb garden. (Photograph by Judith H. Browning, 1989)

Fire Engines Red and Firehorses White

Firefighting history at the New York City Fire Museum

Above: Day of the firehorse and steam engine at Engine Company 30. Photograph circa 1908. (Courtesy of the New York City Fire Museum)

Left: The museum, former home of Engine Company 30. (Photograph © Jeffrey Jay Foxx, 1990)

he fireman on duty in the old New York City firehouse leaned against a railing, trying to catch his breath, then slowly eased down the staircase. "Sorry, heart just doesn't want to pump. An injury to the sac around it."

He looked about 45 years old.

And that was our introduction to the New York City Fire Museum, an inspirational and colorful tribute to the early days, when men just like this one gave their youth and their health, and sometimes their lives, to save people and their possessions from fire. And, of course, the museum pays tribute to the bright red vintage fire engines that helped them do that work.

The New York City Fire Museum, housed in a 1904 Beaux-Arts building, was a working firehouse, called Engine 30, from 1904 to 1959. (Engine Company 30 was one of the first professional firefighting units of New York City, founded October 25, 1865.) The museum quite naturally focuses on New York City, tracing the development of firefighting from the early 18th century until the first years of the 20th century.

Firefighting was a primitive business at first. The main objective was to get people and valuables out of the blazing wooden buildings before the structures collapsed. The most valuable possession? Surprisingly, in Colonial households it was often the bed, which could be dismantled easily, and most of all, the prized and expensive feather mattress.

(By the way, it was Ben Franklin who organized the first volunteer fire company in Philadelphia, Pennsylvania, in 1736. Firefighting was all volunteer until the mid-19th century.)

The water bucket was the equipment of choice for putting out fires during the early 18th century, and the bucket brigade was the order of the day. In many Colonial villages, every household was required to keep two buckets, which were tossed out to the volunteer firefighters as they raced to the fire. The buckets, colorfully decorated and often bearing the owners' names, were heaped into a pile in the town square to be reclaimed after the fire. Examples of these early leather-sheathed buckets are displayed in the museum.

Ah, but people were always inventive when it came to firefighting. Take for example the primitive hand-held water syringe. You will see one of these, a sort of copper and brass torpedo, with a plunger at one end and handles on the sides. It was dipped into a bucket of water; then, while one or two volunteers held it, another pushed the plunger, discharging a few quarts of water. This invention, dating to ancient Rome, was still being used in 18th-century America. Effective? Certainly not.

There had to be a better way to fight fires. Eighteenth-century New Yorkers

had every reason to be terrified, as their buildings were often wooden tinderboxes, huddled together on narrow streets. Even worse, since open fires were a way of life for cooking and for heat, a spark that landed on a wooden floor could turn into a raging blaze within seconds, spreading quickly to other buildings. Women, who had to lean over an open hearth while cooking, were extremely vulnerable, as sparks landing in the folds of their long and cumbersome dresses often exploded into flames. In fact, this was a leading cause of women's deaths during the 18th century.

Fire laws were passed one after another. One, the *couvre feu*, French for "cover fire," required all fires to be covered at night (surviving in the English language as "curfew"). Even so, fires devastated 18th-century New York City in 1712, 1741, 1776, and 1778.

Bucket brigades and small pumps just weren't doing the job. Larger equipment that could hold more water and pump it with more force was in order. Improvement came from London in 1731 with the arrival of the two Newsham hand pumpers resembling bathtubs on wheels. Water was fed into the crude apparatus by the bucket brigades and forced out a gooseneck pipe on top.

Pumpers improved gradually, and you will see an example of a rare 1790s model in the first gallery. It was still just a wooden cylinder on wheels, which functioned very much like an old-fashioned bicycle pump: When the handle was pulled up, water was sucked in, and when the handle was pushed down, the water was forced out. Six men were required to pump this small apparatus after pulling it to the fire.

By the turn of the 19th century, engines pumped by hand and pulled along by volunteers were larger, more powerful,

and more elaborate, but they functioned in exactly the same way as the earliest pumpers. This presented problems because as they became heavier and heavier, more and more volunteers were needed. A pumper weighing several thousand pounds might need 20 or more men lined up, half on each side, vigorously pumping at 60 strokes a minute, up to a remarkable 170 strokes a minute. Exhausted, these men had to be relieved by another team of volunteers, who jumped into line. And keep in mind that these same men had dragged the iron engine all the way to the fire!

Still they must have made an impressive sight, uniformed in bright red and blue, surrounding the brilliant crimson pumper, which was often decorated to a fare-thee-well with gold-leaf striping, engraved brass trim, brass lanterns fitted with stained glass, gleaming brass bells, and perhaps a carved and gilded eagle proudly perching on top.

Since these engines could carry only a limited length of heavy hose, very soon

"Scene at a Fire, 1730." From Costello's *Our Firemen ...* , 1887. This interesting engraving shows the bucket brigade hard at work filling the primitive pumper. Actually this early Newsham pumper is depicted incorrectly, as it was just about the size of a bathtub. Two of these improved pumpers were brought to New York City in 1731, and one of them survives, located at the Firemen's Home in Hudson, New York. In the early 18th century it was housed at City Hall where the first fire companies were headquartered. (Courtesy of The New-York Historical Society, New York City)

hose carriages rumbled alongside, carrying up to 600 feet of hose. As buildings became taller, requiring long ladders, hook-and-ladder trucks joined the procession to fires — all pulled by volunteers. After a few years separate hose companies and hook-and-ladder companies were formed. By 1845 New York City had 39 engine companies, 37 hose companies, and seven hook-and-ladder companies.

You will see one of these hand-pulled hose carriages in the museum. Built in 1857, it is painted ivory with gold striping and has fancy kerosene lamps. On the side is a lively painting of a tiger, symbol of the company.

It stands to reason that as cities grew, the number of fires increased. It became clear that dragging engines to fires and manually pumping them for water pressure had to change. That change began in 1829 with the introduction of the steam engine, fueled by coal, belching clouds of smoke, and capable of pumping on and on, leaving firefighters more time and energy to put out blazes.

The days of sweat-drenched lines of volunteers pumping the great engines

Off to a New York City fire! The steam
engine is drawn by matched white
firehorses, while the hook-and-ladder
carriage is pulled by racing black
horses. Fire fills the windows of the
building behind. Lithograph, circa
1880. (Courtesy of The New-York
Historical Society, New York City)

were coming to an end, although many
volunteer companies converted gradually
to steamers and continued to insist on
dragging the engines to fires. When the
idea was suggested that horses could pull
the ponderous engines, the volunteers
balked, feeling it would be an affront to
the honorable name of the volunteer
firefighter to let horses take over the job.

Affront or not, horsepower was far
more practical than manpower. Little by
little, teams of horses began pulling the
gaily painted steam engines, the gilded
and decorated hook-and-ladder carriages,
and the brass-ornamented hose carriages.

The era of the firehorse had begun,
marking the end of the volunteer fire
department. Because fewer men were
needed, cities and villages could afford to
pay full-time professional firefighters. In
Manhattan the year of change was 1865,
when hand-drawn equipment began to be
adapted to the horse.

It is often written that the era of the
firehorse and firefighter was a romantic
period in American history. Actually, in
the beginning firefighters had no intention of sharing their quarters with horses,
which meant putting up with haylofts,
flies, and the pervading odor of manure.
Why not put their stalls out in back?
Better yet, at a nearby stable? This was
certainly a more pleasant alternative.
Unfortunately, when the fire bell clanged,
the men had to run to the stable to get the
horses, bring them to the firehouse, and
hook them up to the apparatus. A building could burn to the ground before they
got the engine out of the firehouse!

With no small amount of grumbling
and headshaking, the men finally admitted
that the horses had to be stabled near the
equipment. Stalls were built on the
ground floor, where unlucky rookie
firemen were assigned "horse detail."
With a little patience — probably on both

sides — horses and men settled into a comfortable and affectionate partnership.

In the beginning firehorses were always kept harnessed. When the fire bell rang, they were trained to bolt from the stalls and back up to the apparatus, where further adjustments to the harness were made. Good timing, but not good enough.

The quick-release harness, developed in 1873, revolutionized firefighting and was considered one of the two greatest 19th-century firefighting inventions. (The other? The fire pole!)

After the horses had backed up to the engine, the suspended harness was released, falling into place over the horses. After a quick fastening by a firefighter the team was off, often within 30 seconds! (If you've ever wondered why early firehouses have high ceilings, the answer is the quick-release harness.)

The museum gives the firehorse a wonderful tribute. You will see the heavy buckle-on snowshoes and several examples of harness. There are marvelous Ben-Hur photographs of perfectly matched, pure white, three-horse teams racing down the street with a firefighter standing on the engine holding the reins.

Of course you will see those shiny red steam engines perched on surprisingly high and delicate wooden spoked wheels. And you will see a New York City fire chief's horse-drawn carriage built in 1892, light and sleek with a gleaming black body and crimson wheels. There is a chief's sleigh as well, used to whisk him over the snow-piled streets.

Obviously 19th-century firemen and firehorses led exciting and dangerous lives. The horses, accustomed to that excitement, often found retirement boring. There are stories told about former firehorses sedately pulling milk or ice wagons. When they heard the rousing clamor of fire engines, they took up the chase and galloped to the fire while their new owners held on for dear life!

And there was another animal that held a favored place in the firehouse — the firehouse dog. Although Dalmatians were sometimes chosen because they were long-winded and could be trained to keep other dogs away from the galloping horses, usually the firehouse dog was a mutt, pure and simple.

There is a tribute to firehouse dogs at the New York City Fire Museum. In fact, one heroic little dog now lies on his bright red cushion in the museum. That little mongrel dog could climb ladders, slide down poles, and search burning buildings for victims. He rescued scores of New Yorkers, and even though he detested cats, he saved dozens of them as well.

It was finally a hit-and-run driver who ended the dog's years as company mascot, after 10 years of service and numerous bravery medals. It was reported that he dragged himself up on the fire engine's running board before he died. A life worth remembering, don't you agree?

★

The life of the 19th-century firefighter was not all hard work and danger, as you will discover when you climb the stairs to the second floor. Spread before you in a gleaming, grand display, you will see a procession of fire engines. And if you think it looks just like a parade — well, that is exactly what it is. This is a celebration of the ornate fire engines used by the volunteer firefighters and the festive parades in which they starred.

You will probably notice the center engine first, which is one of the most elaborate double-decker pumper engines ever made. Ornamented with gilded dolphins and a patriotic eagle with red, white, and blue ribbons streaming from its

mouth, this resplendent crimson engine was created in 1838 by a master builder, John Agnew, and was displayed in a parade at the unveiling of the Statue of Liberty in 1886.

Following up the rear of the parade are two rare engines: an 1840 mahogany pumper whose shape resembles a piano, and a fancy 1853 hose carriage that resembles a gaily decorated bass drum perched on high spoked wheels.

As you watch this motionless parade, I guarantee that you will almost hear the men calling through the fancy, engraved silver megaphones exhibited alongside — and that in your mind's eye you will see patriotic flags flying and the firefighters, bedecked in grand ceremonial hats and capes, pulling the great gilded engines along the parade route.

The walls of this gallery are covered with "hurrahs!" to the firefighter in every art form. There are scores of posters and engravings and newspaper accounts of 18th- and 19th-century fires.

Second-Class Double Plunger Engine— New Style. The improved horsedrawn steamer pictured here was made for New York Metropolitan 12 Company by Amoskaeg Manufacturing Company in 1866. Engraving after a design by Abraham Hosier. (Courtesy of The New-York Historical Society, New York City)

There is a newspaper article about the 19th-century P.T. Barnum Circus Museum fire in Lower Manhattan. Apparently, Barnum's sideshow attractions leaped, flew, and slithered from the burning museum to the horror of scattering New Yorkers. The 400-pound "Fat Lady" had to be carried from the second floor by a lone firefighter, and how successful he was, we aren't told!

Another story and engraving tell about the devastating 1835 New York City fire that burned 674 buildings in the financial and business center in Lower Manhattan, destroying Wall Street. That conflagration actually touched off a national economic depression. There was one death — a man who was caught in the act of burglarizing a building and was lynched on the spot!

Two walls in this gallery are completely covered with antique fire marks, highly prized by collectors today. These colorful and decorative signs were attached to early buildings to prove they had been insured. If volunteer fire companies put out the blaze in an insured building, the insurance company offered an added reward — a keg of beer and the next firehouse meal. Needless to say, a blazing building bearing a fire mark received prompt attention.

★

The New York City Fire Museum offers a rare glimpse of early New York City and its valiant firefighters. Undoubtedly you will come away with a new admiration for these men, both past and present.

We expressed these thoughts to the fireman who had spoken to us earlier, and this was his response:

"Firemen — well, they're the greatest guys in the world, an altogether different breed of cat. And I guarantee it's the only job where everybody's an hour early for work at least. You know, it's the truth — they're the bravest, the best, a family."

And with that, he turned his full attention to the squawking radio unit at his side, straining to catch the details of a restaurant blaze on lower Broadway.

A parade of steam engines is highlighted on the museum's second floor.
(Photograph © Jeffrey Jay Foxx, 1990)

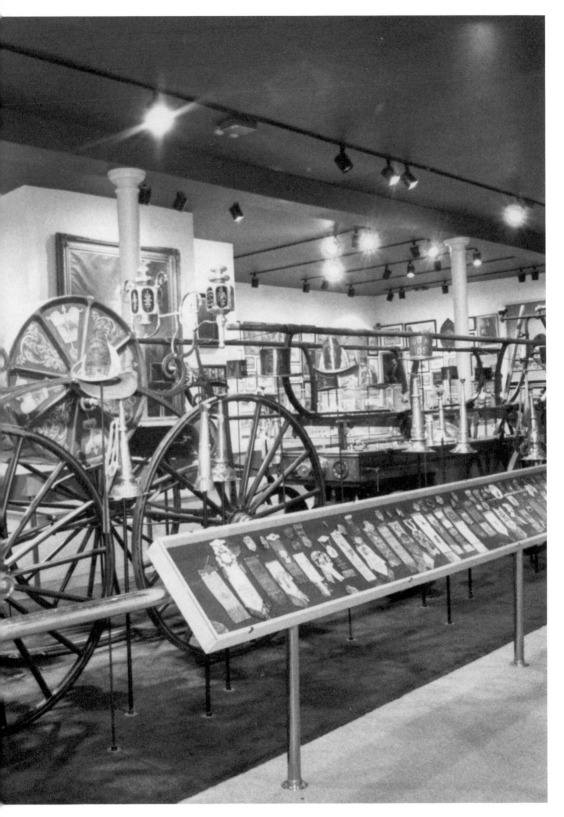

New York City Fire Museum

Housed in the former Engine 30 Firehouse
278 Spring Street
Between Hudson & Varick Streets
New York, NY 10013
212-691-1303

Hours:
Tuesday-Saturday 10:00 a.m.-4:00 p.m.

Closed holidays

Admission:
Free, although a donation is requested

The New York City Fire Museum is a short walk from the sights and restaurants of SoHo (South of Houston Street) and Greenwich Village.

RESTAURANTS

La Margarita

184 Thompson Street at corner
of Bleeker Street
212-533-2410

Monday-Thursday noon-1:00 a.m.
Friday-Saturday noon-3:00 a.m.

• All major credit cards

This comfortable, airy second-floor restaurant, with cactus plants in the windows and fans whirring gently overhead, offers a nice Mexican menu.

We began with a helping of fresh guacamole, served with freshly fried, crispy tostadas and served with a chunky, spicy chili sauce full of peppers and onions.

Enchiladas were well-prepared and plump with chicken and cheese, enlivened with sour cream and salsa verde. The old-fashioned beef enchiladas were winners in a spicy red sauce. Both dishes were prepared to order and served piping hot.

Tamales were also a nice surprise, a nicely seasoned meat center wrapped in tender cornmeal mush and steamed in corn husks.

Chimichangas, made with flour tortillas stuffed with chicken or beef and lightly fried, also had that freshly made flavor. They were served with big dollops of guacamole, sour cream, and refried beans. Tacos al carbon made with marinated steak that was broiled then thinly sliced and rolled in tortillas made a delicious dish, especially as they were served with good rice and beans and garnished with fresh tomatoes, onions, and sour cream.

Special daily lunches and dinners are a bargain at under $7.00 and include various combination platters. (There is even a $3.95 combination platter at lunch only.) Other main courses at lunch and dinner are under $10.00.

By the way, if you can manage to get a table by a window, you will have a wonderful view of the lively parade of Greenwich Village denizens and tourists!

★

See Forbes chapter for additional restaurants.

Firefighters struggle to save New York City's Equitable Building on a freezing night, January 9, 1912. Fire swept up a center stairway, engulfing the entire "fireproof" building, which collapsed. Icicles fringe the puffing steamer engine. (Courtesy of Museum of the City of New York)

D I R E C T I O N S

Subway:
- #1 (Broadway Seventh Avenue local) to Houston & Varick Street Station
- E, C (Avenue of the Americas) to Spring Street Station

Bus:
- M5 (Fifth Avenue / Avenue of the Americas) to Houston Street
- M6 (Seventh Avenue / Broadway / Avenue of the Americas) to Spring Street
- M10 (Seventh Avenue / Eighth Avenue / Central Park West) downtown to Spring & Varick Streets, uptown to Spring & Hudson Streets

Car:
- FDR, Houston Street exit
- West Street, turn at Canal Street

The Forbes Magazine Galleries

From flights of fancy to Fabergé

 alcolm Forbes, the exuberant publisher of *Forbes* magazine, died peacefully in his sleep on February 24, 1990, at the age of 70. Even then, he had a few nice surprises for his employees: He forgave all debts up to $10,000 from the company's lending fund, and he left each employee a gift of a week's salary — just to enjoy life.

Enjoy life — that was Malcolm Forbes' motto. And enjoy life, he did.

Forbes, who sometimes laughingly referred to his qualifications to run *Forbes* magazine as "inheritance," was a mixture of astute businessman and Barnum & Bailey showman. He took over as editor-in-chief when he was just 38 years old, propelling the already successful publication founded in 1917 by his father into a publishing empire with a circulation of 735,000 and a net worth estimated at over $600 million. Other real estate holdings, art investments, and various publications boosted his net worth even higher, valued by some experts at more than $1 billion.

Malcolm Forbes was born in Brooklyn, New York, on August 19, 1919, the third of five children born to Adelaide and B.C. (Bertie) Forbes. The elder Forbes had achieved the American

Above: The Forbes Building today. (Courtesy of The Forbes Magazine Collection, New York)

Right: These mid-19th century houses stood at the corner of Fifth Avenue and 12th Street. They were replaced in 1925 by the MacMillan Publishing Company Building, which was purchased in 1967 by *Forbes* magazine. (Courtesy of The Forbes Magazine Collection, New York)

dream by that time. He had come to the United States as a poor Scottish immigrant and, having amassed wealth in financial journalism, crowned his achievement by founding *Forbes* magazine two years before Malcolm was born.

The son followed suit. At the age of 21 and a recent graduate of Princeton University, in 1941 Malcolm Forbes became owner and publisher of an Ohio newspaper and then founded a second.

Forbes enlisted in the army in 1942, serving as a machine gun sergeant in Europe until he was severely wounded in the thigh during combat in 1944. He spent nine months in a hospital recovering and brought home the Bronze Star and the Purple Heart. After the war Forbes joined his father's magazine as vice president. During the 1950s Malcolm Forbes took the plunge into politics, serving from 1951 to 1958 in the New Jersey Senate. After an unsuccessful bid for the governorship of New Jersey, Forbes returned to the magazine in 1957 to take over the reins as editor-in-chief.

And his collecting days began.

Forbes developed a passion for ballooning. After receiving a commercial balloon pilot's license, he set six world records in hot-air ballooning and was the first to pilot a balloon over the United States from coast to coast in 1973. In the meantime his hot-air balloon collection grew so large and unusual — there was even one shaped like the Sphinx — that he created the world's first hot-air balloon museum at his chateau in Normandy, France.

Malcolm Forbes (1919-1990), Chairman and Editor-in-Chief, *Forbes* magazine. (Courtesy of The Forbes Magazine Collection, New York. Photograph by Harry Benson)

And motorcycles. Forbes had quite a collection, numbering about 70. He relished heating up the highways in black leather and a crash helmet in such far-flung places as China, where he was the first to tour by motorcycle, and in Egypt, where he joyfully circled the pyramids. (Just as a riderless horse in a funeral cortege symbolizes a fallen soldier, Forbes' Harley-Davidson was parked outside the overflowing Park Avenue church on the day of his funeral service.)

With childlike glee Malcolm Forbes began to form other collections — thousands of toy soldiers and hundreds of toy boats. On the serious side, he collected more than 3,000 priceless historical American documents relating to the Presidents as well as other rare historical papers. Through the years Forbes also formed a superb collection of art.

Forbes' homes were a kind of collection as well — a 400-acre Colorado ranch; a ranch in Montana; a New York townhouse; Old Battersea House in London, attributed to Christopher Wren; a Fiji island, Laucala (where his ashes were interred); his 40-acre New Jersey estate, Timberfield; and a palace in Tangier, Morocco, at which he celebrated his 70th birthday, attended by 1,000 of his friends.

And who has not heard about Forbes' world-renowned collection of more than 300 Fabergé works of art, ranging from the Grand Duke Kirill's cuff links to the exquisite and fanciful Easter eggs? Fifty-four Imperial eggs were made by the firm of Peter Carl Fabergé; of these, 45 are known to exist today. The 12 eggs in The Forbes Magazine Collection outnumber the 10 Imperial eggs owned by the Kremlin.

Whether working, playing, or collecting, Malcolm Forbes made life an adventure. As he told his five children, "Life is a gamble, whether it is getting out of bed or getting out of a balloon." Forbes' view of life as a precious gift has become his epitaph: *While Alive, He Lived.*

The Tour

Toy ships dancing over painted waves. This is what the first gallery, *Ships Ahoy*, is all about. And what a great little fleet it is — well over 500 vessels manufactured between 1870 and 1955. Some are masterworks built by famous craftsmen, others are rare antiques, and still others are replicas of historic vessels.

In one glass case, against a photographic nautical backdrop, serene 19th- and early 20th-century ocean liners glide over the motionless sea. You can almost believe that there are tiny crystal chandeliers and grand sweeping staircases inside.

World War I and World War II battleships patrol the painted waters of another fantasy ocean, while streamlined yachts float in a make-believe harbor. Look again. The yachts are replicas of those owned by *Forbes* magazine over the past 30 years.

Just ahead of you there are 19th-century riverboats circling lazily around an island. Listen and you'll hear strains of Mississippi banjo music.

In another glass case submarines prowl the depths of a murky sea above the wrecked hull of the famous luxury liner *Lusitania.* Eerie burbling submarine sounds add to the menacing scene.

Children love these toy ships on their pretend seas, but more often than not adults seem to have their noses pressed against the windows while their offspring whine, "Come on! I wanna see the soldiers now!"

And what soldiers these are, nearly 12,000 troops on display from The Forbes Magazine Collection of more than

Late 19th- and early 20th-century ocean liners make up this toy fleet. (Photograph © Jeffrey Jay Foxx, 1990)

100,000 figures. Malcolm Forbes bought the first soldiers at auction in 1960 — a regiment of World War I doughboys.

You have never seen armies quite like these.

Ancient Aztec warriors savagely slaughter their foes on the temple steps, while the legions of Caesar and Cleopatra fight a fierce battle in another glass case. Alexander the Great leads his troops in a war against the Persians — the year, 331 B.C.

Peer through another window and you will see the world of medieval knights with shining silver-painted armor. Powerful Henry VIII commands his knights in one painted setting, while in another Greeks are trampling the astonished Trojans, who have been deceived by the tiny wooden horse standing nearby.

Even Malcolm Forbes' Colorado ranch becomes a painted backdrop in which cowboys and Indians skirmish, and masked bandits rob the Deadwood stage.

Tiny, silent, and motionless, their bright uniforms a bit scuffed and flaking, these metal armies fight on forever while rousing military marches play on in the galleries. Great fun for everybody!

★

The collection of presidential papers and other priceless historical documents, considered one of the finest privately owned archives of American history, is found in the *Highlights Gallery*. Included is a document signed by Charles II of England in 1664, formally proclaiming Dutch New Netherland with its village port, New Amsterdam, as a province of England (granted to his brother James, Duke of York), to be called henceforth by the name "New York."

Paul Revere's expense report is in the gallery, written in his own hand and dated January 3, 1774. These expenses related to Revere's horseback ride from Boston to New York and Philadelphia to tell the Colonists about the Boston Tea Party. (Bostonians, dressed as Indians, dumped English tea into the harbor in protest against the hated Stamp Act.) John Hancock, who was the first signer of the Declaration of Independence, approved payment, signing his name with a flourish in his distinctively bold script.

There is a letter in the gallery that will make you laugh, although it is very plain Harry Truman was not laughing when he wrote it. Music critic Paul Hume had written a newspaper review sniping at Truman's adored only child, Margaret — and at her singing talent. President Truman was hopping mad when he read it.

President Truman fired off this letter, informing Hume that "a guttersnipe is a gentleman alongside you ... " and "Someday I hope to meet you. When that happens, you'll need a new nose, a lot of beefsteak for black eyes, and perhaps a supporter below!"

President Theodore Roosevelt was another President who did not mince words when explaining how he felt about something. On the subject of Panama he wrote, "When I took Panama, I did not expect Colombia to like my doing it any more that a United States marshal would expect a train robber to enjoy being captured."

On display is the original manuscript of Abraham Lincoln's last address, delivered three days before his assassination. In this powerfully worded speech President Lincoln expressed his great joy that the bloody Civil War had finally ended and the country was united at last. A sad irony is that Lincoln once said he knew his life would not last beyond his one purpose for being on earth, the unification of his country. In fact, Lincoln had frightening premonitions of his death, including a dream in which he saw himself lying in state in the White House.

Other papers on view include a land survey made by 16-year-old surveyor George Washington; a description of the Boston Massacre by Thomas Preston, captain of the British soldiers; and a copy of the Emancipation Proclamation.

But the *Highlights Gallery* is not restricted to presidential papers. Exhibited are Lincoln's top hat and the opera glasses he was using that tragic night at Ford's Theatre when he was assassinated. These historical treasures were nearly taken away from the American public a few years ago — a fact I discovered quite by accident.

I was browsing at a New York auction preview one rainy Saturday. There on a shelf (in a display case to be sure, but people were allowed to handle them) were Abraham Lincoln's top hat and opera glasses. I couldn't believe my eyes.

Were these precious objects going into private hands? It seemed a distinct possibility, and I was dismayed and angry. I wondered who would buy them.

Fortunately, the purchaser was Malcolm Forbes, who felt they should be preserved and exhibited for all Americans to see and remember — perhaps with a sigh of sadness and pride.

★

In the next gallery you will visit the glittering world of Imperial Russia from

A selection of the priceless objects in The Forbes Magazine Collection: the top hat and opera glasses used by President Abraham Lincoln the night of his assassination, April 14, 1865; a signed 1864 photograph of the President with his son, 10-year-old Tad; a 1797 bottle of unopened wine purchased by Thomas Jefferson; a copy of the Emancipation Proclamation; the log of the *Enola Gay*, the plane that dropped the atomic bomb on Hiroshima, Japan, August 6, 1945; the first keys to the White House. (Courtesy of The Forbes Magazine Collection, New York. Photograph by Larry Stein)

the 19th to the early 20th century. This was a time of splendid pastel palaces and gilded royal coaches, when sable cloaks trailed in the snow and the wealthy held newly fashionable cigarettes in diamond-studded holders, tapping ashes into gold ashtrays.

That is, until the death knell was rung by the Russian Revolution in 1917, destroying the world of Imperial Russia. Czar Nicholas II, Czarina Alexandra Feodorovna, and their five children were summarily rounded up and taken to a secret location. They were executed in a barrage of gunfire on July 17, 1918.

But during the time the Czars ruled, the Russian aristocracy and a small wealthy merchant class enjoyed a life of astounding opulence. It is difficult in today's world to imagine a life of such splendor and luxury — unless the dazzling objects can be seen.

And they *can* be seen in Forbes Magazine Galleries; but first, a few words are in order about the life of Peter Carl Fabergé, the man who catered to all of those extravagant whims and fancies.

★

Peter Carl Fabergé's father Gustave started the family business in 1842 in St. Petersburg (now Leningrad). The family

A selection of Fabergé jewelry, including the platinum and diamond Imperial Diadem (#1); the Nobel Necklace (#10, at bottom), made of platinum, diamonds, rock crystal, and silver, owned by the nephew of Alfred Nobel, the famed Swedish engineer who established the Nobel prizes; and the "Snowflake" pendant with a red cross (#14), made of diamonds, rubies, rock crystal, gold, and platinum. (Photograph © Jeffrey Jay Foxx, 1990)

Among the Fabergé objects shown in the case are the ostrich-feather fan owned by Grand Duchess Xenia, sister of Czar Nicholas II; at right, a photograph of the Grand Duchess holding the fan; at left, the Duchess of Marlborough Clock Egg, made of gold, enamel, pearls, and diamonds. (Photograph © Jeffrey Jay Foxx, 1990)

was of French origin but had left France more than 150 years before.

By 1870 24-year-old Carl had taken over the business and was beginning to build his own empire, which by the turn of the century had five branches and employed hundreds of people. Needless to say, such success was not based on Imperial orders alone. At the turn of the 20th century Russia had a booming economy, and many fortunes were made in industry, finance, and agriculture. In addition, Fabergé had customers all over the world, from wealthy New Yorkers to the King of Siam.

Of course, Fabergé was honored to make beautiful objects for the Russian Czars. He received the Imperial nod often from Alexander III and later from his son Nicholas II.

Fabergé supplied the Imperial household with utilitarian objects as well as with the masterworks of jewelry. Not all were jeweled objects. In fact, many were quite simple in design and ornamentation, although they were elegant and refined.

There were fans, perfume bottles, picture frames, cigarette lighters, and cigarette cases. There were hat pins, parasols, lorgnettes, and combs. There were bowls, plates, mirrors, and music boxes.

And there were, of course, the incomparable, exquisite Easter eggs, created to celebrate the most important festival of the Russian Orthodox Church. The first Imperial egg was made for Czarina Marie Feodorovna, given to her by Czar Alexander III on Easter 1885, beginning a tradition of giving Fabergé Easter eggs that continued until the dynasty ended with the assassinations of Nicholas II and Alexandra.

Unfortunately, Fabergé's future and that of his firm were linked to the fortunes of the Russian aristocracy and the Imperial family. His firm was taken over by the "Committee of the Employees of the Company K. Fabergé." Fearing for his life, Fabergé escaped from Russia with the help of the British Embassy. In 1918 Russia's House of Fabergé closed its doors forever.

The gilded and jeweled age of the Russian Imperial court and the House of Fabergé has long since vanished, but it has been brought to life once again in the Forbes Magazine Galleries.

First there are the rather haunting photographs of members of the Imperial family. Some gaze complacently from simple Fabergé frames made of wood or silver, while others seem troubled and sad, in strange contrast to the pearl-encrusted and diamond-inlaid frames.

In one photograph the Czar's sister, Grand Duchess Xenia, holds a rock-crystal, gold, and diamond fan sprouting ostrich plumes. It is the occasion of a grand ball at the Winter Palace in 1903. And in the glass case, next to the photograph, is the same Fabergé fan, fresh and new as it was that snowy night.

A desk ornament, this silver motor car held pens, pen nibs, stamps, and ink. (Photograph © Jeffrey Jay Foxx, 1990)

Among elaborate presentation objects is a silver automobile that is actually a desk set. The radiator is the inkwell, the driver's seat holds stamps, and the trunk holds pen nibs.

Another, a paddle steamer music box, is also fashioned from silver. The donors were Volga shipbuilders, who knew exactly how to please the young, ailing Czarevitch Alexis when they presented a gift that played *God Save the Czar*. This wish for his future would never come true: The boy would never become Czar of Russia.

Presentation gifts and photograph frames represent only a fraction of the dazzling Fabergé objects displayed in the galleries. There are jeweled buttons and bottles, parasol handles and paper knives, exquisite jewelry and dainty animals made of gold, pearls, and precious stones.

And then there are the Easter eggs.

The Cuckoo Egg, presented by Czar Nicholas II to Czarina Alexandra

Feodorovna on Easter 1900, is fashioned of gold and enamel and decorated with pearls and diamonds, and rubies. The "surprise" is a mechanical bird, which crows and flaps its wings every hour.

The gold Coronation Egg, presented by Nicholas II to the Czarina for Easter in 1897, opens to reveal a red enamel and gold replica of the Czarina's coronation coach. A diamond pendant (lost) once hung as a chandelier inside the coach.

The pink enamel and gold Lilies of the Valley Egg, presented by Czar Nicholas II on Easter 1898, is decorated with dainty sprays of lilies of the valley and ornamented with diamonds and pearls. Portraits of the Czar and his two eldest daughters, Olga and Tatiana, rise from the egg when a button is turned.

★

So there you have it — a walk through the many worlds of Malcolm Forbes — from fantasy oceans plied by toy boats and fantasy battles fought by metal men, to invaluable American historical documents and the whimsical Fabergé masterpieces that pay silent homage to Imperial Russia. They — as well as the paintings, the hot-air balloons, and the motorcycles — are reflections of Malcolm Forbes, his imagination, and his zest for life.

Above: Lilies of the Valley Egg, Easter 1898. The miniatures depict Czar Nicholas II and his two eldest daughters, Olga and Tatiana. (Courtesy of The Forbes Magazine Collection, New York. Photograph by Larry Stein)

Left: The Cuckoo Egg, presented by Czar Nicholas II to the Czarina, Easter 1900. Gold, enamel, pearls, diamonds, and rubies. The suprise: a bird that rises to crow and flap its wings on the hour. (Courtesy of The Forbes Magazine Collection, New York. Photograph by Larry Stein)

The Forbes Magazine Galleries

Located on the ground floor of
the Forbes Building
62 Fifth Avenue at 12th Street
New York, NY 10011
212-206-5549

Hours:
Tuesday-Saturday 10:00 a.m.-4:00 p.m.

Closed Sunday, Monday & all legal holidays

Admission:
Free. Children under 16 must be accompanied
by an adult.

Group Tours:
Must make advance reservations. Thursdays
are reserved exclusively for guided tours
offered by the curatorial department for groups
of 10-30 people. Call 212-206-5548.

Portrait of Abraham Lincoln and his
10-year-old son Tad. This photograph,
taken by Anthony Berger in 1864, was
one of the last formal images made of
the President. (Courtesy of The Forbes
Magazine Collection, New York.
Photograph by Larry Stein)

R E S T A U R A N T S

Cent'Anni

50 Carmine Street
Between Bleeker & Bedford Streets
212-989-9494

Lunch:
  Monday-Friday noon-2:30 p.m.
Dinner:
  Monday-Friday 5:30-11:30 p.m.
  Sunday 5:00-11:30 p.m.

- American Express
- Reservations suggested

A tiny storefront restaurant to be sure, but
Cent'Anni is one of my favorites.

First of all, the pastas in this cheerful, casual northern Italian restaurant are sublime,
whether served in a delectable and spicy
tomato sauce with lobster and clams, or in a
buttery, creamy sauce laced with salmon,
tomatoes, and onions.

You can share a pasta dish for your first
course; or you might try a hearty helping of
warm garlicky, tomatoey beans; a delicious
lobster, shrimp, squid, and scallop salad; or
roasted red peppers with anchovies.

Grilled pheasant, chicken, or squab entrees
have been marinated first, split, then grilled
to a crispy, golden turn. Or try a mixed grill
of lamb, rabbit, quail, and sausage — enough
to suit even the most ravenous appetite. The
huge, thick, juicy veal chop (grilled and then
sauteed), is smothered in an aromatic sage
and wine sauce.

Lunch:
  Appetizers $5.00
  Entrees $10.00-$20.00
Dinner:
  Appetizers $7.00
  Entrees $15.00-$25.00

Provence

38 MacDougal Street
Between Prince & Houston Streets
212-475-7500

Lunch:
   Tuesday-Sunday noon-3:00 p.m.
Dinner:
   Tuesday-Thursday 6:00-11:30 p.m.
   Friday & Saturday 6:00 p.m.-midnight
   Sunday 5:30-11:00 p.m.

* American Express
* Reservations suggested

Take a piece of French countryside, and add a memorable little *auberge*. Now look inside the cozy dining room. There you have Provence, except that you have it in the middle of Manhattan.

   Begin with a robust fish soup, fairly ringing with garlic; a zesty eggplant and vegetable terrine glistening with an olive and anchovy vinaigrette; or the rabbit pâté, rich and silky smooth.

   Fish is always a good choice for the main course. Try red snapper bathed in a zingy saffron sauce or a delicate poached sole with sea-urchin butter. Or try the tender lamb or the golden roast chicken wreathed in whole garlic cloves, filling the air with a mouthwatering aroma!

   Lunch or dinner in the little garden is a treat during the summer.

Lunch:
   Appetizers $5.00-$8.00
   Entrees $10.00-$17.00
Dinner:
   Appetizers $5.00-$8.50
   Entrees $14.00-$19.00
   (These prices do not include specials)

John's Pizza

278 Bleeker Street
Between Avenue of the Americas &
Seventh Avenue
212-243-1680

Daily 11:30 a.m.-11:30 p.m.

A lot of people in Greenwich Village say this is the best pizza place in New York. If you'd like to find out, now is the time!

   John's sells 55 different varieties of pizza. I understand the favorite is #20, with sausage, mushrooms, and fresh garlic, but why not try two different slices and compare for yourself! Small pies start at $7.75.

D I R E C T I O N S

Subway:
* IRT #1, 2, 3 to 14th Street &
  Seventh Avenue
* IRT #4, 5, 6 to 14th Street &
  Union Square
* BMT N, R to 14th Street &
  Union Square
* BMT B to 14th Street & Avenue of
  the Americas

Bus:
* M1, M2, M3 (Fifth / Madison Avenues)
* M5 (Fifth Avenue / Avenue of the
  Americas)

Car:
* FDR Drive, East 15th Street exit
* West Street, West 14th Street exit

Theodore Roosevelt Birthplace Museum

Teddy Roosevelt's childhood home and museum

Above: The Theodore Roosevelt Birthplace Museum today. (Courtesy of the Theodore Roosevelt Birthplace National Historic Site)

Left: Theodore Roosevelt's childhood home as it appeared about 1860, when TR was a small child. (Courtesy of the Theodore Roosevelt Collection, Harvard College Library)

y grandfather was there when Roosevelt was nearly assassinated in 1912!" Startled, I turned around to face the speaker, an angular, no-nonsense woman with sparkling brown eyes. She nodded her head toward a glass case holding Roosevelt's white dress shirt, a spectacles case, and the text of one of his speeches.

Tapping the glass, she continued, "Granddad saw the whole thing. TR was standing in an open car — on the way to give a speech. There was a shot, and Roosevelt grabbed his chest. Then he stuffed a handkerchief inside his shirt — this very shirt — to stop the bleeding. The bullet passed through TR's coat pocket and shirt, drilling through his glasses case and his folded-up speech. They saved his life!"

I peered through the glass. She was right. A neat, round hole pierced all three — the starched shirt, the case, and the speech. I asked the sprightly little woman where all of this had taken place.

Folding her arms thoughtfully, she explained, "When Teddy Roosevelt was running for a third term as President — you'll remember that he was a Bull Moose party candidate — he was in Milwaukee, Wisconsin, campaigning. That's where it happened."

I waited as the woman paused, pushing her glasses back on her nose, trying to remember. "I don't recall all the details," she said finally, "but Granddad was a member of the mayor's welcoming committee. Apparently TR wouldn't go to the hospital. In fact, he went right on to the auditorium to give the speech. And do you know why? President McKinley had died because of bungled surgery to remove an assassin's bullet, not from the bullet wound. Roosevelt declared that he was not about to let that happen to him!"

★

This interesting conversation was my introduction to the birthplace of Theodore Roosevelt. As I stood inside the brownstone townhouse, I tried to picture how it must have looked at the time of his birth.

★

It was the year 1858. The house at 28 East 20th Street was located in one of New York City's most fashionable neighborhoods. The street was lined with distinguished townhouses which were enclosed in front by low wrought-iron fences, while well-tended flower beds perfumed backyard gardens. The sounds wafting through the front parlor windows were the clicking of horses' hooves and the clattering of carriages. In the evening gaslights glowed softly, casting shadows over the sidewalks. It must have been a gentle place for the children of the Roosevelt family — Anna, Theodore, Elliot, and Corinne.

I began my visit with a self-guided tour of the museum, which contains the world's largest collection of Roosevelt memorabilia. Here, through Roosevelt's letters, photographs, and personal posses-sions, I learned how "Teedie," as Roosevelt was nicknamed by the family, developed from a sick, weak little boy

into the powerhouse who would one day become an American legend.

As I followed the chronologically arranged glass cases, I was intrigued by the number of rare photographs, among them one of Theodore Roosevelt, Sr. President Roosevelt would write later that his father was "the best man I ever knew ... I never knew any one who got greater joy out of living than did my father, or any one who more wholeheartedly performed every duty ... "

There was an appealing photograph of Roosevelt's beautiful mother, Martha Bulloch, called "Mittie" by the family. She was poised and dignified, dressed in a crisp white linen walking dress. Next to the photograph lay a fragile porcelain cup and saucer, a gift from the young Teedie. Roosevelt adored his mother, whom he described as "a sweet, gracious, beautiful Southern woman."

Another somber photograph shows the funeral cortege of President Lincoln as it passed in front of the Roosevelt home. Leaning out of the upstairs window are two young boys, probably Theodore and his brother Elliott.

Letters and mementos follow Teedie through his childhood, when he was so frail from bouts of asthma and other illnesses that he had to be tutored at home. It was in this home that his father built a gymnasium, reminding the little boy that having a strong mind was not enough; it was necessary to build a strong body. From that day forward TR made good health a primary goal.

There are letters and papers from

TR's shirt, spectacles case, and speech were drilled with bullet holes during an assassination attempt in 1912. (Photograph © Jeffrey Jay Foxx, 1990)

Roosevelt's Harvard years, during which he quickly developed a reputation for his "energy, ability and oddity." After his graduation in 1880, Theodore married 18-year-old Alice Lee, only to lose her within four years following the birth of their daughter Alice. His grief was compounded by the death of his beloved mother on the very same day, February 14, 1884 — Valentine's Day. Roosevelt, then only 25, wrote in his diary, "The light has gone out of my life."

Not long afterward Roosevelt left New York City to go west, where he became a rancher in the Dakota Territory. One photograph taken during this period reveals a robust and healthy cowboy in buckskins. Although the ranching venture was a failure, Roosevelt later wrote that this time in the West brought him two important gifts: a new understanding of the need for a broad national view in politics and excellent health with which to pursue his political vision.

A second marriage in 1886 to Edith Carow after TR's return to New York is richly documented with photographs and letters. Edith had been a close childhood friend, but after a teen-age argument, they had been estranged for years. The nature of the argument was never revealed, but Edith wrote later that she had always known that she would spend her life with Theodore Roosevelt.

Happily married and father to a growing family, finally totaling six children — Alice, Ethel, Theodore, Archibald, Kermit, and Quentin, Roosevelt

---

Climbing the political ladder. A fascinating photograph of Theodore Roosevelt making a speech. Date unknown. (Courtesy of Museum of the City of New York. Photograph by Underwood & Underwood)

quickly moved up the political ladder. Delightful political cartoons document this climb. After a successful tenure as a member of the U.S. Civil Service Commission and two years as president of the powerful New York City Board of Police Commissioners, Roosevelt at the age of 39 became Assistant Secretary of the Navy. (The massive desk used by Roosevelt when he held this office is in the museum.)

During the summer of 1897, while Secretary of the Navy John D. Long was relaxing on several minivacations (heartily endorsed by TR), Acting Secretary Roosevelt was a whirlwind of activity, bombarding anyone who would listen with his views about the need for a strong, modern navy and the deliverance of Cuba and the Philippines from Spanish rule.

The stage was set for TR to turn words into action when the U.S. battleship *Maine*, on a "goodwill" visit to Cuba, was blown up in Havana Harbor at 9:40 p.m. on February 15, 1898. Ten days later, while Secretary Long was once again out of the office — this time for a massage and a long walk to calm his tattered nerves — TR fired off a number of orders, among them a cablegram to Commodore George Dewey in Hong Kong:

"ORDER THE SQUADRON ... TO HONG KONG. KEEP FULL OF COAL. IN THE EVENT OF DECLARATION [OF] WAR [AGAINST] SPAIN, YOUR DUTY WILL BE TO SEE THAT THE SPANISH SQUADRON DOES NOT LEAVE THE ASIATIC COAST, AND THEN [BEGIN] OFFENSIVE OPERATIONS IN PHILIPPINE ISLANDS ... "

Surprisingly, Secretary Long, although upset and embarrassed, allowed the orders to stand. TR had effectively in one afternoon prepared the United States

Navy for war with Spain.

Roosevelt fought in Cuba during the Spanish-American War, commanding the First U.S. Volunteer Cavalry, nicknamed the Rough Riders, during the summer of 1898. Roosevelt's battered uniform (hurriedly ordered from Brooks Brothers!) is in the museum, flanked by a photograph of his men, a curious mix of Ivy League college graduates and cowboys. Some interesting facts: The Rough Riders regiment was in existence approximately five months; the famous charge made by TR and his Rough Riders lasted about one hour; and the famous hill they charged was actually Kettle Hill, not the adjacent San Juan Hill.

TR's years as Governor of New York from 1898 to 1901, his election as Vice President under McKinley, and his sudden succession to the presidency when McKinley died on September 14, 1901, are all documented with fascinating memorabilia. Bright, clever campaign buttons and political cartoons mark his re-election in 1904.

Many colorful stories have been told about Roosevelt. An event that received wide press coverage occurred during a bear-hunting trip to Mississippi. To the delight of the reporters, the "big game" found by the President's guide turned out to be a tiny bear cub, which President Roosevelt refused to shoot. Later a Brooklyn toy shop owner manufactured a number of little brown bears, which he dubbed "Teddy." An early example, shabby from love, is in the museum.

Colonel Theodore Roosevelt in the Rough Riders regiment during the Spanish-American War. (Courtesy of The New-York Historical Society, New York City. Photograph by Underwood & Underwood, 1898)

The museum traces Roosevelt's years after the White House, revealing a man who still searched for adventure and yearned to remain an active and effective leader in world events.

Roosevelt began to travel and to write. One of these expeditions, an exploration along the Amazon River in 1914, was vividly described in his book *Through the Brazilian Wilderness*. More than 2,500 birds and 500 mammals, many never seen before, were brought back for display in New York City's Museum of Natural History. A new river was also discovered, named the Rio Teodoro in honor of Roosevelt.

It was during this adventure that Roosevelt badly injured his left leg, which became dangerously infected, marking the beginning of a decline in his health. Even

The parlor in the Theodore Roosevelt Birthplace National Historic Site. (Photograph © Jeffrey Jay Foxx, 1990)

so, TR later told a friend, "I had just one more chance to be a boy, and I took it."

The last, and one of the most poignant exhibits tells of the death of Roosevelt's beloved son and youngest child, Quentin, whose plane was shot down in World War I. Roosevelt never got over it. There is a photograph of Quentin, and beside it, a grief-stricken letter written by Roosevelt in shaky, nearly illegible handwriting.

Theodore Roosevelt died soon afterward on January 6, 1919, at his home, Sagamore Hill, on Oyster Bay, Long Island. In one of his books, *The Great Adventure*, he had written, "All daring and courage, all iron endurance of misfortune — make for a finer, nobler type of manhood."

Roosevelt had lived a life of daring, from the small to the great events of history. He had been the first President to go up in an airplane and to go down in a submarine and the first to use a typewriter and a camera. TR had been a big game hunter, but he had also been a leader in the cause of conservation. He had explored the world's wilderness, from the American West to Africa and South America, and had written over 50 books. He had played an integral part in world events, from the acquisition of the Panama Canal Zone to mediating between the Japanese and Russians to end the Russo-Japanese War, for which he was the first American to win the Nobel Peace Prize. Theodore Roosevelt had justly earned a lasting place in history as one of the great world leaders.

Tour of the Roosevelt Birthplace

The Roosevelt home is an exact reconstruction of the dignified brownstone in which Theodore Roosevelt was born and in which he lived until he was 14. In 1854 Theodore, Sr., brought his young bride to this house, which had been a gift from his father. All four children were born in the spacious master bedroom overlooking 20th Street.

The neighborhood became less fashionable and more commercial as the 19th century rolled toward its close. In 1872, when Theodore, Jr., was 14, the family moved to 6 West 57th Street. The house at 28 East 20th Street was finally razed in 1916, replaced by a commercial building. However, the brownstone next door, an exact duplicate owned by Theodore, Sr.'s brother, remained intact.

After President Roosevelt's death in 1919, the site of the original Roosevelt birthplace was purchased, and using the adjacent brownstone as a model, the brownstone was reconstructed. Roosevelt's wife and two sisters were instrumental in collecting the furnishings, 40 percent of which were original to the house, while another 20 percent had belonged to other family members. Under the sisters' direction, the rooms were decorated just as they had been when Theodore was a child.

The tour, led by a knowledgeable guide, begins in the Victorian library, with its dark and substantial rosewood furniture, ornate gas chandeliers, and artifacts brought back from a family trip to Europe and Egypt. Roosevelt once recalled that one of his strongest memories of the somber library was the black horsehair upholstery covering all of the furniture. He remembered that the

The "Lion's Room" in the museum. (Courtesy of the Theodore Roosevelt Birthplace National Historic Site)

horsehair had been wretchedly scratchy
to his bare legs, and since the library
had been the only downstairs room in
which the children were allowed to play,
he had spent many hours on that sofa!

The formal dining room, darkened by
heavy green draperies and green carpeting, once overlooked a manicured
back garden. The rosewood Gothic
Revival dining table belonged to TR's
grandfather.

The parlor, overlooking 20th Street,
is light and elegant in contrast, with
intricately carved furniture in the Rococo-
Revival style. A graceful crystal chandelier sparkles above, while a gilded mirror
reflects the soft blues of wallpaper,
carpeting, and upholstery.

Roosevelt once remarked that the parlor had always reminded him of a fairy-
land when he was a child — and was
strictly off-limits. One day he sneaked

Theodore Roosevelt's life is detailed by
numerous objects in the museum.
(Photograph © Jeffrey Jay Foxx, 1990)

★

into the parlor and unhooked a prism from
the chandelier, then hid the sparkling
treasure in his room. His parents were
mystified, and he felt guilty, but not guilty
enough to tell them that he was the one
who had taken the prism!

Upstairs is the nursery, which holds
the original crib and toys used by the
Roosevelt children. The gymnasium was
once located on a porch outside the
nursery window.

A portrait of Theodore's mother
hangs above the mantel in the master
bedroom. The furniture here, all original
to the room, is delicate and refined,
crafted from satinwood and rosewood.

The Roosevelt birthplace is interesting to see, not only because it was
Theodore Roosevelt's childhood home,
but because it allows the visitor to step
back into the Civil War years and those
that followed. The home, with its fine
furnishings, gives an accurate picture of
the life of a wealthy and influential New
York City family. Here, cared for by five
servants and taught by his own private
tutor, frail and sickly "Teedie" began his
climb into the pages of history.

Theodore Roosevelt Birthplace
National Historic Site
28 East 20th Street
New York, NY 10003
212-260-1616

Hours:
Wednesday-Sunday 9:00 a.m.-5:00 p.m.

Tours:
Given approximately every hour, the last one
beginning around 3:30 p.m.

Admission:
• Adults $1.00
• Seniors 63 & over & children under 17 free

The Theodore Roosevelt Birthplace is
administered by the National Park Service,
U.S. Department of the Interior.

Additional Sights

A Stroll Around Gramercy Park
The tranquil greenery of Gramercy Park is just
a half-block away from Theodore Roosevelt's
childhood home. Turn right as you leave the
house, and in a few minutes you will find
yourself strolling beside a fenced park that
resembles a London square — and with good
reason. Samuel Ruggles, who created this
park out of a marsh in 1831, utilized a concept
that had been used in London: he deeded park
plots to those owning building lots around the
park, guaranteeing the owners that the park
would always remain private, for their use
alone. To this day, the most highly prized
Gramercy Park apartments have their "keys to
the park."

Turning left at the park, walk by #3 and #4
on the west side, charming examples of pre-
Civil War (1847) architecture with handsome
doorways, converted gas lanterns, and lacy
ironwork decoration.

Continue your stroll around the park to the
east side. Number 34 is one of New York
City's earliest apartment buildings, built in
1883. Next door is #36, a Gothic Revival
structure built in 1908, hard to miss with its
silvery knights in armor guarding the front.

On the south side there are several fine
examples of 19th-century architecture.
The first is #28, originally owned by Friends
Meeting House. It is now owned by the
Brotherhood Synagogue. This distinguished
Italianate structure was completed in 1859.

The Players at 16 Gramercy Park South was
built in 1845. The celebrated actor Edwin
Booth bought the building. (Yes, Edwin
was related to the infamous John Wilkes
Booth, assassin of President Lincoln. They
were brothers.) He asked the famous architect
Stanford White to remodel it in 1888 as a club
for men in the theatrical profession (although
members included Winston Churchill and
Mark Twain). Notice the filigree wrought-iron
railings, accented by plaques of Tragedy and
Comedy, and the large wrought-iron lanterns.

The National Arts Club at 15 Gramercy Park
South was once owned by Samuel J. Tilden,
Governor of New York and unsuccessful
presidential candidate in 1876, losing to
Rutherford B. Hayes. Architect Calvert Vaux
turned two houses into this brownstone
mansion (1881-1884).

★

Note: Keeping in mind that Theodore
Roosevelt was the president of Police
Commissioners of the City of New York,
why not visit the New York City Police
Museum just down the street, at 235 East
20th? Just read on!

RESTAURANTS

Cafe du Parc
106 East 19th Street
212-777-7840

Lunch:
  Monday-Friday 12:30-3:00 p.m.
Dinner:
  Monday-Thursday 5:00-10:30 p.m.
  Friday & Saturday 5:00-11:30 p.m.

Closed Sunday

• All major credit cards
• Reservations suggested

Lace curtains in the windows and window boxes full of tumbling flowers introduce this charming little restaurant. A highly polished old wooden bar and etched glass partitions between tables create a cozy, private feeling. Add fresh flowers and soft music, and you have an old-fashioned, romantic atmosphere.

Appetizers include a savory duckling pâté with pistachios and green pepper, a half-order of angel-hair pasta with mushrooms in red-wine sauce — rich and delicious — and shrimp with leeks in puff pastry.

Among tempting main courses offered to us were a moist Cornish game hen grilled with raspberry vinegar sauce; a perfectly grilled veal chop, juicy in its orange and raspberry vinegar sauce; and veal in wine sauce with a lively accompaniment of bright yellow and red peppers, carrots, and snow peas, all delicately sauced and seasoned.

Lunch:
  Appetizers $5.95
  Entrees $10.95
Dinner:
  Appetizers $6.95
  Entrees $13.95

Paul & Jimmy's
123 East 18th Street
Near Irving Place
212-475-9540

All-day dining:
  Daily noon-11:00 p.m.
  (Friday & Saturday until midnight)
Prix-fixe menu:
  Monday-Friday 4:30-6:30 p.m.
  Saturday & Sunday 1:00-6:00 p.m.

• All major credit cards

This cheerful, bustling little restaurant has a casual atmosphere and a simple art deco style interior.

The southern Italian dishes are well-prepared, never stinting on the tomatoes, garlic, mushrooms, and peppers required for a lively flavor.

The menu is extensive, with plenty of choices from the offerings of pasta, fish, veal, chicken, and beef. Salad is included with most main courses.

We particularly enjoyed boneless breast of chicken baked with mozzarella, prosciutto, and wine sauce; a filet of sole with garlic, onion, tomato, and wine sauce; red snapper with clams, squid, and shrimp in a light tomato sauce; and spaghetti with garlic, olive oil, and fresh tomatoes, with a liberal dose of spices. All dishes we tried had a bright, zesty flavor, very fresh ingredients, and arrived in healthy portions.

Service is brisk and professional.

Lunch & dinner:
  Appetizers $7.00
  Entrees $10.50
Prix-fixe menu $17.50

Sal Anthony's
17th Street & Irving Place
212-982-9030

Lunch:
  Daily noon-3:00 p.m.
Dinner:
  Monday-Thursday 3:00-10:00 p.m.
  Friday & Saturday 3:00-11:00 p.m.

• All major credit cards

Light-hearted, congenial restaurant. Especially delightful in fine weather to sit at a table outside — wonderful on a summer evening with the lighted silhouette of the Chrysler Building above, watching strollers, savoring historic Gramercy Park.
  The food is Italian, served in generous portions and prepared well. Popular for brunch.
  Prix-fixe lunches for $7.50 and dinners at $17.50 in addition to a la carte.

★

Choshi
Irving Place & 19th Street
212-420-1419

Lunch:
  Monday-Friday noon-2:30 p.m.
Dinner:
  Daily 5:30-10:15 p.m.

• All major credit cards

A sparkling, clean little restaurant, serving inexpensive and good Japanese food — sushi, sashimi, tempura — with lots of spicy green tea. Sit at one of the pristine wooden tables and watch the parade of strollers in this historic area.

Colonel Roosevelt in the Rough Riders regiment, 1898. (Courtesy of Museum of the City of New York)

D I R E C T I O N S

Subway:
• IRT #6 stop at 23rd Street & Park Avenue South
• BMT N stop at 23rd Street & Fifth Avenue

Bus:
• M1, M2, M3 (Fifth / Madison Avenues)
• M5 (Fifth Avenue / Avenue of the Americas)
• M101 and M102 (Third & Lexington Avenues)

Car:
• FDR Drive, East 23rd Street exit
• Twelfth Avenue, West 23rd Street exit

The New York City Police Museum

A history of New York's Finest

he New York City Police Museum, considered one of the finest collections of police memorabilia in the world, was created in 1929 to preserve important police information and objects, and to instill a sense of historic pride in New York City police officers. The museum also serves as a teaching tool for police officers all over the world.

A visit to the Police Museum, which is located at the New York City Police Academy, will take you into the world of "New York's Finest," a term first used for New York police officers in 1875. You will know that you have reached the big, square, modern academy when you look up and see the bright green, navy, and white police flag fluttering alongside the American flag and the New York State flag. You might suddenly find yourself surrounded by groups of fresh-faced, neatly groomed recruits, and here and there you will certainly see a seasoned police officer, whose world-weary eyes tell you he or she has seen everything.

It was a bright June morning for a fascinating adventure when Curator John Podracky and Assistant Curator Police Officer Dominick Palermo met me just

Above: Horse-drawn patrol wagon known as the "Black Maria," as it resembled a 19th-century hearse. Used to transport prisoners to court, and if guilty — to jail. The Bronx, 61st Precinct, circa 1890. (Courtesy of the New York City Police Museum)

Right: New York's Finest today. (Photograph © Jeffrey Jay Foxx, 1990)

inside the Police Museum located on the second floor of the academy. John Podracky, who has written two books about technical photography and once worked with New York City's Municipal Archives, has brought a rich knowledge of New York history and the conservation of early photographs to the Police Museum. Officer Palermo, with years of service as a New York City police officer — some of that time spent as an academy instructor — has brought his deep knowledge of

the police force and love of New York history with him. Together they make a great team.

I had not been in the museum long before the colorful, interesting stories started to flow.

Police officers donned the first regulation uniform in 1854, modeled after special uniforms worn by New York City police officers at the World's Fair of 1853. The police chief, captains, and lieutenants wore a style of double-

The first regulation New York City police uniform. From a drawing in *Gleason's Pictorial Drawing-Room Companion, 1853.* (Courtesy of the New York City Police Museum)

breasted navy wool frock coat that extended halfway to the knee. A double row of shiny brass buttons marched down the impressive coat from a black silk-velvet collar. Sergeants and patrolmen wore similar single-breasted frock coats.

A bright star distinguished every police officer from a distance. The chief wore a large gold star connected by a gold ribbon to a gold shield; captains and lieutenants wore silver stars; sergeants wore copper stars; and patrolmen wore brass. (By the way, "cop" and "copper," slang terms for police officers, can be traced back to those copper stars.)

And as for hats, there was quite a mix! Each police officer was issued a navy cloth cap with a bill, made in the style of a naval officer's cap. For summer weather they wore brimmed straw hats. And for night patrols the policemen wore leather helmets that closely resembled firemen's hats. As a matter of fact, until 1865 when the first New York City professional fire department was organized, the police officers often did double duty as volunteer firemen!

John Podracky told me this story: "During that same era police officers wore celluloid collars on their shirts. An old record book tells us that once a policeman came on the scene of a burning tenement where people were literally hanging out of the windows of the second and third floors. The patrolman raced through that building again and again. The heat was so intense that his wool uniform smoked, and his celluloid collar fused to his neck and had to be surgically removed!"

And two stories about riots: "During the 1890s there were so many riots in New York City that the record books are full of entries about all of the confetti being thrown. Confetti? They meant a confetti of bricks!

"During one New York City riot a mob actually attacked the police station. The officer on duty sat inside, calmly writing in the record book: 'The crowds are smashing through the precinct doors now. I am going to stop writing, take this book, and run out the back exit...' He must have slammed the book shut, shoved it under his arm, and raced out, chased by the howling mob!"

Then the curators began to reminisce about Theodore Roosevelt. They told me that many of the rules and regulations that are operating procedure in New York City today stem from Roosevelt's two years as president of the Board of Police Commissioners, beginning in 1895.

Roosevelt had always admired the London police force and considered it the finest example of law enforcement in the world. He set about reorganizing the New York force after that model. TR changed the police uniform to resemble that of the London bobby. He instituted the night stick and the horse in crowd-control situations. Roosevelt even used the London model to establish the beats that New York patrolmen walked, determining the maximum range that could be covered to give the best protection to citizens. However, there was one change TR decided not to make: Even though London bobbies never carried guns, he determined that New York City officers needed them.

This interesting photograph was taken in 1893 at Fifth Avenue and 23rd Street, just opposite the Flatiron Building. The police officer on the right, Harry Graham, known as Broadway Harry, was famous as the "World's Tallest Policeman" at 6' 6". It was said that he jumped into the East River many times, heroically rescuing people. (Courtesy of the New York City Police Museum)

Speaking of guns, one of Roosevelt's first acts in 1895 as president of the Board of Police Commissioners was to standardize the .32-caliber Colt six-shot revolver as the regulation handgun of the force. (The .38 special Smith & Wesson, Ruger, and Colt revolvers are the regulation handguns used today, and the 9mm semi-automatic pistol is presently being evaluated.) This decision was made because until that time the New York City police officer was allowed to carry any type of gun he happened to own, such as the Union army cap-and-ball revolver and the navy Colt, which were quite often damaged or worn out.

After a tragic incident that took place one cold night on Broadway, an enraged public demanded change. A rabid dog had been menacing people on the street, and a patrolman hurried to the scene, his old revolver in hand. When he half-cocked the gun, it discharged into the crowd, killing a little girl. Roosevelt, responding to the hue and cry of a furious city, moved immediately to standardize the police handgun.

"It is such incidents that change police force policies," said Officer Palermo. "When something happens in the city, we immediately analyze the way we handled the situation and then decide if we should change our procedure to make it better, and if so, how we should do it. That is the ongoing process begun by Roosevelt."

When I asked Officer Palermo to express his thoughts on the police force today, he replied:

"Every now and then when things get hard, we remember that people need us. You know, 85 percent of our job is helping the people of New York City — a sick person or somebody who's lost or frightened. And when we meet even one person who appreciates it, who cares about us, that makes it all worthwhile.

"You can look at the police flag that was adopted in 1919 to see our rich tradition and what we have always stood for. The 24 white stars in a circular constellation represent New York City's original cities, towns, and villages before the 1898 consolidation, when they were absorbed into the city as the five boroughs. The blue field represents vigilance and strength, just as it does in the blue police uniform.

"There are five stripes in the flag, each band representing a borough of New York City. The three bright green stripes symbolize hope and also represent the first green lanterns carried by policemen in 17th-century Dutch New York. That green lantern meant safety to the citizens then, just as the green light placed outside each police station today means safety to New Yorkers.

"And the white stripes? They symbolize integrity and honesty. And no matter what you read now and then in the newspapers, New York officers still hold these values.

"Long ago police officers took their jobs very seriously, and they take them just as seriously now. It has always been an extremely tough job, but ours is a unique and important task. We men and women in blue take care of the people of New York City."

The Tour

Take the elevator to the museum, located on the second floor. The exhibits fill one large room, spilling out into the hallway where there is an international police exhibit — items given by visiting police forces from around the world.

The museum is lined with glass cases that are loaded with fascinating police memorabilia and a horde of weapons taken from criminals. For example, there are exhibits of firearms dating from the 17th century. You will see blunderbusses and pistols owned by pirates, a tiny gambler's pistol that was secured to the under-forearm, and "gentlemen's pistols," so-called because they were secreted in the vest.

A tiny "virtue" pistol was sometimes carried by dance hall girls in their garters, discharged by gently squeezing the palm of the hand. On display also is a single-action revolver with a long, deadly knife hinged to the barrel, which could be

The museum's Assistant Curator, Police Officer Palermo, holds Al Capone's Thompson submachine gun and a Model 1911 Colt .45 pistol from the 1920s. The Model 1911 has been used by the U.S. Armed Services since World War I. (Photograph © Jeffrey Jay Foxx, 1990)

snapped forward in a flash. Another case holds a collection of rare early Colt "Peacemaker" revolvers with a faded photograph alongside that shows General Custer's Indian scout carrying the same make of gun.

The very first Thompson submachine gun used in a New York City murder is in the museum as well. It belonged to the powerful gangster Al Capone and was used during Prohibition to kill New York City mobster Frankie Vale. Capone's strong-arm men from Chicago did it, but there was never enough proof to send them to prison. You will see their photographs alongside one of the luckless Vale.

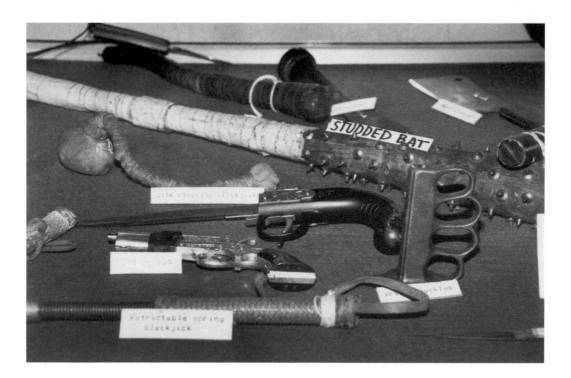

Now take a look at the violin case nearby. Still partially concealed inside is a sawed-off, double-barreled shotgun, used in a 1930s robbery.

Noteworthy are the weapons from the Gun Amnesty Program of 1975, during which people were requested to turn in weapons in their possession. Among them is a World War I aircraft machine gun, which the owner kept in his back yard for many years.

Take a look at the giant box camera used about 1910 to take mug shots. Among several photographs made from the original glass plates is a 1925 mug shot of three men arrested at 4:00 a.m. for stealing compressed gas from a factory. There they sit, as if posing for an early-morning formal portrait, nattily dressed in cashmere top coats and fedoras.

★

Above: Illegal weapons taken from street gang members. (Photograph © Jeffrey Jay Foxx, 1990)

Right: New York's Finest. Photograph circa 1870. (Courtesy of Museum of the City of New York)

Don't miss the glass cases jammed with illegal weapons taken from young gang members — chilling, to say the least! There are evil-looking flails, crudely made spiked balls swinging from chains, baseball bats studded with spikes, razor-sharp long knives, and machetes honed to a fine edge.

And much more awaits museum-goers — all just as informative and fascinating.

The New York City Police Museum
The New York City Police Academy
235 East 20th Street
New York, NY 10003
212-477-9753

Hours:
Monday-Friday 9:00 a.m.-3:00 p.m.

Admission: Free

DIRECTIONS

Subway:
• IRT #6 to 23rd Street & Park Avenue South

Bus:
• M101, M102 (Third / Lexington Avenues)
• M23 (23rd Street crosstown)

Car:
• FDR Drive, East 23rd Street exit
• Twelfth Avenue, West 23rd Street exit

However, there was the hill full in sight, so there was nothing to be done but start again. This time she came upon a large flower-bed, with a border of daisies, and a willow-tree growing in the middle.

"O Tiger-lily," said Alice, addressing herself to one that was waving gracefully about in the wind, "I *wish* you could talk!"

"We *can* talk," said the Tiger-lily: "when there's anybody worth talking to."

Alice was so astonished that she couldn't speak for a minute: it quite seemed to take her breath away. At length, as the Tiger-lily only went on waving about, she spoke again, in a timid voice—almost in a whisper. "And can *all* the flowers talk!"

"As well as *you* can," said the Tiger-lily. "And a great deal louder."

"It isn't manners for us to begin, you know," said the Rose, "and I really was wondering when you'd speak! Said I to myself, 'Her face has got *some* sense in it, though

it's not a clever one!' Still, you're the right colour, and that goes a long way."

"I don't care about the colour," the Tiger-lily remarked. "If only her petals curled up a little more, she'd be all right."

An Auction Adventure for Book Lovers

Buying rare books – and so much more at Swann Galleries, Inc.

Above: An auction at Swann Galleries. (Photograph © Jeffrey Jay Foxx, 1990)

Left: The author's 1872 edition of *Through the Looking-Glass and What Alice Found There*, bought at the Swann Galleries auction described in this chapter. (Photograph by Beth Crowell, 1990)

I had a number of favorite books as a child, but *Alice in Wonderland* topped the list. I can still picture the colorful cardboard cover with its bent corners and timeworn edges. Somewhere along the way, this much-loved, battered copy was lost, so I decided to buy another one for memory's sake. This time, though, I wanted a beautiful copy — an old one — to hand down someday to grandchildren.

The search turned into a fascinating and successful adventure. A distinctive leatherbound volume now lies on my desk — an 1872 edition that bears the original title, *Through the Looking-Glass and What Alice Found There*. I paid $110 for this treasure at Swann Galleries, the oldest and largest American rare book auction house. This is my journal of that experience.

Wednesday, May 6. The Preview.

I took the elevator up to Swann Galleries, located on the building's sixth floor, and as the doors opened, I saw several people busily cataloging books behind a long information desk. The manager of the gallery put me at ease right away.

"Swann Galleries auctions every type of rare and unique printed material, including manuscripts, autographs, maps, and photographs. Of course, all categories of books are included," she explained, "and you needn't be knowledgeable to feel comfortable at previews or sales. Just bring along your love of books!"

As a rule previews are held on Saturday from 10:00 a.m.-4:00 p.m. and from 10:00 a.m.-6:00 p.m. on Monday, Tuesday, and Wednesday. Auctions are usually held on Thursday.

It is advisable to spend an hour or so previewing the books or other materials, using the auction catalog as a guide. The catalog describes each item in clear, precise language. Each book on display has a number corresponding to its catalog description.

Ah! There were two copies of *Alice in Wonderland* listed. One was a deluxe first edition with gilt edges, estimated to bring from $400 to $600. Definitely out of my league. But the other one sounded promising:

Carroll, Lewis. *Through the Looking-Glass and What Alice Found There.* Fifty John Tenniel black & white illustrations. Occasional foxing and soiling. Rebound in red calf. (London 1872) ($110/150)

I slipped the small red volume from the shelf, running my fingers over the smooth leather binding. This was a little jewel of a book, with dainty engravings of Alice as she climbed onto a Victorian mantel and through an ornate looking glass. There were charming illustrations of a disagreeable Queen of Hearts and a dapper rabbit wearing a frock coat and wire-rimmed spectacles.

The foxing (brown spots) and smudges, and the fact that the book didn't have its original binding didn't bother me as they might trouble a puristic collector. Rather I felt that they added charm. After all, it was over 100 years old. I really wanted this book!

"It's a good idea to decide the top price you feel you should pay and jot it down in your catalog," advised a cheerful young woman, who was carefully examining each book and making notes in her catalog. "You'll be less likely to get carried away and pay more than you should." Good advice. I wrote "$130" next to my book's description.

Quickly I scanned the catalog for other tempting children's books and decided to leaf through the most interesting ones and jot down imaginary top bids for these also. It would be fun to find out how many books I could get at the auction if I were really bidding for them!

I decided I would bid $90 for a 1915 edition of Dickens' *A Christmas Carol,* estimated to bring $80/120. A lovely 1905 edition of Washington Irving's *Rip Van Winkle* with 51 color plates, estimated at $100/130, should be worth $110. Within a few minutes, I picked 15 books for my imaginary bidding. I could hardly wait for the auction the next day.

Thursday, May 7. The Auction.
The manager had suggested that I arrive by 10:00 a.m. for the 10:30 auction. There was a friendly, relaxed feeling in the room as I once again stepped through the elevator doors and made my way to the information desk. I was handed a simple card on which I wrote my name and address. Then I was given my bidding "paddle," a numbered card.

A book auction preview. (Photograph © Jeffrey Jay Foxx, 1990)

I strolled toward a small group of folding chairs set up near the bookcases and chose a seat near the back to better watch the bidding action.

At 10:30 sharp, George Lowry, president and auctioneer, strode into the room and took his place behind the podium. Lowry gave simple, clear instructions about bidding, gently encouraging nervous bidders. He explained that he would take bids from the room and would also execute "order bids," written or telephone bids left by hopefuls who couldn't attend the auction. Bidding was very easy, he explained. He would start with the opening bid for the book — $40, for example, and would identify if it was an order bid. Then he would say, "Do I hear $50?" (Bidding increments are listed at the front of the catalog.) In order to bid $50, all I had to do was raise my bidding paddle, showing my number.

Book #1 was held up, a pretty and colorful edition of *Black Beauty* — estimate: $40/60. It sold for $60. One after another, the books were held up, many bringing top bids that seemed to fall between the high and low estimates, although some brought less and some sold for much more. It was fascinating to watch the bidding matches develop among dealers and collectors.

I followed my imaginary top bids with interest. *Rip Van Winkle* brought $130. My bid of $110 would not have been high enough. But *A Christmas Carol* realized only $70, far below my bid of $90. Of the 15 books picked for imaginary bidding, I would have taken away five. Not bad!

At last, #84. My book was held up. There was an order bid for $90. "Do I hear $100?" A paddle went up in the third row. Oh, no! This man had made a number of successful bids already. Probably a dealer!

George Lowry paused. "I have $100. Now do I hear $110?"

I slowly raised my paddle, Number 195, peering over the top.

"The bid is now with Number 195 at $110. Do I hear $120?"

I slanted a glance to the right. The dealer who had made the opening bid fiddled with his paddle. Another pause, which seemed interminable. At last the gavel banged on the podium. "Sold to Number 195 for $110!"

The appealing little 1872 volume with its beautifully rendered illustrations was really mine! Exhilarated, I returned to the information desk to pay. I was advised there would be a short wait while the book was collected and wrapped, and wouldn't I like to go and have a bite of lunch and return later? Pleasantly tired and very hungry, I headed for the elevator to do just that.

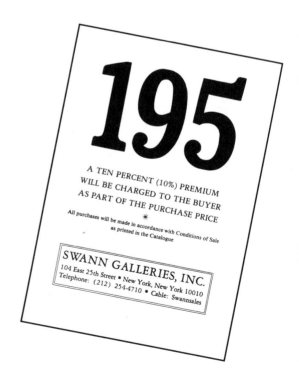

195

A TEN PERCENT (10%) PREMIUM WILL BE CHARGED TO THE BUYER AS PART OF THE PURCHASE PRICE

All purchases will be made in accordance with Conditions of Sale as printed in the Catalogue

SWANN GALLERIES, INC.
104 East 25th Street • New York, New York 10010
Telephone: (212) 254-4710 • Cable: Swannsales

Swann Galleries, Inc.
104 East 25th Street, 6th Floor
New York, NY 10010
Tel 212-254-4710
Fax 212-979-1017

Preview Days: (as a general rule)
Saturday 10:00 a.m.-4:00 p.m.
Monday-Wednesday 10:00 a.m.-6:00 p.m.

Sale Days:
Most Thursdays at 10:30 a.m., September to June, excluding holidays. Sometimes sales are held Thursday evenings, Saturdays, and Sundays. There are a few auctions in July and August.

Swann Galleries auctions every type of rare and unique printed material, including first editions, volumes of travel and exploration, sporting books, historical works, modern literature, illustrated books, children's books, rare and early maps, volumes of medicine, Americana, theatre, scientific books, and books with unusual and fine bindings. In addition, there are two major sales each year of autographs and manuscripts ranging from rare signed presidential letters to autographs of movie stars, as well as sales of fine photographs, photographic literature, Hebraica and Judaica, and works of art on paper.

Call for information about upcoming auctions and to receive a free newsletter, *The Trumpet*, which lists the extended schedule and information about upcoming sales. Auction catalogs are also available by mail (usually $7.00-$15.00), and may be charged on VISA and MasterCard. If a catalog is ordered, a list of prices realized will be mailed after the auction.

Cash, cashier's checks, and certified checks are accepted for immediate delivery of items purchased. Personal checks must clear before purchases are collected unless credit has been established. (Call for details.)

If bidding by telephone, please make arrangements in advance. Note: A 10 percent premium or surcharge is added to the hammer price and is paid by the buyer.

To truly enjoy the rich experience of buying at auction, you should approach this adventure as if you were actually a dealer or collector. This means that it is very important to spend an hour or two on a preview day just looking at the books or other printed material. (Previewing is not permitted on auction day.) Just keep in mind that you don't even have to buy anything to enjoy the thrill of the auction; but if you do, you will always have something to remind you of your adventure!

R E S T A U R A N T S

There are a number of inexpensive restaurants along Lexington and Third Avenues between 25th and 30th Streets. If you are in the mood for exotic food, try the tiny *Tibetan Kitchen* at 444 Third Avenue between 30th and 31st Streets — quite inexpensive. We liked the curry — especially lamb — and the ground meat dumplings.

Also: *Hunan Balcony East* at 386 Third Avenue between 27th and 28th Streets. Clean, simple, and attractive, with good Chinese food at inexpensive prices.

D I R E C T I O N S

See Theodore Roosevelt chapter.

An American Midas of the Gilded Age: Pierpont Morgan

A walk through The Pierpont Morgan Library

 id the United States ever have royalty? "Very nearly," I thought, as I stood in the magnificent marble rotunda of The Pierpont Morgan Library. It was the era of the Gilded Age at the end of the 19th century, a golden time before income taxes, when the Vanderbilts and the Astors built marble summer palaces in Newport and when a businessman could live the life of a Renaissance prince. John Pierpont Morgan was such a man.

The engaging docent turned to me with a smile. "Pierpont Morgan chose a Renaissance model as his inspiration for the Library, which was built between 1902 and 1906 by the noted architect Charles McKim."

I gazed up at the rotunda's richly painted ceiling, the work of Harry Siddons Mowbray, who studied the Renaissance buildings in Rome before beginning his work on the Library. The rotunda's ceiling was inspired by Raphael's ceiling in the *Stanza della Segnatura* in the Vatican and was painted in the same manner to resemble mosaics. The surrounding lunettes were modeled after paintings in the Borgia Apartments in Rome. The entrance to the Library was originally through the rotunda's bronze doors, whose scenes depict events described in the New Testament. The carved lions flanking the steps outside

Above: The Pierpont Morgan Library as it appears today. (Photograph © Jeffrey Jay Foxx, 1990)

Right: The Pierpont Morgan Library, circa 1910. View of original entrance. Visitors now enter the Library through the Annex, completed in 1928. (Courtesy of Museum of the City of New York)

were carved by Edward Clark Potter, who carved The New York Public Library lions. (Visitors now enter the library through the Annex, completed in 1928, occupying land on which Morgan's house once stood.)

I turned to examine a pair of blue columns in the rotunda, discovering that they were carved from lapis lazuli. A second pair of columns once decorated a small, elegant chateau that still stands in the Bagatelle Garden, located in the Bois de Boulogne on the outskirts of Paris. This chateau was built as the result of a wager made in 1779 between the Comte d'Artois (later Charles X) and the queen of France, Marie Antoinette. The count insisted that the chateau and garden could be completed within three months, and the queen said it was impossible. The Comte d'Artois won the wager handily in just 64 days.

Passing between two imposing 15th- and 16th-century marriage chests flanking the doorway, visitors enter the East Room. A graceful expanse of 123 glass-fronted bookcases encircles the mahogany-paneled room, then rises tier upon tier to the lavishly painted ceiling. These brass-trimmed tiers have walkways made with layers of stacked, clear three-inch glass plates, giving them a floating quality. Hidden stairways behind the cases are revealed when a lower bookcase panel swings out.

The East Room's ceiling was modeled on the work of the Italian painter Pintoricchio (circa 1454-1513). Incorporated into the painting are Morgan's birth sign (Aries) and the birth signs of his first wife Amelia Sturges (Aquarius), and his second wife Frances Tracy (Gemini).

A great fireplace centers the far east wall, framed by a 16th-century marble mantel. Above it hangs a Renaissance-style 15-by-24-foot Flemish tapestry,

The Triumph of Avarice. Significantly, the figure is that of Midas, who turned everything he touched into gold!

The East Room is used as an exhibition space for the Library's vast collection and displays objects on a rotating basis. Among them: one of the first Gutenberg Bibles (of three owned by Morgan); the only existing Proclamation made by George Washington in 1789 creating Thanksgiving Day; the Declaration of Independence, one of 22 existing copies in the first state; works of art from the Library's world-famous cabinet of drawings; and the *Stavelot Triptych*, made for Archbishop Wibald, adviser to the Holy Roman Emperor in Constantinople. Also displayed in the East Room is a figure of Eros running a race in honor of the gods of fire, taken from the ruins of Villa Maximia, which was destroyed by Vesuvius in 79 A.D. The East Room is used for six special exhibitions yearly.

Pierpont Morgan did not begin to collect books seriously until after his father's death in 1890. Shortly thereafter he bought a William Thackeray manuscript in Thackeray's own handwriting. Purchases of individual manuscripts including Dickens' *Christmas Carol* and Keats' *Endymion* followed; then, as Morgan's collecting appetite grew, he bought whole collections. In 1902 he acquired an invaluable collection of 700 incunabula (books written before 1501), among them more than 100 precious illuminated manuscripts. He acquired

Pierpont Morgan (1837-1913). From a studio portrait by Edward Steichen, 1903, taken when Morgan was 66 years old. (Courtesy of the Archives of The Pierpont Morgan Library, New York. Reprinted with permission of Joanna T. Steichen)

The West Room of The Pierpont Morgan Library. (Courtesy of The Pierpont Morgan Library, New York. Photograph by Ezra Stoller, Esto Photographics, Inc. 1956)

other collections: fine bookbindings, a number of which are decorated with precious metals and gems; early scientific works; music manuscripts; authors' original manuscripts; letters and documents of historical significance; ancient written records; early children's books; medieval and Renaissance manuscripts; Old Master drawings; poetry; and later printed books.

The Pierpont Morgan Library was built to house this priceless treasure of literature and art. The books lining the walls of the East Room and stored in the vaults would ultimately form one of the eminent research libraries in the world.

Morgan's far-ranging collecting interests extended beyond his library. He began to purchase treasures of every description, yet they had one characteristic in common: They were the best, and often the earliest and rarest.

Morgan collected 15th- and 16th-century masterpieces of Italian majolica. He acquired the finest and most intricate works of the 17th-century German goldsmiths and silversmiths, superb 17th-century ivory carvings, Sèvres and Vincennes porcelains, and 18th-century German Meissen porcelains. And the list went on. He collected tapestries and French furniture. His mammoth collection of ancient art represented nearly every civilization. Other purchases included remarkable collections of watches, oriental porcelains, and Baroque glass.

And the paintings. It was said that everywhere one looked in the house at Prince's Gate in London there were magnificent paintings. Among them were works by Reynolds, Gainsborough, Velázquez, Van Dyck, and Rembrandt. Morgan's collection of portrait miniatures was splendid, from Holbein's painting of Henry VIII (a royal gift to Anne of Cleves) to Hilliard's portrait of the young princess who would become Elizabeth I. These small, exquisite portraits were often set in frames of gold and encrusted with pearls and jewels.

We headed toward the West Room, a dark, luxurious study in which Pierpont Morgan held many of the meetings that shook Wall Street and Washington, D.C. His impressive desk and chair were there, as well as the faded red velvet club chair in which Morgan frequently sat playing his favorite game, solitaire, on a folding card table.

I studied Pierpont Morgan's portrait dominating the West Room from its place above the mantel. The financier glared imperiously from his frame, his formidable demeanor empowered further by the great misshapen nose and piercing hawk eyes.

Who was this man, I wondered, and what events brought him to such a position of wealth and influence?

★

John Pierpont Morgan was born into a wealthy family. His grandfather, Joseph Morgan, left the family tradition of farming and moved to Hartford, Connecticut, building a fortune in real estate, co-founding the Aetna Fire Insurance Company, and dabbling in politics.

Joseph's only son, Junius Spencer Morgan, broadened the financial empire by becoming an international banker. Junius and Juliet Pierpont Morgan had five children, of whom the eldest and only surviving son was John Pierpont, born April 17, 1837.

Young Pierpont spent his childhood and early teenage years in Hartford and Boston, and also attended boarding school in Connecticut. By all accounts the boy was fairly well-adjusted, made average grades, and had a circle of friends. He showed an interest in writing and in business before he was 12 years old. The greatest blight on his young life was a genetic illness that gradually turned his nose into an enormous and fiery red mass, a lifelong embarrassment.

Pierpont Morgan's simple life changed dramatically in 1854 when he was 17. His father became a partner in the merchant-banking firm of George Peabody & Co. in London, moving his family permanently to England. The young Morgan attended schools in Switzerland and Germany, using his free time to explore the cities and study their art and architecture. (During his stay in Switzerland he picked up nearly a barrelful of stained-glass shards that he found lying around churches. It is believed that these shards were used later in the windows of the Library's West Room.)

Fascinating as the young man found Europe, he returned to the United States at the age of 20 to build his career in New York, beginning as an unpaid junior accountant, then starting his own firm four years later. Eventually the firm became the American representative of George Peabody & Co.

Morgan married Amelia Sturges in 1862 when he was 23 years old, fully aware that she was dying of tuberculosis. The marriage was short and tragic, lasting approximately five months from the moment he carried her to the carriage after the wedding until her death in Nice, France. Morgan suffered a brief emotional collapse.

Pierpont Morgan married Frances Tracy three years later, an enduring marriage that produced three daughters and a son. The Morgans lived in several homes during their years together, one of which was a solid, respectable brownstone mansion at 219 Madison Avenue (subsequently razed to make way for the Library Annex). They also spent time at Cragston, a country estate on the Hudson River, purchased in 1872.

From 1871 to 1895 Morgan enjoyed a lucrative partnership with the Drexels of Philadelphia, who controlled an international banking empire. During these years and the years following, Morgan amassed incredible wealth, and with the wealth came immense power, which the portly financier used like a bulldozer. For example, it was Morgan who saw the future of the railroad when it was in its infancy and set out to link as many of the

The East Room of The Pierpont Morgan Library. (Courtesy of The Pierpont Morgan Library, New York. Photograph by Ezra Stoller, Esto Photographics, Inc. 1956)

sprawling, competing lines as he could buy — one way or another.

It was Morgan who founded U.S. Steel Corporation in 1901, a merger that integrated Carnegie Steel Corporation, purchased from Andrew Carnegie and his associates for $420 million. It was Morgan, too, who effected the solution to the gold crisis of 1895 and who provided the leadership that averted a stock market crash and banking failure during the Financial Panic of 1907.

Among other diverse challenges, Morgan attempted to reorganize the banking system to make it less vulnerable. He helped arrange the financing for the $50 million purchase of the Panama Canal Zone during Theodore Roosevelt's administration, and he aided the British government by partially funding the Boer War through American loans underwritten by his firm.

Morgan was also a financial backer of Thomas A. Edison's phonograph. He was president of The Metropolitan Museum of Art. The financier's International Mercantile Marine Trust even owned the *Titanic*. (Luckily, after choosing his personal staterooms, he cancelled his plan to take the maiden voyage.)

And Morgan played as hard as he worked. He floated up and down the Hudson in his opulent black yacht *Corsair**, or he relaxed in one of his private railroad cars, often discreetly accompanied by such famed beauties as Lillian Russell. Another equally luxurious craft, an Egyptian *dehabeah* named the *Khargeh*, waited on the Nile at his pleasure. Here was a man who was a friend of King Edward VII and entertained Kaiser Wilhelm, afterward declaring matter-of-factly, "I have met the Kaiser, and I like him."

Pierpont Morgan died just as he had lived — with grand style. On March 31, 1913, while lying in his personal suite at the Grand Hotel in Rome, he quietly raised his hand to the ceiling, saying, "I've got to go up the hill." Then he closed his eyes and drifted off to sleep.

Even after Morgan's death, his power lived on. The House of Morgan became the banker of the Allied cause, arranging two loans in 1914 and 1915 totaling $600 million.

But what happened to this vast collection after Morgan died? His son, J.P. Morgan, Jr., sold three-fifths of the collection to pay taxes and other debts. Fortunately, a great number of works of art were donated to The Metropolitan Museum, many of which are on view in the medieval galleries. A portion of the superlative collection of decorative arts was given to the Wadsworth Atheneum in Hartford. A series of magnificent Fragonard panels was bought by Henry Frick for $1.2 million, along with Morgan's collection of medieval French Limoges enamels, all on permanent display at The Frick Collection.

And so it was only Pierpont Morgan's magnificent Library that survived intact. Considered one of the wonders of the world when it was completed in 1906, The Pierpont Morgan Library is still one of the finest libraries in the world today.

* Named for a type of fast ship used for piracy. Morgan owned four black-hulled yachts through the years, all named *Corsair* — chosen perhaps because Morgan believed the pirate Henry Morgan was an ancestor.

The Pierpont Morgan Library
29 East 36th Street at Madison Avenue
New York, NY 10016
212-685-0008

Hours:
Tuesday-Saturday 10:30 a.m.-5:00 p.m.
Sunday 1:00-5:00 p.m

Closed Monday & holidays

Admission: (Suggested donation)
- Adults $3.00
- Students & seniors $1.00

The Library:
There is always a special exhibition on view, with several lectures offered during the course of each exhibition.

Tours are given by the Library docents. Group tours of special exhibitions may also be arranged. Call for details.

The museum's attractive gift shop offers unusual gifts and books.

The Area

The Library is located in historic Murray Hill, which was a neighborhood of mansions and pretty brownstones owned by the social elite in the late 19th and early 20th centuries. Murray Hill covers an approximate area from Madison Avenue to Third Avenue, and from 34th to 40th Streets.

If you would like to take a walking tour of the area, here are a few interesting landmarks along these tranquil streets:

The Home of J.P. Morgan, Jr.
The Italianate brownstone at 231 Madison Avenue, on the southeast corner of 37th Street, was built in 1852 for banker Anson Phelps Stokes. The house was purchased by Pierpont Morgan in 1904 and given to his son, J.P. Morgan, Jr. Apparently Morgan's daughter-in-law didn't care to live in the 45-room mansion, with its grand, sweeping staircase, high-ceilinged ballroom, and 22 fireplaces, because the couple spent most of their time at their Long Island home.

The DeLamar Mansion
Northeast corner of 37th Street & Madison Avenue. This rather grand mansion at 233 Madison was built for a Dutch sea captain-turned stockbroker. DeLamar wanted to be Morgan's pal, but Morgan could be quite a snob and considered DeLamar an upstart. At least the unhappy millionaire had this house to console him! It now belongs to the Polish Consulate.

Church of the Incarnation
205 Madison Avenue at 35th Street. At this beautiful if somber church, which is an 1864 brownstone Gothic Revival structure, you will see four fine Tiffany stained-glass windows and a set of Tiffany doors. There are information leaflets at the door.

Anthroposophical Society of America
211 Madison Avenue, between 35th & 36th Streets. Originally Morgan's carriage house.

Circa 1890 Carriage Houses
157 & 159 East 35th Street, between Third and Lexington Avenues.

A String of Turn-of-the-Century Houses
35th Street, east of Park Avenue on the north side of the street. #123, a particularly handsome house built in 1903, was owned by an international banker.

First Home of Newly Married F.D.R. and Eleanor
125 East 36th Street, west of Lexington Avenue. Chosen by Roosevelt's mother, the first indication of her iron-clad control over the young couple.

Sniffen Court
150-158 East 36th, between Third & Lexington Avenues. A cluster of charming brick townhouses arranged in a mews. Converted from carriage houses and stables built in the 1850s by John Sniffen.

Adjacent Twin Homes of Abraham Lincoln's Two Granddaughters
122 & 124 East 38th Street

The Old Print Shop
150 Lexington Avenue at 30th Street. 212-683-3950. A first-rate shop, founded in 1898. Owned by the Newman family since 1928. Has a warm 19th-century feeling; very friendly and helpful owners and staff. A fine selection of antique prints — Currier & Ives, Audubon, maps, town views, flowers, marine, etc.

Additional Sights

If you would like to learn more about Pierpont Morgan's friends and competitors, you might enjoy these museums:

Theodore Roosevelt Birthplace, (chapter 13), The Frick Collection (chapter 20), and Cooper Hewitt National Museum of Design at 2 East 91st Street 212-860-6868 (former home of Andrew Carnegie).

Visit The Metropolitan Museum of Art (Fifth Avenue and 82nd Street 212-535-7710) to see more of Pierpont Morgan's great collection of medieval works of art. The Frick Collection owns the Limoges enamels and the Fragonard panels.

RESTAURANTS

Bien Venue
21 East 36th Street
212-684-0215

Lunch:
    Monday-Friday 11:30 a.m.-2:30 p.m.
Dinner:
    Monday-Friday 5:30-10:00 p.m.

Closed at lunch Saturday & all day Sunday

- All major credit cards
- Reservations suggested

Bien Venue is conveniently located across the street from the Morgan Library. The little restaurant has the true flavor of France, with Norman-inspired stuccoed and lathed walls, small tables, flowers, and the musical French language of the waitresses.

The food is very good, from coq au vin in a wine-rich sauce to the delicate touch used in salmon with capers. Salads are crisp with a delicious house dressing. At lunchtime try the omelets and crepes.

Lunch:
    Appetizers $2.50-$3.15
    Entrees $8.00-$13.25
Dinner:
    Appetizers $3.75-$6.00
    Entrees $13.50-$18.00
    Prix fixe $22.00

Keen's

72 West 36th Street
Between Fifth Avenue & Avenue
of the Americas
212-947-3636

Lunch:
    Monday-Friday 11:45 a.m.-3:00 p.m.
Dinner:
    Monday-Friday 5:30-11:00 p.m.
    Saturday 5:00-11:00 p.m.

Closed Sunday

* All major credit cards
* Reservations suggested

In this turn-of-the-century restaurant J.P.
Morgan, Teddy Roosevelt, Lillie Langtry, and
Diamond Jim Brady dined. The interior is
charming and cozy, with dark paneled walls
covered with 18th-century playbills. Thousands of clay pipes hang from the ceiling, a reminder that long ago a customer often left a
pipe at a restaurant to smoke after dinner.

Ask to see the delightful rooms upstairs.
The Lincoln Room is lined with Lincoln and
Booth memorabilia; the Lambs Club Room is
named for the famous literary and theatrical
club founded in England; the Bull Moose
Room has memorabilia of Teddy Roosevelt
and the Spanish-American War; the Lillie
Langtry Room was dedicated to the glamorous
actress because of the furor she created when
she was not admitted to this restaurant, which
was then for men only. She took her case to
court and won!

The star of Keen's menu is still the mutton
chop, which is absolutely delicious. Seafood is
very good, as is seasonal game. Rack of lamb
and veal chops are succulent and juicy.

Lunch offerings range from simply prepared
salads to more elaborate entrees. On Saturday
evenings end your dinner with coffee and
dessert in front of a cozy fire in the Bull
Moose Room. Lunch per person averages
$25.00-$30.00; dinner, $50.00.

Lord & Taylor

37th Street & Fifth Avenue
212-391-3344

Daily 11:00 a.m.-5:00 p.m.
Monday & Thursday until 7:00 p.m.

Three choices for an inexpensive lunch:
* *The Bird Cage,* fifth floor, for tasty salads,
  soups and sandwiches
* Sixth-floor counter restaurant
* 10th-floor counter restaurant for a hearty
  bowl of soup and roll

★

Genroku Sushi

366 Fifth Avenue
Between 34th & 35th Streets
212-947-7940

Lunch & Dinner:
    Monday-Saturday 11:30 a.m.-8:30 p.m.

Very quick and inexpensive. Fun too, with
Japanese and Chinese dishes presented on a
moving belt at the counter. You just pick your
dish as it speeds by!

D I R E C T I O N S

Subway:
* #6 to 33rd Street
* B, D, N, R to 34th Street

Bus:
* M1, M2, M3, M4, M32 (Fifth / Madison
  Avenues)
* M5 (Fifth Avenue / Avenue of the
  Americas / Riverside Drive)
* M16, M34 (34th street crosstown)

Car:
* FDR Drive, East 34th Street exit
* Twelfth Avenue, West 34th Street exit

Above: Commodore Vanderbilt's red-and-white brick Grand Central Depot, which opened in 1871, was demolished to make way for the present Grand Central Terminal. (Courtesy of The New-York Historical Society, New York City)

Left: Grand Central Terminal today. View at corner of 42nd Street and Vanderbilt Avenue. (Photograph © Jeffrey Jay Foxx, 1990)

Exploring Grand Central Terminal

Basement to ballroom to bird's-eye view

The History

efore 1830 travel from Manhattan's southern tip to Harlem's rolling farm-lands 10 miles away was a journey that required patience, as it could take two hours in a horse-drawn conveyance, an inconvenience that dampened the urge to travel and discouraged settlement of the northern part of the island.

A new transportation system began in 1832 when the New York & Harlem steam-powered trains began to clatter a short distance along the rails in Lower Manhattan. Within a few years the tracks extended to such far-flung destinations as the hamlet of Yorkville (the East 80s) and a bucolic village in Harlem (in the area of 125th Street and First Avenue).

In 1857 the city banned steam locomotives below 42nd Street, acceding to the demands of well-heeled residents who had tired of the noise and pollution. In 1871 Commodore Vanderbilt, the millionaire steamboat-turned-railroad tycoon, having decided to route his passenger trains down Manhattan's East Side, completed an impressive terminal on 42nd Street, Grand Central Depot.

Trains were housed in the depot's giant cast-iron and glass train shed.

By 1902 the city had finally had enough of the trains with their belching smoke, ear-wrenching noise, and soot, and banned steam locomotives within the city altogether, forcing the railroad (which by that time was called the New York Central & Hudson River R.R.) to make drastic changes.

The development of the electric locomotive and sophisticated building innovations just before the turn of the century opened up new possibilities for the New York Central. Why not put the tracks beneath the ground? And it was done — more than 33 miles of track on two levels.

In 1903 a splendid new Grand Central Terminal began to rise above the

Grand Central Terminal as it looked in 1934. View looking north at the corner of 42nd Street and Vanderbilt Avenue. Behind the terminal rises the graceful 1929 New York Central (R.R.) Building (now the Helmsley Building), once the tallest building on Park Avenue. The 59-story Pan Am Building went up in 1963, dwarfing both of these buildings. (Courtesy of The New-York Historical Society, New York City)

subterranean hodgepodge of tracks and noisy trains, opening in 1913. The distinguished Beaux-Arts building was uniquely designed to meet the needs of the railroad passenger, the subway rider, the automobile, and the pedestrian, yet kept them separated in different areas and levels of the terminal. The structure was massive and impressive, and flooded with soft light through 64-foot-high arched windows — a graceful and dignified pavilion for travelers.

The land surrounding the terminal was at last free of the clutter of trains and tracks, and beautification began. Park Avenue was built over the fan-shaped underground train yards as far north as 50th Street. Handsome apartment buildings and hotels rose along the broad avenue and were actually built over those vast subterranean railroad yards. The band of Park Avenue extending from Grand Central Terminal through the 40s developed into a gilt-edged ribbon that existed until World War II. Subsequently ugly, undistinguished, or (as in the case of the 1963 Pan Am Building) towering buildings began to replace the smaller, well-designed structures, finally destroying the elegance that had distinguished this section of Park Avenue.

The Tour

"Well, times have certainly changed since this terminal opened in 1913," I remark to myself as I wait in the Grand Concourse for my tour to start. What a clamor this mob makes! There is so much going on that my eyes never stop moving.

Since it isn't necessary to make a reservation for this tour, and because it is free, I am beginning to wonder if I'm the only one who has heard about it — or if there really is a tour. Then at 12:30 on the dot the guide arrives. Suddenly a small group seems to materialize around him, and I saunter over to join them.

The guide introduces himself and tells us that he is with the Municipal Arts Society, which has been sponsoring these Wednesday tours every week since 1975. He explains that 1975 was a dismal year for Grand Central Terminal, when it nearly succumbed to the wrecking ball to make room for another steel and glass skyscraper. The Committee to Save Grand Central Terminal rescued the terminal by having it declared a landmark. The committee took its case to the Supreme Court and won.

That is why scaffolds are up everywhere now, he continues, and workmen seem to be crawling over everything. The grand old terminal (75 years old in 1988) is slowly being returned to its 1913 glory. In fact, in April 1990 The Metropolitan Transportation Authority, which leases Grand Central Terminal from Penn Central Corporation, unveiled an ambitious plan that would not only restore the structure to its 1913 splendor, but would increase lucrative commercial space from 105,000 to 150,000 square feet, to be used for restaurants, upscale shops, and the like. The project, estimated to cost about $400 million, would continue over a 10-year period. The plan is contingent upon a number of factors; among them, the success of the M.T.A.'s proposal to purchase the terminal, permission to renovate from the City Landmarks Preservation Commission, funds from the city and state, and from private interests.

We listen, some of us taking notes, and I learn later that a newspaper reporter and another writer are in our group. Most are here for the fun of it though — from teen-agers to grandmothers.

Our guide tells us that this concourse is 275 feet long, 120 feet wide, and as

The terminal's Grand Concourse during a mid-morning lull. View of the Vanderbilt Avenue staircase, the information kiosk, and the ticket counters. (Photograph by David Browning, 1990)

high as a 12-story building — larger than the nave of Notre Dame Cathedral. In the early years about 50,000 people a day walked through the terminal, but now over 500,000 people hurry through it each day, and 500 trains arrive and depart daily. "Yet," he continues, "the terminal functions very well. Why?

"Grand Central is obviously a work of architectural genius, but it is also a work of superlative engineering and design, and more than anything else, I hope *that* is what you get out of this tour." So saying, our guide weaves historical and architectural information with entertaining stories and colorful details.

"If you look around, you will see many symbols of travel, which tourists often notice, but New Yorkers rarely do: wings, wheels, anchors, and globes, for example. And if you look straight up, you will see the least obvious of the symbols of travel, but a very important one — the sky — important because ancient travel-

The striking 13-foot-high clock and sculpture group of Mercury, Hercules, Minerva, and an American eagle on the terminal's 42nd Street side. The Pan Am Building rises behind the figure of Mercury. (Photograph by David Browning, 1990)

ers, like the mariners, used the skies to chart their courses."

I scan the ceiling 12 stories above me. Painted on the vaulted expanse are constellations and symbols of the zodiac. I may be imagining it, but I see starlight.

"That ceiling, called *Mediterranean Winter's Night,* has 2,500 stars, some of which are lighted by bulbs. And you will be interested to know that you are looking at the sky as if you are in the heavens looking down on the constellations. Perhaps the artist, who was using a celestial globe, made the mistake."

It seems that this ceiling also played a prominent role in the movie thriller *The House on Carrol Street*. In the movie the spies are seen running on a catwalk suspended between the vaulted ceiling and the roof above. In the final scene one of the spies falls from the catwalk, through the ceiling and down to the floor 125 feet below!

Pointing out numerous architectural details in the concourse of "one of the few remaining classical jewels that we have left in New York City," our guide takes us on a fascinating 90-minute walk, passing first the "Kissing Gallery," so named because in years gone by long-distance travelers were greeted — and presumably kissed — by friends and loved ones when they met in this waiting room.

We climb a flight of surprisingly beautiful stairs as we hear that one staircase, the Grand Staircase on the Vanderbilt Avenue side, was modeled after the Paris Opera House. An elevator whisks us to the sixth floor, and we are rewarded with a rare view of the concourse from a glass-paved corridor.

We hear how ugly additions have changed the beautifully designed terminal, but we also learn how the stately old Grand Central will look when restorations are completed. Even simple cleaning makes a startling difference: The numerous large skylights that bathe the concourse in soft light were cleaned in 1988 by removing tar that had covered them since the blackouts of World War II! We hear that Phillip Johnson, the renowned American architect, once said that this concourse was the most perfectly lighted room in the world, and as I look down, I begin to understand why.

The upper reaches of this enormous building hold other surprises that most New Yorkers never see. High above the noise and moving streams of commuters, we are amazed to enter a tennis club, a green and white and wicker oasis that is open to the public (at about $75.00 an hour!). We watch players bat balls around while we learn about the club's different incarnations. Planned originally as a ballroom and never used, it lay dark and empty for more than 25 years, until CBS-TV studios took it over from the late 1940s to the 1960s.

As we head downstairs and pass the Metro-North Police Headquarters housed in the terminal, we hear another amusing story. Once a very wealthy New Yorker had an opulent duplex apartment right in Grand Central Terminal. The police are headquartered there now, and the chief has an office in the former sumptuous bedroom. And the wine cellar? A perfect holding tank!

Finally, we go outside to discuss the impressive 42nd Street façade of Grand Central Terminal, with its 13-foot-high clock and sculpture group by Jules Coutan of Hercules, Minerva, and Mercury and an American eagle. We learn, among other facts, that Mercury was the Roman messenger of the gods and the patron of travelers and merchants — and even the patron of thieves!

As eddies of pedestrians swirl around us, we stand in a cluster, listening to the last interesting details of history and architecture. I, for one, am sorry the tour is over. It has given me a rare look at New York City as it existed in 1913, and an appreciation of a venerable landmark that bridges the early 20th century to the present day.

Grand Central Terminal
Park Avenue & East 42nd Street to East
45th Street

Meeting Place for Tour:
Concourse level in front of Chemical Bank

Hours:
Every Wednesday at 12:30 p.m.

Admission: Free

• Reservations are unnecessary

Call the Municipal Arts Society for
other interesting tours of New York City
212-935-3960

R E S T A U R A N T S

Oyster Bar & Restaurant
Located in the lower level of
Grand Central Terminal
212-490-6650

Monday-Friday 11:30 a.m.-9:30 p.m.

Closed Saturday, Sunday & holidays

• All major credit cards
• Reservations a good idea, especially for
  the Saloon or the back dining room

You may decide to end your tour in this
restaurant. And why not? The Oyster Bar &
Restaurant has been a real New York institution since Grand Central Terminal opened
in 1913. New Yorkers certainly love it, which
accounts for the huge crowds you will find
here every day. The name of the game is
seafood — and lots of it!

I had a visit with Mario Staub, executive
vice president of the Brody Corporation
(which bought the restaurant in 1974), and
he gave me some remarkable statistics.

"We serve an average of 1,800 to 2,000
persons a day. We offer between 90 to 110
items on the menu every single day, and we
change our menu daily, depending on what we
find at the fish market. We serve absolutely
fresh seafood, nothing frozen, which is why
we are closed Saturday, Sunday, and holidays,
since the market is closed then. Between
6,000 and 8,000 oysters are eaten daily."

You may eat in several different areas, all
interesting: the oyster bar, at one of the four
wooden counters, in the Saloon, or in the big
main dining room with its tiled floors, vaulted
ceilings, and red-checkered tablecloths. The
menu is the same, with such a selection of
seafood that you will have trouble choosing.

There are all sorts of stews and pan-roasts
made with oysters, clams, lobster, and
scallops. Or choose from a huge selection of
fish — every kind you have ever seen in a fish
market — all prepared in a straightforward
manner to bring out the fresh flavor. And,
of course, the oysters. I counted 14 different
varieties, at around $1.35 to $1.95 each, a
must for anyone who loves oysters.

Desserts range from a hazelnut chocolate
cake to a blueberry zabaglione.

Lunch & dinner:
  Entrees $19.50-$25.00
  Salads $3.35

Zaro's Breadbasket
Concourse level, Grand Central Terminal
212-599-1515

Monday-Friday 6:00 a.m.-10:00 p.m.
Saturday & Sunday 6:00 a.m.-8:00 p.m.

If you are in a hurry, this is the place for a
sandwich, yogurt, or pastry. There aren't any
places to sit while you eat, but this is the kind
of food you can carry along very easily.
Choose from deli croissants with an assortment of fillings such as turkey with Swiss
cheese or sausage, $3.25; roast beef, corned
beef, and pastrami sandwiches, $4.75. There
is a frozen yogurt counter, and you can choose
from case after case of tempting pastries.

D I R E C T I O N S

Subway:
- #4, 5, 6 & 7 to Grand Central Terminal

Bus:
- M1, M2, M3, M4 (Fifth / Madison
  Avenues)
- M42 (42nd Street crosstown)
- M101, M102 (Third / Lexington Avenues)
- M104 (Broadway / 42nd Street)

Car:
- FDR Drive East, 42nd Street exit
- Twelfth Avenue, West 42nd Street exit

The terminal's Grand Concourse. The
famous New York Colorama, known
to all as the Kodak Sign, was taken
down in March 1990 during ongoing
restoration. (Photograph © Jeffrey Jay
Foxx, 1990)

The Rink at Rockefeller Plaza

Your chance to skate like a star!

The Story of Rockefeller Center

ockefeller Center was built on 12 acres, from 48th to 51st Streets and from Fifth Avenue to Sixth Avenue (Avenue of the Americas), which until 1801 had been open pastureland. In that year Dr. David Hosack bought the land and additional acreage, transforming 20 acres into Elgin Botanic Garden. (An interesting note: Dr. Hosack attended Alexander Hamilton after the Treasury Secretary was mortally wounded in a duel with Aaron Burr.)

In 1811 Dr. Hosack sold the property to New York State. Three years later the state legislature conveyed the land to Columbia College, the present-day Columbia University. Slowly the acreage filled with a mixture of small buildings, all leased from the college.

In 1928 John D. Rockefeller, Jr., spearheaded a civic group whose goal was to provide land for the Metropolitan Opera Company's new opera house, replacing its deteriorating building at Broadway and 39th Street. Rockefeller formulated a plan with the opera company to build Metropolitan Square, which would have as its centerpiece the

Above: An early-morning skating lesson in the heart of New York City. It is hard to believe, but this little skater and her mother nearly have the rink to themselves! (Photograph © Jeffrey Jay Foxx, 1990)

Right: The rink at Rockefeller Plaza, circa 1935. Laying the water pipes. The golden *Prometheus* sculpture by Paul Manship, erected in 1934, watches over the proceedings. (Courtesy of Museum of the City of New York)

247

impressive Metropolitan Opera House.

Rockefeller's problems began when economic conditions worsened. After the 1929 stock market crash, the Metropolitan Opera Company decided it could not afford to build the luxurious opera house and backed out of the agreement. Private builders who had joined the Metropolitan Square venture also had to retreat for economic reasons, leaving Rockefeller with a $3.8 million yearly lease. Rockefeller decided to go on with the project, and in 1931 he began to shoulder the entire cost of the venture himself. (Rockefeller's immense fortune was securely rooted in the Standard Oil empire founded by his father, John D. Rockefeller.)

Rockefeller developed a plan for a multi-use complex for business and entertainment that would not only put thousands of the Depression's unemployed to work during construction but would continue to employ an army of workers when completed.

A new occupant was found to replace the Metropolitan Opera Company. This tenant was RCA, Radio Corporation of America, manufacturer of radios and components, which also owned NBC, the National Broadcasting Company, and the RKO motion picture studio. The RCA Building would become the new centerpiece of Rockefeller Center.

Demolition of the large area began. Some 228 buildings were razed, and the site was cleared of debris. Thousands of tenants were relocated. Construction began in 1931 and continued until 1940, employing more than 225,000 people on the site and elsewhere and giving a much-needed economic boost to New York City. Rockefeller's investment — $135 million.

The urban complex that emerged is a sophisticated jigsaw puzzle of soaring limestone, steel, and glass buildings,

This photograph shows the Rockefeller Center area before demolition. View from 51st Street and Avenue of the Americas looking east toward Fifth Avenue. At far left is St. Patrick's Cathedral. (Courtesy of Rockefeller Center © The Rockefeller Group. Photograph by Irving Underhill, 1931)

51st St. South Side 6th to 5th Ave C55292
Copyright 1931 by Irving Underhill
RQ-200

fitting snugly and harmoniously next to flower-filled public areas — an elegant mix of retail, office, and open space.

Rockefeller Center is impressive to visitors and New Yorkers alike. From Fifth Avenue the Channel Gardens slice through the middle of Rockefeller Center, delighting the eye with raised flower gardens in summer and sparkling angel sculptures at Christmastime. (The official name of this walkway is the Promenade, but it is usually called the "Channel Gardens" because it separates two buildings, La Maison Française and the British Empire Building, just as the English Channel separates France from England.)

The Lower Plaza lies at the end of the Channel Gardens, a fanciful skating rink in winter and an umbrella-shaded restaurant in summer. The golden figure of *Prometheus* (Paul Manship, 1934) oversees the activities, while colorful flags of the United Nations flutter above him at street level.

The 70-story GE Building (GE bought RCA and dissolved the corporation — hence, the name change), a striking limestone sliver, soars into the sky behind *Prometheus* and is indeed the art deco centerpiece of Rockefeller Center. Another of the Center's art deco masterworks is Radio City Music Hall ® at 50th Street and Avenue of the Americas.

A concourse of shops and restaurants on several levels lies beneath Rockefeller Center. It is a two-mile underground Main Street, stretching from Fifth Avenue to Avenue of the Americas.

Rockefeller Center covers 22 acres now, the result of expansion westward past Avenue of the Americas beginning in the 1950s. A number of skyscrapers were built — Time & Life, Exxon, McGraw-Hill, and 1211 Avenue of the Americas, among others.

There have been other changes in Rockefeller Center. In 1985 Columbia University sold the original 12 acres for $400 million to The Rockefeller Group. Rockefeller Center Properties, Inc., a real estate investment trust, was formed in 1985 to permit public investment in

---

The completed Rockefeller Center, circa 1939. View from Fifth Avenue, looking west. The former RCA Building (now the GE Building) rises behind the Channel Gardens. La Maison Française is on the left, and the British Empire Building is on the right. (Courtesy of Rockefeller Center © The Rockefeller Group)

Rockefeller Center. RCPI has the option to convert the loan into a 71.5 percent ownership interest in the year 2000.

In 1989 Mitsubishi Estate Company of Tokyo paid $846 million for 51 percent of The Rockefeller Group, the company that controls Rockefeller Center. (Mitsubishi did not buy Rockefeller Center outright, as many people think.)

Ownership may change, but it is quite likely that Rockefeller Center will remain just as it is — the finest urban complex of the 20th century, enhanced by Radio City Music Hall, the flower-bedecked Channel Gardens, the glorious Christmas tree, and the delightful skating rink.

The Adventure

I've never ice-skated (although this adventure has convinced me that it is never too late to learn), but I've often gazed down on Rockefeller Center skating rink, wondering if skating there is half as glamorous and exciting as it looks. And how does it feel to skate at Christmas, beneath the grand golden sculpture of *Prometheus* and the sparkling lights of the great Christmas tree?

The answers were waiting for me down on the skating rink.

★

"I was a competitive skater, and this was the first rink I ever skated in. It was beautiful. The people watching and encouraging me made me feel special, made me excel. For me to come back here as manager was realizing a dream." *Carol Olsen, manager*.

"For me it's a real high. It starts when I see the sheet of ice here. There is something thrilling about it — I don't know whether it's a combination of

Prometheus, midtown Manhattan and Fifth Avenue, but it is special ... I've skated in rinks all over the world, but this is still the best. And skating at night is a memorable experience." *C.A. Fine.*

"You've come to the right person because it's my first time here. It's fantastic — the music, and the lights, and the people. And being right in the center of the city makes me feel kind of like a movie star." *R. Roberts.*

"But you would be surprised that a high percentage of the people who come here — all ages — have never skated before. This rink is a perfect place to begin. Just pick a warm, sunny day, take your time, and hold onto the railing. And remember — we give lessons here and rent skates." *Carol Olsen, manager.*

"There is such exhilaration in being here. I look up and see the faces, some people waving at me, the flags fluttering all around, sometimes people taking my picture. You have to do it to understand. It's like being famous." *D. Weitz.*

"If you want to feel the real joy of Christmas, just come skate here under that magnificent tree. I love it at night with all the lights." *N. Johnson.*

I couldn't have described it better.

Rockefeller Center's first Christmas tree with a view of St. Patrick's Cathedral, 1931. (Courtesy of Rockefeller Center © The Rockefeller Group)

The Rink at Rockefeller Plaza
Between 49th & 50th Streets off Fifth Avenue
212-757-5731

Hours:
Mid-October through mid-April
Monday-Friday
9:00 a.m.-1:00 p.m., 1:30-5:30 p.m., 6:00-10:00 p.m.
Weekends
9:00 a.m.-noon, 12:30-3:00 p.m., 3:30-6:00 p.m., 6:30-10:00 p.m.

Admission:
- Adults, per session
  Monday-Thursday $7.00
  Friday-Sunday & holiday season $8.00
- Children under 12 & seniors
  Monday-Thursday $6.00
  Friday-Sunday & holiday season $6.50
- Skate rental per session $4.00
- Ice-skating lessons
  Private, per person, half-hour $19.00
  Semi-private, half-hour $26.00 per group of three

(Rates and schedule, current at book's publication, are subject to change. Call to verify.)

® Radio City Music Hall is a Registered Trademark of The Rockefeller Group, Inc.

RESTAURANTS

American Festival Cafe
20 West 50th Street
Next to the skating rink
212-246-6699

Breakfast:
Monday-Friday 7:30-10:30 a.m.
Weekends 9:00-10:30 a.m.
Brunch:
Saturday & Sunday 10:30 a.m.-3:30 p.m.
Lunch:
Weekdays 11:00 a.m.-3:30 p.m.
Dinner:
Weekdays 4:00-11:00 p.m.

- All major credit cards
- Reservations accepted except during the Christmas season

My friend Pat and I sat at a window table watching the skaters glide onto the ice. Sunshine streamed through the large windows. What a special memory! We were so close to the rink that we could see the sparkling eyes and the laughing faces of the skaters, young and old.

And this is why you will want to go to the American Festival Cafe in winter.

In spring and summer? Try to get an umbrella-shaded table located in the same skating rink area.

The same menu is offered for lunch and dinner, along with many daily specials on the dinner menu. Entrees vary from salads and sandwiches to fairly complicated dishes. Choices may include thick hamburgers with french fries; lobster pot pie; fettuccine with scallops, shrimp, and basil; and poached salmon with pepper relish.

Special thematic menus are offered several times a year. These food festivals have included New Orleans fare, a Texas barbeque, and a chocolate extravaganza.

Another way to enjoy the surroundings is to come for a drink after 4:00 p.m. The restaurant is less crowded, and you will be able to sit at a window table. And speaking of window tables, you must come early — 11:30 a.m. for lunch and before 6:00 p.m. for dinner, if you want to have a good shot at one.

Breakfast:
Averages $10.00 per person
Lunch & dinner:
Appetizers $5.75-$9.25
Entrees $12.95-$19.25

★

The Sea Grill
Rockefeller Center
18 West 49th Street
212-246-9201

Lunch:
Monday-Friday noon-2:45 p.m.
Dinner:
Monday-Saturday 5:00-10:45 p.m.
Pre-theatre dinner:
Monday-Saturday, beginning at 5:00 p.m. with last seating at 6:30 p.m.

• All major credit cards
• Reservations suggested

Here is another memorable way to watch the skaters glide across the rink in winter and have a delicious lunch or dinner outside during warm weather (beginning in May). The seafood dishes, which have an international flair, are getting rave reviews from customers, thanks to the head chef Seppi Renggli, who was formerly at The Four Seasons. And the setting? Elegant and sophisticated. Without a doubt, this restaurant has all the necessary ingredients for a superb New York City dining experience.

Lunch & dinner appetizers $8.25-$14.00
Lunch & dinner entrees $27.00 & up
Pre-theatre dinner $37.00 per person

D I R E C T I O N S

Subway:
• #1 to 50th Street
• #6 to 51st Street
• B, D, F, S to 47th-50th Streets
• E, F to Fifth Avenue
• N, R to 49th Street

Bus:
• M1, M2, M3, M4 (Fifth / Madison Avenues)
• M5 (Fifth Avenue / Avenue of the Americas / Riverside Drive)
• M6, M7 (Seventh Avenue / Broadway / Avenue of the Americas)
• M50 (49th / 50th Streets crosstown)

Car:
• FDR Drive, East 49th Street exit
• West Side Highway, West 57th Street exit

A wintertime view of the Channel Gardens and *Prometheus*. (Photograph © Jeffrey Jay Foxx, 1990)

The High-Kicking Rockettes®

Behind the footlights of Radio City Music Hall®

Above: The dazzling auditorium today. (Photograph © George Le Moine, 1988)

Left: A 1930s photograph of the great stage of the auditorium, showing the curved ceiling and Roxy's dramatic "sunrise" effect. (Courtesy of Radio City Music Hall Productions, Inc. Archives)

A Brief Look Back to 1932, Construction Year

America's future looked bleak on December 27, 1932 — Radio City Music Hall's grand opening night. This had been the worst year of the Great Depression, although President Herbert Hoover was still reassuring Americans that the economy was on the rise.

There were more than one million men out of work in New York City that year. If by sheer luck one of them did land a job, he knew that he would have to watch every penny because in 1932 the average pay was just about $16.00 a week. To be sure, many people in the country made even less. A construction worker could expect under eight cents an hour, clerks often drew $5.00 a week, and miners made about $11.00 a month.

Farmers were no better off, getting less than 25 cents a bushel for wheat, five cents a pound for cotton, two-and-a-half cents a pound for pork and beef, and 40 cents for 200 unblemished apples.

There were 82 bread lines and countless soup kitchens in New York City in

1932, feeding block-long lines of the hungry and dejected. The homeless paid a dime a night to sleep in miserable "flophouses," or they slept in Central Park under newspapers, contemptuously called "Hoover blankets."

In 1932 New York Governor Franklin Delano Roosevelt offered the electorate a "New Deal," and *Happy Days Are Here Again* played for the very first time at the Democratic Convention. After the general election that November, a deflated Herbert Hoover packed his bags and left the White House to the new Democratic President.

And in 1932 a two-hour escape from despair cost 25 cents for an adult ticket to the movies, 10 cents for a child. That was a lot of money during the Depression, but well worth it, especially when it meant having the grandest escape of them all — a golden time in a glamorous place — Radio City Music Hall.

The Tour

My son Mark glanced appreciatively around the immense foyer of Radio City Music Hall. "This is interesting — a kind of 1930s time warp!"

He was absolutely right, and for a good reason. On the brink of destruction in 1979, this handsome building was saved when it was declared an historic landmark. Of course, this meant that in terms of restoration all of its public areas had to be returned to the year 1932, when Radio City Music Hall was completed. Miles of fabric, wallpaper, and carpet were reproduced and installed, murals and mirrors restored, and metalwork replaced. Amazingly, the entire restoration was completed in one short month. It was 1932 once again, during the heyday of art deco design.

The gleaming red marble and gold-leafed Grand Foyer. (Photograph © George Le Moine, 1978)

"This is your chance to learn about art deco," I whispered to Mark. "You'll notice that the architecture and decorative objects here have a geometric simplicity. The style developed in the 1920s and evolved from many sources, among them cubism and art nouveau."

"This must be art deco then," Mark responded, studying the carpet. "It seems to be an Oriental carpet, but there are simple outlines of musical instruments hidden in the design. I can see an abstract guitar and a clarinet."

By that time a small group had gathered, and we joined them just as the guide was saying that the red marble Grand Foyer covers a city block, from 50th to 51st Streets, measuring 150 feet long, 60 feet wide, and a towering 60 feet high. The seemingly delicate crystal chandeliers suspended high above the crowd weigh two tons each. Everything is on a large scale here, he declared, from the king-size mural, depicting the elusive

search for the fountain of youth, which was painted as it lay stretched on a tennis court, to the vast expanse of ceiling, leafed in 24-karat gold. Even the six towering floor-to-ceiling mirrors were backed in gold instead of silver.

As we followed the young guide out of the Grand Foyer, we learned that Radio City Music Hall was the first building to go up in the Rockefeller Center complex. The foundation was laid in September 1931, and the theatre's opening night was December 27, 1932 — just a little over a year from start to finish, with a final cost of $7 million to $8 million.

Without a doubt Radio City Music Hall owes its glamour and style to two men. The first went by the name "Roxy."

John D. Rockefeller, Jr., chose S.L."Roxy" Rothafel as general director of the Music Hall and of the smaller RKO Roxy at 49th Street and Sixth Avenue. Roxy was also to be the "unofficial chief of architecture and construction," a position for which he was uniquely qualified.

Roxy had revolutionized the entertainment industry beginning in 1908 with such innovative ideas as live radio broadcasts of stage shows, as well as the mixed bill, which combined movies with vaudeville acts, live orchestra music, dancers, imaginative lighting, unusual mechanical techniques — and most of all, a megadose of glitz and glitter. Roxy became *the expert* called in by movie theatre owners who had sagging box-office receipts, because Roxy could put a theatre "in the black" in short order. By

The Rockefeller Center construction site, 1932. Radio City Music Hall was the first building to go up and the first to open on December 27, 1932. (Courtesy of Rockefeller Center © The Rockefeller Group)

1927 Roxy was so famous that when he was hired to manage a dazzling new theatre in New York City, it was named the Roxy Theatre and featured the precision dancers, the Roxyettes, (who later moved to Radio City Music Hall with Roxy, becoming the world-famous Rockettes).

Roxy masterminded the design for Radio City Music Hall. He planned the soaring inner spaces, including the dramatic auditorium with its "sunrise" effect, achieved through unusual lighting techniques. From making decisions about innovative stage machinery to staging the great shows, Roxy had the final say.

However, the subtle elegance of the Music Hall's interior decoration was the work of a talented 35-year-old designer, Donald Deskey, who admired the fresh, clean lines of art deco. Deskey decorated the huge interior spaces, including the carpets, draperies, the sweeping stairways, and the furniture. He commissioned the murals as well. Moreover, he accomplished everything in less than a year and managed to keep the final cost at about $50,000.

We entered Roxy's famous auditorium, a gigantic barrel with a ceiling of overlapping arches, each one wider than the last. We were told that an illusion of sunbeams radiating from the golden "sun" of the stage is created when lights are played across the arches. Many effects are possible, even a brilliant rainbow.

The 60-foot-high proscenium arch framing the stage is hung with a shimmering golden curtain weighing three tons and woven from 4,000 yards of fabric, its graceful movement controlled by 13 powerful motors.

As the group settled into a few of the 5,874 plush seats installed in the orchestra section and three mezzanines, the guide explained that the auditorium is nearly a block wide, with a ceiling reaching 190 feet at its highest point. The stage is 144 feet wide and 66 feet deep.

Two huge Wurlitzer organs provide music for the 1.8 million cubic feet of space. They have so many pipes, ranging in size from 32 feet high to the size of a pencil, that eight rooms are required to house all of them.

As we watched and listened, a crew of men swarmed over the mammoth stage, busily working on the next extravaganza, a Walt Disney production on ice. The rink was already in place, as big as a pond, and it took up just a portion of the immense space. Men darted like ants, pulling props here, pushing ladders there.

"How do they get everything on and off that stage?" somebody in the front row asked.

"Good question," the guide responded. "There is a revolving turntable 43 feet in diameter. Three elevators are set into it, and they move props and people around the stage, as well as lift them to various levels or whisk them out of sight to the sub-basement 27 feet below the stage. A fourth elevator lifts the whole orchestra from the sub-basement to stage level. You'll be able to see more of the mechanics when we visit the area below the stage. But before we do that, let's go up on this famous stage so you can feel what it's like to be a Radio City Music Hall star!"

That we did. We stepped into the bright halo of stage lights. We peered into the colossal auditorium with its ocean of seats. We all pretended for just a few minutes that the golden curtain had risen just for us. That experience alone was worth the price of the tour!

Next stop? Donald Deskey's Grand Lounge, located beneath the Grand Foyer and connected by two sweeping stairways with bronze railings. The 200-foot-long,

S.L. "Roxy" Rothafel, seated in the auditorium of Radio City Music Hall, his ever-present megaphone by his side. (Courtesy of Radio City Music Hall Productions, Inc.®Archives)

80-foot-wide lounge is a design in diamonds: A forest of columns sparkles with mirrored diamond prisms; the expanse of carpet is a woven pattern of intersecting diamonds; countless diamonds march across the ceiling, all studded with lights. Diamonds and more diamonds.

To soften these numerous angular forms, Deskey designed bright plastic sofas and chairs and commissioned three large cast-aluminum sculptures depicting well-rounded female nudes. (Roxy tried unsuccessfully to have the rather demure figures banned from the theatre — perhaps as a publicity stunt. The incident received wide press coverage just before the 1932 opening.)

It might seem unusual to visit bathrooms on a tour, but these are delightful examples of Deskey's art deco design. A ladies' powder room is painted with amusing scenes tracing the history of cosmetics from Eve to the 1920s flappers.

The smoking room in the men's lounge is covered with a brown-and-white wall covering entitled "Nicotine," an abstract design of pipes, cigars, cigarettes, and tobacco leaves. Art deco touches are everywhere, from the round mirrors and checkerboard tile floors to the plastic stools in bright Crayola colors.

True to his word, our guide led us next to the hydraulic system, cradled in a mammoth pit 27 feet below the stage. We saw one of the 70-foot-long elevators comprising a section of the giant turntable on the stage. The elevator was supported by a pair of hydraulic pistons, giving it the capacity to lift nearly 27 tons of props or a whole troop of performers.

Next stop? The eighth floor to see the rehearsal hall used by the Rockettes since 1932 and still used today. By the way, some say that Roxy's ghost sometimes roams this floor, checking on the dancers he made famous!

"This is what I came to see," confided a long-legged teen-age girl to no one in particular, as we wound through a maze of hallways and entered the Rockettes' rehearsal hall. We clattered across the wooden floor, casting side glances in a long stretch of mirror.

People are usually very curious about the Rockettes. Are they really exactly the same height? Where are all the gorgeous costumes made? (To create the illusion of equal heights, shorter dancers wear higher hats, and skirt hems are all the same distance from the floor — just one of the secrets revealed on the tour!)

We saw the workroom in which those hats and the glamorous costumes are created, a topsy-turvy room full of dress forms, outstretched patterns, and bolts of cloth. Vintage 1932 sewing machines are still used today, as the seamstresses feel these machines are superior to new ones.

*

By the end of the tour, we had explored the celebrated Music Hall from sub-basement to the loftiest mezzanine tiers. From the director's booth we had peered at the great stage 190 feet below. We had actually stood at eye level with the foyer's gleaming gold-leaf ceiling, just a few feet from the dangling crystal and steel chandeliers — 29-foot-long glittering cylinders. Finally the group had trooped downstairs, laughing and chatting, heels clattering, leaving 1932 and the darkened Music Hall empty and quiet once again.

The glamorous art deco ladies' lounge, located on the first mezzanine level. Designed by Donald Deskey. (Photograph © George Le Moine, 1979)

264

Radio City Music Hall
1260 Avenue of the Americas at 50th Street
New York, NY 10020

Telephone:
212-632-4000 Ask for tour desk
212-632-4210 Group tour information
212-632-4000 Current productions

Throughout the year there is a great variety of entertainment on the Music Hall stage, from *The Magnificent Christmas Spectacular*, which features the Rockettes and runs from November 15-January 6 with four shows daily, to numerous concerts. (Bill Cosby, Madonna, Eddie Murphy, and Sting have played here.) Try to combine your tour with a production to make this adventure complete.

Tour Hours:
Tours are given every hour. During busy times they are offered more frequently, usually every half-hour. (Call to check.)
    Monday-Saturday 10:15 a.m.-4:45 p.m.
    Sunday 11:15 a.m.-4:45 p.m.

Admission:
• $6.50 per person for tour

Music Hall Box Office Hours:
Monday-Saturday 10:00 a.m.-8:00 p.m.
Sunday 11:00 a.m.-8:00 p.m.

Ticket Information: 212-307-7171

Parking:
Discount parking for evening and Sunday performances at the Rockefeller Center lot at 49th Street between Fifth Avenue and Avenue of the Americas.

George A. Le Moine, whose photographs of Radio City Music Hall interiors are included in this chapter, is one of those rare artists with a camera. His work has been exhibited in New York museums and has appeared in magazines worldwide.

For many years Le Moine has worked at Radio City Music Hall and has taken countless splendid photographs of the building, many of which appear in Music Hall production programs.

Additional Sights

GE (formerly RCA) Building
1250 Avenue of the Americas, a short walk from Radio City Music Hall. The art-deco mosaic mural above the entrance is striking. ABC tours are offered. (Information and ticket booths are located on the ground floor, in the center of the building.) There are several inexpensive restaurants in the building.

Whitney Museum of American Art at Equitable Center
787 Seventh Avenue at 51st Street
212-554-1113

Hours:
Monday-Friday 11:00 a.m.-6:00 p.m.
Thursday 11:00 a.m.-7:30 p.m.
Saturday noon-5:00 p.m.

Admission: Free

This bright, airy extension of the Whitney Museum of American Art can be enjoyed in less than an hour. It is worth a trip just to see the four-story-high mural painting by Roy Lichtenstein!

R E S T A U R A N T S

Lattanzi

361 West 46th Street
Between Eighth & Ninth Avenues
212-315-0980

Lunch:
  Monday-Friday noon-2:00 p.m.
Dinner:
  Monday & Tuesday 5:00-10:00 p.m.
  Wednesday & Thursday 5:00-11:00 p.m.
  Friday & Saturday 5:30 p.m.-midnight

Closed Sunday

• American Express
• Reservations suggested
• Busy at lunch & before theatre

This small, brick-walled restaurant has a friendly, relaxed atmosphere with excellent service and delicious food. Among the appetizers are half-orders of pasta: linguini with a spicy white clam sauce; a light capellini primavera with bright ribbons of vegetables; and a richly satisfying bucatini amatriciana with tomato, tangy Italian bacon, and onion. Salads are well-seasoned, and mussels in tomato broth are flavorful.

Main courses include red snapper prepared with tomatoes, onions, peppers, and garlic, and also with vinegar and raisins — both delicious; veal chops were grilled perfectly, and the grilled chicken was tender and moist. Pasta dishes are also available as main courses — always a sure bet.

Lattanzi also offers a special Roman-Jewish menu after 8:00 p.m. — many unusual and creative dishes.

Lunch:
  From 15-20 percent less than dinner menu
Dinner:
  Appetizers $5.95-$11.95
  Entrees $14.95-$23.95
  Pasta around $13.95

The Rainbow Room

30 Rockefeller Plaza, 65th Floor
212-632-5000

Brunch:
  Sunday noon-2:30 p.m.
Dinner:
  Tuesday-Thursday 5:30 p.m.-1:00 a.m.
  Friday & Saturday 5:30 p.m.-2:00 a.m.
  Sunday 5:00-midnight

If you've ever fantasized about going back in time to the soignée 1930s, dinner and dancing at the Rainbow Room is your chance. There isn't another experience in New York City quite like it.

The Rainbow Room has just been restored to its former art deco elegance — to the tune of $20 million. The result is a smart room with aubergine and mirrored walls, forest-green carpeting, and round tables arranged on brass-railed tiers so that every table enjoys a spectacular view of New York City's tapestry of lights. And don't forget the marvelous dance-band music and the revolving dance floor; the waiters in pink, pale blue, and mint green tailcoats with satin lapels and velvet collars; and hostesses in ankle-length tapered skirts and bolero jackets. What glamour! What fun!

The surprise is that the Rainbow Room is so intimate in feeling — not as large as you might imagine. There is a comfortable feeling imparted by the 1930s architecture, which must be catching, because everyone is friendly and relaxed, from the maitre d' to the waiters.

Appetizers we've tried: crisp salads composed of wild greens and garden flowers, a spicy crab cake with warm tomato vinaigrette, chilled cream of sorrel soup, and truffled pâté of veal.

Main courses may include a nice crisp duckling with kumquats; breast of pheasant stuffed with vegetables in a port wine sauce; grilled double lamb chops; a fricassee of scallops, shrimp, and lobster on fresh pasta; and boned quail stuffed with fois gras.

As for desserts, choices have included rhubarb and strawberry pie with candied-ginger whipped cream, a frozen hazelnut souffle with hot chocolate sauce inside, and a nice chocolate fudge cake.

Sunday brunch $34.50
Fixed price pre-theatre dinner $38.50
Dinner:
    Appetizers $10.00-$16.00
    Entrees $26.00-$42.00

Note: There is an additional $15.00 per person entertainment charge for dinner and dancing in the Rainbow Room, but it does not apply to the pre-theatre dinner.

★

Rainbow Promenade
30 Rockefeller Plaza, 65th Floor
212-632-5000

Monday-Friday 3:00 p.m.-1:00 a.m.
Saturday noon-1:00 a.m.
Sunday noon-11:00 p.m.

• "Little Meals" served ($8.00-$25.00)

★

Rainbow and Stars
30 Rockefeller Plaza, 65th Floor
212-632-5000

In the mood for dinner at a smart cabaret? Try *Rainbow and Stars*, which also offers a beautiful 65th-floor view overlooking Central Park. 30 Rockefeller Plaza, 65th floor

Tuesday-Saturday two seatings:
• 7:00 p.m. dinner & 9:00 p.m. show
• 10:30 p.m. supper & 11:15 p.m. show

$35.00 cover charge plus an a la carte menu, about $100-$125 per person

Information for Rainbow Restaurants
• General Information: 212-632-5100
• Reservations: 212-632-5000
• Parking: 49th Street between Fifth Avenue & Avenue of the Americas

• American Express
• Reservations necessary

★

The Carnegie Delicatessen
854 Seventh Avenue at 55th Street
212-757-2245

Daily 6:00 a.m.-4:00 a.m.

• No credit cards
• No reservations

Humorous, informal, noisy, festive — the Carnegie Deli is all of these.

This is a New York experience. You wait in line while waiters scurry around you lugging mouthwatering, gigantic sandwiches to the boisterous crowd. You sit at a little table jammed against three others — so close that there's a lot of listening to everybody else. Is it interesting? You bet it is! On one side of us two choreographers were planning a big production number for a Broadway musical. On the other side a famous movie critic was shooting the breeze with some writer friends.

Try a corned beef or pastrami sandwich on rye — great mounds of tender, juicy meat overflowing onto the plate, $8.45. And don't leave without a big slab of velvety rich cheese-cake, $4.75. Unless you are ravenous, two can share. A sandwich, coleslaw, and coffee or tea total about $12.00 at lunch or dinner. The Carnegie Deli also serves good breakfasts for about $6.00.

Cafe Cielo

881 Eighth Avenue
Between 52nd and 53rd Streets
212-246-9555

Brunch:
    Sunday noon-4:00 p.m.
Lunch:
    Monday-Friday noon-3:00 p.m.
Dinner:
    Monday-Thursday 5:00-10:30 p.m.
    Friday & Saturday 5:00-11:30 p.m.
    Sunday 5:00-10:00 p.m.

• All major credit cards

What a nice surprise it is to find this Northern Italian restaurant in the theatre district. Sleek and understated, this restaurant exudes good cheer and happy times and is popular with the Broadway and music world, as well as with New York politicians — and with good reason — the food is good, and the atmosphere is inviting.

I've tried the salad made with arugula, endive, and roasted pine nuts in a tangy lemon-lime vinaigrette — fresh and crisp. A chicken broth with eggs, spinach, and parmesan cheese was light and tasty. Rigatoni in a light, creamy tomato sauce spiked with basil and capers was a very nice beginning.

Entrees include red snapper with dilled mustard sauce; tortellini filled with a light seafood mousse, garnished with shrimp and bathed in a golden broth; well-prepared grilled swordfish with olives, capers, tomatoes, garlic, and oregano; and scallops with prosciutto and sage, gently bathed in a lively marsala wine sauce. There are several good pizza choices as well.

Lunch & dinner:
    Appetizers $5.50-$11.00
    Entrees $10.50-$24.00

La Reserve

4 West 49th Street
212-247-2993

Lunch:
    Monday-Friday noon-3:00 p.m.
Dinner:
    Monday-Thursday 6:45-10:30 p.m.
    Friday & Saturday 6:45-11:00 p.m.
Pre-theatre dinner:
    Monday-Saturday 5:30-6:45 p.m.

• All major credit cards
• Reservations suggested

La Reserve has a dignity, courtesy and low-key comfort found in fine restaurants that have maintained high standards for a long time.

The prix-fixe lunch offers such appetizers as tangy avocado vinaigrette, a sprightly and colorful vegetable pâté; entrees such as Dover sole with mustard and chive sauce; Black Angus beef with madeira sauce (deliciously juicy in the deep, rich sauce); and grilled red snapper with tomato, garlic, and herbs (perfectly prepared with a delicately spicy flavor). Desserts were nicely prepared: chocolate or white mousse with a raspberry sauce, various delicious cakes, and a delightful pineapple souffle.

Offerings on the dinner menu include a velvety rich lobster soup with morel mushrooms, succulent duck with ginger, a hearty loin of venison, and a crispy roast chicken with forest mushrooms. There is a "menu gastronomique" of nightly chef's specials.

Prix-fixe lunch $31.00
Pre-theatre dinner $40.00
Prix-fixe dinner $49.00 (after 7:00 p.m.)

D I R E C T I O N S

See The Rink at Rockefeller Plaza chapter.

Steel King of the Gilded Age, Henry Clay Frick

A tour of The Frick Collection

The History

 enry Clay Frick was born in 1849 in West Overton, Pennsylvania, a farming community about 50 miles from Pittsburgh. Clay, the son of a farmer and the grandson of a prosperous miller and whiskey distiller, spent his early years working on his father's farm and attending several small country schools. Although the boy made average grades, excelling only in math, he was an able child with a determination to succeed in business, even confiding to his friends that he intended to become a millionaire.

When Clay reached the age of 12, his formal education all but ended, totaling approximately 11 months during his teenage years. The boy began the first of a series of clerking jobs when he was 13 years old, doing well at sales, although his interest lay in bookkeeping. At last his grandfather, whom he greatly admired, offered 19-year-old Clay the prized position of chief bookkeeper in the family distillery at a salary of $1,000 a year.

Above: Residence of Henry Clay Frick. Designed by Thomas Hastings and completed in 1914. After Mrs. Frick's death in 1931, the mansion was partially remodeled, and extensions were made before opening to the public in 1935. A further extension was completed in 1977. This photograph was probably taken shortly after completion of the mansion in 1914. (Courtesy of Museum of the City of New York)

Right: The Frick Collection today, the former residence of Henry Clay Frick. (Photograph © Jeffrey Jay Foxx, 1990)

Frick was at last moving toward the success he had envisioned as a child.

However, there was one aspect of Clay's life over which he had little control. He was handicapped by a recurring, painful illness, thought to be inflammatory rheumatism or "chronic indigestion," which plagued his early years and nearly took his life when he was 25. Frick managed to regain his health after that critical seven-week illness — a fortunate outcome, as the young man had already begun to build his empire.

As a matter of fact, by the time Frick was 21 years old, he had set the course for his life. With three partners, two of whom were cousins, Clay entered into the coal mining and coke industry, forming Frick & Co.*

After purchasing coal lands, the partners were faced with the problem of acquiring additional working capital to build coke ovens. In 1871 Frick boarded a train to Pittsburgh and paid a call on powerful Judge Mellon of The Mellon Bank. Mellon must have believed the coking process could become an invaluable and lucrative part of the steel industry, because he quickly agreed to lend Frick & Co. $10,000 with which to buy 50 coke ovens, subsequently agreeing to a further loan of $10,000.

Frick & Co. prospered, even surviving the industrial crisis that followed the Panic of 1873 (although Frick recalled nearly 50 years later that it had been "an awful time"). By 1879 the company owned more than 2,000 acres of promising coal lands, with an expectation of having more than 1,000 coke ovens by the following year. On December 19, 1879, Frick's 30th birthday, he had another

reason to celebrate: He had fulfilled his ambition to become a millionaire.

In 1881 32-year-old Clay Frick was introduced to beautiful Adelaide Howard Childs, a member of a distinguished Pittsburgh family. Within three months they were engaged, and three months later they were married. Not long afterward the couple moved into their new home, Clayton, which was to remain their permanent residence in Pittsburgh, and Frick gradually began to fill the gracious house with works of art.

During the 1880's Frick's wealth, influence, and power increased rapidly. A business alliance formed with Andrew Carnegie and his brother Thomas led to a reorganization of Frick & Co., creating H.C. Frick Coke Company in 1882, in which the Carnegies ultimately acquired 50 percent ownership. Great expansion was on the horizon for the profitable company, which owned more than 8,000 acres of coal lands and approximately 3,000 ovens.

In 1889 Carnegie chose 40-year-old Frick as "The Man" to reorganize Carnegie Brothers & Co. As chairman, Frick proved he was indeed the right man, engineering in 1890 the acquisition of a formidable competitor, Duquesne Steel Works.

In 1891 Frick became chairman of the newly formed Carnegie Steel Company, and in the years that followed, he maintained an uneasy and often quarrelsome alliance with Andrew Carnegie. Through Frick's adroit management, the remaining essential links in the steel industry were added to the Carnegie chain. Although Carnegie balked, Frick arranged for the acquisition of iron ore mines in the Lake Superior region. Since transportation for the ore was needed, a decrepit railroad was overhauled, and a fleet of steamers was bought to carry the tons of ore to the

*Coke, the fuel used in the manufacture of steel, is produced by the distillation of coal in ovens.

steel mills. Under Frick's able leadership, Carnegie Steel Company became an industrial colossus, owning all facilities needed for steel production.

It should be noted that although Frick was deeply involved in business matters as chairman of Carnegie Steel Company during the 1890s, his interest in art never waned. Between 1895 and 1900 Frick acquired a work of art approximately every month.

During the late 19th century Frick was faced with new problems when union strikes flared. Finally one of these strikes blazed into riots against the Carnegie Steel Company. It was during these riots that 43-year-old Frick was nearly assassinated in 1892. A crazed Russian anarchist entered the chairman's office in Pittsburgh, fired two shots into Frick's neck, then stabbed him three times. Somehow Frick survived the attack, and eventually he recovered completely.

In 1900 Frick's long partnership with Carnegie ended in a bitter argument. During the angry exchange, Carnegie made it quite clear that he had the power to force Frick to relinquish his one-sixth interest in Carnegie Steel, at a price determined at "book value" by the company, an amount much lower than the true value. The case was finally settled out of court, and Frick received $15 million, although he had been ousted as chairman of both Carnegie Steel Company and H.C. Frick Coke Company. The two men never spoke to each other again from the day of the argument in 1900 until their deaths in the same year, 1919.

Approximately 16 months after Frick was forced out as chairman of the companies he had served for so many years, Carnegie's giant corporation was absorbed by J. Pierpont Morgan's United States Steel Corporation. Shortly after the formation of the gigantic steel trust, Frick

Henry Clay Frick (1849-1919).
(Courtesy of Museum of the City of New York)

was elected to the board of directors, a powerful position he held until his death.

After the turn of the century, Frick's interest in collecting began to develop a new focus when he visited the Wallace Collection in London, an 1894 bequest to the British nation. Frick envisioned creating a similar museum as a gift to the American public — paintings, furniture, and other works of art placed in the personal setting of his own home.

In 1914 the Frick mansion on 70th Street and Fifth Avenue was completed, and the Fricks moved from the residence they had leased for nine years, the former

Vanderbilt mansion at 640 Fifth Avenue. Paintings were hung and the objects placed in their final home.

Frick received great pleasure from seeing his collection displayed in this beautiful setting, and he would often tip-toe downstairs late at night to walk quietly through the rooms. This mansion and these splendid works of art were to become a monument to Henry Clay Frick, a man who fulfilled his lifelong dream of success and shared that dream with the American people.

The Tour

"You know, I believe the Frick is my favorite museum," my sister-in-law Earlene confided softly. We had stopped to gaze at The Frick Collection's small garden designed by the noted landscape designer, Russell Page. It was June, and the flower beds overflowed with pink caladiums; a wreath of waterlilies floated in the square reflecting pool.

We left the noise and heat of the city streets as we climbed the steps and entered the museum. It was cool and quiet there, a respite from our hectic activities. From the Entrance Hall we passed through the East Vestibule to the South Hall. We stopped there, delighted

View of the grand staircase. At left: French neoclassical longcase regulator clock (1767), veneered with tulipwood and kingwood and decorated with gilt-bronze mounts; *Mother and Children* (circa 1875), Pierre-Auguste Renoir. On landing: American Aeolian pipe organ. The organ screen was designed by Eugene W. Mason of Carrière and Hastings and installed in 1914. (Copyright The Frick Collection, New York)

as always by the wonderful pictures.

Among the canvases were two remarkable paintings by Jan Vermeer (1632-1675), *Officer and Laughing Girl* (circa 1655-1660) and *Girl Interrupted at her Music* (circa 1660), both suffused with white light. There was a saucy portrait of 27-year-old Marie-Jeanne Boucher, dressed in a gown of white taffeta, pink ribbons and lace, painted in 1743 by her husband François Boucher (1703-1770), who in 1765 would be appointed *Premier Peintre* to Louis XV. Another splendid work hung on a wall near the grand staircase: a charming *Mother and Children*, painted in the 1870s by Pierre-Auguste Renoir (1841-1919) and considered one of his masterpieces.

Crossing the East Vestibule, we passed through the Anteroom and entered the Boucher Room. The eight panels, *The Arts and Sciences*, were painted by Boucher about 1752 for the beautiful mistress of Louis XV, Madame de Pompadour, and installed at Château de Crécy near Chartres. The panels depict children pursuing such adult interests and occupations as poetry, astronomy, hunting, chemistry, and architecture — all of which were interests of the accomplished marquise. The panels were removed sometime before the château was destroyed in 1830.

We gazed a moment at the posthumous watercolor portrait of Mrs. Frick, imagining how much she must have enjoyed having these Boucher panels in her second-floor boudoir in which they were formerly installed. We also took a few minutes to admire the Vincennes and Sèvres porcelains in the Boucher Room, discussing Madame de Pompadour's role in starting the manufactory at Vincennes and afterward at Sèvres.

We entered the inviting dining room, brightened with vases of colorful summer flowers. On one wall was Thomas Gainsborough's (1727-1788) romantic masterpiece *The Mall in St. James's Park* (probably 1783), a graceful composition of strolling Londoners, including ladies of fashion and their smart military escorts. An amusing note: At least one figure lurking in the background is purportedly a gravekeeper!

Among the six 18th-century English portraits lining the walls is a dashing *General John Burgoyne*, painted about 1766 by Sir Joshua Reynolds (1723-1792). General Burgoyne surrendered to General Horatio Gates at Saratoga, New York, in 1777 during the Revolutionary War. This battle was the turning point of the war, as France was convinced the patriots could win and signed a treaty of alliance with America.

Another interesting Gainsborough portrait, painted about 1782, is of *Grace Dalrymple Elliott*, who was considered a great beauty, although quite free with her charms. After her marriage at the age of 17 to wealthy physician John (later Sir John) Elliott, 18 years her senior, Mrs. Elliott took a number of lovers. Her disenchanted husband divorced her after five years of marriage, after which she became the mistress of the Earl of Cholmondeley, then of the Prince of Wales (who, she claimed, fathered her daughter), and later, of the Duc d'Orleans.

Miss Mary Edwards, bejeweled and dressed in a scarlet damask gown, was painted in 1742 by William Hogarth (1697-1764). Mary Edwards was one of the wealthiest women of her day, having had control of a great estate from her 24th year. Strong and self-assured, she decided to take steps to annul her marriage, as her profligate husband was recklessly going through her fortune. Her decision was a courageous one for the time, because after the annulment their only son

was illegitimate in the eyes of the law and society. Miss Edwards died at 38, leaving her estate to her son.

★

Adjacent to the dining room is the West Vestibule, in which we paused to look at Boucher's *The Four Seasons*, completed by the artist for Madame de Pompadour in 1755. The ivory-skinned coquettes in the four panels, *Spring, Summer, Autumn*, and *Winter* resemble Madame Boucher, as did many of the women in Boucher's paintings by the mid-1750s.

★

We entered the Fragonard Room, named for the series of panels installed there: *The Progress of Love*, depicting love from the chase to the conquest, painted by Jean-Honoré Fragonard. These masterpieces of rococo art were bought by Frick from the estate of Pierpont Morgan.

Four large panels in the series, *The Pursuit, The Meeting, The Lover Crowned*, and *Love Letters*, were commissioned by Madame du Barry, the elegant, mercurial mistress of Louis XV. Fragonard painted the panels between 1771 and 1773 for Madame du Barry's chateau at Louveciennes, overlooking the Seine west of Paris.

The panels, which were installed in the chateau's garden dining pavilion, were for some reason rejected by Madame du Barry, perhaps because she felt the rococo style was unfashionable. The panels were returned to Fragonard, who kept them for 18 years, finally installing them in 1790 in the home of his cousin Alexandre Maubert in Grasse. Fragonard subsequently completed the salon with two large panels, four narrow hollyhock panels, and four overdoors.

The furnishings and porcelains in the Fragonard Room are quite beautiful. Among the pieces: a French commode with fine pictorial marquetry, completed in 1769 for the bedroom of Madame Victoire, the daughter of Louis XV; a suite consisting of two sofas and *fauteuils* (circa 1760-1765), covered with Beauvais tapestry depicting pastoral scenes; a small French mechanical reading and writing table, made about 1781, inset with dainty blossom-sprinkled, pink-banded Sèvres porcelain plaques; a small gilt-bronze tripod table, (circa 1783), inset with exquisite Sèvres porcelain floral plaques, the top plaque depicting a beribboned basket holding roses, trailing morning glories, and other summer flowers — considered a masterpiece of the Louis XVI period; and a rare Sèvres porcelain potpourri container in the shape of a masted ship, with two matching vases (circa 1759).

★

Among the splendid works of art in the adjacent Living Hall are two oil paintings on oak panels by Hans Holbein the Younger (1497/1498-1543), court painter to Henry VIII. *Sir Thomas More,* painted in 1527, depicts the eminent statesman who held among other offices that of Speaker of the House of Commons and later of Lord Chancellor to Henry VIII. Sir Thomas More wears a favorite gold chain around his shoulders, an emblem of service to the king, which he wore constantly. It is believed that the chain was removed for the last time when More was sent to the tower in 1534 and beheaded on July 6, 1535, because he opposed the king's antipapal policies.

The other oil portrait by Holbein (circa 1532-1533), portrays Thomas Cromwell when he was Henry VIII's Master of the Jewels. The powerful, sinister Cromwell, who was responsible for Sir Thomas More's execution, later served as Lord Great Chamberlain to Henry VIII, an office he lost a year later (in 1540), when he was beheaded.

Other paintings in the Living Hall include El Greco's *St. Jerome*, painted between 1590 and 1600; a portrait of the influential Italian writer *Pietro Aretino,* painted about 1550 by Titian (1490-1576); Titian's sensitively rendered *Portrait of a Man in a Red Cap*, completed about 1516; and *St. Francis in the Desert* (circa 1480), a masterpiece painted by Giovanni Bellini (1430-1516), under whom Titian studied.

Among the noteworthy works of decorative art in this gallery are numerous bronze sculptures and porcelains.

★

In the Library we immediately felt the presence of distinguished Henry Clay Frick, whose 1943 posthumous portrait by J.C. Johansen (1876-1964) hangs above the mantlepiece, a gift from the Frick's daughter, Helen Clay Frick.

Among the 18th- and 19th-century paintings hanging in the paneled Library is a lyrical *Lady Hamilton as 'Nature'*, painted in 1782 by the popular English portraitist George Romney (1734-1802). Daughter of a blacksmith, the beautiful and eccentric Emma Lyon was mistress, then wife, of Sir William Hamilton, British Ambassador to Naples. After meeting Admiral Horatio Nelson in 1793, she became his mistress as well until Nelson's death in 1805. Although both Hamilton (who died in 1803) and Nelson left money to Emma in their wills, she spent it recklessly, finally drifting into poverty. She spent a year in debtor's prison, from which she escaped in 1813, two years before her death.

The sparkling 1827 portrait *Julia, Lady Peel* reveals a lively, intelligent woman whose face is framed by a jaunty hat with scarlet plumage. Her portrait was painted by Sir Thomas Lawrence (1769-1830), president of the Royal Academy and celebrated portraitist in Europe and England.

Julia was married in 1820 to Sir Robert Peel, who later became Prime Minister, a love match that endured until his death in 1850. Lady Peel died in 1859. This portrait hung in the Peel's country estate in Staffordshire until about 1896 when it was sold by the third baronet, Sir Robert Peel.

Other noteworthy paintings in the Library are portraits by Gainsborough, Reynolds, and Raeburn, and a 1795-1796 portrait of George Washington by Gilbert Stuart (1755-1828). In addition, there are landscape paintings by John Constable (1776-1837) and Joseph Mallord William Turner (1775-1851).

★

The North Hall, which adjoins the Library, is another intimate gallery of paintings, among them a dazzling 1845 portrait, *Comtesse d'Haussonville,* by Jean-Auguste-Dominique Ingres (1780-1867). The thoughtful countess (1818-1882) faces the viewer, hand to her chin. Her blue silk taffeta gown almost seems to rustle in the silent hall. The silken sheen of her red satin hair ribbon and the milky glow of her skin are reflected in the mirror behind her. The countess was an accomplished writer, whose published works included a biography of Byron.

★

The large West Gallery is lined with numerous superb works of art, far too many to describe in this chapter. I offer some of my favorite paintings:

Among canvases by Rembrandt Harmensz van Rijn (1606-1669), is the powerful and brooding *Self-Portrait* of 1658, one of 60 self-portraits, this one painted when 52-year-old Rembrandt was ill and bankrupt (although the artist's financial situation improved after 1660, allowing him to live out his days rather comfortably). Another Rembrandt painting is of pensive, world-weary Dutch merchant-trader *Nicolaes Ruts*, clad in luxurious furs — perhaps symbolizing his trade with Russia — and holding a sheet of paper whose message has been blurred except for the date 1631, the year in which the portrait was painted.

There are marvelously robust paintings by Hans Hals (1581/1585-1666), who worked in Haarlem, Holland. Canny wisdom marks the gaze of the prosperous-looking subject in *Portrait of an Elderly Man* (circa 1627-1630), his paunch softened by the rich folds of his velvet suit; while in *Portrait of a Painter* (circa 1650-1655), Hals' subject leans on his chair back, captivating the viewer with his direct, nonchalant gaze. His sophisticated pose is heightened by the cloak casually thrown over one shoulder.

There is a large, remarkably beautiful Vermeer, *Mistress and Maid* (circa 1665-1670), which freezes forever a moment of reflection — or is it concern? The mistress, dressed in a sumptuous sable-trimmed yellow garment, her ears, hair, and neck ornamented with pearls, looks up from a letter she is writing. The mistress, the maid, and the note held by the maid are bathed in shimmering light. (This was the last painting purchased by

278

Frick before his death in 1919.)

King Philip IV of Spain was painted by Velázquez (1599-1660), court painter and friend to the king. This 1644 painting, which portrays the king dressed in the elegant garments he wore during a victorious battle against the French, was painted immediately after the victory. However, as the portrait reveals in the king's tentative, sidelong glance, Philip IV was a weak, ineffective ruler, whose chief success was attained in his patronage of the arts.

Other outstanding works of art in the West Gallery include paintings by Corot, Van Dyck, Turner, Constable, Veronese, David, Cuyp, Goya, as well as works by El Greco, La Tour, Hobbema, Bronzino, and Ruisdael.

The Library. From right: *Mortlake Terrace: Early Summer Morning* (1826), Joseph Mallord William Turner; *Henry Clay Frick*, posthumous portrait, (1943), John C. Johansen; *Fishing Boats Entering Calais Harbor* (circa 1803), Joseph Mallord William Turner; *Lady Taylor* (circa 1780), Sir Joshua Reynolds; and *Salisbury Cathedral from the Bishop's Garden* (1826), John Constable. (Copyright The Frick Collection, New York)

The West Gallery holds a number of bronze sculptures and other works of decorative art, including eight walnut Italian Renaissance cassoni, which were used as storage chests.

★

The adjacent Enamel Room is a small paneled coffer holding enamels crafted in Limoges, France, between approximately 1500 and 1650, bought from the estate of J. Pierpont Morgan in 1916. Resembling liquefied jewels, the vibrant colors of the enamels seem to glow in the light of the two large display cabinets.

Notable Italian sculptures and paintings dating from the 14th and 15th centuries are displayed in this room.

★

We entered the East Gallery after passing through a graceful Oval Room (containing four large canvases — two by Sir Anthony Van Dyck and two by Thomas Gainsborough).

Of four large canvases by American artist James Abbott McNeill Whistler (1834-1903) lining the East Gallery walls, there is a poetic portrait of *Mrs. Frederick R. Leyland*, painted between 1872-1873.

The West Gallery. Paintings clearly visible in this view, from right: *The Education of the Virgin* (circa 1650), attributed to Étienne de la Tour; *Portrait of a Man* (circa 1660), Frans Hals. At far left: *Allegory of Wisdom and Strength* (circa 1580), Paolo Veronese. On the 17th-century Herat carpet stands an Italian Renaissance table. Displayed on the large table are two 16th-century Italian bronzes. (Copyright The Frick Collection, New York)

Her back turned to the viewer, Mrs. Leyland's face is seen in profile, hands behind her back, looking quite ethereal in a white gown and floating pink robe.

The wealthy Leylands were Whistler's chief patrons until the tempermental artist completed the famous Peacock Room (in the Freer Gallery, Washington, D.C.) for their London house and was abusive when they disapproved of his work. Leyland was a primary creditor during Whistler's bankruptcy proceedings in 1879.

There are two splendid paintings by Sir Anthony van Dyck (1599-1641) in the East Gallery. (Van Dyck, considered one of the two greatest 17th-century Flemish painters, was greatly influenced by the other, Peter Paul Rubens, and was briefly his assistant.) One of the paintings portrays *Paola Adorno, Marchesa di Brignole Sale*, a member of one of the most celebrated Genoese families, who gazes thoughtfully at the viewer from one large canvas. She stands in regal splendor, gowned in white satin, which is ornamented with row upon row of gleaming gold braid.

There are three portraits by Francisco de Goya y Lucientes (1746-1828). One painting is of *Don Pedro, Duque de Osuna*, who lived from 1755 until 1807 and was one of the most celebrated figures in Spain during his lifetime. Of long and noble lineage, great wealth, superior intelligence and education, Don Pedro was Lieutenant General of the Armies and Ambassador to the Viennese Court and was awarded numerous honors, among them the Order of the Golden Fleece, conferred by Charles IV.

★

In addition to the paintings discussed, there are splendid works of art in the East Gallery by Maris, Millet, van Ruisdael, Lorrain, Cuyp, David, Degas, Corot, Turner, and Grueze.

★

It was time to rest now. We headed for the pleasant greenery of the central Garden Court where we sat on a stone bench near the reflecting pool and listened to the fountain's musical cascade. Frick had certainly been right, we decided. The serene beauty of this mansion did make the study of art a personal and memorable experience.

The charming small garden designed by Russell Page. (Photograph © Jeffrey Jay Foxx, 1990)

The Frick Collection

1 East 70th Street
New York, NY 10021
212-288-0700

Hours:
Tuesday-Saturday 10:00 a.m.-6:00 p.m.
Sunday 1:00-6:00 p.m.

Closed Monday & major holidays

Admission:
- Adults $3.00
- Students & seniors $1.50
- Children under 10 years old not admitted

Lectures:
An introductory slide lecture is given
Tuesday-Friday, at 11:00 a.m., from
September-May. By appointment.
   Call for a schedule of special subject
lectures.

Concerts:
Concerts are performed on selected Sunday
afternoons at 5:00 p.m. in the Music Room
(except during the summer, when concerts are
given in the Garden Court). Tickets are free
but must be reserved at least three Mondays
in advance.

RESTAURANTS

The Pembroke Room

Lowell Room
28 East 63rd Street
212-838-1400

Breakfast:
   Daily 7:00-10:30 a.m
Lunch:
   Daily noon-2:30 p.m.
Afternoon tea:
   Daily 3:30-6:30 p.m.
Brunch:
   Saturday & Sunday noon-2:30 p.m.
(Dinner is not served)

- All major credit cards
- Reservations suggested

This pretty dining room, located on the second
floor of the Lowell Hotel, is the perfect place
for breakfast, lunch, or afternoon tea.
   In warmer weather the lace curtains stir
gently in the open windows. In winter the
room is cozy in spite of its formality.
   The menu is refreshingly interesting, with
such entrees as pompano with orange papaya
sauce, seared tuna steak with fresh basil and
tomatoes, broiled lamb chops with pistachio
pesto, and sea scallops with porcini mushrooms, sundried tomatoes, and arugula.
   Among the lighter dishes offered: sandwiches, scrambled eggs with asparagus, warm
chicken salad, fresh fruit salad, and tuna salad.
   Service is very friendly and professional.
This is a romantic, peaceful dining room that
will give you a feeling of the 19th century.

Breakfast $12.00-$15.00
Lunch:
   Appetizers $8.00-$12.00
   Entrees $14.00-$26.00
Tea (sandwiches, scones, & pastries) $15.50

Madison Grill

746 Madison Avenue
Between 64th & 65th Streets
212-861-8820

Daily 11:00 a.m.-midnight

- All major credit cards
- Reserve during busy hours, although getting
  a table is not usually a problem

This festive and busy restaurant offers a wide
range of nicely prepared dishes. Appetizers
include well-prepared lobster bisque, onion
soup, and a refreshing mozzarella, tomato, and
red-pepper salad.

Hefty deep-dish chicken pot pie is full of
chunky chicken and vegetables. Chicken
Breast Raphaelo, made with avocado and
Russian dressing, is satisfying and offers a
pleasant contrast in flavors.

Want dessert? You might try key-lime pie
or peach melba.

Tables are small and close together. It is
hard not to hear the lively conversations
around you, and the restaurant can be noisy.
But this is a nice place to choose if you want
to watch the fashionable drift in for lunch or
dinner and have a view of the Madison
Avenue crowd parading outside.

Lunch:
    Appetizers $4.95-$9.95
    Entrees $10.50-$19.50
Dinner:
    Entrees $11.00-$25.00

La Côte Basque

5 East 55th Street
212-688-6525

Lunch:
    Monday-Saturday noon-2:30 p.m.
Dinner:
    Monday-Friday 6:00-10:30 p.m.
    Saturday until 11:00 p.m.

Closed Sunday

- All major credit cards
- Reservations necessary

La Côte Basque is rated year after year as one
of the best New York City restaurants, a favorite of the chic, the famous, and the powerful.
What a pleasant surprise to walk through the
door and discover a restaurant that resembles a
cozy French country inn, its creamy walls and
dark wooden beams brightened by masses of
mixed flowers, and an array of delicious desserts spread on a wide table. Cheerful murals
of the French seaside are painted as though
viewed through canopied windows.

If you love beautifully prepared and
presented food, chef-proprietor Jean-Jacques
Rachou, who is a master of classic French
cuisine, will not disappoint.

The fish soup is reduced to a rich blend of
flavors and perfumed with garlic. A succulent
lobster, shrimp, and scallop melange is laced
with a delicately seasoned lemon sauce and
presented in a puff pastry scallop shell. A
seafood salad appetizer is a combination of
lobster, crab, and shrimp with a lively tarragon
mayonnaise, placed inside a wreath of bright
vegetables.

Entrees include a juicy and crusty roast
chicken in a piquant mustard sauce; a splendidly rich sole, intensified by a silky fish
mousse and two elegantly reduced sauces; and
perfectly pink and tender rack of lamb.

Desserts. What a selection! The Grand
Marnier souffle with raspberry sauce is
delightfully delicate. A chocolate mousse is
densely delicious and perfumed with Grand
Marnier. In springtime refreshing *fraises du*

bois and raspberries are mixed for another tempting dessert.

There are other pleasures to enjoy at La Côte Basque. Service is extremely courteous and efficient. The rooms are softly lighted with generously spaced tables. It is easy to carry on a conversation even when the restaurant is full, and diners relax quickly and have a very good time.

Prix-fixe lunch $32.00
Prix-fixe dinner $55.00

★

Le Train Bleu

Bloomingdale's Department Store
59th Street and Lexington Avenue, 6th Floor
212-705-2100

Brunch:
  Monday-Saturday 11:00 a.m.-noon
Lunch:
  Monday-Saturday noon-4:30 p.m.
  Thursday evening only until 7:30 p.m.
Afternoon tea:
  Monday-Friday 3:00-4:30 p.m.

• All major credit cards &
  Bloomingdale's charge
• Reservations suggested

Leave it to Bloomingdale's to create a store restaurant that actually has good food, professional service, and an exotic and romantic theme for its decoration.

Le Train Bleu is done up just like a turn-of-the-century railroad dining car. The appointments look authentic: burnished brass chandeliers with fluted glass shades, old-fashioned ceiling fans, and overhead brass racks (on which neatly folded coats are stored — a great idea!). There are mirrors galore and plush green velveteen chairs that add just the right note of luxury. In fact, the whole car is swathed in a lively Kelly green. So why is it called the Blue Train? No matter — the effect is dashing and sophisticated.

We started with a colorful, well-seasoned salad. A special cream of lettuce soup was unusual and enticing. There was a delicious pasta carbonara, full of Italian bacon and aromatic with garlic. Grilled sole was enhanced by a golden dill sauce. A grilled salmon was just as tasty, prepared with a delicate green-pea butter sauce. Chef's salads are also good, and there are always assorted omelets for lighter fare.

Also in a lighter vein is the brunch, served before noon. The brunch provides a quiet interlude from hectic shopping at a small price and includes a glass of wine with a choice of an omelet, waffle, or grilled brie and ham sandwich.

Mayfair tea is served from 3:00-4:30 p.m. and seems just the right thing to do on a fantasy train. A glass of sherry, sandwiches, and sweets are served. Or, if you prefer, choose an afternoon snack — chicken salad or a cheese and cracker plate.

Lunch:
  Appetizers $4.50-$8.00
  Entrees $14.50-$17.50
Brunch & afternoon tea under $10.00

D I R E C T I O N S

Subway:
• IRT #6 (to 68th Street)

Bus:
• M1, M2, M3, M4 (Fifth / Madison
  Avenues)
• M66 (66th Street / 67th Street crosstown)
• M30, M72 (72nd Street crosstown)

Car:
• FDR Drive, East 71st Street exit
• Henry Hudson Parkway, West 72nd
  Street exit

285

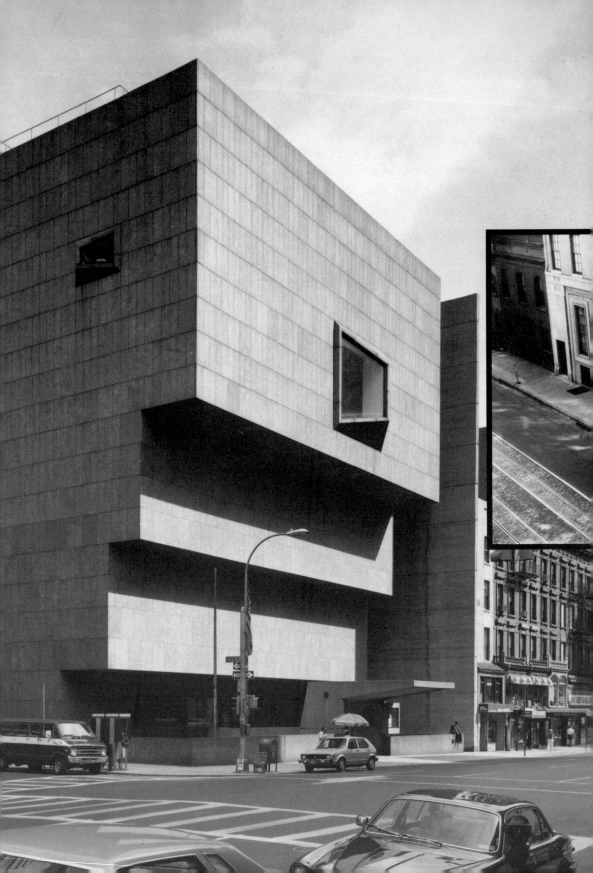

American Art – A Walk Through the 20th Century

Whitney Museum of American Art

Above: A circa 1931 photograph showing the museum's first building located at 10 West 8th Street, which opened to the public on November 18, 1931. (Courtesy of Whitney Museum of American Art, New York, NY)

Left: A view of the museum's third and present building located at 945 Madison Avenue. An award-winning design by Marcel Breuer, completed in 1966. (Courtesy of Whitney Museum of American Art, New York, NY. Photograph by Jerry L. Thompson)

ithout a doubt the Whitney Museum of American Art offers one of New York City's best learning experiences in contemporary art. In a little over an hour, the tour entitled *Highlights of the Permanent Collection* takes the visitor through the world of American art from the early 1900s to the present.

Since its founding in 1930 the museum has developed one of the most comprehensive collections of 20th-century American art in the world. The tour, using many of these great works of art as illustration, explains the American artistic movements that developed during the 20th century — and the social and political events that influenced and enriched them.

The Tour

I was standing in the third-floor oval gallery waiting for the 1:30 p.m. tour to begin. The small gallery was dominated by a monumental bronze sculpture of a voluptuous *Standing Woman* by Gaston Lachaise, originally cast in 1927. Lachaise called the figure, which was inspired by his future wife, " ... the glorification of the human being, of the human body, of the human spirit, with all there is of daring magnificence."

Hanging near the bronze was the portrait of Gertrude Vanderbilt Whitney, founder of the Whitney Museum of American Art. Robert Henri painted this whimsical portrait in 1916, capturing her languid grace and artistic nature.

Exactly on time, the young docent strode briskly into the gallery. With a welcoming smile, he enthusiastically accompanied us on a journey through 20th-century American art.

Our first stop was a gallery devoted to the Ashcan School, which flowered at the beginning of the 20th century. This school of New York City artists had grown tired of the romanticized subjects and impressionistic scenes of 19th-century painting and chose instead to depict the everyday life of everyday people. They painted subjects from the real, sometimes unpleasant world, subjects once regarded as beneath the consideration of artists — the backyard of a tenement house or a cluttered street where children played kickball. Yes, even an ashcan was considered a worthy subject, and critics gleefully attached the name to the group of artists.

As we moved to the next gallery, I was captivated by the guide's lively

Representative works of art from the
Permanent Collection: From left:
Mahoning (1956) by Franz Kline,
Standing Woman (1912-1927) by Gaston
Lachaise, *Dial* (1956) by Philip Guston,
Quasantania (1941) by Louise
Bourgeois, and *Number 27* (1950) by
Jackson Pollock. Installation view of
*20th Century American Art: Highlights of
the Permanent Collection III*. (Courtesy
of Whitney Museum of American Art,
New York, NY)

descriptions and by the precise pictures he created with words. For example, to explain the idea of cubism, the first new art movement to dawn in Europe at the turn of the 20th century, he asked us to imagine ripping all the sides of a shoebox apart, then putting them flat on a table. In this way we would be able to see all sides from the same vantage point.

Using the museum's 1915 painting *Chinese Restaurant* by Max Weber as an illustration of an American artist's synthesis of cubist techniques, the docent showed us that the artist had torn apart and rearranged the restaurant. The black-and-white tiled floor, a table, and a white tablecloth had become flat, geometric shapes flipped up to the front of the canvas. Suddenly we were also able to see the faces of diners, the awning, and the red-flocked wallpaper as fragmented, one-dimensional forms.

My Egypt, painted by Charles Demuth in 1927, was offered as an exceptional example of the American precisionist movement. Pennsylvania grain storage elevators were transformed by Demuth's clean, linear painting style and crisp, precise vision of reality into Egyptian pyramids, symbolizing America's endur-ing economic strength and agricultural abundance.

Next — a splendid Georgia O'Keeffe painting. "It is easy to understand early abstractionist work if you think of a camera with a zoom lens focusing on a tiny part of an object," the docent explained as he stood beside *Flower Abstraction*, painted in 1924. "Or think of it in another way: Imagine that you are holding this flower in your hand and looking at one small section with a magni-fying glass." He continued by explaining that Georgia O'Keeffe said she could get to the true meaning of things only through the process of simplification. She felt that abstraction was the intangible thing in herself expressed only through her painting. And in answer to questions about the great size of her flowers, she once remarked that if she painted flowers very, very big, even busy New Yorkers would have to stop and look!

Surrealism, an art and literary movement that began in the early 1920s, was concerned with exploring and depicting the subconscious mind. As we gazed at the dreamscape *Fear*, painted in 1949 by Yves Tanguy, we were asked to consider, from a surrealist's viewpoint, what we do when we "doodle" on a piece of paper. "When you doodle," the docent explained, "you are trying to free the unconscious mind from everyday reality, trying to free it from religious, social, and cultural mores." He added that when a person draws a doodle, then expands on the image he sees, he is developing images that are surrealistic — the dreamscape of his innermost thoughts.

Abstract expressionism. Who exemplifies it more than Jackson Pollock, the acknowledged leader of the movement? As we stood in front of *Number 27,* painted in 1950, a huge canvas whose surface was covered with a tangle of pink, yellow, black, and white webs, we learned that it was the work of abstract expressionists that catapulted American art into worldwide acclaim.

Pollock said his aim was to express his feelings, not just to illustrate them. He wanted the act of creating a painting to be as important as the finished product.

"Imagine this, if you will," the docent explained. "Pollock throws the canvas on the ground. He runs and jumps and dances as he is painting. It is the psychic energies he is creating that become a release of anxieties. Because of the way they worked, you will often hear these artists referred to as action painters. It

was no longer good enough to document emotion. The artist had to act it out."

The next light-filled gallery was lined with huge canvases. Some were vast sheets in one color, while others were explosions of several bold colors. These were the color-field paintings. Again the docent used imagery. He told us that these abstract expressionist artists wanted us to become encompassed by a work of art, engulfed by it. These monumental canvases were meant to create an environment that the viewer could quietly contemplate.

We walked to a large color-field painting by Mark Rothko, another important figure in the abstract expressionist movement. Rothko said that his work was about human emotion, about tragedy, ecstasy, and doom. As we stood before his powerful *Four Darks in Red* of 1958, a composition of wide horizontal bands, we were encouraged to use our imaginations to become a part of the somber, brooding painting. And we did. Quietly we were drawn into the great expanse of horizontal forms. We did contemplate. And we had a better understanding of the artist's intent.

In the last gallery we enjoyed pop art. Jasper Johns challenged our senses and raised questions about reality and perception with *Three Flags*, painted in 1958. Stripped of both symbolism and fluttering imagery, then stacked one on another, the stylized, board-stiff flags form a geometric composition. They have been transformed into an aesthetic object.

George Segal's *Walk, Don't Walk* of 1976 links the real world with a world of imagination and dreams. The white plaster figures are forever caught in time, eyes closed as though in a trance, eternally standing on a street corner, while in the world of reality, time moves forward, and the pedestrian signal light blinks unceasingly, *Walk — Don't Walk — Walk — Don't Walk —*

Last was the silkscreen painting by Andy Warhol, who in *Green Coca-Cola Bottles* of 1962 commented about the lives we lead and about mass production, which has played an important role in the American lifestyle. Warhol wrote, "A Coke is a Coke and no amount of money can get you a better Coke than the one the bum on the corner is drinking. All the Cokes are the same and all the Cokes are good. Liz Taylor knows it, the President knows it, the bum knows it, and you know it."

Warhol, like the others, tried to make us re-examine the way we perceive art and the world in which we live— indeed, to make us re-examine the meaning of art itself.

George Segal, *Walk, Don't Walk,* 1976. Plaster, cement, metal, painted wood, and electric light. 104 x 72 x 72 inches. (Collection of Whitney Museum of American Art, New York, NY. Purchase, with funds from the Louis and Bessie Adler Foundation, Inc., Seymour M. Klein, President, the Gilman Foundation, Inc., the Howard and Jean Lipman Foundation, Inc., and the National Endowment for the Arts 79.4. Photograph by Jerry L. Thompson)

This chapter can describe only a few of the 20th-century American art movements and paintings covered during an hour-long tour by one of 20 knowledgeable docents. The tour is worth taking more than once, as each docent offers a different viewpoint and may discuss different artworks in the permanent collection. The works of art described in this chapter may not be on view when you visit, as they are periodically rotated among the museum's four branches.

Whitney Museum of American Art

945 Madison Avenue at 75th Street
New York, NY 10021
212-570-3600 or 212-570-3676

Hours:
Wednesday-Saturday 11:00 a.m.-5:00 p.m.
Tuesday 1:00-8:00 p.m.
Sunday noon-6:00 p.m.

Closed Monday, New Year's Day, July 4, Thanksgiving & Christmas

Admission:
- Adults $5.00
- Seniors $2.50
- Children under 12 with an adult, high school & college students with current I.D., free
- Museum is free on Tuesday from 6:00-8:00 p.m.

Highlights of the Permanent Collection tours are offered free with admission on Tuesday at 1:30 p.m., 3:30 p.m., and 6:15 p.m.; Wednesday, Thursday, and Friday at 1:30 p.m. and 3:30 p.m.; Saturday and Sunday at 3:30 p.m.

Other Gallery Tours:
Special Exhibition tours are usually given on Tuesday, Wednesday, and Thursday at 2:30 p.m.; Saturday and Sunday at 2:00 p.m. Check schedule at Lobby Information Desk for changes.

Private Group Tours and Foreign Language Tours:
Call 212-606-0395 Monday 10:00 a.m.-1:00 p.m. and Thursday 1:00-5:00 p.m. for information, cost, and reservations.

Seminars with Artists:
An interesting series of informal visits with New York artists and critics is held each spring and fall, Tuesdays at 6:00 p.m., 10 seminars per semester. Call Coordinator of Public Education Programs for details.

R E S T A U R A N T S

Whitney Museum Garden Restaurant

Lower level of the museum
212-570-3670

Wednesday-Saturday 11:30 a.m.-4:30 p.m.
Tuesday 1:00-7:00 p.m.
Sunday noon-5:00 p.m.

- All major credit cards
- Reservations are unnecessary

This airy restaurant overlooking the outdoor sculpture court offers simple, freshly prepared lunches — soup, salads, sandwiches, and desserts. Chicken salad, prepared a different way each week, can be very tasty. Sandwiches (such as an open-face beef sandwich offered as a special recently) are usually very nice. Omelets, prepared in a variety of ways, are plump, tender, and well-seasoned. As for desserts, a chocolate cake and pecan pie we had recently were excellent. The restaurant offers wine, beer, and mixed drinks.

If you want to spend several hours at the Whitney, lunch here is pleasant and relaxing. Certainly the prices (generally under $15.00 per person) are inexpensive for New York.

Little Mushroom Cafe

1439 Second Avenue at 75th Street
212-988-9006

Brunch:
   Saturday & Sunday 11:45 a.m.-4:30 p.m.
Dinner:
   Daily 5:00-11:00 p.m.
Earlybird dinner:
   Daily 5:00-7:00 p.m.

• American Express

A bright, fresh Thai cafe in Italian dress with its peach-sherbert walls, sleek modern chairs, and marble-topped tables. It may be dressed Italian, but its personality is pure Thai, even if pasta dishes are on the menu.

The prices are modest, so it's certainly worth having a Thai-Italian adventure. Just pick the authentic Thai dishes, and you'll have a pleasing meal.

Teriyaki chicken on a skewer with spicy peanut sauce as a dip is a tasty appetizer. *Tom yum koong* is a delightfully tangy shrimp soup.

Sauteed chicken breast and shrimp Thai-style with fresh basil, onion, and chili is a nice dish, and the chicken with spicy coconut curry sauce has a lively, rich flavor. We enjoyed *pad thai*, stir-fried rice topped with sauteed chicken or shrimp with vegetables, scallions, and ground peanuts. All of these dishes were well-prepared and spicy without being overwhelming, using a flavorful combination of colorful and aromatic ingredients.

Service is courteous and speedy. In summer try a small table outdoors.

Brunch $7.95
Lunch & dinner:
   Appetizers $2.95-$5.95
   Entrees $7.00-$14.95
   Earlybird dinner $7.95

DIRECTIONS

Subway:
• IRT #6 to 77th Street & Lexington Avenue

Bus:
• M1, M2, M3, M4 (Madison / Fifth Avenues)
• M30, M72 (72nd Street crosstown)

Car:
• FDR Drive, East 71st Street exit
• Henry Hudson Parkway, West 72nd Street exit

Gaston Lachaise, *Standing Woman,* 1912-1927. Bronze. 70 x 28 x 16 inches. (Collection of Whitney Museum of American Art, New York, NY. Purchase 36.91. © 1927, G. Lachaise. Photograph by Jerry L. Thompson)

"O Sole Mio!"

A Venetian gondola ride on Central Park Lake

The History

 n the middle of the 19th century 840 undeveloped acres still remained in the heart of Manhattan — an inharmonious mix of meadows, whiskey stills, ponds, squatters' huts, woods, pig wallows, swamps, and bone-boiling works.

The city acquired the land in 1856 for $5.5 million and began to clear the acreage. By 1858 work had begun to transform the wide swath of countryside into Central Park, a masterpiece of landscape design conceived by Frederick Law Olmsted and Calvert Vaux. Their plan, which they called Greensward, was the winner among 33 entries in an 1857 competition.

By the time the park was completed nearly 20 years later, thousands of tons of earth and rock had been moved around or carted away, dramatically changing the terrain. Central Park was a rich and varied landscape — from rolling meadows to a wild tangle of woods called the Ramble; from the bucolic mirror of a lake for boating to the formal Conservatory Garden; from the sedate Mall, lined with trees and statuary, to wild stretches of rocky terrain laced with wildflowers.

This tour will show you the heart of Central Park: the Terrace and its centerpiece, Bethesda Fountain. The Terrace, with its formality and elegance, was

Above: Central Park Lake, 1880s. The idea of having a gondola on Central Park Lake is not new after all! The Terrace and Bethesda Fountain are shown in the background. (Courtesy of The New-York Historical Society, New York City. Photograph from the Bagoe Collection)

Right: Central Park Lake is just as tranquil, and the gondola ride just as delightful today. (Photograph © Jeffrey Jay Foxx, 1990)

meant to tie together the elements of classical design with those of nature's wild beauty.

If you stand on the upper level of the Terrace, you will see just how this was accomplished. Look south. The Mall slices the center of the park with its canopy of regimented trees and formal statues of Columbus, Shakespeare, Robert Burns, and others. Hidden behind the trees is the Pergola, an old wisteria arbor, and the Naumburg band shell, where summer concerts are held. You could be looking at an English park.

Now look north. The peaceful rock-bordered Central Park Lake is fringed with willows and dotted with rowboats. It is quiet and serene. You could be miles in the country. Beyond, on the lake's north shore, the lush and densely over-grown Ramble hides its maze of winding paths and obstructs the view of Vista Rock and Belvedere Castle, which were the northern focal points of the Mall's axis in the Greensward design.

The Terrace is a tie that binds the civilized and the wild into harmony.

The Terrace, Central Park. An
1878 engraving after a painting by
C. Rosenberg. Recently restored,
the Terrace once again resembles this
19th-century engraving. (Courtesy of
Museum of the City of New York)

Previous pages: Central Park, circa
1864. A fascinating lithograph that
shows the design of the park as con-
ceived by Olmsted and Vaux. At upper
right: The reservoirs. Center: Central
Park Lake, Bethesda Fountain, and the
Mall. Lower right: Fifth Avenue
begins to develop. Upper left: The
West Side is still countryside. (Courtesy
of Museum of the City of New York)

The Gondola Ride

The glossy black gondola slid through the
soft, bright water of Central Park Lake.
My son Mark and I sank into the cush-
ioned seats and listened to Ron Mattia,
our gondolier.

"This is an authentic Venetian gondola, 25 years old. Two Venetian gondo-
liers actually came here to teach some of
us how to handle this gondola. There's
something else that will probably surprise
you: There was actually a gondola for
rent on this lake in the 19th century."

We could have been in the 19th
century ourselves on this summer evening. It was 6:00 p.m., but the water still
sparkled with sunshine. A woman
holding a lacy blue parasol waved to us as
her suitor rowed her through the quiet
water. Two merry, laughing young men,
attired in dapper white suits and straw
boaters, rowed another rented rowboat.

But we were the center of attention in
our dashing gondola! A photographer
kneeling on the willow-draped bank took
our picture. We were even saluted by a
trio of young cadets who strode down the
path in crisp formation.

Two bright fluttering flags drew my
attention to the newly restored Terrace
and Bethesda Fountain on the south bank.
Designed by Calvert Vaux and Jacob
Wrey Mould, the Terrace was begun in
1859, the same year the lake was carved
out. How well Vaux and Mould succeeded. With its grand twin staircases, its
arcades, and the splendid fountain, the
Terrace is a palatial, open-air reception
hall. Wonderful to see.

Ron followed my gaze. "That bronze
statue in the center of Bethesda Fountain
was made by Emma Stebbins around
1870. She called it *Angel of the Waters*
after a passage in the Bible that says a
pool called Bethesda in Jerusalem was

often visited by an angel, who gave the water a healing power. All who bathed there after the angel's visit were miraculously cured of any illness. That pool in Jerusalem was located near a sheep market, just as Bethesda Fountain is located near Central Park's Sheep Meadow, where sheep grazed until 1934."

Our sleek gondola glided quietly through the sun-spangled water. A small, graceful bridge arched over us — Bow Bridge, a gentle curve of cast-iron interconnecting circles, also designed by Vaux and built in 1879 (restored in 1974). And above it, behind a mass of trees, rose the imposing green copper roof peaks of the Dakota Apartments.

Built in 1884, the luxurious Dakota was thought to be so far north that people laughed and said it might as well be in Dakota Territory, that wild and desolate place somewhere in the West. The Dakota, which resembles a battered and slightly dingy castle on the outside, still holds opulent apartments, some with grand ballrooms. There have been many famous residents, among them John Lennon, who was shot and killed in front of the building. Just across the street is Strawberry Fields, an area in Central Park dedicated to Lennon and restored by his wife, Yoko Ono.

Ron pointed to a young boy lazing on a granite outcropping, a Huckleberry Finn in bare feet and cut-offs, holding a string fishing pole. "You'd be amazed at the fish that people catch here! Bass, perch, catfish — some a foot long — and they use everything for bait, from English muffins to fancy lures!"

As Ron turned the long gondola around in a smooth arc, he told us that sunset rides are romantic and memorable. And on a moonlit night the lake is as smooth as a mirror, reflecting the sparkling lights of Central Park South. Only

Skating in Central Park Lake, circa 1895. The Dakota, completed in 1884, is seen at right, and the Hotel Majestic, completed in 1895, is at center. The Majestic was demolished, replaced by the Majestic Apartments in 1930. (Courtesy of Museum of the City of New York)

the gentle lapping of water and the sleepy croaking of frogs can be heard in the quiet night.

Our gondola ride was nearly over. The Boathouse Cafe, from which we had started this delightful adventure, was once again in view. We could see the wide wooden deck filled with blue umbrella-shaded tables. We heard relaxed conversations and smelled the tangy aroma of Italian food drifting over the sunlit water.

A plate of savory pasta seemed just the right finish to a Venetian gondola ride.

Ron, jaunty in his red-and-white striped shirt and straw boater, helped us onto the deck just as a garlicky, buttery scent wafted to us. "Have one of those pastas for me," he sighed, as he clambered back into the gondola. "Delicious!"

The 72nd Street Boathouse and Cafe
Overlooking Central Park Lake

May or June through October, depending
on the weather.

Boathouse Gondola Rides:
- Evenings 6:00-11:00 p.m.
- $30.00 plus tax per half-hour. The gondola
  will carry as many as six people.
- Reservations are a must. Call 212-517-2233

Boathouse Bike Rentals:
- March-November, weather permitting
  Weekdays 10:00 a.m.-6:00 p.m.
  Weekends 9:00 a.m.-6:00 p.m.
- $6.00 an hour for a three-speed bike.
  Must leave a credit card or driver's license
  as security.
- $8.00 an hour for a 10-speed bike. A $20.00
  deposit required. Call 212-861-4137

Boathouse Rowboat Rentals:
- April-October, weather permitting
  Weekdays 10:00 a.m.-5:30 p.m.
  Weekends 10:00 a.m.-6:30 p.m.
- $7.00 an hour, $1.75 each additional
  quarter-hour. A $20.00 deposit required.
  Call 212-517-2233

Free Evening Transportation:
Every evening from 6:00 p.m. the Boathouse
Cafe offers free rides to and from the restaurant in a charming replica of a San Francisco
trolley car. Customers are picked up every 20
minutes at the park entrances along Fifth
Avenue from 72nd Street to 90th Street. You
can't miss the dark green trolley car trimmed
in gold and red, with *Boathouse Central Park
Cafe* emblazoned on its side.

Additional Tours:
Leaving the Boathouse Cafe, turn right,
following the path next to the street, which
will lead you around the lake and over Bow
Bridge. Turn around (facing Fifth Avenue)
and follow the first path to the right, which
leads to the Terrace and Bethesda Fountain.
To return to Fifth Avenue, follow the street
adjacent to the Terrace at 72nd Street.

★

The Urban Park Rangers of the New York
City Parks and Recreation Department offer
numerous free New York City tours, many of
them in Central Park. For current tour
information call 212-427-4040.

RESTAURANTS

Boathouse Central Park Cafe
Near 72nd Street
Overlooking Central Park Lake
212-517-2233

Monday-Thursday noon-9:00 p.m.
Friday-Saturday noon-11:00 p.m.
Sunday 11:30 a.m.-9:00 p.m.

- Open late March-early November
- All major credit cards
- Reservations taken for six or more people
  at lunch and for four or more at dinner
- Same menu all day

The unforgettable setting on Central Park Lake
makes this restaurant a special treat. A wide
menu of Northern Italian food is served.

Choose from such appetizers as roasted
peppers on grilled country bread, warm goat-
cheese salad, or grilled eggplant with sun-
dried tomatoes, pine nuts, and basil.

Main courses include grilled shrimp with a
tangy anchovy-caper sauce, cold poached
salmon with fresh basil mayonnaise, and an
Italian omelet stuffed with tomatoes, onions,
garlic, and mushrooms.

Among the pasta dishes are ziti bathed in a creamy sauce with prosciutto, peas, and sun-dried tomatoes; a tasty fettuccine with scallops in lemon sauce; and a lively linguini al pesto.

It is hard to resist such dessert temptations as chocolate cake in a raspberry sauce, which is a rich dark-and-white chocolate confection, and strawberries in a Marsala wine sauce.

Appetizers $6.00-$18.00
Entrees $10.00-$19.00

D I R E C T I O N S

Subway:
• IRT #6 to 68th Street & Lexington Avenue

Bus:
• M1, M2, M3, M4 (Fifth / Madison Avenues)
• M30, M72 (72nd Street crosstown)

Car:
• FDR Drive, East 71st Street exit
• Henry Hudson Parkway, West 72nd Street exit

The Mall, 1894. The Mall looks very much like this today. (Courtesy of Museum of the City of New York. Photograph by J.S. Johnston)

A Day with the Tiffanys, Father and Son

The New-York Historical Society and The Metropolitan Museum of Art

Above: Tiffany & Co., Fifth Avenue and 37th Street, circa 1910. Tiffany & Co. moved to its present location in 1940. (Courtesy of Museum of the City of New York)

Left: Tiffany & Co. today, located at Fifth Avenue and 57th Street. (Photograph © Jeffrey Jay Foxx, 1990)

he following chronicle of the Tiffanys begins in the year 1837, when the world-famous co-founder of Tiffany & Co., Charles Lewis Tiffany, opened the first small "fancy goods" store at 259 Broadway in Lower Manhattan, a city of contrasts then as now: quiet, gaslit streets and fashionable districts, as well as raucous, rough-and-tumble neighborhoods. The narrative ends in 1933 with the death of the millionaire merchant's son, Louis Comfort Tiffany, master of stained-glass artworks. The city was a radically different place by that time, caught up in an era of machinery and the Depression, and suspended between two world wars.

Charles Lewis Tiffany was the son of a Connecticut textile mill owner, who instilled in Charles the attributes of hard work, good moral values, and sound business judgment. He also gave 25-year-old Charles and his partner, John Young, $1,000 with which to start a business, a considerable sum in 1837.

Although 1837 was the year of a financial panic, the two young men struck pay dirt with their small store. From paltry three days' receipts of $4.98 following the opening of Tiffany & Young, the partners rapidly expanded inventory until they offered something for everyone: saddles, walking canes, buggy whips, dishes — even suits of armor!

Tiffany was known to step across the line of good taste from time to time, however, if it meant hearing the music of ringing cash registers. When P.T. Barnum had to kill a rogue elephant in his circus, he sold the carcass to Tiffany, who made an assortment of leather goods out of the hide. The mobs of purchasers had to be controlled by the police.

In 1858 Tiffany bought miles of a broken section of the first trans-Atlantic telegraph cable, chopped it into three-inch pieces, and sold the tiny inscribed souvenirs to hoards of delighted customers. Again, the cash registers did double-duty!

It was during those early years that Tiffany developed the store's distinctive blue packaging and Tiffany logo. Why blue? It was simply the most fashionable color of the time. And the logo was copied from the storefront's gilded wooden sign.

Tiffany & Young didn't sell canes and buggy whips very long. By 1841 English silver and European porcelains enriched the inventory after a third partner, John L. Ellis, joined the company, bringing in additional capital. Beginning in 1845 gold jewelry was made in the store's own goldsmithing shop. Six years later, when New York's foremost silver manufacturer, John C. Moore, joined the company, Tiffany & Co. began designing and making its own unique silver objects, a move that led to international acclaim and overwhelming financial success.

And jewels. Who can forget the diamonds, emeralds, rubies, the bright array of semiprecious stones, and pearls? Fascinating stories are linked to Tiffany's plunge into the world of fine jewelry.

Pearl jewelry is an interesting example. Before the development of the cultured pearl, natural pearls were extremely rare and expensive, and for that reason they were considered the ultimate symbol of refinement, good taste, and social status. Soon the company offered a handsome selection of pearl jewelry for those who had "arrived" and those who were still climbing.

Mary Todd Lincoln was one of Tiffany's important customers who was determined to have Tiffany pearls to flaunt before the Washingtonians who ridiculed her. She got her way, even if she had to settle for the less-expensive seed pearls. The President-elect purchased a matched set as a gift: a parure, a pair of bracelets and necklace. The new First Lady proudly wore her Tiffany jewelry to her husband's 1861 inauguration. The cost: $530. (Nearly a hundred years later President Eisenhower asked for a discount and was told that President Lincoln didn't get one!)

Tiffany & Co. began selling diamond jewelry in a dramatic way. By the mid-19th century revolutions had taken their toll on the noble and wealthy of Europe. In France continued political turmoil had caused diamonds to depreciate to approximately half their worth. Tiffany & Co. took advantage of a rare opportunity. While on a buying trip to Paris, John Young purchased the crown jewels of Maria Amelia, wife of deposed King Louis Philippe of France. When the jewels went on display in the store, Tiffany was given the title "King of Diamonds" by New York City newspapers, and the company reaped international acclaim.

Empress Eugenie, the consort of Napoleon III (Emperor of France from 1851 to 1870), had such a passion for jewels that they spangled her gowns. She apparently decided her welfare was worth more than her treasure, because she left her jewels when she fled France in 1887. Tiffany & Co. bought more than $500,000 worth of her jewels at a public sale held

An interior view of Tiffany & Co.
(Photograph © Jeffrey Jay Foxx, 1990)

by the Ministry of Finance, delighting its customers — the Astors, among others.

Diamonds and more diamonds were made available to Tiffany & Co. after they were discovered in South Africa in the 1870s. The store's showcases were soon filled with the brilliant stones. Sales were brisk, as diamonds were considered the height of fashion from the latter part of the 19th century until the beginning of World War I. In fact, the sparkle was so intense in the first tier of the Metropolitan Opera House that this area was, and is, known as the Diamond Horseshoe.

In 1878 the Tiffany Diamond was discovered in South Africa, an extraordinary canary diamond, which in its uncut state weighed 287.42 carats. It took a year for Tiffany & Co. to cut the exquisite yellow diamond into the famous cushion shape of 128.51 carats with 90 facets, but the result was a diamond of inestimable worth. (The Tiffany Diamond is permanently on view on the first floor of the Fifth Avenue store.)

Rubies and emeralds have been highly prized since ancient times, but until the late 19th century almost all other colored stones were considered unacceptable for jewelry — that is, until Tiffany & Co. changed the public's perception of "suitable" stones.

The guiding spirit behind this radical change in jewelry was a young mineralogist, George Kunz, who in 1879 at the age of 23 joined Tiffany & Co. Kunz, who had an extraordinary knowledge of colored stones, their scientific properties, and where they could be found, immediately set out to discover exciting new stones in appealing and unusual colors. He brought back a rainbow of semiprecious stones, which Tiffany's designers set into creatively designed jewelry —

aquamarines, topazes, turquoises, and blue sapphires, among others. The jewelry sold extremely well and began Tiffany's tradition of experimentation with unusual stones.

Kunz assembled a large collection of fine American colored gemstones, which was exhibited by Tiffany & Co. at the Paris Exposition of 1889. Afterward Pierpont Morgan bought the collection (see chapter 16 for more about Morgan), and he subsequently donated it to the New York Museum of Natural History, forming the core of the Hall of Meteorites, Minerals and Gems, still one of the most popular attractions at the museum.

From its unpretentious beginning on lower Broadway, the company had made four moves, always following the northward move of the affluent neighborhoods. After relocating to 550 Broadway in 1854, the company was headquartered at Union Square on 16th Street beginning in 1870. In 1905 Tiffany & Co. moved to a splendid new building at 37th Street and Fifth Avenue, designed by McKim, Mead & White in the style of a 16th-century Venetian *palazzo* (still standing, although the façade has been unattractively altered). In 1940 Tiffany's made its final move to its present impressive building, located at 57th Street and Fifth Avenue.

By the turn of the 20th century Tiffany & Co., with branches in London and Paris, was one of the most successful stores in the world. Charles Tiffany died in 1902, leaving a legacy of success and fame to his son, Louis Comfort, who was then 54 years old and had attained great success and fame in a totally different field, the world of art. This must have been a great surprise and a relief to his father, as Louis had not been the most promising child.

Now let us meet the son, Louis Comfort Tiffany.

★

From the beginning Louis was a mediocre student who disliked school. He was strong-minded and rebellious as well, and his frustrated father finally sent the boy to military school, where he spent several years in abject misery.

Freed at last from school at the age of 17, Louis announced that he was never going to college, another disappointment for his father. And yet another — Louis said he wanted absolutely nothing to do with business and Tiffany & Co. What did he want to be? An artist. Charles Tiffany was hard-pressed to understand his strong-willed son, to say the least!

But Louis Comfort Tiffany always did things his own way. When he was barely 17 years old, he packed his brushes and sailed for Europe.

Louis saw the best side of Europe — and why not? He saw it through the eyes of youth, wealth, and privilege. He painted, studied art, and browsed through museums and cathedrals. He traveled to Italy and was enthralled by the early Christian mosaics in the ancient capital of the Byzantine Empire, Ravenna. He was just as captivated by the 12th- and 13th-century leaded-glass windows at Chartres Cathedral in France.

As it turned out, Louis was wasting neither time nor his father's money. In fact, Louis was an artistic Midas. Every venture he touched seemed to have a golden gleam.

Almost immediately the young artist's paintings began to sell. Not only did they sell, but the European critics

---

Louis Comfort Tiffany (1848-1933). (Courtesy of The New-York Historical Society, New York City. Photograph by Pach)

liked them. While Tiffany was still in his 20s, he established himself as a successful artist in Europe and in the United States.

But there were new worlds to conquer. Louis kept thinking of the Italian mosaics and the jewel-like colors of the medieval leaded-glass windows he had seen. The windows were completely different from those created by 19th-century artisans, who enhanced inferior colored glass by applying powdered colored glass to the surface and fusing it into place. Tiffany wondered why he couldn't bring the superb workmanship found in medieval windows into the present by putting vivid colors *into* the glass once again.

When Tiffany made a decision, he acted on it immediately. In the mid-1870s he began to experiment with metallic oxides and other chemicals to create a brilliantly colored glass, teaching himself as he went along. Eventually he began to make leaded-glass windows, a number of which were sold to churches.

At 30 years of age, Louis was already a success in two fields. Then he began to notice that more and more huge mansions were lining the fine avenues of New York City. Louis realized that wealth did not necessarily anoint people with good taste. Why not offer them guidance? Why not become a decorator?

In 1879 Tiffany set up a decorating business, completely unruffled by the fact that he had neither training nor experience. He was an instant success, with such prestigious clients as Cornelius Vanderbilt and Mark Twain. Within four years Tiffany was asked to decorate the White House.

The decorating business expanded at an astounding rate. By 1902 the company, renamed Tiffany Studios*, was a beehive of showrooms and workers. Tiffany Studios offered something for everyone — an exclusive line of fabrics and carpets, lighting fixtures, furniture, antiques, paintings, pottery, glassware, and mosaics. Tiffany Studios even followed its customers to the grave, offering a full range of tombstones and mausoleums!

★

Tiffany began making blown glass as a natural evolvement from his work with leaded-glass windows. It made business sense as well, as there were great quantities of leftover glass that could be used.

Under Tiffany's guidance, blown glass took the sinuous, flowing forms of nature and echoed the graceful shapes of Japanese porcelains. Tiffany was also inspired by ancient glass, especially by the milky iridescent surfaces found on long-buried glass objects. He experimented, finally creating a similar patina on his glassware, and began turning out these pieces in great numbers. This venture too was overwhelmingly successful. His glassware, which he called "Favrile" (derived, he said, from a word meaning to "fabricate" or "make by hand"), was critically acclaimed, ensuring his lasting fame in the art nouveau movement.

The name art nouveau was coined by S. Bing, an art dealer who promoted Tiffany's work as well as that of other avant-garde artists in his Paris gallery, Le Salon de l'Art Nouveau, which opened in 1895. This "new art" drew its inspiration from many sources, including the Arts

* Just as Charles Tiffany had created Tiffany & Co. when he was a young man, his son Louis formed his first company in 1878 when he was 30 years old. This company was reorganized several times under such names as Louis C. Tiffany & Company and Tiffany Glass Company before it became Tiffany Studios.

and Crafts Movement of the 19th century, which venerated fine handmade crafts and art. Another inspiration — nature's gently flowing lines. Japanese art, which epitomized fine craftsmanship and a delight in natural forms, was highly regarded as well.

Tiffany's next triumph wasn't long in coming, evolving naturally from his glassmaking experience and his delight in watching the ways in which light affects the colors in glass. Another fortuitous circumstance came into play: Thomas A. Edison had perfected the incandescent electric lamp by 1879 — and Tiffany knew Edison. By the early 1890s Tiffany had decided to make electric lamps with blown-glass and leaded-glass shades.

Now here was an object that was beautiful, but even more than that, it was useful. Tiffany envisioned every home in America glowing in a jeweled light that also softened the early lightbulb's glare. His timing was exactly right, and the electric light was his ally.

From the beginning of production in the mid-1890s, Tiffany's blown-glass lamps (made just as the glassware was blown) and his leaded-glass lamps (using the techniques of the leaded-glass windows) were astounding successes. Tiffany's designers and assemblers couldn't fill the orders quickly enough.

Tiffany developed creative marketing methods to sell his lamps. Bases and shades could be mixed and matched according to the customer's taste. In fact, the customer could design the lamp — for a price — and have it assembled. At the height of production more than 500 different shades and bases were available. Tiffany & Co. even sent out a mail-order catalog, allowing customers the convenience of choosing at home. (L.C. Tiffany maintained a department for his merchandise in his father's store.)

When Louis Comfort Tiffany's father died in 1902, both father and son were remarkable successes. Louis, already wealthy in his own right, inherited another fortune and a position as vice president and art director in his father's world-famous Tiffany & Co. He was at the height of his success. And yet, just as the first brisk breezes rustle branches high in the treetops, there were indications that winter was coming for art nouveau and for Tiffany. There were disturbing murmurs that Tiffany's art was too ornate, too flamboyant, too busy. The spare, the geometric, the abstract were admired — blasts of cold, fresh air that would finally mean the end of Tiffany Studios.

Tiffany, who had always been artistically farsighted, ignored the warning signs. Of course, he could afford to do so, protected as he was by immense wealth. Even though his empire had begun to falter by 1913, he continued to guide Tiffany Studios as before.

In 1932 Tiffany Studios filed for bankruptcy. Tiffany returned to his grand estate, Laurelton Hall on Oyster Bay, Long Island, his monument to art nouveau. There he sat, surrounded by his windows, antiques, and mosaics, living out the last of his 85 years.

When Tiffany died in 1933, there was very little left of his vast fortune, and there were very few who admired his work. Laurelton Hall, which had functioned as a gathering place for artists, was finally sold in 1948. Nine years later, when the mansion caught fire and burned for three days, few people really cared. After all, everyone said, art nouveau was dead and buried, wasn't it? Who would possibly be interested in Louis Comfort Tiffany or his art?

Representative lamps from The New-York Historical Society exhibit *The World of Tiffany: Lamps from the Egon Neustadt Collection of Tiffany Lamps*

Left to right:
   Poinsettia Floor Lamp
   Crimson Peacock Lamp
   Lily Pad Lamp
   Pineapple Lamp

(Courtesy of The New-York Historical Society, New York City. Photographs by Sundak Inc., Stamford, CT)

Tour of the World of Tiffany: the Egon Neustadt Collection of Tiffany Lamps

New York City is rich in treasures of Tiffany art. They are found everywhere: in museums, in shops specializing in Tiffany antiques, in churches, even in restaurants and hotels. Begin this homage to the Tiffanys at The New-York Historical Society.

★

Many people don't know that the stately New-York Historical Society is the oldest museum in New York City, founded in 1804. The Society's first home was historic Federal Hall (see chapter 2), and its members included John Adams, Thomas Jefferson, Washington Irving, and Noah Webster. The New-York Historical Society houses remarkable historical and artistic gems, among them the Neustadt Collection of Tiffany lamps. On display are 132 superb examples, along with five leaded-glass windows.

New York orthodontist Egon Neustadt and his wife Hildegard began collecting Tiffany lamps in 1935, shortly after Tiffany's death, when there was little interest in Tiffany's work. Dr. Neustadt gave his collection to the Society a few years ago. Before his recent death the amiable Dr. Neustadt, who lived in a brownstone nearby, was apt to turn up on Sunday afternoons to give impromptu tours to surprised and delighted visitors.

The Neustadt Collection is beautifully organized and creatively displayed in darkened galleries, in which row after row of cast-bronze lamps are crowned with glowing domes of color.

As you enter the gallery, you will see a display of glass shards, illustrating the

Autumn Landscape, 1923. The window
may be seen in the American Wing of
The Metropolitan Museum of Art.
(Photograph © Jeffrey Jay Foxx, 1990)

The Neustadt Collection is divided
into seven sections, organized to show the
progression of lampshade designs from
the simplest forms to the most complex.

Favrile Blown Shades: one-piece shades,
blown using the centuries-old glassmaker's method: The Tiffany glassmaker
blew gently through one end of a long
tube, creating a bubble of glass from the
molten "gathering" at the other end.

Geometric Shades: simplest leaded-glass
shades, constructed using uncomplicated
designs with straight lines, emphasizing
symmetry and repetition.

Transition to Flowers: Bands of naturalistic flowers and leaves appear in the
geometric design. These shades required
the cutting of glass into curved shapes
and necessitated more complicated
bonding techniques. Especially pretty are
shades with delicate dogwood blossoms
and daisies.

Flowered Cone Shades: Geometric
patterns disappear, and most glass fragments are irregular in shape. Dragonfly
lamps are displayed in this section, with
dragonflies superimposed like pieces of
jewelry on the surface of each leaded-
glass shade. Naturalistic or stylized floral
patterns are important. Examples include
a daffodil shade and a shade with clusters
of grapes entwining on an arbor.

Globe Shades: Shades curve horizontally
and vertically, requiring precise selection
and cutting of each glass piece. Beautiful
examples include a shade with brilliant
red poppies and emerald leaves, one of
the most popular Tiffany designs. Another best-selling design was the peacock-
feather lamp, which could be ordered with
a base cast in the form of feathers. The

great variety of glass colors and textures
that Tiffany created, among them striated,
ribbon, plaid — even glass that simulates
shirred fabric.

A Tiffany leaded-glass landscape
panel at the entrance provides an insight
into his technique of using layerings of
glass in different colors and textures to
achieve perspective and richness of hues.
This impressionist work is also a tribute to
Tiffany's talent as a painter.

Take a few minutes to study the pages
from a Tiffany lamp album of 1907.
These framed advertisements show the
various designs for lampshades and bases
available at the turn of the century, along
with the low 1907 prices!

★

most valuable example in the collection is a globe-shaded floor lamp, which has a refined design of pale dogwood blossoms against a soft amethyst ground.

Irregular Lower Borders: shades of increased technical and artistic complexity, with an uneven lower rim following the design's outline. Examples include a grape-cluster shade, whose grape bunches dangle from an arbor, the grape globes creating the lower rim.

Irregular Upper and Lower Borders: shades whose upper and lower rims follow the contours of the design. Romantic wisteria shades are highlighted, with fragile cut-out bronze stems and drooping purple blossoms outlining both rims. The rarest lamp, a rather somber lamp of apple blossoms and a spider-web, is featured in this section.

★

Before continuing this Tiffany tour, browse through the other outstanding galleries. The Society's treasury of American history and art includes American period rooms, a remarkable collection of silver, an extensive art collection, an exhibition of New York carriages, and John James Audubon's original watercolors, from which engravings were made for publication in *Birds of America.*

★

Now take a quick bus ride to The Metropolitan Museum of Art at 82nd Street and Fifth Avenue, which is just across Central Park. (Get on the bus at 81st Street and Central Park West.) More Tiffany masterpieces are waiting for you there.

Tour of the American Wing in The Metropolitan Museum of Art

The indoor garden of the American Wing is a quiet and peaceful setting for several large works of art from Tiffany Studios:

Autumn Landscape, a leaded-glass window completed in 1923, depicts a tranquil lake fringed by the russet colors of autumn leaves.

The large *Landscape Fountain*, a 1905 composition in glass mosaics, is a romantic scene of a waterlily-sprigged pond and floating white swans. Highlighted against an iridescent sky are cypresses and an orchard (which may remind you a bit of Van Gogh). This fountain was sold at auction in 1938, only to remain crated and forgotten in a warehouse for nearly 40 years.

The entrance loggia of Laurelton Hall (circa 1905) is found in the American Wing, having been spared when the mansion burned. How exotic it is, with columns whose capitals are garlanded by colorful ceramic flowers. The design and bright colors, the iridescent mosaic entablature, and the amber glass lanterns may give you the feeling of ancient buildings in Egypt or Crete, or perhaps some lost civilization. (Tiffany, who was fascinated with ancient times and faraway lands, also designed Laurelton Hall's hanging gardens, a three-storied domed fountain court, and a rather strange, moody octagonal Oriental room on the second floor.)

Now climb the ornate cast-iron 1893 Chicago Stock Exchange Building staircase, a noteworthy example of Gilded Age craftsmanship. A large collection of glassware and silver is displayed on the balcony, including pieces from Tiffany & Co. and Tiffany Studios.

Although the exhibits change periodically, you will probably see the famous *Magnolia Vase* and *Viking Punch Bowl* of 1893, two extravagantly ornate pieces made by Tiffany & Co., which received rave reviews at the Chicago World's Columbian Exposition that year.

Be sure to see the case of Tiffany Studios glassware. One vase, whose base forms a green, leafy stem crowned by a pink tulip bowl, is imaginative and charming, as is a fan-shaped vase executed in the design and rich colors of peacock feathers. Another vase simulates molten lava, and yet another has the iridescence of dragonfly wings.

As you leave the American Wing, passing through the Medieval Sculpture Hall, you will see 13th- and 14th-century examples of leaded-glass windows. These windows exemplify the stained-glass masterworks that Tiffany admired and sought to emulate.

Notice also ancient examples of iridescent glass in the cases lining the corridors leading back to the main entrance. Tiffany had his own collection of ancient glass on which he modeled his glassware.

★

Now, last, but certainly not least, take a pleasant bus ride along Fifth Avenue to Tiffany & Co., at 57th Street and Fifth Avenue. (The bus stops in front of the museum.)

What fun it is to browse among the cases of gleaming silver, sparkling crystal, porcelains, and jewelry. Just Imagine: Tiffany & Co. was 150 years old in 1987 and still carries on in much the same way it did in the 19th century, a living tribute to the genius of Charles Lewis Tiffany.

Left: The entrance loggia from Tiffany's mansion, Laurelton Hall. Exhibited in the American Wing of The Metropolitan Museum of Art. (Photograph © Jeffrey Jay Foxx, 1990)

Right: *Landscape Fountain*, a 1905 glass mosaic artwork. Exhibited in the American Wing of The Metropolitan Museum of Art. (Photograph © Jeffrey Jay Foxx, 1990)

The New-York Historical Society

170 Central Park West
Between 76th & 77th Streets
New York, NY 10024
212-873-3400

Hours:
Tuesday-Sunday 10:00 a.m.-5:00 p.m.

Admission:
- Adults $3.00
- Seniors $2.00
- Children under 12 $1.00

Library

A major research library of American
history; free with admission to The New-York
Historical Society. 212-873-3400 ext. 221

Hours:
Labor Day to Memorial Day
   Tuesday-Saturday 10:00 a.m.-5:00 p.m.
Memorial Day to Labor Day
   Monday-Friday 10:00 a.m.-5:00 p.m.

Group Tours:
Reservations required. Free guided tours of
the permanent and temporary exhibits may be
arranged.

Handicapped:
Call the Society for information

The Metropolitan Museum of Art

Fifth Avenue at 82nd Street
New York, NY 10028
212-535-7710 for recorded information

Hours:
Tuesday-Thursday & Sunday
   9:30 a.m.-5:15 p.m.
Friday & Saturday
   9:30 a.m.-8:45 p.m.

Closed Monday

Admission: (Suggested donation)
- Adults $6.00
- Students & seniors $3.00
- Free to members & children under
  12 with adult

Group Tours:
Advance reservations required:
212-570-3916. Numerous individual audio
tours and free group walking tours.

Handicapped:
Many special programs. Call for information
212-879-5500 ext. 2063

Tiffany & Co.

Fifth Avenue & 57th Street
New York, NY 10022
212-755-8000

Hours:
Monday-Saturday 10:00 a.m.-5:30 p.m.

Additional Sights

Tiffany Studios produced hundreds of leaded-glass windows for churches and synagogues in New York City. These are a few of the finest that remain:

St. Michael's Episcopal Church
Amsterdam Avenue at 99th Street. Tiffany designed the entire chancel of the sanctuary — seven apse windows above the altar (each five feet wide by 25 feet high), an inlaid marble altar, railings, and pulpit. In the smaller Chapel of the Angels: a glass mosaic, two Resurrection windows, marble altar, and railings. Call ahead 212-222-2700.

Church of the Incarnation
Madison Avenue at 35th Street, 212-689-6350. By Tiffany Studios: Oak and bronze doors, as well as five windows, including *The Twenty-Third Psalm* . (This somber and interesting 19th-century Gothic church is just a block from the Pierpont Morgan Library.) Informative leaflet describing the windows. Generally open daily except Thursday, 9:00 a.m.-1:00 p.m.; however, it would be wise to call first, especially during the summer.

Church of the Ascension
Fifth Avenue between 10th and 11th Streets, 212-254-8620. One window, *The Resurrection*. Open daily noon-2:00 p.m.

Temple Emanu-El
Fifth Avenue and 65th Street, 212-744-1400. Beautiful landscape window. Open daily 10:00 a.m.-4:30 p.m.

First Presbyterian Church
124 Henry Street at Clark Street in Brooklyn Heights, 718-624-3770. Six memorial windows; half-dome window over pulpit of mosaics. Call Monday-Thursday to make an appointment to see the windows.

R E S T A U R A N T S

The Metropolitan Museum of Art Restaurant and Cafeteria
Fifth Avenue at 82nd Street
212-570-3964

Restaurant Hours
Lunch:
    Tuesday-Sunday 11:30 a.m.-3:30 p.m.
Dinner:
    Friday-Saturday 5:00-8:00 p.m.

Cafeteria Hours
Breakfast:
    Tuesday-Sunday 9:30-10:30 a.m.
Lunch:
    Tuesday-Sunday 11:30 a.m.-4:30 p.m.
Dinner:
    Friday-Saturday 5:00-8:00 p.m.

• Reservations suggested on weekends

The Metropolitan Museum Restaurant offers a surprisingly tranquil lunch oasis in the crowded museum. Service is professional, tables are uncrowded, and the food is appetizing.

Typical offerings: a daily fish choice such as sole meuniere, always garnished with nicely prepared vegetables; a tasty duck and pear salad with mango chutney; a seafood chef's salad; and a daily omelet (a brie and chives combination recently sampled was quite good). There is a nice selection of desserts.

Lunch $8.00-$14.00
Dinner $10.00-$17.00

The cafeteria offers both hot and cold dishes. There are always chef's salads, fruit salads, and made-to-order sandwiches. Hot main courses in hearty proportions change daily and may include meatloaf, chicken pie, smothered chicken, and lasagna.

Tavern on the Green

Central Park West at 67th Street

212-873-3200

Brunch:
Saturday & Sunday 10:00 a.m.-3:30 p.m.
Lunch:
Monday-Friday noon-3:30 p.m.
Pre-theatre:
Monday-Friday 5:30-6:45 p.m.
Dinner:
Monday-Sunday 5:30-11:00 p.m.

- All major credit cards
- Reservations suggested
- Valet parking

Warner LeRoy, owner of Tavern on the Green, is the son of Mervin LeRoy, producer of *The Wizard of Oz*. Maybe that explains the fanciful exuberance of this restaurant.

The Crystal Room is a flamboyant greenhouse with splendid views of Central Park through walls of windows. Flowers are everywhere: in bouquets, in the carpet design, and in overflowing planter boxes. This huge, glass-enclosed dining room is a modern addition to an historic Central Park landmark, which was a sheepfold until 1934, used to shelter sheep that grazed on Sheep Meadow in Central Park. The original sheepfold is now the Chestnut Room, a delightful dining room with a beamed ceiling and brass-and-copper chandeliers. This room offers a lovely view of the tree-shaded terrace. (LeRoy obviously admires Tiffany too. There are many reproductions of Tiffany artworks in the restaurant.)

Tavern on the Green is lavish and fun and extremely popular, even with children, who love the festive Disney-World sort of atmosphere. The food is good too. Considering the great number of people served each day (over 1,500), we were amazed at the quality and preparation of all the dishes we tried.

Appetizers included a rich, garlicky lobster bisque and a flavorful New England clam chowder. The house salad was tossed with walnut-oil vinaigrette and was full of walnuts, apple chunks, and cheese, mixed with fresh greens — quite delicious.

Main courses included a sauteed red snapper on a bed of Chinese cabbage, bathed in a piquant lemon wine sauce. The grilled sea bass was equally succulent, prepared with fennel, lemon chutney, and a spicy black bean relish. Other winners: the juicy grilled chicken in a rich and spicy marinade, the roast leg of lamb in a tasty veal broth, and the sauteed venison, prepared in a deep red-wine sauce with barley pilaf.

Desserts included a velvety chocolate truffle cake with mocha sauce; chocolate supreme with cocoa cream, chestnuts, and cappuccino sauce; a poached-pear, oven-glazed and splashed with rum cream sauce; and a strudel served with Armagnac ice cream.

Lunch and brunch dishes also include a variety of egg dishes and sandwiches such as a nice lobster on a brioche and a thick and juicy hamburger surrounded with a heap of crisp french fries. (Hamburgers served at dinner also.)

In nice weather it is a treat to have a drink or dine on the terrace at a white wrought-iron table under a tree encircled with flowers. In the evening the trees are spangled in tiny white lights.

Brunch $7.00-$26.00
Lunch:
Appetizers $4.50-$13.00
Entrees $11.75-$24.00
Three-course prix fixe $13.50-$18.50
Dinner:
Appetizers $7.00-$14.00
Entrees $11.50-$32.00
Pre-theatre dinner:
Three-course prix fixe $19.60-$23.50

Sarabeth's Kitchen
423 Amsterdam Avenue at 80th Street
212-496-6280

Second location
1295 Madison Avenue
Between 92nd & 93rd Streets
212-410-7335

Breakfast:
 Tuesday-Friday 8:00 a.m.-3:30 p.m.
Brunch:
 Saturday & Sunday 9:00 a.m.-4:00 p.m.
Lunch:
 Tuesday-Friday 11:00 a.m.-3:30 p.m.
Afternoon tea:
 Tuesday-Friday 3:30-5:00 p.m.
Dinner:
 Monday-Thursday 6:00-11:00 p.m.
 Friday & Saturday 6:00 p.m.-midnight

- All major credit cards
- Reservations suggested for dinner

This busy little restaurant has a loyal follow-ing. Its reasonable prices, good food, and lively, cheerful atmosphere are the reasons.

Salads may include a warm chicken salad on a bed of mixed greens with roasted pine nuts, and a sliced jumbo shrimp salad on a bed of greens — both well-seasoned and fresh.

Examples of imaginative and tasty sand-wiches: a tender smoked roast chicken salad and a grilled smoked fresh mozzarella with tomatoes and avocado.

Soups are always a good bet. I've had a fresh tomato and basil soup, an aromatic pumpkin soup, and a creamy spinach soup — all satisfying and delicious.

There really is a Sarabeth, whose recipes and constant attention to detail have made this little restaurant and another at 1295 Madison Avenue extremely successful.

Breakfast $3.00-$9.00
Lunch $4.00-$11.00
Dinner:
 Appetizers $3.50-$7.00
 Entrees $14.00-$19.50

D I R E C T I O N S

To The New-York Historical Society

Subway:
- #1 to 79th Street & Broadway
- B, C to 81st Street

Bus:
- M7 (Seventh Avenue / Broadway / Avenue of the Americas)
- M10 (Seventh / Eighth Avenues / Central Park West)
- M79 (79th Street crosstown)

Car:
- Henry Hudson Parkway, West 79th Street exit
- FDR Drive, East 71st Street exit

To The Metropolitan Museum of Art

Subway:
- IRT #6 to East 77th Street
- IRT #4, 5 to East 86th Street

Bus:
- M1, M2, M3, M4 (Fifth / Madison Avenues)
- M79 (79th Street crosstown)
- M86 (86th Street crosstown)

Car:
- FDR Drive, East 71st Street exit
- Henry Hudson Parkway, West 79th Street exit
- Parking in garage at 81st Street & Fifth Avenue

From the museum to Tiffany & Co.

Bus:
- M1, M2, M3, M4 (Fifth / Madison Avenues)

Bidding
on History

A New York City
antiques auction

t is a bitter February afternoon, a Tuesday. The sidewalks already have a thick padding of snow, and the sky is white with flakes. The doors of William Doyle Galleries open with a *whoosh* and a blast of icy air, letting in a few more people to preview the Wednesday auction. And I am one of them.

The gallery is festive under clusters of sparkling chandeliers, all tagged for the auction tomorrow. It is warm here, and cheery, with the hum of conversation, the crisp rustle of auction catalogs, the soft sounds of furniture drawers being opened, crystal being picked up then set down, metal brushing against metal.

There are tableloads of crystal, cases of porcelains, and a friendly jumble of furniture — a nice mix of antiques in all price ranges.

I stand a minute, leafing through the catalog. Each item is described here, along with the price the gallery feels the object will bring — a range between two estimates. Of course, many pieces are "hammered down" below or above the estimates given.

I saunter over to an inlaid mahogany tea table. This is a slim-legged beauty, described in the catalog as "American Federal-style mahogany oval tea table ($300-$500)." This tells me that the table

Above: The fun begins! Previewing at William Doyle Galleries. (Photograph © Jeffrey Jay Foxx, 1990)

Right: Japanese Imari porcelains from the author's collection — bought at auction, of course! (Photograph by Beth Crowell, 1990)

is in the *style* of American furniture made from the end of the American Revolution until the early 19th century, but the word "style" tells me that the table wasn't actually made during that period. Even so, the table is well-proportioned with a nice veneer — a good buy.

Speaking of good buys, the experts have plenty of tips for auction-goers:

Never buy at auction without pre-viewing, and once there, carefully examine the object you are considering for such imperfections as cracks, chips, improper repairs, and "marriages" (a combination of elements from different pieces to make a new unit — usually applies to furniture, but sometimes to crystal and silver). If unsure, ask a staff expert for help.

Ask yourself, "Will this piece fit into the space I'm considering?" Borrow a tape measure, and write down the dimensions to take home. Just remember: Nothing will haunt you more than to discover you've bought a disaster that is two feet too long for the wall, dwarfs everything else in the room, or won't even go up the stairway.

And think about repairs. Your prize may have a peeling veneer that could cost more to repair than the piece is worth, or perhaps even worse, is impossible to repair. Again, ask for advice.

Buying for investment? Be sure you like it! Values go down just as fast as they go up.

Keep in mind that dealers can unload their mistakes. You probably can't.

Now go home. Picture the object nestled among your treasures. Will it really harmonize with what you have? Is there room for it? Do you really need it? Now is the time to be sensible, because emotions can run high at auction!

If you still want the object, the next step is to decide how much you are willing to pay, using the gallery estimates as a guideline. Remember that there are additional costs: Auction houses usually add a surcharge of 10 percent, and sometimes more, based on your final bid. Don't forget city and state taxes. Finally, add 5-10 percent for emotional leeway.

If you keep these tips in mind, you should certainly be well-armed to enter the auction fray.

"All right, what about this tea table?" I ask myself. "Will it fit into the space beside the sofa? No — too high. In front? No, I don't need it in front. In fact, I don't need that table at all."

I notice a good-looking pair of English Georgian-style crystal decanters ($150-$250) next. I'm leaning over, getting a closer look, when an ample body wedges in beside me.

"I *do* like *those*!" He beams at me over wire-rimmed glasses, then scrutinizes the decanters, carefully running his fingers over them, feeling for chips. "Lydia-a-a!" he demands in a thunderous voice. "Come over here and check these decanters. They've got What's-Her-Name Wallace written all over them!"

Off he struts, looking like a prime turkey, barely breaking his stride as he flips over a small chair to peer at its underpinnings.

This is one reason I'm here today — to soak up auction atmosphere and people-watch. I've attended many previews and auctions through the years, as I once owned an antiques store. But it was all business then. Today I'm here for the pure pleasure of it, and it has been hard to choose among the auction houses, because each one has a distinct personality and is exciting in its own way.

More treasures to examine at a William Doyle Galleries preview. (Photograph © Jeffrey Jay Foxx, 1990)

I also go to previews because they provide an excellent free education in fine works of art and antiques. Where else is a person allowed to touch — or even hold — museum-quality works of art? As dealers and collectors know, inspecting fine objects is vital to learning, but it is also extremely important to know how an object *feels*. An antique has a certain softness of surface, for example, or a different weight, or a subtle tapering. The craftsmanship peculiar to antique furni-

ture can be studied by opening a drawer, or examining a chair frame, or gently rubbing the surface of a table.

One more reason to attend previews: Superb collections, expertly and lovingly assembled over many years, wind up at auction. These collections often include privately held art treasures. The finest paintings, drawings, and prints. Incredible porcelains, rare furniture, and other splendid works of art representing the masterpieces from every age and country.

And now the auction at William Doyle Galleries! (Photograph © Jeffrey Jay Foxx, 1990)

Then there is the auction itself, an adventure in pure theatre. The air is electric with excitement. The bidders are the players in the drama: a mixture of the serious, the frivolous, the fashion plates, and the peculiar. The rest of us — another motley mix — have come to view the whole colorful spectacle!

I'm reflecting on all of these favorable aspects of the auction scene when I notice a young couple methodically examining each and every object. The woman, dressed in a black suede suit that announces "I assure you, I am expensive," has the elongated, hungry look of a woman who has denied herself and is proud of it. He, on the other hand, is garbed in what he undoubtedly considers to be shabby English elegance. Both have been to the hairdresser, which has cost them a bundle.

They stake a claim next to me, then they immediately launch into a ruthless critique of a pair of gilded candlestick table lamps ("So-o-o pretentious! We should get them for Emily!") and of an English mahogany Pembroke table ("Dreary! Dreary! Dreary! Perfect for the Wilsons!"). A 19th-century pine slant-top desk seems to pass muster ("Just too adorable!").

I edge away and amble over to the information counter where I pick up an absentee bidding sheet. A gentle-eyed woman behind the counter encourages me with "I hope you get the item you want, dear. Just fill in your name, address, etc., write down the item number and the highest bid you want to make, and sign it. We'll do your bidding for you!"

As I fold the sheet and put it away, I catch sight of a fine Italian walnut and satinwood corner cabinet, circa 1900, ($800-$1,200). I stroll over to run my fingers over the honey veneer.

My gaze drifts upward. Is that a

pencil drawing by the American impressionist Mary Cassatt hanging above the cabinet? It is indeed. I am studying the beautiful little sketch when I feel a tap on my arm. A tiny, fragile-looking woman peers up at me.

"Excuse me, but would you give me your opinion about these chandeliers? I just can't make up my mind!" She waves a set of neatly manicured fingernails vaguely above her.

We talk over the chandeliers. (Exchanging viewpoints is not at all unusual at auction previews.) The woman gives me a detailed description of her apartment. We decide against the 19th-century French gilt metal and crystal chandelier ($250-$350) and settle on the gleaming Dutch brass six-light chandelier ($600-$900). The woman shyly thanks me and then turns to scribble notes in her catalog.

I have a decision to make as well. Should I bid on the brass lamp decorated with unusual reliefs resembling Mayan faces ($200-$300)? It isn't antique, but the brass has a patina that develops only with time — 20 or 30 years, I'd say. It would be nice to have that lamp on my desk as I write my book — a memory of this day.

I gather up my notebooks and my catalog and stand a minute, savoring this auction preview. Then, with a last appraising look at the lamp I want (which I do win the next day for $250), I pull on my gloves, button my coat, and step into the wintery twilight.

The brass lamp with Mayan reliefs, bought at auction by the author. (Photograph by Beth Crowell, 1990)

Auction procedure, rules, and services vary from gallery to gallery, but here are a few general guidelines:

Check Approval:
Call the gallery's credit manager before the day of sale to establish credit references if you would like to pay by personal check. Otherwise, payment will be made by cashier's check, certified check, travelers check, cash (or sometimes by unconfirmed personal check, which must clear before purchases are released). Some galleries ask for a deposit the day of sale with the balance due the next day; others allow more time for payment and pick-up of merchandise. Be sure to ask.

Bidding

In Person:
Register your name, address, and credit references to obtain a numbered paddle, either before or during the sale. You will raise this paddle each time you bid. The auctioneer will call out your number if yours is the highest bid.

By Order Bid:
If you can't attend the auction, you may fill out a bid form at the desk, writing down the highest bid you will offer for a "lot" (the term used for an item or group of items sold as one entity). A gallery representative will bid for you and will try to get the lot for you at the lowest possible bid, continuing to bid until your maximum has been reached.

By Telephone:
You may bid by telephone when your lot goes up for sale, but you must make arrangements well in advance, as facilities are often quite limited. Arrangements must often be confirmed in writing 24 hours before auction.

By Agent:
Anyone — friend or professional — may act as your agent, bidding as you would bid.

Bidding Increments:
How are bidding increments decided? Will a bid exceed the previous bid by $10? By $50? By $100? At what price does bidding start?
Procedures vary. An auctioneer might, for example, open the bidding at one-third to one-half the estimated value of the lot with bidding increments 10 percent or less over the last bid. The auctioneer has final say over the bidding. The best bet is to call the auction house and ask about its procedure.

The Successful Bid:
If you are attending the auction, you'll know at once if you've won your lot because the auctioneer will call out your paddle number. If you've placed an order bid, telephone the gallery after the sale.

Collecting Merchandise:
Purchases must be picked up within a specified time to avoid storage charges, usually three days. Check with the cashier. After you have paid for your merchandise, the cashier will give you a receipt allowing you to pick up your merchandise. Ask about pick-up hours.

Additional Services:
Galleries will usually make shipping arrangements for you, especially helpful if you are shipping out of the country.
Galleries usually offer written evaluations of an object's monetary worth for insurance, taxes, etc. A fee is charged. Informal verbal appraisals are often given without charge. These services extend to objects that have not been purchased at the auction house.
Several auction houses offer free lectures on a variety of subjects. Both Sotheby's and Christie's offer informative and entertaining lectures.

Some auction houses offer a restoration service for objects bought at their auctions, and galleries will often give buyers free con-servation tips as well as pre-auction restoration estimates on furniture.

Some auction houses publish first-rate books about antiques and works of art. Call for a list. Christie's and Sotheby's both offer a wide range of publications.

A Partial List of New York City Auction Galleries

Note: Auction houses will give preview and auction information by phone or will send information by mail. In addition, the Friday edition of *The New York Times* has a section devoted to upcoming previews and auctions.

Christie's
502 Park Avenue
New York, NY 10022
212-546-1000

- Special events & lectures: call main number
- Catalogs: 718-784-1480, or write:

  Christie's Catalog Department
  21-24 44th Avenue
  Long Island City, NY 11101

- Auctionline: 212-371-5438 for 24-hour auction and exhibition information

Christie's East
(A Christie's offshoot for less expensive items)
219 East 67th Street
New York, NY 10021
212-606-0400

- Auctionline: 212-371-5438, for information about upcoming previews and auctions

Lubin Galleries
30 West 26th Street
New York, NY 10010
212-924-3777

The Manhattan Galleries
221 West 17th Street
New York, NY 10011
212-727-0370

Phillips Auctioneers
406 East 79th Street
Off First Avenue
New York, NY 10021
212-570-4830

Sotheby's
1334 York Avenue at 72nd Street
New York, NY 10021
212-606-7000

- 24-hour auction and exhibition information: 212-606-7245
- Catalogs: 1-800-447-6843

Swann Galleries, Inc.
104 East 25th Street
New York, NY 10010
212-254-4710
(See Swann Galleries chapter)

Tepper Galleries
110 East 25th Street
New York, NY 10010
212-677-5300

William Doyle Galleries
175 East 87th Street
New York, NY 10128
212-427-2730

R E S T A U R A N T S

The Summer House
50 East 86th Street
212-249-6300

Brunch:
 Saturday & Sunday 11:30 a.m.-3:00 p.m.
Lunch:
 Monday-Friday 11:30 a.m.-3:00 p.m.
Dinner:
 Daily 5:00-11:00 p.m

- All major credit cards
- Reservations suggested

The Summer House has the cozy quality of an old-fashioned tea room — a carousel horse in the window, cabbage-rose wallpaper, and the contented chatter of friends who obviously meet here often for lunch.

Appetizers include a tasty fresh mozzarella salad with basil, black olives, tomatoes, and olive oil; a creamy broccoli soup; and a healthy portion of crisp mixed greens with a well-seasoned vinaigrette dressing. Soups change daily and are nicely prepared.

Main courses might include a delicately seasoned curried chicken salad; a Russian egg and salmon plate garnished with caviar and sour cream on brown bread; a turkey club with lettuce, tomato, and bacon, served with a creamy Thousand Island dressing; and a homey chicken pot pie. There is always a nice choice of omelets, such as the unusual bacon and chutney combination — quite flavorful.

I always save room for dessert here, and I am especially fond of the moist carrot cake, although I still remember a deep, velvety chocolate cake I had a year ago!

Lunch:
 Appetizers $4.50-$9.00
 Entrees $8.50-$12.50
Dinner:
 Appetizers $4.50-$9.50
 Entrees $10.50-$19.50

Indian Tandoor-Oven Restaurant
175 East 83rd Street
Corner of Third Avenue
212-628-3000

Daily noon-11:30 p.m.

- All major credit cards

This tiny restaurant serves the whole range of Indian dishes at very reasonable prices, including oven specialties cooked over charcoal in an Indian clay oven; delicious curry dishes; dishes prepared with cream, almond, and sweet spice (kurma); or with green peppers, onions, tomatoes, and spices (jalfrazie); or with spinach and spices (shaag). All are served with an aromatic rice, onion relish, and hot mint sauce.

Lunch & dinner:
 Appetizers $2.35-$7.50
 Entrees $4.95-$15.95

D I R E C T I O N S

Subway:
- IRT #4, 5, 6 to 86th Street & Lexington Avenue

Bus:
- M101 & M102 (Third / Lexington Avenues)
- M86 (86th Street crosstown)

Car:
- FDR Drive, 96th Street exit

Historic Gracie Mansion

Home of the mayors

The History

hen I first visited Gracie Mansion during the summer of 1989, Mayor Edward I. Koch's photograph laughed merrily from a silver frame in the kelly-green study. Many changes have taken place since that June day. Mayor David N. Dinkins and his wife Joyce now call the lovely old mansion their home. They, like the previous mayor, Ed Koch, and the six mayors who preceded him, will fill the historic house with the things they love — family heirlooms, photographs, books — all of those favorite treasures that give a home its unique personality and make it welcoming to visitors.

★

I certainly felt at home that balmy June day as I sat in the cheerful study talking to David Reese, the mansion's curator — a young man with 19th-century courtesy and charm, and with a number of years of experience in architectural history and preservation, including five years as director of the Abigail Adams Smith Museum in New York City. Then one fine day he received a call from

Above: Gracie Mansion today.
(Photograph © Jeffery Jay Foxx, 1990)

Left: Gracie Mansion, circa 1915. Shows the house in decline when it was managed by the New York Parks Commission. Dilapidated shutters and railings had been pulled down, and the house was being used as a refreshment stand, as the sign "ice cream" indicates. (Courtesy of Museum of the City of New York)

Gracie Mansion, a call that marked a decidedly interesting turn in his career.

"I always have to be prepared for the unexpected, because I never know what is going to happen. There is never a typical day," David Reese explained, adding that this made his work all the more enjoyable. He told me that although Gracie Mansion is the mayor's home, it is also an extension of New York City government. Hundreds of official events — breakfasts, press conferences, dinners, receptions, and even outdoor barbecues — are held at the mansion each year. In addition, the house is open for public tours.

Because Gracie Mansion is used so heavily — more than 22,000 people visit the house each year — the curator's responsibilities include the constant refurbishing of the mansion, which is an ongoing project of reupholstering, replacing, and repainting. Another responsibility is the study and preservation of the fine antiques and works of art lent by private collectors and museums. Then there is the "meeting and greeting" of visitors — David has met everyone from heads of state to Dolly Parton.

"The former mayors certainly left their own indelible stamps on this house," I remarked. "But tell me — before that time — were the previous owners of the property dynamic, interesting?"

As the minutes ticked by on that sunny June afternoon, I sat back in a comfortable chair, sheltered by the walls of a house nearly 200 years old — the silent observer of so much of America's history — listening as David Reese began to weave the fascinating story.

★

From 1646 to 1896 — exactly 250 years — the high, select 11 acres of land on which Gracie Mansion now stands were owned successively by six men. During half of that time, from 1646 until 1770, the property was held in turn by the first two owners, Dutch landholders and their families. The 11-acre tract, which was used for farming, comprised just a portion of the land owned by these men.

In 1770 the 11-acre parcel was sold to Jacob Walton. Considered the finest of locations for a country estate, the property was a prime slice of land running from present-day East 86th Street to East 89th Street. Walton's ownership marked the end of the land's peaceful, bucolic years. It would soon play an unexpected role in the American Revolution.

The proud owner, Jacob Walton, was a wealthy, prominent New Yorker, who was a member of the New York General Assembly and vice president of the New York Chamber of Commerce. He had enhanced his position in society further by marrying Polly Cruger, who was from another prosperous merchant family.

In spite of Walton's ties and devotion to New York, he was a Loyalist, an unfortunate leaning in view of the events that were about to unfold. He was no fool, however, and after building a handsome two-storied house, he had a secret tunnel constructed — a brick-lined passage leading to the East River, his safeguard in the event a hasty retreat to a waiting ship proved necessary. (This tunnel lay hidden, a secret of the past, until it was accidentally discovered in 1913 by a park foreman.)

As fate would have it, the Waltons never used that tunnel. General George Washington, realizing the strategic importance of the site, forced the family to evacuate the house in 1776. American Minutemen immediately built a fort on the land, and after installing a battery of heavy guns, they waited for British sails to appear on the East River. That time was not long in coming. In October of 1776 the British bombarded the fort, destroying the house. British soldiers occupied the land.

Meanwhile the Waltons, who waited anxiously outside the city, mourned the loss of their beloved home. They were never to enjoy their land again, as they died within eight days of each other in 1782, the year before the British surrendered the site.

The land lay vacant, waiting for its next owner, the once well-tended garden growing wild around the remains of the foundation of the Walton house and the battered fort. Sixteen years came and went; then in 1798 a new chapter began to unfold in the mansion's history.

David Reese set the stage, describing New York City at the turn of the 19th century. "We often think that thrifty, cautious Yankee traders were living quietly at that time. Not true. New York was free-wheeling and highly speculative, just as it is today. People came to New York to make money; they made huge fortunes, and they lost them."

This was the New York City that Scotsman Archibald Gracie found when he arrived in 1784. He was 29 years old and already becoming "a man of parts," a successful merchant trader.

Soon after Gracie moved to the city, he formed a mercantile company; then, upon hearing that riches were a certainty from the tobacco trade, he moved to Petersburg, Virginia. He found the life there uncivilized and dismal, and the climate unbearably hot and humid, but he also found a treasure trove in the tobacco trade. He stayed in Virginia eight years, returning to New York City afterward to live in high style with his young bride.

Gracie and his wife, Hetitia, who was a granddaughter of Connecticut Governor Thomas Fitch, enjoyed a life of plenty

Archibald Gracie (1755-1829). Miniature on ivory, circa 1890. (Courtesy of The New-York Historical Society, New York City)

in New York — plenty of money, ships (21 of them), and children, eight in number. They had many influential acquaintances as well. The Gracies entertained Alexander Hamilton, President John Quincy Adams, John Jay, and the Marquis de Lafayette, among others.

In 1798 Gracie decided to give his family a home in the country. He felt that it was important to have a "country seat" away from the bustling activity, the dirt, and noise of the city, which probably seemed congested, as nearly 60,000 residents lived in a concentrated area at the southern tip of Manhattan Island.

Between the thriving downtown area and the northern tip of Manhattan lay miles of rolling green farmland, much of it owned by a few wealthy families, who had already built fine country houses along the East River shoreline. These

were the old, prominent families who ruled New York society. Gracie decided to join their ranks.

So it was that in December of 1798 Archibald Gracie bought the 11 acres of Walton property for the tidy sum of $5,625. In 1799 he began construction on a rather modest house when compared with those of his neighbors, but it was a well-proportioned two-storied structure, perfectly square, with two chimneys. The Gracies delighted in their country house, and surrounded by their young children, they spent summer days on the tree-shaded lawn, enjoying the clean and sparkling river.

By 1809 additions, including an impressive parlor, had nearly doubled the house in size. Additions and improvements were made through the years, until at last the country seat of Archibald Gracie was splendid indeed. Graceful Chippendale-style railings embellished the eaves and porch. Fine gardens and a stand of magnificent trees surrounded the house. A long promenade looped over the rolling lawn, whose green expanse sloped to a stone sea wall. A fanciful bathing pavilion perched near the river. An orchard, a greenhouse, a two-storied stone stable, and an ice house completed the estate, which was enclosed by a pristine white picket fence.

While the country estate was being enlarged and refined, Gracie was also building an elegant house on downtown Pearl Street, the most fashionable of locations — completed in 1806. His fortune seemed secure. In fact, the fortunes of most New York City merchants and shippers had been rising rapidly, reaching a peak in 1806. It was then that the tides of fate rushed in, engulfing Gracie and all that he owned.

The French and British had been battling on the seas even before war was declared between them in 1803, but by 1806 it was apparent that American merchant ships were to be targets for both countries. Napoleon threatened seizure of any ship sailing to England, while Britain threatened all ships that traded with France. Finally, in desperation President Thomas Jefferson requested Congress to place an embargo on trade with all foreign nations, which lasted from 1807 to 1809.

American ships were dead in the water. One after another the merchant shippers lost their fortunes. Archibald Gracie was one of the unlucky ones, losing over a million dollars during this period. Then, when he felt things couldn't get worse, they did. America declared war on England on June 19, 1812. By the next year the British had seized four of Gracie's ships.

Curiously, during the years that Gracie's fortune was draining away, he continued to live in a luxurious manner. He built expensive new offices and bought three new ships. He even began construction on a lavish new downtown residence, which he completed in 1812.

Yet it was after the war that Gracie made his most disastrous mistake. In 1817, determined to compel France and England to pay reparations for the lost ships, he sailed to Europe, where he spent two fruitless years petitioning both governments. Meanwhile, his son and son-in-law, who had been left in charge of

the business, began to speculate wildly and lost the remainder of Gracie's fortune. Then, compounding the disaster, they borrowed hundreds of thousands of dollars, using Gracie's properties as security.

By 1820 Archibald Gracie was worth $20,000. In 1823 his company, Archibald Gracie and Sons, was bankrupt, and all of his property was sold, including the beautiful country house on the hill.

Archibald Gracie spent his remaining years continuing to press his claims against the governments of England and France. Although he lived to see the modest claims against England settled, the merchant trader died a broken man in 1829 at the age of 74.

★

Two more men were destined to buy Gracie Mansion. Joseph Foulke, who had made a fortune by the time he was 30 years old, was also a merchant shipper. Unlike Gracie, however, Foulke managed to keep his money and his country house, which he enjoyed for 34 years with his wife and 10 children, eventually selling the property to Noah Wheaton in 1857.

As it developed, 1857 was the wrong year to buy Gracie Mansion, as it was the year of a severe financial panic. No sooner had Noah Wheaton installed his family in the gracious house than he began to suffer the first of several financial reverses that plagued him for most of the 39 years he owned the house. During these years Gracie Mansion was neglected, slowly sinking into a shabby, deteriorated condition. Wheaton's daughter finally saved the day — and the house — by marrying an enterprising realtor, enabling Wheaton to spend his declining years happily puttering about the house until his death at the age of 85. The year was 1896.

For a number of years New York City had cast covetous eyes on the Gracie property, which was located on the northern border of East River Park. (In 1908 East River Park was renamed Carl Schurz Park in honor of the German immigrant who became U.S. Senator and Cabinet member during the Hayes administration, among other achievements.) In 1896 the city acquired the land through condemnation proceedings, placing it under the jurisdiction of the New York Parks Commission until 1942. These were years of various indignities to the house, which was used as a concession area and comfort station for the park, as well as for a storage area. Fortunately, the Museum of the City of New York occupied Gracie Mansion from 1923 to 1932, pulling it out of complete decay with a renovation.

It was Park Commissioner Robert Moses who changed Gracie Mansion's downhill slide. After ordering a careful restoration in 1934, Moses proposed a plan that would ensure the future of the mansion, making it an extension of city government by making it the mayor's home. With some reluctance the first occupant moved into the house in 1942. He was Mayor Fiorello LaGuardia, who, by the way, said quite soon afterward that he was enjoying the house immensely.

★

This then is the chain of historic events leading to the present day. Mayor Koch was instrumental in securing the mansion's future, establishing the Gracie Mansion Conservancy in 1981, a non-profit organization which has overseen a sensitive and historically accurate restoration of the house and has been dedicated to its preservation.

It is Mayor David Dinkins' turn now — and undoubtedly he and Mrs. Dinkins will continue the revitalization of this grand old mansion, just as they will continue to welcome the thousands of visitors each year into the beautiful and historic home.

The Tour

The mansion that visitors see today is the culmination of three separate building phases, beginning with Archibald Gracie's construction of the original house in 1799. During the second building period ending in 1810, Gracie completed a wing that doubled the house in size, adding a formal parlor and additional upstairs bedrooms.

The third construction period was begun during the administration of Robert F. Wagner, Sr., who was mayor from 1954 to 1965. The plan for this wing was the inspiration of Mayor Wagner's wife, Susan, and is named in her memory. This final wing effectively separated large official functions from the mayor's private quarters in the original mansion. The new wing, completed in 1966, includes a large reception room or ballroom, a sitting room, and a library.

★

As the tour begins, and visitors climb the steps of the stately Federal house, they usually pause to gaze at the handsome façade, which after careful research was recently painted a muted yellow with green shutters. Graceful railings edge the eaves and porch roof.

The tour begins in the golden-yellow ballroom, its lofty ceilings bordered by deep, richly detailed white moldings. The

design of the ballroom harmonizes so well with the Federal architecture of the original house that it is hard to believe the room is a modern addition.

Among the fine antiques in the ballroom are a superb 1785 Irish crystal chandelier and numerous crystal sconces. Especially noteworthy is a bull's-eye mirror, surmounted by a fierce gilded eagle, one of the largest made during the Federal period (circa 1785-1825). The symbol of American hospitality, the pineapple, is found throughout the ballroom on the sconces and the carved capitals of the fluted columns.

Adjoining the ballroom is a small reception or sitting room, which is often used for small meetings or as an overflow room for larger parties and receptions. Decorated in an airy beige and ivory, the walls of this small room are lined with antique Hudson River engravings. Among other antiques are two important Federal card tables and a Directoire chandelier, made during the years of the French Revolution.

The third room in the new wing is decorated as a library, with walls of hollyberry red. The library is centered by a Gothic Revival table which actually belonged to the Gracie family, lent to the mansion by the great-great-grandson of Archibald Gracie. An early 19th-century English Regency chandelier hangs above the table.

Of special interest is an arresting portrait of Mrs. William Gracie (Archibald Gracie's daughter-in-law), painted in 1815 by John Trumbull. Beautiful Elizabeth Wolcott Gracie, daughter of a Connecticut governor, died six years after her 1813 marriage to William, and her funeral was held in

Gracie Mansion. (It was also during this time that William bankrupted his father's business.)

The tour continues in the original mansion, which has been restored as it might have looked in the early 19th century. According to the docent, the Conservancy decided to restore this portion of Gracie Mansion to resemble the house during the time of Archibald Gracie — but to make it seem as though succeeding generations of Gracies had lived there until the end of the 19th century, adding their own furnishings and favorite objects. For this reason, visitors see antiques and decorative objects that span approximately 100 years.

The spacious entrance hall (originally two rooms in the 1799 house) has been wallpapered in a sprightly beige and ivory stripe. The floor was painted to resemble marble, *faux marbre*, as was fashionable during the Federal period, and is centered with a design of a mariner's compass.

Among the outstanding antiques are splendid Federal painted side chairs, each decorated with a different seascape, and a rare five-back painted settee, made in New York City about 1805.

The centerpiece of the entrance hall is the Federal doorway, original to Gracie's 1799 house. When Gracie added the north wing, this doorway was moved from the south elevation to the east, changing the frontage to face the East River.

Adjacent to the entrance hall is the mayor's study, a comfortable and cheerful room that features dentil molding and an original Gracie mantel. (Most of the mantels in the mansion are original to the house, but only the mantel in the study is in its original location.)

The entrance hall at Gracie Mansion.
(Photograph © Jeffrey Jay Foxx, 1990)

The dining room is decorated with a splendid 1830 French handpainted wallpaper, whose landscape is entitled *Classical and Modern Scenes of Paris*. The colors are vibrant and glowing, primarily because the paper was imported by a New York family during the early 19th century and for some reason was never used. It was rolled up and placed in their attic, in which it lay forgotten until surprised descendants found it and subsequently sold it to the Conservancy.

A rosewood-veneered sideboard stands in the dining room. Apart from its value as a fine example of early 19th-century furniture designed in the French manner and attributed to the French cabinetmaker Charles-Honoré Lannuier, the sideboard is important because it was owned by Archibald Gracie's family.

A colorful multistripe carpet adds a festive note to the dining room. Called Venetian Stripe, it is a reproduction of a design that was quite popular in the 19th century.

The drawing room or parlor is decorated in a style greatly admired during the mid-19th century and reflects a delight in pattern-on-pattern design, the more the better — patterned wallpaper, draperies, upholstery fabric, and carpeting.

In contrast, the furniture is restrained and well-proportioned. For example, there are four chairs from the workshop of Duncan Phyfe (1768-1854), the celebrated Scottish-born cabinetmaker who owned a prosperous business on New York City's Partition Street (now Fulton Street) from 1795 to 1854.

Other furnishings include a pair of Hudson River chairs, made about 1820, and a superb 1815 looking glass. Lining the walls are numerous paintings by New York artists as well as canvases depicting New York subject matter.

The tour continues upstairs, where

Gracie Mansion dining room.
(Photograph © Jeffrey Jay Foxx, 1990)

visitors see three bedrooms, each one decorated in a different manner. A delightful folk art bedroom is decorated with wide Federal-red moldings, early rope beds (utilizing stretched ropes instead of springs), and navy-and-ivory woven coverlets. Colorful blue-and-white gingham curtains brighten the windows.

Another spacious and cheerful bedroom is distinguished by maple *faux* bamboo furniture, considered suitable for country houses at the end of the 19th century and reflecting the continuing taste for all things Oriental.

★

The tour ends with an exhibition of the world of merchant trade as seen through the eyes of Archibald Gracie. This seems an appropriate finish to the history-rich walk through a 19th-century house built from New York City's merchant trade — a house that has stood through nearly 200 years of New York City's changes and growth, and functions so well today in the fast-paced life of New York City's mayor.

Gracie Mansion

East End Avenue at 88th Street
New York, NY 10128
212-570-4751

Tours:
Tours given every Wednesday from March
until mid-October. You must reserve.

Group Tours:
For information call 212-570-4751

Tour Hours:
10:00 a.m., 11:00 a.m., noon, 2:00 p.m.,
3:00 p.m., and 4:00 p.m.

Admission: Free

RESTAURANTS

Little Nell's Tea Room

343 East 85th Street
Between First & Second Avenues
212-772-2046

Brunch:
  Saturday & Sunday 11:00 a.m.-3:00 p.m.
Lunch:
  Monday-Friday noon-2:00 p.m.
Afternoon tea:
  Daily 2:00-5:00 p.m.
Dinner:
  Daily 6:00-11:00 p.m.

- All major credit cards
- Reservations suggested

Little Nell's is exactly what an old-fashioned
tea room should be — all pink with ribbons
and flowers — pink tablecloths and napkins
and dainty bouquets of spring blossoms.

There is a harp in the corner, waiting to be
played on Saturday and Sunday evenings. The
atmosphere is cozy and quiet, a good place to
be when you want to talk.

An imaginative menu is offered for lunch
and dinner, and the dishes are prepared with
flair. Appetizers include homemade soups —
I chose a rich, flavorful lettuce and watercress
soup laced with onions — tangy and velvety
and absolutely delicious. Plump, stuffed
mushrooms in a pool of rich, wine-laced
cream sauce were mouthwatering. Pasta
brimming with bright vegetables and bathed
in spicy tomato sauce was zesty and fresh.

Pasta is also a good choice for a main
course. The rigatoni Romano was prepared
with a creamy tomato sauce full of fresh
Romano cheese. The sauteed filet of chicken
arrived on a bed of angel hair pasta, sauced
with wine, mushrooms, and garlic — just
wonderful! The grilled marinated Cornish
hen was crisp, golden, and juicy.

Brunch dishes include such tempting
choices as eggs Benedict, coddled eggs with
sausage and bacon, pasta dishes, potato
pancakes with scallions and sautéed mushrooms, and coddled eggs with lox and dill.
There is always an array of pretty — and good
— desserts, such as an ivory cake, layered
with creamy mocha custard.

If you come for afternoon tea, choose from
cucumber, chicken, salmon, shrimp, watercress, and parsley-butter finger sandwiches;
tender scones with Devonshire cream and jam;
and a selection of 18 teas, including apricot
and raspberry.

Brunch:
  $3.95-$10.95
Afternoon tea: $12.95
Lunch:
  Appetizers $2.95-$5.25
  Entrees $7.95-$12.50
Dinner:
  Appetizers $3.50-$6.95
  Entrees $13.95-$18.95

DIRECTIONS

Subway:
- IRT #4, 5, 6 to 86th Street & Lexington Avenue

Bus:
- M15 (First / Second Avenues)
- M86 (86th Street crosstown)
- M31 (York Avenue)
- M79 (79th Street crosstown)

Car:
- FDR Drive, 96th Street exit

A 1935 record drawing of Gracie Mansion from the Historic American Building Survey ordered by Park Commissioner Robert Moses in 1935. (Courtesy of the Gracie Mansion Conservancy)

Building the Largest Gothic Cathedral in the World

The Cathedral of St. John the Divine

The Story of Construction

I saw the cathedral for the first time on a hot August day. I was trudging up Amsterdam Avenue, thinking more about the sweltering heat and the street noises than of my visit — that is, until I approached the great west façade.

High on its pedestal of steps was a cathedral right out of the 13th century, with its blackened stone blocks, intricate carvings of saints, and massive bronze doors. Yet the cornerstone was laid to begin construction on St. John's Day, December 27, 1892.

The Cathedral of St. John the Divine is an astonishing 601 feet in length (the length of two football fields), 177 feet high to the ridge of the nave roof (a 17-story building), and covers 121,000 square feet. When it is finally finished, it will be the largest Gothic cathedral in the world. (Although St. Peter's in Rome is larger, it is not a cathedral.)

The story of construction is a fascinating one. As early as 1828 there were New Yorkers who reasoned that whatever Europeans had done, Americans could do, and that extended to building a great cathedral. They realized that the project would be an awesome task. After all, the European cathedrals had taken hundreds

Above: The 1927 Ralph Adams Cram design for St. John the Divine. View of south façade. Still to be completed are the west towers, the great crossing, the transepts, and the choir roof. Cram was the noted architect of more than 100 churches, including chapels at West Point and Princeton and St. Thomas Church on Fifth Avenue. (Courtesy of Museum of the City of New York)

Right: The bustling activity of New York City today, set against the peaceful majesty of the cathedral. (Photograph © Jeffrey Jay Foxx, 1990)

of years to finally reach completion.

There were problems to overcome from the very beginning. Since the immense structure had to rest on bedrock, excavation continued until it was reached. Two years later and 72 feet down, workers found bedrock at last.

The arduous task of construction finally began. The decision was made to build the stone cathedral using medieval techniques as often as possible — a time-consuming plan, to say the least. A carver might use as many as 150 different tools to carve one stone figure — one sculpture out of thousands needed.

Finding the money was a problem from the start. The decision had been made never to borrow funds. When money ran out, construction stopped. Unfortunately, money constantly ran out, especially during the Depression and World Wars I and II. Construction halted

The beautiful west façade of the Cathedral of St. John the Divine. (Photograph © Jeffrey Jay Foxx, 1990)

entirely from 1941 to 1979.

In spite of these difficult problems, two-thirds of the cathedral has been completed. Four areas still remain unfinished: the transepts, or arms of the cross (medieval cathedrals were almost always built in the shape of a cross); the two rectangular towers that will rise above the west façade; the great crossing, the vast space at which the transepts meet the body of the cross; and the choir roof.

These problems and other challenges faced a new dean in 1972. When the Very Rev. James Morton arrived, he brought with him the dream that the cathedral could play a vital role in meeting the economic and cultural needs of the community, as well as spiritual needs.

Dean Morton's dream comes true every single day. St. John the Divine fairly explodes with programs and activities, ranging from a soup kitchen to a crisis intervention center. There is an activities program for youngsters, a telephone reassurance program for seniors, and a thrift shop. All of these and others flourish with the help of a great many volunteers.

Along with the religious services offered each day, there are numerous musical events, lectures, plays, art exhibitions, and other stimulating programs scheduled constantly. With all of these activities going on, how could there be any time or money left to recommence the work on the cathedral? It has been done, but not without extraordinary effort.

The first problem was to find the craftsmen, and the solution was an imaginative one. A master builder, master carver, and stone cutter arrived from England to teach apprentices, who were often young people from the neighborhood. A stoneyard was set up on the cathedral grounds, and the painstaking work was begun.

When will the monumental cathedral be finished? It could take a hundred years; yet that is a short time. Many medieval cathedrals required 300 years or longer.

Meanwhile, visitors are encouraged to watch ongoing work at the stoneyard. For a brief time they will leave 20th-century Manhattan and enter the world of the medieval stone mason.

The Tour

Before you enter the Cathedral of St. John the Divine, take a few minutes to study the intricate west façade. Every carving, every design element, forces the eye skyward. The pointed arches, the narrow shafts of statuary, and the 14-foot-high stone cross above the central portal direct the eye heavenward. This is one of the glories of Gothic architecture.

Of special interest are the fine central bronze doors depicting scenes from the Old and New Testaments. These doors, each weighing three tons, were cast and fabricated in Paris by the prominent bronze founder, Barbedienne.

The eight stone carvings flanking the far left portal are heroic in size, each eight feet high and weighing 7,000 pounds. These figures symbolize the Christian martyrs, while the ninth figure on the central post is of St. Peter.

Rising nine-and-a-half feet above the choir roof is a bronze statue of St. Gabriel blowing his trumpet. Gutzon Borglum, who sculpted this figure, is better known for creating the monumental heads of the four Presidents on Mt. Rushmore.

After entering the cool, shadowy cathedral, you will immediately notice the overwhelming silence, especially in contrast to the buzz saw of noises outside. But it is the immensity of the cathedral that may stay in your memory long after you complete your visit.

Before you begin the tour, go to the information desk for a plan of the cathedral, as well as an information sheet. The simple plan clearly shows the incomplete design in the shape of a cross.

★

The narthex, located at the base of the cross, is an entry area meant to give the visitor a moment to shed earthly cares and thoughts.

Ahead is the nave, divided into five aisles and soaring 124 feet high, equivalent to the height of a 12-story building. This is a fine example of Gothic architecture, with its slender supporting piers rising 100 feet and culminating in the graceful vaulted ceiling.

One of two sets of splendid 17th-century tapestries hangs in the nave. This set, depicting New Testament scenes, was woven in Mortlake, England, from cartoons (full-scale paintings used as patterns for the tapestries) painted by Raphael in 1513. The original cartoons were created for Charles I and are owned by the British Crown.

Bays flanking the nave, 14 on each side, symbolize the various earthly and spiritual pursuits of mankind.

Beginning on the near left, they are *Sports, Arts, World Crusaders, Education, Law* (fine example of an altar screen, a reredos), *The Church, Historical and Patriotic Societies, and Fatherhood.*

Beginning on the near right they are *All Souls* (powerful memorial sculpture of Holocaust victims), *Missions, Labor, The Press, Medicine* (reredos), *Monastic Life, Armed Forces, and Motherhood.*

The superb rose window on the west front is 40 feet in diameter and is composed of 10,000 pieces of glass in rich

hues of lapis and ruby. The stained-glass
windows above the bays are also of
superior quality.

    Behind the nave lies the crossing, the
intersection of the body of the cross and
the transepts. Each transept, when completed, will be 125 feet in length. The
unfinished crossing is covered by a

An interior view of the great bronze
doors on the west façade. (Photograph
© Jeffrey Jay Foxx, 1990)

351

temporary tile dome constructed in 1909. This dome is noteworthy, as it covers a huge space and is totally unsupported from beneath.

The second set of 17th-century tapestries hangs in the crossing. These 12 tapestries were commissioned by Pope Urban VIII and were woven on the Barberini looms in Italy from cartoons by Romanelli. The scenes depicted are from the New Testament.

An intricately carved marble pulpit in the Gothic style stands in the crossing. The choir lies behind the crossing and is backed by eight towering granite columns, each 55 feet high, six feet in diameter, and weighing 130 tons. The columns were completed and put into place in 1903, even before the walls of the cathedral were begun.

Beautiful stained-glass windows can be seen behind the columns, high in the ambulatory wall. These windows depict the vision of New Jerusalem in the Revelation to St. John the Divine.

Ten larger-than-life stone figures of the Apostles by Gutzon Borglum are found outside the choir.

Two massive gilt-bronze menorah candelabra can be seen flanking the high altar, each weighing more than a ton. These were modeled after those used in the Temple of Jerusalem.

To the right of the high altar is the Magna Carta Pedestal, which once supported an historic altar. In 1214 the barons swore before the altar to obtain the Great Charter from King John guaranteeing English liberties.

A wide walkway or ambulatory begins beside the choir and continues in a horseshoe pattern behind the high altar. Radiating from the ambulatory are a baptistry (left of the choir) and seven quite beautiful chapels.

The baptistry was given by the Stuyvesant family in 1928. (A member of this eminent Dutch family, Peter Stuyvesant, lived from 1592 to 1682 and was the last Director General of New Amsterdam before it became New York.) Objects relating to early Dutch history in New York are displayed in the baptistry.

Each of the seven chapels is dedicated to a different ethnic group. Of particular interest are the stained-glass windows and gates of ornate ironwork. The cathedral information sheet explains each chapel's important features in detail.

★

Before you leave the cathedral, be sure to visit the gift shop. You will find unique items, which are primarily religious in nature; among them, a puzzle of the great rose window, cathedral architectural prints, original cathedral photos, and interesting replicas of stone carvings found in St. John the Divine. The shop is a pleasure to visit.

A Biblical garden, featuring plants found in the Holy Land before and during the life of Christ, may be visited during the growing season. Ask for directions at the information desk.

Finally, see the stoneyard, a memorable experience and one you will probably never have again.

The first choir, circa 1911. In 1940 the semi-dome was replaced by a Gothic vault. (Courtesy of Museum of the City of New York)

The Cathedral of St. John the Divine

1047 Amsterdam Avenue
Between 110th & 113th Streets
New York, NY 10025
212-316-7540

Hours:
Daily 7:00 a.m.-5:00 p.m.

Services: (Several each day)
For hours call 212-316-7540

Current productions, lectures, etc.:
• Box Office, call 212-662-2133
    Daily 9:00 a.m.-5:00 p.m.
• Public Affairs, call 212-316-7542
    Daily 9:00 a.m.-5:00 p.m.

Gift Shop Hours:
Daily 9:00 a.m.-5:00 p.m.

Stoneyard

Amsterdam Avenue at 112th Street
Go through fence gate at left of the cathedral

Hours:
Monday-Friday 10:00 a.m.-3:00 p.m.

★

Don't miss the *Peace Fountain*, located in a small park near the cathedral. This large, fanciful work of art is dedicated to all of the children on earth. A giant bronze crab, a storybook sun, a deer, and a mythical winged creature are combined into a sculpture at least 20 feet high, resembling something out of *Alice in Wonderland*.

R E S T A U R A N T S

V.T. Restaurant, Inc.

1024 Amsterdam Avenue
212-663-1708

Tuesday-Friday 11:30 a.m.-11:30 p.m.
Saturday (lunch only) 11:30 a.m.-3:00 p.m.
Sunday 11:30 a.m.-10:30 p.m.

• Cash & checks only

Diagonally across the street from the cathedral the weary sightseer can find a friendly haven at this unpretentious Southern Italian family-style restaurant.

The menu is extensive and typical of restaurants of this genre, including all kinds of pasta dishes, well-prepared and served in generous portions. Other main courses include stuffed peppers, meat loaf, and six different veal dishes. Among the other offerings are pizzas, sandwiches, and salads.

Entrees $5.95-$14.95

★

Hungarian Pastry Shop & Cafe

1030 Amsterdam Avenue
212-866-4230

Weekdays 8:00 a.m.-11:00 p.m.
Saturday & Sunday 9:00 a.m.-11:30 p.m.

• Cash only

The Hungarian Pastry Shop & Cafe is the place to go for such energy-lifting drinks as hot cider, Hungarian coffee flavored with almonds and cinnamon, or a fragrant spiced tea.

Try one of their pastries: flaky strudels, black forest cake, or an "almond bombe," made with almonds, chocolate, and rum.

Cafe St. John

1018 Amsterdam Avenue
Corner of 110th Street &
Amsterdam Avenue
212-932-8420

Lunch:
   Monday-Friday 11:30 a.m.-3:00 p.m.
Dinner:
   Monday-Friday 6:00 p.m.-1:00 a.m.
   Saturday noon-1:00 a.m.
   Sunday noon-midnight

• American Express

This little restaurant just recently opened its doors and already seems to be doing a booming business. The decor is simple, the food is good, and the service is efficient and cordial. Main courses range from excellent hamburgers to nicely prepared lemon scallops and chicken in wine sauce.

Main courses $9.95-$14.95

★

Ideal Restaurant

2825 Broadway
Corner of 109th Street
212-866-3224

Monday-Friday 11:00 a.m.-11:00 p.m.
Saturday & Sunday noon-11:00 p.m.

• American Express, MasterCard & VISA

Would you like to try Cuban food? This little restaurant offers a wide menu of savory dishes served in a friendly atmosphere.
   You might start by having Cuban tamales with meat sauce and green peppers. Main courses include Pollo Ideal, a healthy portion of chicken accompanied by a tasty combination of rice and red beans, garnished with sauteed peppers and onions. Try a nicely prepared filet mignon or chicken cordon bleu, Cuban-style. For the adventurous — mondongo, a spicy tripe stew.

Lunch & dinner:
Appetizers $2.95
Entrees $9.00-$14.00

DIRECTIONS

Subway:
• #1 stops at 110th Street & Cathedral Parkway

Bus:
• M5 (Fifth Avenue / Avenue of the Americas / Riverside Drive)
• M11 (Columbus / Amsterdam Avenues)
• M3, M4 (Fifth / Madison Avenues)
• M104 (Broadway)

Car:
• FDR Drive, East 116th Street exit
• Henry Hudson Parkway, West 96th or West 125th Street exit

Ulysses S. Grant, Napoleon of the Civil War

Grant's Tomb tells the story

Above: Funeral procession of President Grant, August 8, 1885. View of Fifth Avenue, west side, looking south from 34th Street to 29th Street. On that corner stands Marble Collegiate Church, built in 1854. Marble Church, whose minister was for many years Dr. Norman Vincent Peale, flourishes today under its pastor, Dr. Arthur Caliandro. (Courtesy of The New-York Historical Society, New York City)

Left: Grant's Tomb today. (Photograph © Jeffrey Jay Foxx, 1990)

The History

t was a blistering summer day in New York City. August 8, 1885. The funeral procession of President Ulysses S. Grant. Black bunting draped buildings on either side of Broadway and Fifth Avenue. At least a million mourners pressed against the barricades, jammed the open windows, even filled the swaying trees until the branches cracked.

More than 60,000 soldiers marched along the street in formation according to rank. Following the horse-drawn catafalque were President Grover Cleveland, his cabinet, members of the Supreme Court and Congress, the state's governors, and 8,000 New York City dignitaries. The marchers formed a great, slow river seven miles long.

This was the greatest funeral procession ever witnessed by the American people, surpassing that of Abraham Lincoln. To those who lined Broadway and Fifth Avenue that day or who walked behind the catafalque, Ulysses S. Grant was the hero who saved the Union from destruction, the man who brought peace.

What happened during the following 100 years to change the understanding of Grant? Most Americans today have only sketchy knowledge of Grant's life, often remembering that he was a Civil War general who drank too much and later was a President who damaged his honorable name by an administration full of corruption. However, perhaps they also remember that Grant played out the American dream, proving that anyone can rise from the ranks — and can even become President of the United States.

Grant's beginnings were humble enough. Born in Point Pleasant, Ohio, on April 27, 1822, the first child of Jesse and Hannah Grant, Hiram Ulysses grew up in Georgetown, Ohio, in a modest brick house across the street from the tannery owned by his father. A lucrative business, tanning, but an ugly, brutal one that the young boy hated.

Ulysses lived in this small Ohio town for 16 years with a demanding, difficult father, a peculiar (some said disturbed) mother, two brothers, and three sisters. The young boy seemed to have few attributes. He was small, wiry, unattractive, and quiet. He did have three things in his favor — determination, riding skills, and a father with grand ambitions on his behalf.

That father saw to it that his eldest son had a good, solid education, and even managed to get the 17-year-old boy an appointment to West Point. Ulysses grabbed the chance, his ticket out of a lonely, boring life.

Above: Pedestrians and carriages on Riverside Drive on a sunny afternoon, circa 1897. Shows Grant's Tomb several months after dedication. At long last President Grant's body was moved from the temporary tomb and interred here on a cold, blustery day that kept many from attending the dedication. (Courtesy of The New-York Historical Society, New York City. Photograph by Robert Louis Bracklow)

Ulysses Simpson Grant* quickly discovered that he disliked West Point, although he easily passed his courses and held a place in the middle of his class. Other than his superb horsemanship, there was nothing about Ulysses S. Grant that indicated greatness. Indeed, much later few of his classmates could recall anything about him.

The climb to fame was long and hard and full of misery. After Grant's graduation from West Point in 1843 and his first taste of battle during the Mexican War of 1846-1848, which wrested the Southwest and California from Mexico, there were 12 degrading, unhappy years. Grant's military career was going nowhere, and he resigned his commission in 1854. Every business he tried turned to dust. It was widely rumored that he was a drunkard. (Grant did drink periodically, possibly linked to bouts of depression.)

The only bright spot in Grant's life during this dismal time was his family — his wife, Julia Dent Grant, and their four children, the last born in 1858. Julia, born into a prosperous St. Louis family, was strong, loving, and stable — fortunate traits, as their marriage had to survive many difficult years.

During those desperate days people later recalled that Grant always seemed to be brooding, his 5-foot-8-inch frame often slumped over a piece of wood he constantly whittled into splinters. He was usually garbed in a faded blue army coat and frayed trousers, stuffed into cracked and dirty boots. He wore a worn-out black hat that shaded sad blue eyes and a half-smoked cigar constantly jutted from his determined mouth.

Grant finally hit bottom in 1858, having failed again, this time at dirt farming on land owned by Julia's father. He asked his father for a job, something he had sworn he would never do, and in 1860 moved his wife and four children to Galena, Ohio. Grant, at the age of 38, became a clerk in one of his father's leather goods stores.

Within months his life changed dramatically. In April 1861 a town meeting was called in Galena. Its purpose was to recruit soldiers, and the only professionally trained soldier present was the former Captain Grant, who was asked to preside over the meeting and later to be in charge of recruitment.

By June Grant had been recommissioned as a colonel. By August he was a brigadier general. The clothes were still rumpled, but people in Galena said there was something different about the man. For one thing, the hunched posture was gone. But it was far more than that — Grant was a rising star, and he knew it.

The Civil War
General Grant's Command Begins
1861-1863
Battles won: Fort Henry, Fort Donelson, and Shiloh, Tennessee; Vicksburg, Mississippi; Chattanooga, Tennessee.

I saw an open field ... so covered with dead that it would have been possible to walk across the clearing, in any direction, stepping on dead bodies, without a foot touching the ground.

Ulysses S. Grant

With sureness of purpose Grant divided the Confederacy. He was 41 when President Lincoln promoted him to the rank of commander of all forces in the West. On March 9, 1864, Grant rose to the rank of lieutenant general, subordi-

---

* (A name-change from Hiram to Simpson, his mother's maiden name, which occurred because there was a mistake on the West Point appointment papers)

nate only to President Lincoln, a rank held by just one American before him: George Washington.

General Grant was a formidable leader. He seemed to be everywhere during a battle, lounging easily astride one of his powerful, fast battle stallions. The general wore a faded, old blue uniform; a dusty and rumpled black hat shaded his eyes. No trappings of rank except his general's stars. No sword. He liked to ride among his troops, to be one of them. Make no mistake, his men knew he was in command. General Grant accepted only total victory, and he did whatever he had to do to achieve it.

The art of war is simple enough. Find out where your enemy is. Get at him as soon as you can. Strike at him as hard as you can and as often as you can, and keep moving on.

Ulysses S. Grant

The Wilderness Campaign
1864-1865

Grant mounted the final nine-month campaign of the war with the intention of overcoming General Lee and eliminating the principal Confederate army. Making his headquarters with the Army of the Potomac in northern Virginia, Grant became the commander of all the Union armies, holding Robert E. Lee's forces in a stranglehold, while his generals mounted relentless and savage offensive thrusts in the remaining theatres.

The telegraph system with its vast network (eventually over 15,000 miles of lines) allowed Grant to direct and communicate with his generals and to follow the battles on all fronts. With great satisfaction he learned at the beginning of September 1864 that General William Sherman had burned Atlanta, Georgia, beginning the bloody "March to the Sea"

that culminated in the fall of Savannah, Georgia, that December. The 33-year-old general, Philip H. Sheridan, was equally successful in his Shenandoah Valley campaign in Virginia. On December 15, 1864, Grant received a telegraph message that General George H. Thomas was winning a decisive battle at Nashville, Tennessee. On April 3, 1865, Richmond, capital of the Confederacy, fell.

General Robert E. Lee, surrounded and unable to retreat, surrendered to Union forces on April 9, 1865. The two great generals met in a farmhouse at Appomattox Court House, Virginia. Lee was aristocratically resplendent in a new gray uniform, his sword sheathed in a scabbard worked in gold. Grant, disheveled and dirty, apologized for his dress. The two men talked of their days at West Point and during the Mexican War, then quietly shook hands. Grant silenced the rejoicing Union gun salutes. He later wrote that he had "felt like anything rather than rejoicing ... "

Ulysses S. Grant was a great hero in 1865, and every American knew his face — aged by war, angular, strong, with the eyes of a warrior who had seen too much killing. His beard was still present, but trimmed neatly; and the ever-present cigar still jutted determinedly from the stern mouth. This was the face that had stared from posters and newspapers during the war. Grant had become one of the first media stars, thanks to that new process of 1839, photography.

The general was surprised and pleased by the throngs of cheering admirers who snatched at his clothes and strained to touch him. A sea of uplifted faces raptly followed his short, modest speeches. In their midst was an Olympian hero who had saved the Union.

Grant was 43 years old. He knew that he would be the next President.

362

★

Ulysses S. Grant's war years were his glory years. During the remaining years his great popularity began a slow, often humiliating decline. Grant had been a brilliantly successful warrior, but he soon discovered that he was embarrassingly ignorant and naive in the world of politics and finance.

During his eight years as President (1869-1877), Grant seemed unable to correctly judge the men he chose for government positions and unable to accurately assess the countless issues that faced him during Reconstruction. The firm, clear decision-making ability he had possessed as a battle commander he somehow lost as President.

Scandals erupted throughout Grant's administration, starting with a gold speculation scandal in which members of his own family, perhaps even his wife, took part and culminating in a Wall Street panic dubbed "Black Friday." The affair was apparently a mystery to Grant until the very end. Other scandals followed with sickening regularity.

Grant failed a great test of his presidency, Reconstruction of the South after the Civil War. Caught between the radical Republicans in Congress who sought social transformation and the diehard former Confederates who opposed any reform, Grant provided ineffective leadership. By the end of his administration the impetus for racial equality was gone.

General Ulysses S. Grant. Bust portrait, circa 1864. Probably taken in Matthew Brady's studio. Photograph from *The Civil War Album* pp. 19-20. (Courtesy of The New-York Historical Society, New York City)

Grant's disasters followed him from the White House. After a brief, abortive try for a third term, the Grants settled in New York City at 3 East 66th Street in a handsome brownstone. Then, as now, life in New York City was expensive, and Grant began to worry about finances. He decided to entrust all of his life savings, $100,000, to his son's Wall Street firm, Grant & Ward. Little did he know that Ward was involved in improper stock manipulations. The scheme was uncovered, and Grant & Ward failed, dragging other brokerage firms and banks down with it. Grant, who was by that time 62 years old, was disgraced and lost everything he had.

It was that very summer, when Grant was so physically and emotionally weakened, that he discovered he had cancer of the throat. How could he ensure Julia's financial security? He decided to write his memoirs.

Amazingly, this taciturn man wrote with grace, style, and power. His memory was flawless. The details of his war years were vivid and fresh.

As Grant's pain turned to agony, he wrote steadily. In May 1885, he managed to complete the two-volume epic, the *Personal Memoirs of U.S. Grant*, which was published by his friend Samuel Clemens (Mark Twain), who made certain that Julia received a handsome return from the bestselling book.

At 8:00 a.m., July 23, 1885, Grant's terrible suffering was over. His heroic struggle to protect Julia had been a stunning success. Julia received more than $450,000 in royalties during the remaining 17 years of her life. She lived comfortably in Washington, D.C., until her death on December 14, 1902, at the age of 76. She was laid to rest beside her husband in the great granite mausoleum on Riverside Drive in New York City.

The Tour

It soars 150 feet above you from its island of grass and trees — Grant's Tomb — the monument most people have heard about but surprisingly few have visited. You are looking at the largest mausoleum ever constructed in America.

Before you climb the double tier of wide steps, take a few minutes to study the imposing architecture, which is, simply stated, a gigantic cube surmounted by a great, column-ringed cylinder beneath a cone-shaped roof. The southward-facing portico is supported by 10 towering fluted Doric columns whose lower sections are seven feet in diameter. Eight thousand tons of granite, brought by rail from Maine, were used to complete the façade. (During construction so many visitors began to chip away bits of granite for souvenirs that a high fence was placed around the tomb to prevent wholesale damage.) Work began in 1891, and the tomb was finally completed in 1897 at a cost of $600,000.

You will immediately understand why this site was chosen for Grant's last resting place when you look westward. The view of the Hudson River and the green Palisades of New Jersey is splendid and still totally unobstructed. It is interesting to know that in 1885 there was controversy over the choice of this site, as the land, which is now West 122nd Street and Riverside Avenue, was considered too far out in the countryside.

The monument you see today was designed by New York architect John Duncan and was modeled after the tomb of Mausolus (from which *mausoleum* was derived), one of the seven wonders of the ancient world, as well as the tomb of the Roman Emperor Hadrian. Although Duncan's basic design was realized, much of the splendid ornamentation was never completed. Funds dwindled, then ran out during the long years of construction. Meanwhile, Ulysses S. Grant's body lay in a temporary brick tomb nearby.

Duncan's design had called for immense bronze exterior sculptures — an equestrian statue of Grant centering the steps in front of the portico, four large figures above the portico, another at the rotunda level, and an immense sculpture of Victory in a chariot drawn by four horses at the tomb's pinnacle. In addition there was to be a dramatic approach from the Hudson River, a triumphal arch, a railroad station, and a dock for steamers.

Instead you will see a plaque above the entrance inscribed with the words, *Let Us Have Peace*, a plea made by Grant during his first inaugural address. Two large figures flank the plaque, said to symbolize Victory and Peace. Two eagles in flight guard the wide steps, and a large red flag emblazoned with four stars, signifying Grant's rank as general, floats in the sky to the right of the tomb. That is all of the exterior ornamentation, but it seems enough — perhaps what Grant would have chosen for himself.

The monument's interior, which was modeled on Napoleon's tomb at Les Invalides in Paris, is sheathed in marble. Centering the rotunda is an open crypt containing the sarcophagi of the general and Julia Grant. The sarcophagi are of red granite from Wisconsin, and each weighs eight and one-half tons. Many visitors discover that this is the surprising answer to the timeworn question "Who is buried in Grant's Tomb?" General Grant insisted that his wife lie by his side in death as in life, yet he realized that because he was an idolized public figure, this wish might be denied. New York City officials assured Grant's family his wish would be carried out if they chose New York City as the site. The decision was made, which infuriated a number of other states.

In the colonnade surrounding the crypt there are niches holding the busts of the generals under Grant's command — Sherman, Thomas, McPherson, Sheridan, and Ord. The bronze busts were sculpted by artists in the WPA program in 1938.

The three nine-foot by 18-foot murals placed in the lunettes high in the rotunda were designed by Allyn Cox, the muralist who designed a section of the frieze at the Capitol in Washington, D.C. These three murals were dedicated in 1966.

The mural on the left side of the rotunda represents the Battle of Chattanooga, which led the way to the invasion of Georgia. It was after this battle that President Lincoln gave Grant command of all Union armies. Generals Grant and Thomas are seen on horseback, watching the army fight its way to victory at Missionary Ridge.

The mural on the right depicts the Battle of Vicksburg, which divided the Confederacy in half. Grant, again astride his battle horse, watches his officers. Vicksburg and the Mississippi River are seen in the background.

The final mural depicts the surrender at Appomattox. This famous scene, often depicted, shows the handshake between the two great generals, Grant and Lee.

As you stroll around the rotunda, you will see numerous photographs of Grant as he rose through the ranks of power, well-written biographical and historical information, and fascinating material about the tomb's construction. Be sure to read the engrossing biography of Richard T. Greener, the distinguished educator and first black graduate of Harvard, who was a major force behind fund-raising for this monument.

★

Before you leave Grant's Tomb, take a few minutes for a stroll outside. You will see imaginative free-form sculptural benches inlaid with tile mosaics. Here the 19th century meets the 20th century. In 1972 a community participation project was begun under the direction of the National Parks Service. Community residents were encouraged to build the benches and to design and complete the colorful mosaic pictures. As you follow the ribbon of undulating colors, you will be charmed — or dismayed — by the flowers, butterflies, even a scene of a yellow cab amid New York skyscrapers. Whether you find them in harmony with Grant's Tomb or not, you will find them unusual and interesting. In any case, the project was judged a success in terms of the harmony that developed among the neighborhood adults and children, giving a new meaning, perhaps, to Grant's famous words, *Let Us Have Peace*.

Grant's Tomb

Riverside Drive & West 122nd Street
New York, NY 10027
212-666-1640

Hours:
Wednesday-Sunday 9:00 a.m.-4:30 p.m.

The National Park Service Ranger on duty will be happy to give you an informal tour when you visit.

Grant's Tomb is located in a neighborhood called Morningside Heights, an area bounded by the Hudson River on the west, Morningside Park on the east, 125th Street on the north, and 110th Street on the south. Morningside Heights is the home of Riverside Church, just a half-block away from Grant's Tomb, which has a world-famous carillon composed of 74 bells, including the largest bell ever cast. Individual tours are offered every Sunday. 212-222-5900

When the weather is nice, you are allowed to picnic across the street from Grant's Tomb at pretty Sakura Park.

RESTAURANTS

Terrace Restaurant

400 West 119th Street
Between Amsterdam Avenue &
Morningside Avenue
212-666-9490

Lunch:
   Tuesday-Friday noon-2:30 p.m.
Dinner:
   Tuesday-Saturday 6:00-10:00 p.m.

Closed Sunday & Monday

- All major credit cards
- Reservations suggested
- Free valet parking in the evening

I had heard that the Terrace Restaurant was one of the best-kept secrets in New York City. Not true. This excellent restaurant is extremely popular and is a favorite with a long star-studded list of celebrities from Broadway to the world of politics.

First, the atmosphere. Quiet, intimate, and elegant. Handsome decor in burgundy with a mirrored wall. An authentic French feeling. A fine view looking north.

Of course, the food. First-rate all the way. The classic French cuisine is prepared with elegance and imagination.

First courses include a warm lobster salad with succulent lobster chunks served in a silky sauce; grilled prawns and homemade pasta, deliciously sauced and seasoned; smoked Scottish salmon with a rich mousse of smoked trout; a zesty roasted eggplant, tomato, and sweet pepper terrine.

Main courses we've tried include baby chicken roasted with whole garlic and thyme and bathed in natural juices; rich, mouthwatering rabbit in a garlic-laced red-wine sauce; flavorful and moist salmon; and sole, enriched with a seafood mousse and surrounded by a velvety sauce.

Desserts are just as good. They may include a chocolate marquise, a dense square truffle with a luscious pistachio cream sauce flecked with bits of the crunchy pistachios; or a trio of the best sorbets we've ever had — mango, pear, and raspberry, with crisp lacy cookies.

Lunch:
   Appetizers $7.50-$12.00
   Entrees $11.50-$18.00
   Prix fixe $25.00
Dinner:
   Appetizers $9.50-$21.00
   Entrees $25.00-$29.00
   Prix fixe Tuesday-Thursday $44.00

Sylvia's
328 Lenox Avenue
Between 126th & 127th Streets
212-996-0660

Monday-Saturday 7:30 a.m.-10:15 p.m.
Sunday 1:00-7:00 p.m.

• No credit cards

Although the restaurant is some distance from Grant's Tomb, it may be conveniently and quickly reached by taking bus #BX15 from West 125th Street and Riverside Drive to Lenox Avenue and 125th Street.

Sylvia's is the little cafe in the heart of Harlem long famous for its Southern cooking; its casual, dark, Southern-diner interior; and for its customers — who vary from sleek sophisticates and show business greats to busloads of bedraggled tourists, with a good measure of the seedy and the strange thrown in.

As for the food? Well, you can get plenty to eat for under $15.00. People seem to steer toward the fried chicken, barbecued ribs, fried pork chops, or ham. Every meat comes with a choice of vegetables such as black-eyed peas, sweet potatoes, simmered greens, or mashed potatoes. If you're expecting home cooking like Aunt Martha's from South Carolina, you may be disappointed. But you won't be disappointed by the parade of characters who file in and out. (We saw a man swathed in mink to his boot soles, a bevy of gorgeous models who ate like construction workers, and Sylvia herself, balancing loaded plates, dressed in a slinky leather dress. Meanwhile outside, a vintage Rolls Royce hugged the curb, waiting for three burly men in Brooks Brothers suits.)

Breakfast $2.00-$5.50
Lunch & dinner $6.50-$10.95

DIRECTIONS

Subway:
• #1 to 125th Street & Broadway

Bus:
• M4 (Fifth / Madison Avenues)
• M5 (Fifth Avenue / Riverside Drive)

Car:
• From Henry Hudson Parkway, take 125th Street exit. (You will actually be on 133rd Street.) Turn right, following street that runs parallel to the parkway. Watch for a narrow street straight ahead that abruptly runs uphill. This is Riverside Drive. Grant's Tomb is at the top of the small hill.

Parking:
• Available along the street

Ulysses S. Grant. Engraving from a painting by Thomas Nast, 1881. (Courtesy of The New-York Historical Society, New York City)

Distant Hoofbeats, Echoing Drums

National Museum of the American Indian

ust as a kaleidoscope's vivid, unique patterns are shaped by densely packed shards of brilliant glass, the National Museum of the American Indian's vast holdings offer more than one million dazzling artifacts, each with its own special identity, and spanning 11,000 years — easily the largest and finest institution in the world dedicated to the Indian cultures of North, Central, and South America.

The museum was founded in 1916 by George G. Heye, a man of foresight and wealth (an inherited oil fortune), who realized that the Indians' way of life was disappearing at an alarming rate. He decided to document that way of life by collecting and preserving it. In 1897 Heye began to acquire ancient artifacts, photographs, items of everyday life, works of art, weapons, and religious objects — all preserved for future generations.

At present, only one percent of this valuable collection is open to the public in a neoclassical building that is part of a cluster of turn-of-the-century buildings located at Audubon Terrace, 155th Street and Broadway, named for John James

Above: National Museum of the American Indian. (Photograph © Jeffrey Jay Foxx, 1990)

Right: Founder of the museum, George G. Heye, shown with his wife, Thea, and Zuni Indians from New Mexico. Taken in front of the museum January 25, 1923. (Photograph courtesy of National Museum of the American Indian, Heye Foundation)

Audubon, the noted naturalist and artist who lived nearby. Unfortunately, although the building is handsome, it lacks the space to display the museum's great collection, the bulk of which must be stored in a Bronx warehouse.

All of this will change shortly. The museum has recently become a part of The Smithsonian Institution and will ultimately occupy a new building on the Mall in Washington D.C. It will also operate an exhibition facility in the Custom House at Bowling Green in Lower Manhattan. The Custom House, completed in 1907, is the most important Beaux-Arts building in New York City.

Until these facilities are completed, it will be hard for any visitor to complain about the present museum, in which more than 10,000 artifacts and works of art are displayed on three floors, overflowing with so many diverse and unusual objects that it would take a day to study even a small portion of them.

It must have been a monumental task to organize such a collection into understandable units. This has been ably accomplished by dividing the exhibits into broad geographical areas.

The first floor has as its focus North American Indian life from the Atlantic coast to the Northern Plains and the Great Lakes.

The second floor examines the remainder of the North American continent and includes a large wing devoted to North American archaeology.

The third floor concentrates on the

This image, from the museum's collection of more than 86,000 photographs, is a studio portrait of Swift Dog, a Sioux Indian. (Courtesy of National Museum of the American Indian, Heye Foundation. Photograph by F. A. Rinehart, 1898)

tribes of Central and South America, and includes a gallery of archaeological treasures.

Each broad geographical area is further divided into exhibits highlighting the tribes that flourished there. All aspects of everyday life are documented by well-chosen and often rare artifacts. How did the people spend their days? What did they wear? How did they worship? How did they wage war and make peace? Through clear, colorful presentation, Indian life leaves the dusty pages of history books and enters the present.

A good example is the first exhibition seen by visitors as they enter the museum. A tier of brightly lit cases brings the early Iroquois to life, a powerful confederacy of six nations that inhabited the northeastern woodlands. They were unified by a great military skill (thanks in part to guns that they received by trading fur pelts to the Dutch) and by a superb government, whose concepts were so enlightened it is believed that a number of the ideals were incorporated into the United States Constitution.

Among numerous Iroquois artifacts are beautifully crafted women's garments with porcupine quills as decoration, examples of intricate beadwork, fine silver jewelry, and "live" masks carved from living trees and believed to contain supernatural powers.

In contrast to the Iroquois, the Sioux tribes of the Northern Plains led a completely different way of life, especially after acquiring horses first brought into North America by the Spanish.

In the vast landscape of the plains, these tribes followed migrating herds of buffalo, and their culture emphasized bravery and warfare. Sioux warriors were known for their ferocity and daring. Among them were three Sioux leaders who combined forces to destroy Custer and his men at the Battle of Little Bighorn in 1876: Crazy Horse, Rain-In-The-Face, and the medicine man, Sitting Bull.

Sioux warriors considered colorful dress an outward expression of bravery. The war bonnet, believed to have originated with the Sioux, was an important symbol of courage and prestige. Before 1880 the headdress was worn only by chiefs and war leaders and was restricted to ceremonial or other great occasions or battle. War bonnets' tails gradually lengthened after the Indians acquired horses, developing into long, flowing trailers made of feathers from the golden or bald eagle or the wild turkey, designed to blow in the breeze as the rider sat astride his galloping horse. (The 12 feathers from the golden eagle's tail could have the trade value of a good horse.)

Among other exceptional Sioux objects in the collection are the well-worn war club of Sitting Bull, the Medicine Society bonnet worn by Crazy Horse, and rare, sacred medicine bundles, containing as many as 100 religious objects, which were opened before any important undertaking such as a battle or a long journey.

The tomahawk, so popular in Indian lore, is featured in another first-floor exhibit. Surprisingly, tomahawks often have ornamentation of European design. Some have elaborate silver decorations; others have delicate brass inlay; many have heads that are pierced with intricate designs.

There is an interesting explanation: although the Algonkian *tomahak* originally referred to any hammer, club, or ax, by the mid-17th century almost all tomahawks had metal ax heads made by French, English, and American smiths and traded to the Indians.

Tomahawks later developed another use. In addition to warfare, the tomahawk, with a pipe bowl joined to

Works of art and other objects belonging to tribes from the northwestern coast of North America. At center: A house post from Quatsino Sound, Vancouver, British Columbia. The 11-foot-high post was placed inside the home. (Photograph © Jeffrey Jay Foxx, 1990)

the opposite side of the ax blade, was used by Indian envoys to make peace and negotiate treaties. After the mid-19th century these valued symbols of Indian life lost importance and were reproduced and sold as gift items.

Another practice common to many tribes, the taking of scalps, is the focus of another exhibit. Probably developed from ancient religious beliefs, the taking of scalps became a ritual of intertribal warfare, and scalps were sometimes kept as amulets. (Much has been written about the scalping of settlers and others by Indians, but the "white man" took many Indian scalps, sometimes for bounties.)

★

Ancient Indian life is documented in a series of displays on the second floor. One of the most interesting is devoted to Spiro Mound, located near Spiro, Oklahoma.

U.S. Custom House, Bowling Green.
Photograph taken in 1908, a year after
completion. This Beaux-Arts masterwork of Cass Gilbert, the architect of
the Woolworth Building and New
York's U.S. Court House, will be used
as an exhibition facility of National
Museum of American Indian. (Courtesy of Museum of the City of New
York. Photograph by Irving Underhill)

Excavations at Spiro Mound unearthed relics of people who lived in the
region for 10,000 years off and on,
including artifacts of Indians who lived
there from 800 A.D. to 1400 A.D. Evidence of a vast network of trade was
uncovered by excavations, which revealed
such diverse treasures as engraved conch

shells from the Gulf of Mexico and
copper utensils from the Great Lakes. A
cache of pearls was found, as well as
extremely refined pottery and sculptures.

The ugliness of human greed was also
uncovered. The Spiro Mound area was
relentlessly torn apart in modern times by
amateur gravediggers, who destroyed
most of the great works of art and, con-
sequently, information about the past.
This wholesale desecration finally led to
the passage of an act that regulated
archaeological excavations.

Among other noteworthy exhibits on
the second floor are those dedicated to the
Navajo and Apache Indians of the Southwest. The Navajo and the related Apache
tribes left west-central Canada and mi-
grated to the Southwest in the early 16th

century. These warlike Indians were a threatening deterrent to settlement of the Southwest until the latter part of the 19th century. (The Apache warrior Geronimo finally surrendered to the United States Army in 1886.)

Among the fascinating objects: Apache medicine hats, painted with mystical symbols and covered with amulets, giving the wearer the ability to see into the future and to heal the sick, among other powers; Navajo concho belts; the buckskin war cap of Geronimo (1829-1909), thought to have been given to him by his daughter; and Geronimo's colorfully beaded cane.

The striking pottery vessel in the form of a jaguar was made in Costa Rica sometime between the late 15th and early 16th centuries. From a special museum exhibit entitled *Where the Jaguars are Exhalted*. (Photograph by David Browning, 1990)

Life in Central and South America is recorded by an outstanding and varied collection of artifacts and works of art exhibited on the third floor. Several cases display objects from the Jivaro, Amazonian inhabitants of tropical forest areas in eastern Ecuador and north-central Peru. Among the items are blowguns and darts, made from the ribs of ivory-nut palm leaves, which would be coated with

deadly curare poison; a monkey-skin drum used in courting dances; war clubs; and colorful headdresses.

Other objects from Central and South America include red-slip pottery found in graves near ancient Colombian homesites; outstanding clay figures of the Bahia period (500 B.C.-500 A.D.) from the northern coast of Ecuador; Inca drinking vessels; an Aztec stone head of a jaguar from Mexico (15th-early 16th century), its teeth bared menacingly; and a striking pottery jaguar vessel from Costa Rica (15th-early 16th century), with rattle legs and spotted markings depicted as tiny animal heads.

★

The museum's photographic collection of approximately 86,000 images is unsurpassed in its documentation of Indian life. After the process of photography was discovered in 1839, the Indian was a favorite subject, relentlessly recorded by professional and amateur photographers. This interest, sometimes to the point of exploitation, resulted in countless images recording the Indian way of life.

The museum offers special photographic displays, often accompanied by recordings of authentic Indian chants.

A recent exhibit highlighted studio portraits made around 1900, including photographs of famous Indian leaders.

★

Just as a kaleidoscope rotates, revealing ever-changing patterns and colors, so do the museum's exhibits change with every glance — all different, all fascinating: a set of Apache playing cards; Sioux war shields, made from the hides of trophy bull buffalos; a bear cult knife, fashioned from a bear's jawbone; a glass case full of charms, fetishes, and objects used in magic rituals; and a South American jungle war shield covered in a tapestry of bright parrot feathers.

★

Each work of art celebrates in color and design the Indian of the Americas — and each rare artifact holds within it the story of a remarkable past.

Clay figures from the northern coast of Ecuador 500 B.C.-500 A.D. (Photograph by David Browning, 1990)

National Museum of the American Indian

155th Street & Broadway
New York, NY 10032
212-283-2420

Hours:
Tuesday-Saturday 10:00 a.m.-5:00 p.m.
Sunday 1:00-5:00 p.m.

Closed Monday & major holidays

Admission:
• $3.00 for adults
• $2.00 for students & seniors

Group Tours:
Special gallery talks may be arranged for groups. For appointment call: 212-283-2420

The museum library, located at 9 Westchester Square, Bronx, N.Y., is open to the public by appointment. It is a superlative research library, with more than 40,000 books and other materials concerning the archaeology, ethnology, and history of the native peoples of the Americas (212-829-7770).

The museum gift shop has a nice selection of items relating to the Indian culture and history: silver and turquoise jewelry, pottery, belt buckles, and Navajo rugs, as well as a number of books.

Demonstrations by Indian artists and performances by Native Americans are given throughout the year. Lectures are offered on many subjects. Call for details.

Additional Sights

The Hispanic Society of America and the Numismatic Society are also located at Audubon Terrace and are well worth visiting.

Hispanic Society of America

212-926-2234

Hours:
Tuesday-Saturday 10:00 a.m.-4:30 p.m.
Sunday 1:00-4:00 p.m.

Admission: Free

A fine collection of Hispanic art, including superb paintings by El Greco, Goya, and Velázquez; ancient Roman glass; Renaissance furniture; Iron Age and prehistoric pottery.

American Numismatic Society Museum

212-234-3130

Hours:
Tuesday-Saturday 9:00 a.m.-4:30 p.m.
Sunday 1:00-4:00 p.m.

Admission: Free

One of the world's largest collections of coins, paper currency, medals, and medallions. Interesting and informative displays.

DIRECTIONS

Subway:
• #1 to 157th Street
• A, B to 155th Street

Bus:
• M4 (Fifth / Madison Avenues)
• M5 (Fifth Avenue / Avenue of the Americas / Riverside Drive)

Car:
• Henry Hudson Parkway, West 158th Street exit

Historic House, with its own Ghost Story

The Morris-Jumel Mansion

Above: Morris-Jumel mansion, circa 1890. (Courtesy of The New-York Historical Society, New York City)

Left: Morris-Jumel Mansion today. (Photograph © Jeffrey Jay Foxx, 1990)

It was a cloudy Sunday in September. I had taken the brick walk that wound around to the front of the Morris-Jumel Mansion, the only surviving pre-Revolutionary house in Manhattan. As I stood looking up at the great house, my first thought was that it had the same abandoned beauty that empty plantation houses must have had after the Civil War.

Paint was peeling from the portico's two-story-high columns and from the house itself. The graceful balcony needed repair. The door, with its handsome leaded-glass sidelights and fanlight, had an appearance of shabby dignity.

It was obvious that the grounds had once been manicured. There had been fragrant flower gardens, perhaps even a formal geometric garden. Now the property looked forgotten. Overgrown bushes crowded the winding walk, and tangled vines crept over the ground.

I climbed the front steps, wondering what lay behind the door of this venerable old house.

Once inside the spacious entrance hall, I could almost feel the events that had taken place in the house. Festive parties and gracious dinners. Colorful and stimulating conversations. The rustle

Eliza Bowen Jumel, nearing her 80th year. Traces of her youthful beauty are still quite evident. Lithograph made in Paris, France, circa 1854. (Courtesy of The New-York Historical Society, New York City)

rounded by approximately 130 acres of prime land. There they built Mount Morris, whose elegant Georgian design was undoubtedly inspired by the work of architect-builder Roger Morris, the colonel's father.

The entrance hall was long and wide, with lofty ceilings divided by two broad, stately archways. Opening onto the entrance hall were a front parlor for receiving guests, a back family parlor, and a graciously proportioned dining room.

A grand drawing room lay at the end of the hallway, perhaps the first octagonal room built in the Colonies. Splendid and refined, the drawing room had windows that commanded views of the Hudson and Harlem Rivers and featured a fireplace that could be seen all the way down the long hallway. A festive, blazing fire must have been a welcoming sight to visitors as they entered the house.

The remaining floors were used by family and servants. The bedchambers on the second floor, generous in size and handsome in proportion, adjoined another large hallway. It is quite likely that the third floor was occupied by both slaves and servants.

For a few years this distinguished Palladian-style house rang with the laughter of the four Morris children as they ran through the garden. The rooms were enlivened by the soft murmur of guests' voices as they visited with Colonel and Mrs. Morris in the beautiful drawing room.

It was the American Revolution that put an end to this pleasant life. Colonel Morris was British, after all. He sailed to England, while his wife and children fled to her family's estate in Westchester County, New York.

For a time the mansion was empty, silent. Then in mid-September 1776 after two disastrous defeats, the Battle of Long

of taffeta gowns and sparkling laughter beneath candlelit chandeliers. These elegant rooms had once echoed with the voices of great historical figures, secret war plans, and later, had been the stage for the life of a fascinating and controversial woman, Eliza Bowen Jumel.

Washington Heights, as this area of northern Manhattan is known today, was rolling countryside in the middle of the 18th century. It was here in 1765 that British Colonel Roger Morris and his American wife, Mary Philipse, chose a site for their country house on one of the highest elevations in Manhattan, sur-

Island (at least 1,500 casualties) and the Battle of Kip's Bay (a narrow escape), Washington's troops assembled in Upper Manhattan, and General Washington used the house as his headquarters until October 18. It was here that the first small victory won by Washington's army was planned, the Battle of Harlem Heights. Later the mansion fell into British hands, occupied in turn by the British, including General Henry Clinton, and Hessian soldiers under General Baron von Knyphausen.

The Revolutionary War was brought to a close with the British evacuation in 1783. Empty once again, the mansion was seized and sold by the new American government's Commission of Forfeiture, after which the house served as a tavern. President George Washington returned to the mansion for an informal meal on July 10, 1790, accompanied by Secretary of State Thomas Jefferson, Vice President John Adams, Secretary of the Treasury Alexander Hamilton, Secretary of War Henry Knox, and the wives of the cabinet members.

A fascinating new chapter in the mansion's history began in 1810 when beautiful Eliza Bowen Jumel and her husband Stephen bought the house.

There are individuals whose lives are so dramatic that they take on a fictional quality, and Madame Jumel created this kind of life for herself. She was born Eliza Bowen in Providence, Rhode Island. Not much is known about her early years

in Providence, but when she left that conservative town, she left a murky past and an illegitimate baby son, George Washington Bowen.

Eliza made her way to New York City, where she may have lived for a time with a French sea captain. Eventually she set her sights higher, becoming the mistress of Stephen Jumel, a wealthy French wine merchant and ship owner. In 1804 the worldly Eliza Bowen became Madame Stephen Jumel.

In 1810, when the Jumels' lives became intertwined with the history of the mansion, the great house had been languishing for a number of years. The Jumels set about restoring and decorating the mansion in the refined and elegant Federal style. When the work was completed, they sailed to France.

While there, the Jumels became involved in another drama. Just after Napoleon's calamitous loss at Waterloo

Aaron Burr (1756-1836). Oil portrait by James Van Dyck (1834), painted shortly after Burr's brief marriage to Eliza Bowen ended. Burr, depicted at the age of 78 , died two years later. (Courtesy of The New-York Historical Society, New York City)

on June 18, 1815, the Jumels met with the defeated emperor to propose a daring plan: They offered to help him escape to America aboard one of Stephen Jumel's ships. For some reason, Napoleon did not agree to the plan, although the Jumels probably did aid the Bonaparte family financially and also bought a number of their possessions, including furniture belonging to Napoleon.

Stephen Jumel remained in France for 13 years. Eliza left the country several times, exiled once by Louis XVIII for expressing her views in support of Napoleon. She left France for the last time in 1826, two years before her husband's departure.

Madame Jumel brought home to the New York mansion her treasure trove of decorative objects and furniture, and she began an elaborate refurbishing of every room, this time in the fashionable High Empire style.

Eliza Jumel's French acquisitions included roll after roll of exquisite hand-painted wallpaper, a design for almost every room in the mansion. Silk damask draperies were installed — swagged and tasseled in the formal Empire style. At last the decorations were finished, a perfect backdrop for her Napoleonic furniture.

Was this splendid mansion the setting for smart dinner parties, for refined afternoon teas of polite conversation over dainty pastries? Certainly Madame Jumel must have entertained, although she was never accepted by the elite of New York society because of her colorful past. Then too, she was a woman alone, with a

Hallway interior today. Beyond the second archway is the octagonal drawing room. (Photograph © Jeffrey Jay Foxx, 1990)

husband far away in Paris — perhaps cause for more gossip. In any event, it was during this time that Eliza Jumel met Aaron Burr, who had served as Vice President of the United States under President Thomas Jefferson.

Details about Madame Jumel's relationship with Burr are vague. Scandalmongers spread unpleasant rumors about Stephen Jumel's untimely death in 1832 after a carriage accident. They insinuated that Madame Jumel had been "negligent" in her care. Then in 1833 New York City buzzed with the news that Eliza Jumel had married Aaron Burr in the front parlor of Stephen Jumel's home — and just a year after his death.

Unpleasant stories plagued the marriage. There were gossips who spread the word that Eliza had married the 77-year-old Burr for his fame and position in society — and that he cared only for her money. Vicious tongues wagged that the Jumel woman might be the wealthiest woman in America, but she would never be accepted by polite society. And as for Aaron Burr! He had disgraced himself by killing Alexander Hamilton in a duel and by his treasonous behavior in conspiring to carve out an independent nation for himself in the West.

The marriage ended in a separation six months later. Aaron Burr died on September 14, 1836, the day the official divorce decree was finally granted.

Alone once again, Eliza Jumel lived on in the splendid mansion. She traveled to Europe. She managed her business affairs. And then, when Eliza was in her 70s, her mind began to weaken, to play strange tricks. Her behavior became increasingly peculiar. Yet Eliza endured many long years before she died in 1865 at the age of 91.

Madame Jumel remains a mystery more than 125 years after her death. Did she spend her final years repenting her early life, as some have written? And what of the persistent stories that Eliza Jumel's restless ghost still inhabits the elegant, faded mansion?

The Tour

"A lot of people come to this house to find out if it's haunted," Barbara, a staff member, casually remarked. "There's always a story. That's why I like working here so much!"

She recalled a strange incident. A woman had come to the mansion with her 19-year-old daughter one October afternoon. She told Barbara that many years before, when her daughter was four years old, they had visited this mansion. They were alone in a room when suddenly they felt a cold draft. The child exclaimed that there was a beautiful woman dressed in a blue gown standing beside her. The mother saw no one.

"Tell me more!" I urged.

Barbara laughed. "You never know what people are going to tell you! A lady came in one day and told me that Aaron Burr was living inside her cat!"

With or without Madame Jumel's ghost, the Morris-Jumel Mansion is a fascinating adventure into the 18th and 19th centuries. The architecture, the furnishings, and the historical events that occurred there make the trip memorable.

★

The tour of the mansion begins in the front parlor, in which Madame Jumel married Aaron Burr in 1833. This reception parlor is decorated in the ornate Empire style, which reflected Emperor Napoleon's taste for classical grandeur. The style flourished from approximately

The front parlor as it appears today.
(Photograph © Jeffrey Jay Foxx, 1990)

1810 until 1840, relying heavily on
designs from ancient Egypt, Rome, and
Greece. The rectangular furniture, which
was sometimes massive and elaborate,
was made of rich woods with gilt-bronze
mounts and used such decorative motifs
as sphinx heads, torches, wreaths, griffins,
and the Napoleonic symbols of the bee,
the crown, and the letter *N*. The sumptuous style evoked the pomp and splendor
of Napoleon's court and soon filtered into

the great homes of Europe, England,
and America. The front parlor's suite of
American Empire furniture is a good example of this style: twelve chairs and a
heavy, intricately carved sofa with great
lion's paw feet.

Other interesting pieces in the front
parlor include an 1820 mahogany and
satinwood desk that belonged to Aaron
Burr; a brass fireplace fender, once owned
by Revolutionary War general, Marion,

the Swamp Fox; and an ormolu chandelier, said to have been a present from Napoleon to French General Moreau.

Opposite the parlor is the handsome dining room decorated in the Federal style. The Federal period, which began in America following the Revolutionary War, derived its name from the new American federation. The birth of a new nation ushered in a period of elegant decoration in America.

Federal furniture designs were directly influenced by the Scottish architects Robert and James Adam and English cabinetmakers George Hepplewhite and Thomas Sheraton. This classical style was influenced by designs from ancient Greece, Rome, and Pompeii, featuring such graceful motifs as bellflowers, wheat sheaves, ovals, swags, and fans. In contrast to the heavy Empire style, furniture in the Federal style was generally graceful

The drawing room, perhaps the first octagonal room built in America. (Photograph © Jeffrey Jay Foxx, 1990)

and refined, with features such as slender, tapering legs and subdued wooden inlays.

Federal period decoration in the dining room is exemplified by the subtle yellow wallpaper, enhanced by a linear design of wheat sheaves; a graceful mahogany table (circa 1800); and a superb suite of mahogany furniture made by Duncan Phyfe, the eminent New York cabinetmaker.

At the end of the long entrance hall is the most elegant room in the mansion, the drawing room, decorated as it would have appeared in 1765, the year in which the mansion was built. The walls are hung with handpainted Chinese wallpaper, expensive and rare in 18th-century America. Rose silk damask swags accent the six windows, and the same rose silk upholsters the chairs that line the walls. A fine Oriental carpet covers the floor.

On the second floor the hallway is dominated by a large oil painting of Eliza Jumel. Painted in Rome in 1854, when she was in her late 70s, the portrait reveals a woman with a sweet, rather sad face, her auburn hair demurely covered by a lace, ribbon-trimmed day cap. Drifts of white lace ornament her wrists, and a white lace shawl drapes over the shoulders of her blue-green silk gown. Standing beside Madame Jumel are her grandnephew and grandniece, William and Eliza Chase.

Madame Jumel's bedchamber is decorated in the High Empire style. Imperial blue and gold are everywhere — on the walls, the blue satin window swags, the upholstery, the bed hangings, and in the geometric carpeting.

The mahogany sleigh bed in Madame Jumel's bedchamber is said to have belonged to Napoleon when he was First Consul. It has been draped in a manner that was fashionable during the early 19th century with a *couronne-de-lit*, or bed crown, a drapery affixed to the wall on one side of the bed, often surmounted by a gilt crown. This bed has been crowned by a carved and gilded swan.

A pair of blue satin slipper chairs flanking the fireplace in this bedchamber once belonged to Queen Hortense of the Netherlands. Queen Hortense was the daughter of Josephine and the mother of Napoleon III.

Adjacent to Madame Jumel's bedchamber is a boudoir, one of the first designed for an American house, elegantly decorated in the Empire style as well. This room had many functions in 19th-century France. It was a dressing room, a room in which to recline and read, and curiously, a room for entertaining. It was even fashionable to have a portrait painted in the boudoir.

The bedchamber occupied by Aaron Burr during his short stay is cheerful and handsome, its papered walls enriched by deep-red damask bed hangings and draperies. A Southern carved canopy bed, circa 1830, dominates this room.

To the rear of the second floor is the room used by General Washington during his brief occupation of the mansion in 1776. This room afforded views in all directions, an important factor in its choice as an office. Simply decorated as it might have been in 1776, it has scrubbed wideboard flooring, a slantfront desk, a Windsor chair, and a mahogany architect's table.

On a hallway wall is a photograph of Queen Elizabeth and Prince Phillip, a reminder of their visit to this historic mansion during the 1976 bicentennial celebration. An interesting fact: Queen Elizabeth is distantly related to George Washington.

A pleasant ending to the tour is a stroll on the grounds. A wide brick walk winds around to a sunken Colonial Revival herb and rose garden, planted

Madame Jumel's bedroom, decorated in the High Empire style. The bed is believed to have belonged to Napoleon when he was First Consul. (Photograph © Jeffrey Jay Foxx, 1990)

with herbs that would have been found there in the 18th century.

The rosebushes are planted in a charming design, rather shaggy in appearance now. Four circles of boxwood hedge are centered with another circle, all five of them filled with fragrant pink teacup rosebushes. Around the whole is another large circle of boxwood hedge.

The rest of the garden must have been lovely once. For the present, however, the grounds are overgrown — a kind of lost garden of lilacs, yews, herbs, and roses.

The Morris-Jumel Mansion has been maintained as a museum by the Washington Headquarters Association since 1904. The city, which owns the structure, has just begun a major renovation of the mansion. This is a fortunate turn of events, because this beautiful but timeworn house is one of New York City's historical treasures.

Morris-Jumel Mansion
1765 Jumel Terrace
New York, NY 10032
212-923-8008

Hours:
Tuesday-Sunday 10:00 a.m.-4:00 p.m.

Admission:
- Adults $3.00
- Seniors & students $1.00
- Children under 12 free

Group Tours:
Call for information

The Morris-Jumel Mansion is located in Roger Morris Park one block east of St. Nicholas Avenue at West 160th Street and Edgecombe Avenue. Adjacent to the park is another historical landmark, Sylvan Terrace, charming pale yellow row houses built in 1882.

Additional Sights

Trinity Cemetery
This cemetery, a short walk from the Morris-Jumel Mansion, was the rural cemetery for Wall Street's Trinity Church. A large area of rather steep hillside from Riverside Drive to Amsterdam Avenue and from 153rd to 155th Streets was designated as Trinity Cemetery in 1881. Madame Jumel is interred here in a hillside crypt at the end of the main pathway on the right. John James Audubon, the naturalist-artist, and Clement Moore, who wrote *The Night Before Christmas,* are buried here as well. (We were told that the cemetery is often closed, but if you are lucky, the big iron gates off 153rd Street and Broadway will be open.)

Directions to Trinity Cemetery:
From the Morris-Jumel Mansion, walk west to Broadway. Walk south (left) to 153rd Street, turn west (right) one-half block to entrance of Trinity Cemetery.

This walk along Broadway will take you past Audubon Terrace at 155th Street, where several museums are housed in turn-of-the-century Beaux-Arts buildings: *National Museum of the American Indian, Hispanic Society of America,* and *American Numismatic Society Museum.* (See previous chapter for details.)

R E S T A U R A N T S

El Espagnol
3825 Broadway
Between 160th & 161st Streets
212-795-2893

Open 24 hours a day, 7 days a week

- MasterCard, VISA

A short stroll from Morris-Jumel Mansion, this lively little place is brimming with people, cheerful noise, and mirrors everywhere. Very casual and reasonably priced. Typical dishes are Spanish sirloin $12.00, garlic shrimp $12.50, fried chicken $6.00, banana with crisp fried pork, $7.00. Especially good is a huge seafood creole for one person (plenty for two) at $20.50. The color and vitality of the street spill over into this cafe, which makes the experience a lot of fun.

Wilson's
1980 Amsterdam Avenue at 158th Street
212-923-9821

Daily 6:00 a.m.-9:00 p.m.

• No credit cards

An easy walk from the mansion, this family restaurant is very popular in the neighborhood. Serves a wide selection of dishes, from soups and sandwiches to daily hot specials.

Breakfast approximately $3.00
Lunch & dinner $4.00-$10.00
(steaks $18.75)

Special menu on Sunday, which is slightly more expensive.

D I R E C T I O N S

Subway:
• IRT #1 (marked 242nd Street) to West 157th Street
• IND B (marked Washington Heights) to West 163rd Street

Bus:
• M2, M3 (Fifth / Madison Avenues)

Car:
• Henry Hudson Parkway, 158th Street exit

Trinity Cemetery. (Photograph © Jeffrey Jay Foxx, 1990)

Wander Through a Sunlit Monastery

A medieval masterpiece – The Cloisters

The History

 s you walk through the cool, shadowy halls and sunlit gardens of The Cloisters, you will be drawn into the last centuries of a remote time, an era that spanned nearly a thousand years, stretching from ancient times to the Renaissance in Europe — the Middle Ages.

This was a world of knights in armor and moat-ringed castles, but it was also the world of the Catholic church and powerful European monasteries. Within the massive stone walls of The Cloisters, you will enter that monastic world.

Amble beneath a 12th-century stone church doorway from Spain, rescued as it lay disintegrating in a grassy field. Study the 13th-century stone figures of kings, which were torn from a monastery doorway and lost for centuries. Or examine intricately carved stone columns, found standing like sentinels in the crumbling ruin of a French monastery. These last fragments of European churches and monasteries, remnants of rare medieval

Above: The Cloisters today.
(Photograph © Jeffrey Jay Foxx, 1990)

Right: The Cloisters as photographed in 1977. (Courtesy of The Cloisters, The Metropolitan Museum of Art)

393

The 12th-century Cuxa Cloister from the 9th-century French Benedictine monastery of Saint-Michel-de-Cuxa in the Pyrenees. (Photograph © Jeffrey Jay Foxx, 1990)

art and architecture, surround you at The Cloisters.

And as you gaze around, you may wonder, "How did The Cloisters, which so closely resembles a medieval monastery, come to rest high on a hill in Manhattan?"

That is quite an interesting story — a story that first unfolded in France.

During the early 1900s an American sculptor, George Grey Barnard, was living in France and trying to earn a living as an artist. He enjoyed exploring the countryside, but he was appalled at what he found. Architectural works of art were crumbling to dust in meadows, in lonely valleys, and on isolated mountaintops, the sites often chosen for medieval

monasteries. Barnard began trying to save what he could, dragging them home, one after another.

When World War I ignited, Barnard returned to the United States, bringing with him these neglected shards of medieval architecture — literally tons of stone. He created his own small museum near the present museum and began sharing this wealth of art with Americans.

John D. Rockefeller, Jr., stepped into the story in the 1920s when Barnard decided to sell his collection. Rockefeller, realizing the importance of the art (he had his own splendid medieval collection), donated the necessary funds to The Metropolitan Museum of Art. Rockefeller also donated 40 works of art from his own collection and land for a museum — a perfect site high on a hilltop in northern Manhattan with beautiful views of the sparkling Hudson River.

Now the questions began. How could those great stone fragments be displayed effectively and artistically?

What form should the museum take?

The final design, created through inspired collaboration between architect Charles Collens and Metropolitan Museum personnel (primarily James J. Rorimer), was that of a medieval monastery, to be built around four cloisters whose architectural elements had been collected by Barnard. The museum's name evolved from that design, and The Cloisters, a branch of The Metropolitan Museum of Art, was completed in 1938.

★

What is a cloister? Simply, a monastery's rectangular garth (courtyard open to the sky), along with the covered, arcade-edged walkway surrounding it.

The Western European cloister was centered in the monastery complex and was usually built on the sunny south side of the monastery's church, surrounded by buildings used by the monks for living and working. These buildings included the refectory in which meals were eaten, the chapter house used for formal meetings, the second-floor dormitory, workshops, storerooms, and sometimes the library and sacristy.

The cloister's garth, which was often planted as a grassy, tree-shaded oasis bordered with flower beds, was a welcome, restful center to the workday and was used in many ways, from informal discussions, meditation, and study, to simple tasks such as washing clothes. What pleasure the cloister must have brought, especially in cold northern climates, protected as it was from wind and flooded with warm, bright sunshine.

Although The Cloisters is a 20th-century structure, the museum looks and feels for all the world like a medieval monastery, with its galleries and great halls clustered around the four garden cloisters. Yet the museum is not an exact copy of a medieval monastery and was never intended to be. (For example, although a monastery usually had several gardens and often an orchard, it generally had only one cloister, unless the complex was quite large.) The goal was to combine the many architectural fragments and works of art into a harmonious whole, while creating the feeling of monastic life during the Middle Ages. And this it has done very well.

The Tour

When you visit the museum's chapels, galleries, and cloisters, you will be viewing a great number of architectural artifacts that were carved during the closing centuries of the Middle Ages, which in its entirety spanned an approximate period from 500 A.D. to 1350 A.D. You will be seeing Christian architecture created when the European monastic orders were at the zenith of power and influence, and their monasteries and churches reflected that wealth and power. In many cases when you see an architectural fragment, you will be viewing the last vestige of a great building, the rest having long since crumbled into ruin.

Because there is such diversity in the architectural elements and other works of art, The Cloisters is a fascinating study in contrasts. In the Romanesque Hall, for example, there are three carved stone doorways, each from a different French church, illustrating the evolution in style (Romanesque to Gothic) from the mid-12th to mid-13th centuries. A proud lion and ferocious dragon glare from two colorful 13th-century Spanish frescoes, while a pair of 13th-century Italian stone lions crouch beneath.

In the soft light of a two-storied

chapel (modern, but in the Gothic style), soaring shafts of 14th-century stained-glass windows contrast with massive stone tombs, their carved stone knights and ladies forever sleeping on top, while lions (courage) or dogs (fidelity) rest beneath their feet.

Among the numerous art-filled chambers is the newly renovated ground-floor Treasury, in which each object is a unique jewel of medieval art. One example in the splendid collection is the priceless *Book of Hours* (circa 1413), an exquisitely illuminated volume owned by Jean, duc du Berry, who was the brother of Charles V of France.

On the first floor is another treasure for which the museum is renowned — a set of rare and beautiful tapestries, known as *The Hunt of the Unicorn,* or simply the Unicorn Tapestries. Although some theories suggest they were woven around 1500 in Brussels, the series of seven tapestries is still clouded in mystery, as the identity of the original owners has never been discovered. By 1680, however, the tapestries were documented possessions of French nobility, the La Rochefoucauld family, and lined the bedroom walls of a townhouse in Paris. By 1728 records indicate that they were installed in the family chateau south of Paris. The tapestries remained there until 1793 when peasants invaded the chateau during the French Revolution, stripping them from the walls. The priceless works of art were put to use in their barns, used as coverings for stored vegetables.

For more than 50 years the tapestries lay in the barns slowly disintegrating. Finally, in the 1850s a La Rochefoucauld descendant who had inherited the chateau heard about some unusual "old curtains" heaped in a servant's barn. Although the tapestries were found in a sorry state, restoration was successful (except the fifth

tapestry, which had been nearly destroyed), and they were reinstalled in the chateau. The tapestries remained in the La Rochefoucauld family until 1923, when John D. Rockefeller, Jr., bought them and donated them in 1937 to The Metropolitan Museum of Art.

These exquisite tapestries now line the walls of a room so closely resembling the chamber in a chateau that when you stand in front of the massive 15th-century French limestone fireplace and gaze through the expanse of late Gothic windows, you may forget you are in a museum. The incomparable tapestries will surround you in glowing, luminous color, telling not one, but three stories in intricate and lively detail.

On the first level the tale is of a medieval hunt. Noblemen with their horses and grooms, surrounded by houndskeepers and hunting hounds, trail the rarest prey, the legendary unicorn. Finally capturing and slaughtering the creature, they carry it triumphantly back to the castle.

On another level the story is of worldly love, courtship, and marriage. The unicorn, or noble lover, undergoes great trials to prove his undying love for the noble lady. He is chained by love at last in the final tapestry, bathed in the ruby juices of the pomegranate, a symbol of fertility.

The third story is a religious one. The unicorn symbolizes Christ, who is

Entrance to the transept of the 13th-century French monastery church, Moutiers-Saint-Jean. Photograph taken about 1938, shortly after completion of The Cloisters. In 1940 two lost figures of kings were replaced on either side of the doorway, found by chance in a French private garden. (Courtesy of Museum of the City of New York)

captured by his tormentors and in agony is crucified. The noble lady is the Virgin Mary. In the final tapestry the unicorn is Christ who has risen and is in Paradise. The pomegranate tree becomes the symbol of Christ and of eternal life.

The *Nine Heroes Tapestries* in the adjoining room were woven about 1385, probably in Paris. These large tapestries depict three Christian heroes (Arthur, Charlemagne, and Godfrey), three Hebrew heroes (David, Joshua, and Judas Maccabeus), and three pagan heroes (Hector, Alexander, and Julius Caesar). Portions of the three tapestries, containing four of the original nine figures, have been lost; however, the surviving portions are masterpieces of medieval art.

Among the countless museum treasures are those for which The Cloisters is named — the four cloister gardens. These delightful gardens are completely different in theme and design and were taken from different French monasteries; yet all contain plants — herbs, flowers, or trees — that were found in medieval gardens.

The 12th-century Cuxa Cloister, largest of the four, lies at the heart of the

---

Left: The Gothic Chapel. Although the chapel appears to be medieval, it is a modern structure, housing rare 14th-century stained-glass windows and medieval tombs. (Photograph © Jeffrey Jay Foxx, 1990)

Previous pages: the Unicorn Tapestries. Right: the first of the seven tapestries, depicting the start of the hunt. Left: the third tapestry, depicting the unicorn in flight, pursued by hunters and dogs. Above door: fragment of the fifth tapestry in which the maiden captures the unicorn. Center: the sixth tapestry, in which the unicorn is slain. (Photograph © Jeffrey Jay Foxx, 1990)

museum on the first floor, exactly as it would have been located in a medieval monastery, although there is no church at The Cloisters. Of geometric design, the garth is divided into four grassy rectangles rimmed in bright flowers. A tree centers each quadrant: a crabapple, a pear, a cornelian cherry, and a hawthorn. Columns with capitals carved in fanciful designs support the arcade, and a stone fountain stands at the center of a cross formed by stone walks. This is a tranquil, sunny cloister, often filled with strains of medieval music.

The early 13th-century St. Guilhem Cloister has been reconstructed as an indoor winter garden, offering a spring display of grass, shrubs, and flowering plants during winter's bleakest days.

The late 13th- or early 14th-century Bonnefont Cloister on the lower level overflows with more than 250 species of medicinal, aromatic, seasoning, and dyeing plants, all plentiful in medieval gardens, illustrating gardens found in monasteries in addition to the garth — the kitchen and infirmary gardens. Three plants used exclusively to dye the wool in the tapestries are found in this garden: madder, used for red; woad for blue; and weld, from which yellow was taken.

Four venerable quince trees stand in the middle, a splendid sight in the fall when the limbs droop with the heavy golden fruit. (In addition to their supposed curative powers, quinces were used in numerous sweetened dishes.) Of interest is a "wattle," a style of medieval fence made from woven branches, which decorates the garden.

The 15th-century Trie Cloister garden on the lower level is a beautiful living tapestry, having been planted with the flowers, trees, and shrubs depicted in the Unicorn Tapestries. Of more than 100 species of flora depicted in the tapestries, about 50 species are found in this garden. Perhaps because the Trie Cloister garden is centered with a fountain, it most closely resembles the second tapestry in the series, which depicts the unicorn dipping his horn into the water of a fountain.

Of special interest in the Trie Cloister garden are columns whose capitals have been carved with Biblical stories. At the garden's center stands a beautiful fountain surmounted by a cross, which has been carved with the figures of Christ, Mary, and John on one side and St. Anne with Mary and Christ on the other.

★

The cloister gardens do much to impart the feeling of medieval monastic life. As you wander through the museum, perhaps you will suddenly catch a glimpse of a cloister through an open doorway, its medieval arcade casting geometric designs of light and shadow. Or drawn into the sun-splashed garden, you will hear the music of water as it spills from a 13th-century stone fountain and mingles with birdsong. These memories may be just as lasting as those of the great works of medieval art at The Cloisters — and rightly so.

The early 13th-century St. Guilhem Cloister, now used as an indoor winter garden. (Photograph © Jeffrey Jay Foxx, 1990)

The Cloisters
Fort Tryon Park in northern Manhattan
New York, NY 10034
212-923-3700

Hours:
Tuesday-Sunday
  March-October 9:30 a.m.-5:15 p.m.
  November-February 9:30 a.m.-4:45 p.m.

Closed Monday, January 1, Thanksgiving
Day, Christmas Day

Admission: (Suggested donation)
• $6.00 adults
• $3.00 seniors & students
• Children under 12 free

This fee includes same-day admission to
The Metropolitan Museum of Art, Fifth
Avenue at 82nd Street.

Tours:
Tuesday-Friday at 3:00 p.m.
Sunday at noon

Group Tours: Reserve in advance

Handicapped:
Call in advance 212-923-3700

★

Recommended Reading:
From the museum's gift shop: *A Walk
Through the Cloisters*, by Bonnie Young,
which details many of the museum's treasures.
Numerous beautiful pictures taken by photog-
rapher Malcolm Varon.
   The Unicorn Tapestries, is based on a study
of the tapestries by Margaret B. Freeman,
Curator Emeritus of The Cloisters. Adapted
by Linda Sipress.
   Sweet Herbs and Sundry Flowers, by Tania
Bayard. A fascinating analysis of the four
gardens and the plants growing there.

Special Events:
Call for information about performances of
medieval music and gallery talks. Usually
offered at noon and 2:00 p.m. on Saturday.
   The holiday seasons are special times at
The Cloisters, with beautiful garden and floral
displays. During the Christmas season
medieval music is performed in the galleries,
usually on Saturdays. There are activities for
children. Call for details.

D I R E C T I O N S

Subway:
• IND A Train to 190th Street & Overlook
  Terrace. Exit by elevator and take #4 bus
  (Fort Tryon Park – The Cloisters).

Bus:
• The #4 Madison Avenue bus (Fort Tryon
  Park – The Cloisters) will take you to the
  door of the museum and will also give you a
  bit of sightseeing along the way.

Car:
• Henry Hudson Parkway north, The Cloisters
  exit (first exit after George Washington
  Bridge).

The reconstructed 12th-century Langon
Chapel, from the French church of Notre-
Dame-du-Bourg, located southeast of
Bordeaux. (Photograph © Jeffrey Jay
Foxx, 1990)

Restaurants

Below 30th Street

Bridge Cafe *(page 119)*
South Street Seaport
279 Water Street at Dover Street
212-227-3344
Italian/American/fish

Bo Ky *(page 103)*
80 Bayard Street
Between Mott & Mulberry Streets
212-406-2292
Vietnamese

Cafe du Parc *(page 206)*
106 East 19th Street
212-777-7840
French

Carmine's *(page 118)*
South Street Seaport
140 Beekman Street
212-962-8606
Italian/fish

Cent'Anni *(page 190)*
50 Carmine Street
Between Bleeker & Bedford Streets
212-989-9494
Northern Italian

Choshi *(page 207)*
Irving Place &19th Street
212-420-1419
Japanese

Fraunces Tavern Restaurant *(page 45)*
54 Pearl Street
Corner of Pearl & Broad Streets
212-269-0144
American

Hunan Balcony East *(page 223)*
386 Third Avenue
Between 27th & 28th Streets
212-725-1122
Chinese

John's Pizza *(page 191)*
278 Bleeker Street
Between Avenue of the Americas &
Seventh Avenue
212-243-1680

La Margarita *(page 174)*
184 Thompson Street
Corner of Bleeker & Thompson Streets
212-533-2410
Mexican

La Tour D'Or *(page 86)*
14 Wall Street, 31st Floor
212-233-2780
Continental

Paul & Jimmy's *(page 206)*
123 East 18th Street near Irving Place
212-475-9540
Italian

Provence *(page 191)*
38 MacDougal Street at Prince Street
212-475-7500
French

Say Eng Look *(page 102)*
5 East Broadway
212-732-0796
Shanghai

Sal Anthony's *(page 207)*
17th Street & Irving Place
212-982-9030
Italian

Tai Hong Lau *(page 103)*
70 Mott Street
Between Canal & Bayard Streets
212-219-1431
Cantonese

Tibetan Kitchen *(page 223)*
444 Third Avenue
Between 30th & 31st Streets
212-679-6286

20 Mott Street *(page 103)*
20 Mott Street
Between Pell & Bowery Streets
212-964-0380
Chinese dim sum

Y.S. (Hop Woo) *(page 103)*
17 Elizabeth Street
212-966-5838
Chinese

From 30th to 60th Street

American Festival Cafe *(page 254)*
20 West 50th Street
Next to Rockefeller Center skating rink
212-246-6699
American/Continental

Bien Venue *(page 234)*
21 East 36th Street
212-684-0215
French

The Birdcage *(page 235)*
Lord & Taylor
37th Street & Fifth Avenue
212-391-3344
Sandwiches & salads, etc.

Cafe Cielo *(page 269)*
881 Eighth Avenue
Between 52nd & 53rd Streets
212-246-9555
Northern Italian

The Carnegie Delicatessen *(page 268)*
854 Seventh Avenue at 55th Street
212-757-2245
Sandwiches/soups, etc.

Genroku Sushi *(page 235)*
366 Fifth Avenue
Between 34th & 35th Streets
212-947-7940
Japanese/Chinese

Keen's *(page 235)*
72 West 36th Street
Between Fifth Avenue & Avenue of the Americas
212-947-3636
American/Continental

La Côte Basque *(page 284)*
5 East 55th Street
212-688-6525
French

Lattanzi *(page 267)*
361 West 46th Street
Between Eighth & Ninth Avenues
212-315-0980
Italian

La Reserve *(page 269)*
4 West 49th Street
212-247-2993
French

Le Train Bleu *(page 285)*
Bloomingdale's
59th Street & Lexington Avenue, Sixth Floor
212-705-2100
Continental

Oyster Bar & Restaurant *(page 244)*
42nd Street & Park Avenue
Lower level of Grand Central Terminal
212-490-6650
Fish

Rainbow Promenade *(page 268)*
30 Rockefeller Center
GE Building, 65th Floor
212-632-5100
"Little meals"

The Rainbow Room *(page 267)*
30 Rockefeller Center
GE Building, 65th Floor
212-632-5100
Continental

Rainbow and Stars *(page 268)*
30 Rockefeller Center
GE Building, 65th Floor
212-632-5100
Continental

The Sea Grill *(page 255)*
18 West 49th Street
Rockefeller Center
212-246-9201
Continental

Zaro's Breadbasket *(page 245)*
42nd Street & Park Avenue
Concourse level of Grand Central Terminal
Sandwiches/baked goods/yogurt

From 60th to 90th Street

Boathouse Central Park Cafe *(page 302)*
Overlooking Central Park Lake near 72nd Street
212-517-2233
Italian

Indian Tandoor-Oven Restaurant *(page 331)*
175 East 83rd Street
212-628-3000

Little Mushroom Cafe *(page 293)*
1439 Second Avenue at 75th Street
212-988-9006
Thai/Italian

Little Nell's Tea Room *(page 344)*
343 East 85th Street
Between First & Second Avenues
212-772-2046
English/Continental/afternoon tea

Madison Grill *(page 284)*
746 Madison Avenue
Between 64th & 65th Streets
212-861-8820
American/Continental/sandwiches, etc.

**The Metropolitan Museum of Art
Restaurant** *(page 319)*
Fifth Avenue at 82nd Street
212-570-3964
American/Continental

**The Metropolitan Museum of Art
Cafeteria** *(page 319)*
Fifth Avenue at 82nd Street
212-570-3964
American/sandwiches, etc.

The Pembroke Room *(page 283)*
Lowell Hotel
28 East 63rd Street
212-838-1400
American/Continental/afternoon tea

Sarabeth's Kitchen *(page 321)*
423 Amsterdam Avenue at 80th Street
212-496-6280
American/sandwiches, soups, etc.

The Summer House *(page 331)*
50 East 86th Street
212-249-6300
American/sandwiches/soups, etc.

Tavern on the Green *(page 320)*
Central Park West at 67th Street
212-873-3200
American/Continental

**Whitney Museum Garden
Restaurant** *(page 292)*
Whitney Museum of American Art
Madison Avenue at 75th Street
212-570-3670
Light dishes/sandwiches/salads

Above 90th Street

Cafe St. John *(page 355)*
1018 Amsterdam Avenue
Corner of 110th Street
212-932-8420
American/Continental

El Espagnol *(page 390)*
3825 Broadway
Between 160th & 161st Streets
212-795-2893
Spanish

Hungarian Pastry Shop & Cafe *(page 354)*
1030 Amsterdam Avenue
Between 110th & 111th Streets
212-866-4230

Ideal Restaurant *(page 355)*
2825 Broadway
Corner of 109th Street
212-866-3224
Cuban

Sarabeth's Kitchen *(page 321)*
1295 Madison Avenue
Between 92nd & 93rd Streets
212-410-7335
American/sandwiches/soups

Sylvia's *(page 367)*
328 Lenox Avenue
Between 126th & 127th Streets
212-996-0660
Southern soul food

Terrace Restaurant *(page 366)*
400 West 119th Street
Between Amsterdam & Morningside Avenues
212-666-9490
French

Wilson's *(page 391)*
1980 Amsterdam Avenue at 158th Street
212-923-9821
American

V.T. Restaurant, Inc. *(page 354)*
1024 Amsterdam Avenue
Between 110th & 111th Streets
212-662-1708
Southern Italian

Brooklyn

Botanic Garden Terrace Cafe *(page 162)*
Brooklyn Botanic Garden
1000 Washington Avenue
718-622-4433
Sandwiches/salads, etc.

Brooklyn Museum Cafe *(page 162)*
Brooklyn Museum
200 Eastern Parkway
718-638-5000
Sandwiches/salads, etc.

Harbor View *(page 133)*
1 Old Fulton
Corner of Water Street
Brooklyn Heights
718-237-2224
Italian

River Cafe *(page 132)*
1 Water Street
Brooklyn Heights
718-522-5200
American/Continental

Slades *(page 148)*
107 Montague Street
Brooklyn Heights
718-585-1200
American/Italian

Acknowledgments

I was extremely fortunate to have had a group of outstanding individuals working with me during the production of this book:

I particularly wish to thank Cheung/Crowell Design for the dedicated and superior direction of the book's design and production.

Special thanks go to Midge Bacon for her excellent work as copy editor.

Three talented professional photographers contributed a great number of the images found in this book. I am grateful to Jeffrey Jay Foxx, George Le Moine, and Phil Cantor for their beautiful photographs.

I would also like to thank Marilyn Chernin for the word processing of this book.

★

Very special thanks go to my husband David for his outstanding photographs and for the numerous hours he spent reading copy and encouraging me in countless ways.

I would also like to thank our son Mark for his careful, accurate fact-checking and for his help in researching material.

Finally, I give loving thanks to my mother, to whom I owe my determination and sense of adventure.

During the three years I spent in researching and writing this book, many individuals working in museums, public and private institutions, and businesses offered assistance in numerous ways. My grateful thanks go to all of these people:

Benjamin W. Bacon, *Civil War historian*

Brooklyn Botanic Garden:
Laurie Oswald, *Director of Public Affairs*
Gretchen Beckhorn, *Assistant to the Director*

The Brooklyn Historical Society:
Linda Wagner, *Public Relations Director*
Claire Lamers, *Assistant Head Librarian*

The Brooklyn Museum:
Michelle Menendez,
Public Information Department

Richard Campagna, *publisher and attorney*

The Cathedral of St. John the Divine:
The Very Reverend James Parks Morton

Nina Cheung

Eastern Press, Inc.:
Richard Kaplan

Esto Photographics, Inc.:
Erica Stoller

Farm Hands/City Hands:
Wendy Dubit

The Federal Reserve Bank of New York:
Margaret Carmody,
    Chief of Public Information
Bart Sotnick, *Staff Director,*
    Press and Community Relations

Forbes Magazine Galleries:
Margaret Kelly, *Curator*

Fraunces Tavern Museum:
William Ayres, *Director*

Valerian A. Ginter, *urban historian*

Gracie Mansion:
David Reese, *Curator*
Peggy Cohen, *tour director*

Harvard University, Houghton Library:
Wallace Dailey

Karen Jackson, *professor of history*

Joan Strait Kratky, *proofreader*

The Legal Aid Society:
Susan B. Lindenauer, *General Counsel*

The Metropolitan Museum of Art:
Ruth Gales, *Office of Public Information*

The Morris-Jumel Mansion:
Susanna Elliot, *Curator*

The Municipal Arts Society:
Peter Laskowich, *tour guide*

Museum of the City of New York:
Gretchen Viehmann,
Rights and Reproductions

National Museum of the American Indian:
Elizabeth Beim,
   Development and Public Affairs Officer
Marty de Montano, *Office of Indian Information*

The New York City Fire Museum:
James Selby, *Director*
Louis Scrima, *Curator*

The New-York Historical Society:
Wendy Shadwell, *Director, Print Room*
Dina Alcure, *Public Relations Department*
Diana Arecco, *Photographic Services*

The New York City Police Department:
Lieutenant Raymond O'Donnell,
Office of Public Information

The New York City Police Museum:
John Podracky, *Curator*
Police Officer Dominick Palermo,
   Assistant Curator

The New York Public Library:
Wayne Furman, *Office of Special Collections*

Nancy Pearsall, *Brooklyn Heights historian*

The Pierpont Morgan Library:
Carla Berry, Aithne Aialo-Padin,
and Susan Eisner Eley,
   Public Affairs and Education Department
Betty Whiddington, *Docent*

Radio City Music Hall:
Paul Fenton, *Business Affairs*
Jaime Ramos and Andrew Rodgers, *Archives*
Orlando Powers, *tour guide*

The Rockefeller Group:
Celeste Torello, Amy Trotta, and Bevin Maguire,
Public Relations Department

Allen G. Schwartz, *former Corporation
Counsel of the City of New York*

South Street Seaport Museum:
Kathleen Madden, *Director of Public Affairs*

Swann Galleries, Inc.:
Carolyn Bierenbaum,
Public Relations Director

The Theodore Roosevelt
Birthplace National Historical Site:
John Lancos, *Site Manager*

Trinity Parish:
Phyllis Barr, *Parish Archivist and Museum Curator*

The Whitney Museum of American Art:
Linda Daitz,
   Director, Public Education Department
Anita Duquette,
   Manager, Rights and Reproductions
Mary Ellen Klein,
   Public Education Department
Aileen Silverman,
   Assistant, Rights and Reproductions

William Doyle Galleries:
Mary Alice Adams,
Public Relations Department

Selected Bibliography

Albion, Robert Greenhalgh. *The Rise of New York Port (1815-1860)*. New York: Charles Scribner's Sons, 1939.

Bayard, Tania. *Sweet Herbs and Sundry Flowers: Medieval Gardens and the Gardens of The Cloisters*. Boston: David R. Godine for The Metropolitan Museum of Art, 1985.

Beale, Howard K. *Theodore Roosevelt and the Rise of America to World Power*. Baltimore: The John Hopkins Press, 1956.

Bell, James B., and Richard I. Abrams. *In Search of Liberty: The Story of the Statue of Liberty and Ellis Island*. Garden City, New York: Doubleday and Company Inc., 1984.

Bining, Arthur Cecil, and Thomas C. Cochran. *The Rise of American Economic Life*. New York: Scribner, 1964.

Blumenson, John J.G. *Identifying American Architecture*. New York: W.W. Norton and Company, 1977.

Board of Governors of the Federal Reserve System. *The Federal Reserve System, Purpose and Functions*. Washington, D.C., 1984.

Boatner, Mark M. III. *The Civil War Dictionary*. New York: David McKay Company, 1988.

Bolton, R.P. *New York City in Indian Possession*. New York: National Museum of the American Indian, Heye Foundation, 1975.

Bowen, Catherine Drinker. *Miracle at Philadelphia*. Boston: Little, Brown and Company, 1966.

Bowman, John S., executive editor. *The Civil War Almanac*. Bison Books Corp., 1982.

The Brooklyn Museum. *The Great East River Bridge 1883-1983*. New York: Harry N. Abrams Inc., 1983.

Brouwer, Norman. "The Port of New York, 1860-1985: Moving Goods Within the Port," *Seaport* (Spring 1987), pp. 30-35.

Brouwer, Norman. "The Port of New York, 1860-1985: Steam Conquers World Trade Routes," *Seaport* (Summer 1988), pp. 36-41.

Canaday, John. *Metropolitan Seminars in Art*, 12 volumes. New York: The Metropolitan Museum of Art, 1958.

Commager, Henry Steele, and Allan Nevins, editors. *The Heritage of America*. Boston: Little, Brown and Company, 1951.

Cook, Clarence C. *A Description of the New York's Central Park*. New York: Benjamin Blom Inc., 1972.

Culbertson, Judi, and Tom Randall. *Permanent New Yorkers: A Biographical Guide to the Cemeteries of New York*. Chelsea, Vermont: Chelsea Green Publishing Company, 1987.

Cunliffe, Marcus. *George Washington: Man and Monument*. New York: NAL Penguin Inc., 1958.

Davidson, Bernice, and Edgar Munhall, compilers of texts. *The Frick Collection: An Illustrated Catalogue*, volumes 1 and 2. New York: The Frick Collection, 1968.

De Tocqueville, Alexis. *Democracy in America*. New York: Doubleday and Company, Inc., 1968.

Downs, Joseph. *American Furniture in the Winterthur Museum*, 2 volumes. New York: Bonanza Books, 1962.

Federal Reserve Bank of New York. *The Basics of Foreign Trade and Exchange*. New York, 1985.

Federal Reserve Bank of New York. *The Story of Money, Coins, and Currency*. New York, 1985.

Flexner, James Thomas. *George Washington in the American Revolution*, 4 volumes. Boston, Toronto: Little, Brown and Company, 1967.

Foote, Shelby. The *Civil War: A Narrative*, 3 volumes. New York: Random House, 1974.

Freeman, Margaret B., and Linda Sipress. *The Unicorn Tapestries*. New York: The Metropolitan Museum of Art, 1974.

Gody, Lou, editor-in-chief. *New York City Guide*. New York: Octagon Books, 1970.

Goldberger, Paul. *The City Observed: New York, a Guide to the Architecture of Manhattan*. New York: Random House, 1979.

Goldhurst, Richard. *Many Are the Hearts: The Agony and Triumph of Ulysses S. Grant*. New York: Reader's Digest Press, 1975.

Goldstone, Harmon H., and Martha Dalrymple. *History Preserved: A Guide to New York City Landmarks and Historic Districts*. New York: Simon and Schuster, 1974.

Goodbody, John C. *One Peppercorne: A History of the Parish of Trinity Church*. New York: The Parish of Trinity Church, 1982.

Graff, Henry H., editor. *The Presidents: A Reference History*. New York: Charles Scribner's Sons, 1984.

Graff, M.M. *Central Park, Prospect Park: A New Perspective*. New York: Greensward Foundation Inc., 1985.

Handlin, Oscar. *The Statue of Liberty*. New York: Newsweek, 1971.

Harris, Jonathan. *A Statue for America*. New York: Macmillan Publishing Company, Four Winds Press, 1985.

Harvey, George. *Henry Clay Frick, the Man*. New York: The Frick Collection, 1936.

Johnson, Allen, and Dumas Malone, editors. *Dictionary of American Biography*, volume 7. New York: Charles Scribner's Sons, 1931.

Johnson, Curt. *Battles of the American Revolution*. New York: Bonanza Books, 1975.

Johnson, Harry, and Fredrick S. Lightfoot. *Maritime New York in Nineteenth-Century Photographs*. New York: Dover Publications Inc., 1980.

Johnson, Roger T. *Historical Beginnings: The Federal Reserve*. Boston: Banking and Public Services of the Federal Reserve Bank of Boston, 1982.

Kammen, Michael. *Colonial New York: A History*. New York: Charles Scribner's Sons, 1975.

Kelly, Margaret. *Highlights From The Forbes Magazine Galleries*. New York: Forbes Inc., 1985.

Koch, Robert. *Louis C. Tiffany: Rebel in Glass*. New York: Crown Publishers Inc., 1982.

Kouwenhoven, John A. *The Columbia Historical Portrait of New York*. Garden City, New York: Doubleday and Company, 1953.

Lancaster, Clay. *Old Brooklyn Heights: New York's First Suburb*. New York: Dover Publications, 1979.

Leopold, Richard W. *The Growth of American Foreign Policy: A History*. New York: Alfred A. Knopf, 1962.

Lockwood, Charles. *Manhattan Moves Uptown*. Boston: Houghton Mifflin Company, 1976.

Lyman, Elizabeth. *The Story of New York*. New York: Crown Publishers Inc., 1964.

Mackay, Donald A. *The Building of Manhattan*. New York: Harper and Row, 1987.

Mails, Thomas E. *The Mystic Warriors of the Plains*. Garden City, New York: Doubleday & Company, Inc., 1972.

McCormick, Robert. *Ulysses Simpson Grant*. New York: The Bond Wheelwright Company, 1950.

McCullough, David. *The Great Bridge*. New York: Simon and Schuster, 1972.

McFeely, William S. *Grant: A Biography*. New York: W.W. Norton and Company, 1981.

McKay, Richard C. *South Street: A Maritime History of New York*. New York: G.P. Putnam's Sons, 1934.

Mensch, Barbara. *The Last Waterfront: The People of South Street*. New York: Freundlich Books, 1985.

Montgomery, Charles F. *American Furniture*, 2 volumes. New York: Bonanza Books, 1968.

Morris, Edmund. *The Rise of Theodore Roosevelt*. New York: Coward, McCann and Geoghegan Inc., 1979.

Morris, Richard B. *Encyclopedia of American History*. New York: Harper & Brothers, 1953.

Oliver, John W. *Henry Clay Frick: Pioneer-Patriot and Philanthropist 1849-1919*. The Historical Society of Western Pennsylvania, 1949.

O'Toole, G.J.A. *The Spanish War: An American Epic, 1898*. New York, London: W.W. Norton and Company, 1984.

Paul, Tessa. *The Art of Louis Comfort Tiffany*. New York: Exeter Books, 1987.

Pine, John B. "The Story of Gramercy Park, 1831-1921," reprinted from *Valentine's Manual*. New York: Gramercy Park Association, 1921.

Purtell, Joseph. *The Tiffany Touch*. New York: Random House, 1971.

Reier, Sharon. *The Bridges of New York*. New York: Quadrant Press Inc., 1977.

Reynolds, Donald Martin. *The Architecture of New York City: Histories and Views of Important Structures, Sites, and Symbols*. New York, London: Macmillan Publishing Company, Collier Macmillan Publishers, 1984.

Rice, Kym S. *Early American Taverns for Entertainment of Friends and Strangers*. Chicago: Regnery Gateway and Fraunces Tavern Museum, 1983.

Roosevelt, Anna Curtenius, and James G.E. Smith, editor. *The Ancestors: Native Artisans of the Americas*. New York: National Museum of the American Indian, 1979.

Rosebrock, Ellen Fletcher. *Walking Around in South Street*. New York: South Street Seaport Museum, 1974.

Sack, Albert. *Fine Points of Furniture: Early American*. New York: Crown Publishers, Inc., 1940.

Satterlee, Herbert L. *J. Pierpont Morgan: An Intimate Portrait*. New York: The Macmillan Company, 1939.

Schuberth, Christopher J. *The Geology of New York City and Environs*. Garden City, New York: National History Press, 1968.

Shapiro, Mary J. *Gateway to Liberty*. New York: Vintage Books, Random House, 1986.

Sims, Patterson, and others. *Whitney Museum of American Art*. New York: Whitney Museum of American Art, 1985.

Sinclair, Andrew. *Corsair, The Life of J. Pierpont Morgan*. Boston, Toronto: Little, Brown and Company, 1981.

Smith, Gene. *Lee and Grant*. New York: McGraw-Hill, 1984.

Still, Bayrd. *Mirror for Gotham*. New York: New York University Press, 1956.

Tiffany and Company. *Charles L. Tiffany and the House of Tiffany & Co*. New York: Union Square, Tiffany and Company, 1893.

Tiffany, Nelson Otis. *The Tiffanys of America: History and Geneology*. New York: Nelson Otis Tiffany, 1901.

Trachtenberg, Alan. *Brooklyn Bridge: Fact and Symbol*. New York: Oxford University Press, 1965.

Ulmann, Albert. *A Landmark History of New York*. New York: D. Appleton-Century Company, 1939.

Van Der Zee, Henri and Barbara. *A Sweet and Alien Land*. New York: The Viking Press, 1978.

Wheeler, George. *Pierpont Morgan and Friends: The Anatomy of a Myth*. Englewood Cliffs: Prentice-Hall, Inc., 1973.

White, Norval. *New York: A Physical History*. New York: Atheneum, 1987.

White, Norval, and Elliot Willensky. *American Institute ofArchitects Guide to New York City*. New York: Collier Books, 1978.

Williams, T. Harry. *Lincoln and His Generals*. New York: Alfred A. Knopf, 1952.

Wolfe, Gerard R. *New York, a Guide to the Metropolis: Walking Tours of Architecture and History*. New York: McGraw-Hill Book Company, 1988.

Young, Bonnie. *A Walk Through The Cloisters*. New York: The Metropolitan Museum of Art, 1979.

Phi Beta Kappa, teacher, antiques dealer, and antiquarian bookseller — Judith Browning has been all of these. Through the years there has been another recurring theme as well — a delight in delving into history to discover the countless exciting adventures hidden in the past.

Judith Browning's taste for historical adventures has taken many forms: exploring the hidden back-street shops and colorful marketplaces in Europe and the Far East in search of antiques for her store; traveling on her own to Egypt to sail down the Nile and circle the pyramids on a camel's back; and flying alone to Kyoto, Japan, to visit the centuries-old Buddhist monasteries and sleep in a 15th-century ryokan.

Twenty years of living in and near Manhattan have brought her into the world of New York City and its rich past, as her goal for many years was to have a memorable city adventure once a week. There was only one restriction — the adventure had to be one that she had never taken before in her life. It was those varied, fascinating one-day adventures that eventually sowed the seeds for this book.

And Judith Browning's latest adventure? Creating a publishing corporation. She is president of Corsair Publications, Inc.